METAL
RULES
THE
GLOBE

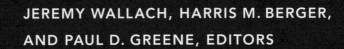

JEREMY WALLACH, HARRIS M. BERGER,
AND PAUL D. GREENE, EDITORS

METAL
RULES
THE GLOBE

HEAVY METAL MUSIC
AROUND THE WORLD

DUKE UNIVERSITY PRESS Durham & London 2011

Printed in the United States of America on acid-free paper ∞
Designed by Jennifer Hill
Typeset in Chaparral Pro and Avenir by Tseng Information Systems, Inc.

Library of Congress Cataloging-in-Publication Data appear
on the last printed page of this book.

Duke University Press gratefully acknowledges
the College of Liberal Arts at Texas A&M University, which
provided funds toward the production of this book.

I BELIEVE THAT HEAVY METAL HAS MORE MEANING NOW THAN
EVER BEFORE. CONSIDERING THE CURRENT STATE OF THE
WORLD, BEING YOUNG IS A VERY INTIMIDATING EXPERIENCE.

—ROB HALFORD OF JUDAS PRIEST (UNITED KINGDOM), 1985

METAL IS WORLDWIDE, MAN.

—WALEED "BLOOD MASTER" RABIAA OF ACRASSICAUDA (IRAQ), 2004

CONTENTS

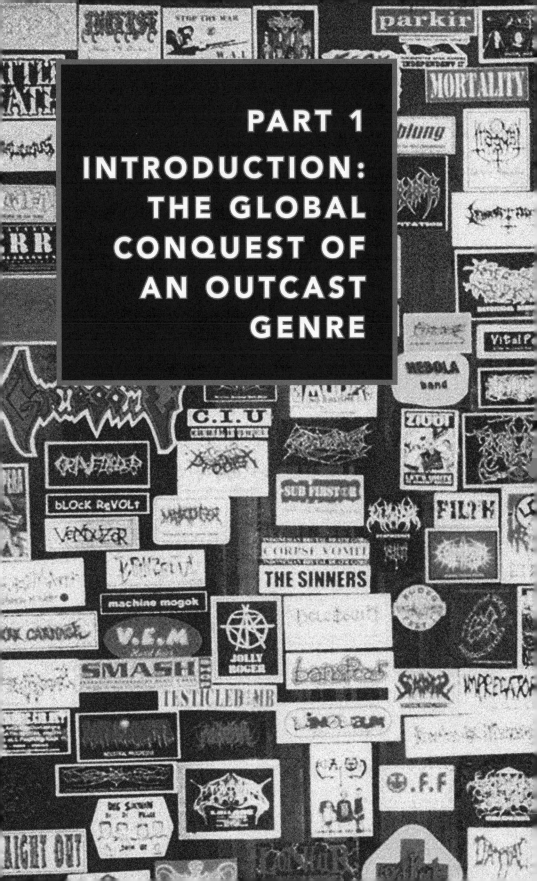

PART 1
INTRODUCTION: THE GLOBAL CONQUEST OF AN OUTCAST GENRE

AFFECTIVE OVERDRIVE, SCENE DYNAMICS, AND IDENTITY IN THE GLOBAL METAL SCENE

Jeremy Wallach, Harris M. Berger,
and Paul D. Greene

We would like to thank all our fans and friends all over the world, from Jakarta to Moscow!!—Sepultura, 1993 (liner notes for the album *Chaos A.D.*)

We are here because we cannot live without our music. Every drumbeat I hear reminds me of the beat of my heart.—Sameh Youssef, a twenty-three-year-old computer science student attending a heavy metal concert outside Cairo (quoted in "Rockin' in the Islamic World," 2006)

Come! Bang your heads to the Dark Rock N' Roll!!!—Holy Flesh Records press release for *Dark,* a cassette by the Indonesian black metal band Bealiah (ca. 2000)

The band takes the stage and launches into its first song. The music is distorted, pounding, and brutal, and it is so loud that it seems to fill in the space between the musicians and the audience members. Sweat pours down the singer's face as he bellows the lyrics in a voice that is half rasp, half scream. The instrumentalists—bass guitarist, electric guitarist, and drummer—gnash their teeth and grimace as if in pain as they concentrate on bashing out their parts. Some in the predominantly, but not exclusively, male audience respond to the music with moshing (a dance involving intentional collisions with other dancers) and headbanging (rhythmic up-and-down movements of the head and neck), their flailing bodies contorting to the beat. Performers and audience are dressed alike—jeans, T-shirts, and long hair or buzz cuts—and they play their roles at the concert as though their lives depended on it. And perhaps, in a sense, they do. Metal around the world has become a viable mode of resistance, of identity assertion, and of self-empowerment, often in the face of powerful, totalizing, and even life-threatening forces.

The concert described above took place in 2002 in Cleveland's Grog Shop, the venerable rock club in that city's trendy Coventry Village section, but it could easily have taken place in Tokyo, Kathmandu, Jakarta,[1] Tel Aviv, Rio de Janeiro, Beijing, Oslo, or any number of other sites the world over in the last fifteen years. Yet the fact that metal music, fashion, and behavior exist in all these places does not necessarily imply that they mean the same things in these quite different cultural contexts. The chapters in this book demonstrate that in every setting, metal is embedded in local cultures and histories and is experienced as part of a complex and historically specific encounter with the forces of modernity. The globalization of metal is well upon us, and with this book we hope to both investigate the specific, variable meanings of heavy metal music and culture for metalheads around the world and contribute insights into the large-scale social processes that have facilitated the music's dramatic worldwide expansion.[2]

METAL GOES GLOBAL

The term *heavy metal* has come to denote a cluster of rock music styles that emphasize loud, distorted guitars; prominent and aggressive drums; emotionally extreme singing techniques; and musical complexity and esotericism (unlike punk, for instance). Frequently misunderstood and maligned in its countries of origin, heavy metal music has in the last four decades become a potent source of meaning and identity for young and no-longer-so-young people across the planet. These fans have stayed loyal to the music despite societal disapproval, occasional moral panics, censorship, and even government harassment and violence.[3] *Metal Rules the Globe* is the first academic book to explore the broad swath of metal's worldwide growth and examine why this often devalued, censored, and ridiculed music genre has attracted so many devoted fans in far-flung locales.[4] Fans and musicians initially developed connections across vast distances through transnational networks of photocopied fanzines, paper correspondence, audio-cassette trading, concert tours big and small (see Waksman, this volume), and a loosely shared canon of "classic" metal albums; now they use e-mail, Web sites, blogs, YouTube, and MP3s to further these connections. In the process, they forged a new, globally deployed music culture. The worldwide metal ecumene is an imagined community in Benedict Anderson's sense of the phrase (1983), though it is constituted through reading 'zines, listening to recordings, watching videos, and attending concerts, rather than through reading newspapers or novels.

Globalization is certainly nothing new in the history of heavy metal. From the beginnings of the genre in the 1970s, metal has been transnational in scope, emerging simultaneously in the United Kingdom and the United States. In the 1980s, it grew deep roots in continental Europe, Australia, and Japan, and during the 1990s the genre expanded dramatically throughout the world in ways that defied all expectations. And metal shows no signs of slowing down in the new millennium. Published in the early 1980s, the *International Encyclopedia of Hard Rock and Heavy Metal* (Jasper et al. 1983) had only 15 entries (out of 1,500) for bands originating from outside Europe, North America, and Australia.[5] In mid-2007, the online *Encyclopaedia Metallum* contained listings for 47,626 metal bands from 129 countries. And the list continues to grow.

METAL AND GLOBALIZATION THEORY

Phenomena of globalization have attracted an enormous amount of attention from researchers in the last three decades. Malcolm Waters pointed out seventeen years ago that globalization is a process that unfolds simultaneously in economic, political, and cultural dimensions and should be understood as encompassing differing domains of social life in order to account for phenomena as diverse as global tourism, diasporic communities, multinational corporations, mass communication technologies, consumerism, and financial speculation (1995). Worldwide interconnectedness is of course hardly a new phenomenon. However, such linkages between people on grand geographical scales have been accelerating rapidly in recent decades in the context of a planet-wide spread of neoliberal, "free market" capitalism facilitated by the post–cold war preeminence of the United States.[6] Likewise, the global dissemination, appropriation, and adaptation of music forms have been happening for centuries, but these processes have accelerated considerably in recent decades due to the advent of mass media technologies and the formation of extensive social networks for music production and distribution, including the grassroots-based but far-flung networks responsible for the dissemination of metal music and culture.

Despite hopes held by some that globalization processes would realize certain utopian potentials, leading to, for example, a transnational capitalist democracy of world citizens, it is evident that globalization unfolds in uneven and in some cases sharply disempowering ways. While ideas about human rights and democracy have spread rapidly and while many economies around the world have benefited from foreign investment and increased global interconnectedness, rigid patterns of exclusion have also emerged. Entire segments of humanity—rural peasants, refugees, urban slum dwellers, industrial workers in the developed world—have been excluded from these emerging economic and cultural systems and have been locked into spirals of isolation, exploitation, and unemployment. While many studies of globalization and its costs attempt to reduce the phenomenon to a straightforward dialectic between "local" and "global" cultural processes, certain more recent works—especially those of Jean and John Comaroff (2005), Manuel Castells (2000), and Anna Tsing (2005)—have revealed the complex and even paradoxical ways that globalizing forces have transformed everyday life around the world. Moreover, directing exclusive attention to local-global dynamics obscures the importance of regional and national levels of cultural production, levels that remain salient "frameworks of flow" (Hannerz 1992) in almost everyone's daily life. Indeed, rather than fading into irrelevance, nation-states have adopted new roles in the global system, often maintaining or increasing their hold on the imaginations of their citizens.

Ethnographic studies have documented how globalization emerges through the interplay of differing actors with diverse visions and agendas. These conflicting globalization projects are manifested in specific social and material interactions in the lives of locally situated agents. Indeed, social existence around the world increasingly unfolds within what Anna Tsing calls the "friction . . . of worldly encounter" (2005, 1), filled with both desires for what globalization has to offer and anxieties about how customary lifeways may be inexorably shaped by it. We suggest that globalization has presented at least two broad challenges to world cultures. First, with the expansion and growing influence of global institutions, transnational networks, and translocal communities, individuals have increasingly become critical of the traditions and values of their immediate families, communities, and nations. Second, transnational capitalism has rapidly and sometimes violently transformed entire cities and regions, from the sudden and wholesale introduction of franchise fast-food chains to the restructuring of entire industries. In response to these two interrelated challenges, some have turned to religious or ethnonational extremisms in the quest for guarantors of personal security during uncertain times. Thus, as

Manuel Castells (2004) argues, one paradoxical result of rapid globalization is that many people retreat into individuated identities, dividing the world into rigid us/them dichotomies. In this book, we suggest that metalheads around the world are responding to these twin challenges of globalization in ways that reject both conformity to a new global capitalist order *and* narrow fundamentalisms based on ethnicity, religion, or locality. As the chapters in this volume demonstrate, when musicians and fans around the world align themselves with a transnational metal community, they begin to stake out stances (Berger 2009) and identities that are sharply opposed to certain local or national customs and values, while strengthening their rootedness in others. In every case discussed here, heavy metal fandom serves as a viable cultural and affective alternative for disempowered youths, one that is often just as critical of globalization's tendency to bring with it crass consumerism, class divisiveness, and uneven development as it is of the authority of traditional norms of behavior. In this context, the scholarship on "multiple" or "alternative" modernities is useful for understanding metal's worldwide spread.

METAL, MODERNITY, MUSIC

Through at least the middle of the twentieth century, anthropologists, development theorists, and intellectual historians had viewed modernity as a set of social, political, and economic processes emerging in Western Europe, including such wide-ranging phenomena as industrialization, the rise of the nation-state, secularization, Enlightenment individualism, mass media technologies, changing gender roles, and an increased pace of social change. Where these older theorists of modernity saw these phenomena as inevitably linked together and necessarily spreading from Western Europe to the rest of the world, more recent scholars such as Charles Taylor (1995) and Dilip Gaonkar (2001) argue that these various features do not necessarily implicate one another, that modernity can take varying, culturally specific forms, and that the spread of social change does not only move from the West to the rest. Inspired by Milton Singer's groundbreaking 1972 study, *When a Great Tradition Modernizes*, and drawing on the ideas of the multiple modernities theorists, a range of scholars from Arjun Appadurai (1990) to Giovanna Del Negro (2004) have understood expressive culture as an arena in which the meanings of such social changes are negotiated. We carry forward this tradition to view heavy metal in this manner—as a key site in which social agents publicly think about and debate modernity's wrenching social changes. In reflecting on the conditions of their lives, metalheads critique both the officially sanctioned versions of social change and the totalizing, regressive attempts at its wholesale rejection. In crafting new meanings (new visions of gender identity; new relations between the local and, in Amy Shuman's phrase, the "larger-than-local" [1993]; new visions of the person's relations to the modern nation-state) heavy metal musicians and fans from differing parts of the world forge related but distinct responses to modernity.

With the wide geographical growth of metal, both its musical style and its culture have expanded, and new metalheads situated in diverse settings have sounded their own particular aesthetics and sociopolitical concerns, many of which are discussed in the following pages. Despite significant differences across national and regional metal scenes, though, *all* metalheads, regardless of their preferred subgenre or subgenres, view metal as the opposite of light entertainment. To them, it is a form of serious music that endorses a particular set of values. In the words of a middle-aged Deep Purple fan from Russia, "There are some bands that are out there for entertainment [that is, pop music bands outside of metal], but there are others that have moral content, like Deep Purple . . . It makes me feel good that the youth of this country are learning about it" (quoted in Cullison 2004; see Bushnell 1990, 82–94, for an excellent discussion of the place of heavy metal in the former Soviet Union).[7] The following chapters make clear that no matter where it is found, metal music answers the question of how ethics (that is, formulations of the proper way of being in the world) fit into a disenchanted universe by offering a promise of community and significance built around powerful emotions and amplified sounds. Of course, one of the paramount values of metal culture is the music itself and rich aesthetic experiences.[8] Lack of attention to aesthetics, a problem that plagues popular music studies in general, is therefore an especially conspicuous omission when analyzing heavy metal (Clinton 2010). As Keith Kahn-Harris notes in his landmark study of extreme metal, "music has a more paramount place in the extreme metal scene than is the case in other scenes such as the goth or punk scenes, where other practices such as fashion or activism are just as important" (2007, 154). Thus, as a site of sonic pleasure, the focus of a social group, and a means of negotiating modernity and social change, metal is a phenomenon of great aesthetic and sociopolitical complexity.

If the globalization of metal has been going on for some time, it was not until the early 1990s that this music attracted the attention of scholars.[9] Three foundational texts ground the scholarly literature in this area: *Teenage Wasteland: Suburbia's Dead End Kids* by Donna Gaines (1991), *Heavy Metal: A Cultural Sociology* by Deena Weinstein (1991), and *Running with the Devil: Power, Gender, and Madness in Heavy Metal Music* by Robert Walser (1993a). These books—especially Walser's, which remains a cultural studies classic—had a transformative effect on metal scholarship, which until then tended to privilege dismissive or bemused outsider perspectives that were often little better than those of the sensationalistic mass media. Eschewing both impassioned but vague pronouncements about heavy metal and superficial outsider treatments in favor of careful, sympathetic research, the early 1990s "power trio" of Gaines, Weinstein, and Walser inspired books by Harris M. Berger (1999a), Susan Fast (2001), Chris McDonald (2009), Natalie Purcell (2003), Glenn Pillsbury (2006), Keith Kahn-Harris (2007), and Steve Waksman (1999, 2009) that include detailed, nuanced accounts of metal fans and their music. Taken together, the research contained in these books, along with that found in dozens of contemporaneous scholarly articles and edited volumes, richly draws out insider perspectives on heavy metal and its culture by deploying the methods of ethnography, social history, and musical and cultural analysis.

Until now there has been relatively little research on metal scenes outside the Anglo-American context—sites where metal scenes have developed and continue to emerge in varying, unpredictable forms, nuanced by local and regional sociocultural forces. Recent studies of metal scenes in the non-Anglophone world have revealed a complex identity politics in Bali, where scene participants contrast the music's values with those of "hedonistic" tourists and trend-following peers (Baulch 2003, 2007); a metal scene in Cairo, reborn after a brutal government crackdown in 1997, where Iron Maiden's ancient-Egypt-themed *Powerslave* album is regarded as a sacred text (Harbert 2007; see also "Rockin' in the Islamic World" 2006); a small scene in Alcalá de Henares, Spain that revolves around two bars that play metal albums and videos (Conover n.d.); a large, active scene in Aracuja, Brazil where metal is by far the dominant underground rock genre (Ribeiro 2004, 2009); and a long-standing scene in Turkey, where metal music and fashion, especially when embraced by women, continually

10   provoke the ire of religious conservatives (Ayik 2008; Hecker 2008, 2009). Of these studies, only a few, such as Baulch's, have gone beyond the initial stages of research, but they point to some of the diversity of world metal scenes, and the chapters in this volume seek to complement and extend their work.[10]

FUNDAMENTAL ISSUES IN GLOBAL METAL RESEARCH

In this section, we outline four important themes explored by the chapters in this volume, ones that we hope will guide future research into global metal phenomena. These are the analyses of metal's distinctive sounds; the varied cultural meanings that metalheads ascribe to those sounds; the social dynamics of local scenes in which metal is created, consumed, and lived; and the diverse, situated performances of identity in metal.

MUSIC, SOUND, AND EMOTION:
HEAVY METAL'S AFFECTIVE OVERDRIVE

Taken together, the musical qualities that characterize heavy metal offer listeners musical experiences invested with serious, weighty, or powerful emotions. This is key to the music's global appeal. Throughout metal history, its musics and songtexts have become considerably more diverse.[11] Today, heavy metal is performed and listened to in well over fifty different languages, and many local musical styles and instruments have been incorporated by metal musicians, including Afro-Brazilian percussion and Xavante Indian chants in the Brazilian metal of Sepultura (Avelar, this volume), *qin* and *zheng* zithers and East Asian pentatonicism in the Chinese metal of Tang Dynasty (Wong, this volume), Balinese gamelan in the death metal of Eternal Madness (Wallach 2005a, 148–51), the Arab *oud* in the Israeli extreme metal of Orphaned Land (Kahn-Harris 2007, 113; LeVine 2008, 117), and Anatolian folk music elements in songs by the Turkish metal legend Pentagram (Ayik 2008). Nevertheless, certain core musical qualities continue to characterize the genre, providing a musical center of gravity to the growing and diversifying global scene. Some commonly shared features include the distinctive timbre of the heavily distorted electric guitar; either soaring or raspy and unpitched vocals (including shouting, shrieking, and growling); prominent use of a Western drum set, often with a heavy emphasis on double-bass drums; and energetic and prominent guitar figuration, in the form of the virtuosic melodic expression of classic heavy metal guitar solos or the fast-paced riffs of thrash metal (cf. Kahn-Harris 2007, 30–34). Borrowings from Western classical music, including the use of florid arpeggiated runs in guitar solos, can also be heard (cf. Walser 1993a, 57 ff.; 1997), although such devices seem to be becoming less common as metal's globalization increases. This may be because Western classical music is not a frame of reference for all of metal's audiences around the world or because most of the metal scenes outside of Europe and America draw heavily on "underground" thrash and post-thrash metal, subgenres that tend to emphasize fast tempos and high energy but not Western classical borrowings.

In 1993 Robert Walser wrote, "The most important aural sign of heavy metal is the sound of an extremely distorted electric guitar" (1993a, 41), and that timbre is no less central to heavy metal today. Although similar timbres can be found in other musical genres, such as punk and hard rock, the distorted "heavy" guitar sound remains a central and defining feature of heavy metal, and a musical performance that lacks this timbre probably would not be considered part of the metal scene. The most common technique for producing distortion is to send a very powerful signal through the pre-amp or power amp stage of a guitar's amplifier. Unable to reproduce the sound accurately, the circuitry adds a noise component to the signal that we call distortion. Such distortion was originally eschewed as an undesirable result of sloppy sound engineering. As early as the 1940s, though, blues guitarists began to see distortion as a valuable feature of amplified sound, and later musicians and engineers began to devise techniques deliberately to produce it (Hicks 1999, 14). Since the 1960s, specially designed effects devices have been commonly used to produce distorted timbres. As Walser argues (1993a, 42), distortion came to be seen as the vehicle for exhilarating experiences of power: a musical experience so intense that it overflows its own channels of transmission.

In terms of acoustics, guitar distortion often involves a flattening of the signal's dynamic envelope, because the waveforms are clipped by the limitations of the transmission channel. In a perception study focusing on American metalheads, Harris M. Berger and Cornelia Fales found that the experience of "heaviness" in heavy metal music is correlated with the flatness of the dynamic envelope of guitar sounds, such that sounds with flatter envelopes were perceived to be "heavier" sounds (Berger and Fales 2005). Distinctive heavy metal overdrive techniques not only produce distortion but also signal compression and sometimes feedback, with the result that notes can have virtually endless sustains. Because under most circumstances a continual input of energy is required to make notes sustain, the use of distortion adds to the sense that there is tremendous energy and power in heavy metal.

Guitar distortion is associated with, and often supplemented by, overflows of other channels of musical communication and experience. One example of this lies in the sheer loudness of the music. While heavy metal scenes around the world vary in terms of volume, most tend toward the loud to extremely loud end of the dynamic range.[12] Listening to such powerfully amplified music can overwhelm a person's ability to process musical sound accurately, an experience analogous in many ways to that evoked by distortion. Further, the timbres produced by metal singers often contain a noise component. Though only occasionally produced by electronic means, the tone quality of these vocals is sometimes referred to as "distorted," and metalheads often think of these raspy or rough-timbred vocal sounds as analogous to those of distorted metal guitars. A variety of heavy metal singing styles have emerged that feature distorted vocal sounds. In the classic and power metal subgenres, singers often perform in the tenor range and favor a bright tone; some use distortion as an occasional effect to signal the intensity of particular passages, while others have a consistently rough tone color. Doom metal vocalists are known for intoning their songs in a deep, raspy bass, while singers in the thrash and death genres often use the full pitch range and employ intensely distorted timbres. (See Hagen's chapter in this volume for a discussion of black metal vocal techniques; see Berger 2004 for a discussion of timbre and ornamentation in heavy metal vocals.)

Other sonic features are also typical of heavy metal music. Guitarists use "power chords"—chords generally comprised of a root, a perfect fifth or fourth, and the octave, usually played on the instrument's lower-pitched strings. When played with distortion at high volumes, power chords often produce resultant tones below the pitches actually played (Walser 1993a, 43). This expands and deepens the aural experience into the bass range, giving a sense of weight to the music. In thrash metal and its variants, this effect is heightened through the use of downtuned guitars and complemented by low-pitched vocals and loud double-bass drumbeats (see Kahn-Harris 2007, 32–33). Frequently, instrumental passages featuring dissonant intervals and parallel harmonies strain toward ambiguous tonality and, in some cases, atonality (see Harrell 1994; Berger 1999a, 184–99,

218–22; Berger 1999b; Hagen, this volume). Heavy metal often uses the four-beat meter typical of many global popular musics. In perceptual practices, though, metal musicians may shift their focus of attention from the rhythmic pulses to the backbeats (the second and fourth beats of the measure; Berger 1997; cf. Walser 1993a, 49), and in many varieties of metal, musicians experiment with odd meters. Further, many styles of heavy metal explore extremely fast or slow tempos, sudden and dramatic shifts in tempo, and percussive devices such as the thundering gallop of palm-muted rhythm guitar parts in thrash metal and the "blast beat" drumming patterns of black metal (see Hagen, this volume).

The sheer volume and rich timbres of metal fill the audible sound spectrum and can generate a kind of sonic and affective saturation. The music can even fill one's awareness to such an extent that, while listening, it becomes impossible to think about or feel anything else, an experience of *affective overdrive*. In this collection we maintain that through heavy guitar distortion, volume, speed, tendencies toward atonality, and distorted vocals, metal explores extremes of human expression, gesturing toward escape, empowerment, or transgression.[13]

AFFECTIVE OVERDRIVE AND CULTURAL MEANING

Affective overdrive is the common denominator in most of the world's heavy metal scenes. Interpreting the meanings that metalheads around the world ascribe to such an overdrive is a complex issue, though, and one of the key themes of this volume. Berger's *Metal, Rock, and Jazz* (1999a), an ethnography of underground metal (what would now be called "extreme metal," see Kahn-Harris 2007) in Akron, Ohio, provides a starting point for this particular inquiry, and we will review it here in some detail. Berger's study showed that Ohio scene participants interpret the meaning of their music's emotional intensity in an oppositional fashion—that is, in contrast to other music styles and scenes alive in their social world. For Akron metalheads in the early and mid-1990s, the music genres played on mainstream radio were the main "other" against which they defined their music, and these radio-friendly styles were widely disparaged by metalheads as nothing more than musical fluff. Hard rock and Top-40 pop were musically unsophisticated and lacking in intense emotional expression, the metalheads said, while other forms of commercial radio music (from hip hop to country and beyond) were felt to be unworthy of comment. Aside from metal, hardcore punk was the primary form of rock-based, non-mainstream music popular in Ohio at the time, and though the metal-heads had a higher tolerance for punk than pop or commercial rock, they did not fully embrace it. With its transgressive songtexts, rough vocal tim-bres, and aggressive style, hardcore punk was something that metalheads could not dismiss as auditory pabulum. However, metalheads felt that the emotional intensity of hardcore was too frequently linked to explicit politi-cal ideologies. Hardcore bands may run the political gamut from far-left to far-right, but the metalheads felt that despite these differences most punk music shared a tendency toward preachy, dogmatic songtexts and the punks themselves had an intolerant attitude toward the views of others. In contrast, the metalheads claimed that extreme metal was more individu-alistic and emphasized tolerance, personal responsibility, and individual choice.[14] While these themes were not always evident in songtexts, which frequently focused on images from fantasy literature or the occult, they were central to the larger metal scene and crucial for the interpretation of its music's affective intensity.

The broadly individualistic themes Berger encountered in the Akron scene are linked to metal's affective overdrive by a specific set of musi-cal uses. To listeners unfamiliar with the music, metal may seem to focus solely on the expression of rage and aggression. Closer inspection, how-ever, reveals a far broader palette of affective valences, and this is key to the music's meaning. Rage and aggression are certainly present in metal, but songs and performances also offer sadness, fear, depression, grandeur, drama, and a kind of affectively neutral but intensely powerful energy. What is absent are the lighter emotions—the perceived emotional pabu-lum of commercial music—and the perceived heavy-handed politics of punk.[15]

The spectrum of serious and intense feelings that this music explores, the Ohio metalheads said, stemmed from the nature of everyday life. With-out raising the kinds of political explanations common to the left or the right, metalheads often stated that their daily experience was one of stul-tification and domination. From an educational system that was more about social control than learning, to a world of mindless factory work, dead-end service sector jobs, or unemployment, one was constantly con-fronted by people and situations that held one down. Every day, one bit back anger, frustration, sadness, and rage, and over time these feelings built up, leaving a person apathetic and blocked. Playing or listening to metal, as scene participants explained, allowed one to explore those emotions, unearth the rage and sadness that developed in daily experience, and free repressed energies. Metal's affective overdrive was about taking control of one's life, an expression of freedom in the face of society's attempted imprisonment. Berger found that while metal tends to focus on liberating the individual, Ohio metalheads also had a deep commitment to the idea of their scene as a community, and the musicians and fans spent hours playing and rehearsing, traveling to shows, engaging in correspondence, and doing the work necessary to create and maintain both local and widespread social networks. (This orientation is typical of most metal scenes around the world.) In this context, the growing globalization of their music was a profound encouragement to metalheads in Akron. Discussing the Brazilian band Dorsal Atlântica, the Akron guitarist Dann Saladin celebrated metal's global dissemination: "That's the future. . . . [Metal is] an international language. It's a bond between me and five guys in fucking Brazil that I've never met before . . . And I can't speak their language, and they probably can't speak mine. But there's a bond there . . . It's my only hope for the future" (Saladin quoted in Berger 1999a, 274). In sum, the aesthetic exploration of serious emotions, individualism, and musical community were the meanings at play in Akron's metal scene, and other ethnographic studies of Western metal (for example, Kahn-Harris 2007; Olson 2008) suggest that they are widely present in other scenes as well.

The assertion Berger encountered—that metal music's affective overdrive is an antidote to complacency and apathy—is also widespread in world metal. A Chinese metalhead told Cynthia P. Wong that listening to metal for the first time was "like waking from a dream" (Wong, personal communication, August 20, 2008) and Vietnamese metal bands sing songs of self-uplift and empowerment that challenge their culture's stereotypes of rockers as apathetic, lazy drug users (Gibbs 2008, 21; see also Olsen 2008). In Indonesia, metalheads valued their music's ability to provide a productive outlet for the anger and frustration they felt under the Soeharto dictatorship; their scene was part of a cultural ferment that contributed to the toppling of that regime (Wallach 2005b).

METAL, DEINDUSTRIALIZATION, AND INDUSTRIALIZATION

While some metal bands do explicitly link the stultifications of everyday life to larger social contexts, that task has primarily been the concern of metal's scholars. Weinstein, Walser, Gaines, and Berger have observed that metal in the West has a predominantly, though not exclusively, working-class audience and that the music first emerged in those parts of the United States and the United Kingdom that suffered from deindustrialization—the process by which the industrial infrastructure of a region is dismantled by business interests in their relentless search for cheap labor and unfettered control of workers and production. Deindustrialization began in the manufacturing heartlands of America and Britain during the 1960s, but its effects—increased unemployment and underemployment, economic insecurity, a weakening of unions, and a crumbling civic infrastructure—weren't widely felt on the ground until the 1970s, the period of metal's initial emergence. The majority of studies of metal have linked the social frustrations that metalheads identify to these broad economic and social trends. It is worth reiterating here that in both its dissemination and its key social contexts, metal has been a product of globalization from its start: in the United States and the United Kingdom, industry declined and plants were eventually shuttered after profits were milked from factories there and invested in Latin America and Asia; at the same time, metal music was being spread around the world by media technologies and the transnational music industry.

The contexts outlined above are central to Weinstein's interpretation of the meanings that non-Western metalheads bring to their music. Outlining the history and demographics of extreme metal's worldwide dissemination, Weinstein's chapter in this volume observes that the music has failed to achieve popularity in the rural communities of the developing world, and that the bulk of its audience can be found among working-class youth in regions that have or had an industrial base. Since it is dependent on media technologies and a consumer culture, she argues, extreme metal is the music of those who live under conditions of modernity but do not get to experience its benefits—young men and women working in the factories of developing countries without access to the protections that unions afford or a hope for upward mobility, and those in developed countries who see before them only a life of unemployment or poorly paid service-sector jobs. With its distorted electric guitars and intense amplification, metal situates itself in the contemporary world and embraces technology as a means of powerful emotional expression. Metalheads, however, do not celebrate modernity but rather use its technology to express their estrangement from it. In short, the central claim of Weinstein's chapter is that extreme metal is a key music of the global proletariat, and henceforth we will refer to this idea as the Weinstein Hypothesis.

Acknowledging differences among the world's extreme metal scenes, Weinstein distinguishes two broad trends in the music's global dissemination. The subgenre of death metal has developed a more or less uniform sound around the world; black metal (a subgenre whose name refers to its focus on evil and the occult, not its racial makeup), however, often combines the musical style and imagery of Western extreme metal with that of the traditional cultures in the regions to which it has spread. While non-Western black metal may employ indigenous musical structures or celebrate the heroes of local myths or legends, the music can in no way be mistaken for that of a folk revival. Though it may draw on images of the pre-modern to critique contemporary life, black metal's overwhelming distortion and crushing amplification situate it firmly within the present. Despite their differences, both death metal and black metal are, Weinstein argues, working-class responses to the predations of modernity.

A number of chapters in the book develop these themes, considering the Weinstein Hypothesis and advancing the program of research outlined by Weinstein. Wallach's study of the metal scenes of Indonesia, Malaysia, and Singapore shows how the industrialization of those countries from the 1970s through the 1990s led to the emergence of a disenfranchised working class whose everyday experiences were similar in key ways to the experiences of Americans and Britons confronting *de*industrialization. He finds that on the ground, the feelings of rage and frustration engendered by the exploitive industrialization of the developing world have much in common with the feelings of powerlessness and aggression engendered by deindustrialization in the United States and the United Kingdom, and metal's emotional overdrive emerged in Indonesia, Malaysia, and Singapore as a response to these conditions. Qualifying the Weinstein Hypothesis, Wallach's chapter shows how heavy metal comes to function as a unique and appealing vehicle of youth identities that are not burdened by religious or authoritarian pressures of conformity, traditional culture, or mainstream commercialism.

A different set of dynamics plays out in Nepal, which is the focus of Greene's chapter. Greene shows how the audience for metal in this country comes from white-collar backgrounds, not the working classes. While contemporary metal expresses rage at the political instability and violence that wracked Nepal from the late 1990s to 2006, the powerful influence of religion on Nepali life is also an important focus of this scene's music, and Nepali metal rails against the substantial familial responsibilities that Hinduism places on the individual and the limits it imposes on his or her ability to explore romantic relationships or new types of spiritual experiences. Would-be cosmopolitans, Nepali scene participants see Western metal as both a means of transgressing the boundaries of traditional Hinduism and a lifeline to the wider world of modernity from which they have been excluded. Comparing the differing social contexts of Nepali, Indonesian, and Western metal, Greene suggests that the transgression of boundaries—both auditory and social—is the theme that unifies the diverse local manifestations of the global metal scene.[16]

Despite the economic and religious differences between the countries, the issues that Rajko Muršič's chapter identifies in Slovenian metal and Albert Bell's chapter describes in Maltese metal are strikingly similar to those in Greene's Nepal. In Slovenia, metal is popular largely among educated youth in depressed industrial areas, and the most significant frustrations that the music addresses are the limitations imposed by traditional Slovenian culture and the Catholic Church. These themes play out in Malta as well, where metalheads seek to embrace modernity and use their music to express their discontent with Catholicism, traditional mores, and the narrow spectrum of politics at play in the island's national government.

If, as Greene argues, metal's affective overdrive is everywhere about transgressing boundaries, a comparison of this set of European and Asian case studies with the existing scholarship on metal in Anglophone countries suggests that the music is also about the unfulfilled desire for the benefits of modernity in both its economic and social dimensions, especially rising material affluence, the emancipation of the individual, and social justice. In the United States and the United Kingdom, metalheads are not only frustrated by dead-end jobs and crumbling cities; they see that the rich in their countries have gotten richer and the poor, poorer. A sense of relative deprivation—of being excluded from the economic benefits that an industrial economy has brought to others—and a desire to lead a life of one's own choosing are at the heart of Anglo-American metal. Idelber Avelar sees a similar situation in Brazil. Describing metal there as a response to the political and economic failures of the 1980s, Avelar writes that the music developed "in a milieu fully exposed to modernization but excluded from its fruits" (Avelar 2001, 132; quoted in Weinstein, this volume). In the Nepali, Slovenian, and Maltese cases, metalheads are, in contrast, focused more on the social dimensions of modernity than on the economic ones. Here, metal expresses a desire for the freedom that moder-

nity promises from the domination of everyday life by religion and tradition. Taken in its broader context, metal can therefore be interpreted as a
music, not only of the global proletariat, but of anyone who is frustrated
by the unkept promises of modernity and willing to embrace a marginalized, transgressive culture to express those feelings. It is the music of the
modern project unfulfilled.[17]

As we suggested above, metal bands often syncretize elements of their
traditional culture with metal's sounds and style. These local-global metal
"alloys" do not merely incorporate musical elements or figures from indigenous folklore. They can also draw on concepts from the country's classical philosophy or aesthetics. In so doing, they represent new ways in
which metal's affective power is given distinctively local meanings. Chapters by Cynthia P. Wong, and Kei Kawano and Shuhei Hosokawa explore
these issues.

Wong shows how ideas from classical Chinese philosophy infuse the
aesthetic of the Beijing metal band Tang Dynasty. Yoking metal's affective
overdrive to traditional ideals of masculinity in China, Tang Dynasty creates a space in which young men can generate a unique type of homosocial
bond and explore new gender constructions in contemporary Chinese culture. The role of ideas from classic Japanese aesthetics in the genre discourses of fans, journalists, and music industry figures is richly discussed
in Kawano and Hosokawa's chapter. They show how scene stalwarts draw
on traditional Japanese notions of stylistic purity to sharply mark the generic limits of metal and give a distinctive meaning to their music. This
musical boundary maintenance also helps to shape the scene dynamics of
metal in Japan, a point that we will discuss in more detail below.

Sharon Hochhauser's chapter explores a rather different way in which
metal's affective overdrive is connected to new ideologies and meanings.
Historically, metal has had little connection with the racist right,[18] but in
the last dozen years, white supremacist groups in Canada and the United
States have worked to change that. Using sophisticated Internet marketing techniques, they have constructed a new subgenre of metal, "hatecore,"
in an attempt to harness metal's affective power to serve their ideological
interests. Seeking to build a worldwide alliance among "whites" from countries around the world, this new subgenre of metal represents the potential for a reactionary realignment of centers and peripheries in the globalization of metal—a highly disturbing new dynamic (cf. Corte and Edwards
2008).[19]

The relationships among metal scenes do not only play out in terms of the meanings that the musicians and fans bring to the music. Metalheads are indeed eager to discuss musical sound and the emotional intensity it evokes (see Berger 1999a, 200–77; Berger 2004; Kahn-Harris 2007, 51–54), but they are also deeply concerned with the role of their local or national scene in the broader context of metal around the world (Berger 1999a, 273–75; Kahn-Harris 2002, 2007; Wallach 2003a).[20] Complex processes play out here, and understanding the social dynamics of metal scenes is a project that not only speaks to scholars and fans of this music, but to anyone interested in the formation of popular music scenes, the globalization of culture, or, most broadly, the relationship between expressive culture and its social base.

Research to date strongly suggests that the emergence and growth of local metal scenes in various countries around the world tend to follow a common trajectory. The maturation of local scenes results from flows of knowledge from more established scenes to newer ones, coupled with a desire among scene members to apply this knowledge constructively. This cumulative process of "metallification" is, like "modernization," fundamentally reflexive (Waters 1995, 16–17). As scenes develop, the number of metal subgenres represented tends to increase and the stylistic boundaries between them become clearer. The music is also more likely to be kept separate from non-metal genres, though there are some significant exceptions to this. In general, playing covers of songs by favorite international bands eventually gives way to attempts to write and perform original songs in the local vernacular (see Wallach 2003a). According to this logic, the scenes in Nepal and China are in an early stage, while those in Indonesia, Malaysia, and Singapore have undergone more extensive metallification; indeed, these scenes are quite large and variegated. As more scenes sprout up and thrive in East Asia, Southeast Asia, the Indian subcontinent, Latin America, Eastern Europe, the Middle East, and other places, it is possible that the current Western dominance of this music could eventually give way to a more equitable balance of musical and cultural influence in the global metal ecumene. Until then, however, global metal will exemplify not only the serendipitous consequences of the global dissemination of cultural forms, but also persistent inequalities in the world system.

The phenomenon of scene dynamics raises numerous questions. What is the full range of social and cultural conditions that lead to the emergence of metal scenes in particular countries? How do large-scale social forces and structures within the scene itself affect the scene's development? How have bands from small scenes learned to compete on the global stage with those from larger ones? How do the legacy of colonialism and contemporary forms of economic and political domination shape the growth of metal scenes in the developing world? How have the transnational, national, and independent sectors of the music industry shaped the growth of metal scenes in different countries? In the United States and United Kingdom, metal has had a complex, volatile relationship with the mainstream music industry: classic 1970s bands, 1980s "lite" or "pop" metal acts, and nü-metal artists in the 1990s all attained mass success, while extreme metal was largely marginalized by the mainstream music business. How has this relationship played out in other regions of the world?[21]

Questions of community and scene dynamics are central to all the chapters in the volume, and history is an important starting point for the authors' analyses. Deena Weinstein's chapter gives an overview of the globalization of metal from the 1970s to the present, and each of the subsequent contributions furthers her discussion by detailing the dissemination of recordings and live performances into the country or region that it examines and the history of the scene or scenes there. While grounded in a common interest in history, the authors apply differing theories and methods to explore their local scene's dynamics. Keith Kahn-Harris's study draws on Pierre Bourdieu's notion of cultural capital to compare the ways in which Israeli and Norwegian extreme metal bands jockeyed for position in the wider world of metal in the 1990s. Kahn-Harris shows how Norwegian metal bands in the 1980s and 1990s combined anti-Christian rhetoric with musical innovations to forge the subgenre of black metal. In so doing, they became the first metal bands from a non-English-speaking country to catapult themselves into the center of global metal. As the 1990s wore on, they further entrenched their position as transgressive firebrands by directing anti-Semitic rhetoric at Jewish Israeli metal bands. Hampered by this, as well as by social and economic factors specific to their country (compulsory military service, political instability, a relatively weak currency), Israeli bands never became a major force in metal's wider world. From a careful comparison of the two cases, Kahn-Harris develops a sophisticated analysis of the role of cultural capital in the emergence of music scenes and the relationship between centers and peripheries in the global flow of culture.

Focusing on dominant players in the history of metal and the scenes of

22   large nation-states, the chapters by Steve Waksman and by Kawano and
Hosokawa explore socioeconomic dynamics very different from those of
the marginalized Israeli scene. Waksman's study discusses the international concert tours of two seminal metal bands in the 1970s—Kiss and
Led Zeppelin.[22] Waksman reveals how the economics of concert promotion in this period and the emergence of the sports arena as a venue for
rock performance led to the development of Kiss's tours of Asia and Latin
America—a key moment in the globalization of heavy metal. This history
is contrasted with an examination of Led Zeppelin's musical borrowings
from Celtic, Indian, and Arab traditions and the band's own worldwide
travels in the 1970s. Exploring both the financial and cultural factors in
these two distinct forms of musical globalization, Waksman shows how
the economics of the music industry and ideologies of exoticism and imperialism helped to shape the initial wave of metal's global spread. Likewise attending to music industry structures and issues of culture, Kawano
and Hosokawa's chapter explores the scene dynamics of metal in Japan. As
we suggested above, Kawano and Hosokawa show how classical Japanese
notions of style and purity are taken up by fans, journalists, and music industry workers to draw particular genre boundaries for heavy metal. Discussing the relationship between transnational and national record labels,
the authors explore the practices by which bands, both Japanese and foreign, are signed, marketed, distributed, and promoted in Japan, revealing the unique nature of metal in a country that boasts the second largest
music market in the world (see also Stevens 2008).

   The chapters by Rajko Muršič, Albert Bell, and Dan Bendrups explore
the metal scenes of small countries and the contrasting dynamics that take
place there. Muršič's study traces the history of metal in Slovenia. Unlike
Israeli metal, which, Kahn-Harris reports, is highly organized and unified, Slovenian metal is fragmented into separate regions, subgenres, and
styles. Record company support and concert revenues are limited there,
and Muršič shows how, despite the lack of scenic infrastructure, heavy
metal continues to develop and diversify in Slovenia, continually straining
toward international markets. Even smaller and more marginalized are the
metal scenes on the islands of Malta and Rapanui (Easter Island), and Bell
and Bendrups respectively offer intimate, personal glimpses into their dynamics. A long-standing participant in the Maltese scene, Bell shows how
heavy metal emerged on the island as a response to and vehicle of globalization and modernity. Unlike the fragmented Slovenian scene, the one in

Malta displays a high degree of unity, despite the adherents' embrace of a wide range of subgenres. Emphasizing the creativity of the scene's participants, Bell's discussion shows how a sense of estrangement from mainstream Maltese culture keeps the island's metalheads engaged with the scene and active in its reproduction and maintenance.

With a population of only four thousand, Rapanui is a society on the furthest edges of globalization. Bendrups shows how the members of Nako, a band from this isolated Chilean territory in Polynesia, came to appropriate metal as a way of dealing with their social position in a marginalized region within a political entity itself already marginalized by processes of empire. Without even the limited and flexible institutional coherence that the term "scene" designates, Nako (which means "marrow" in the local language) and its cohort form what one might refer to as a "proto-scene," and Bendrups's discussion of this fascinating micro-social formation suggests the cultural and musical dynamics that play out at the far edge of metal's knowledge flows.

IDENTITY: IMAGES OF GENDER, ETHNICITY, AND NATION IN METAL

One of the striking aspects of the global transmission of heavy metal music is that it frequently comes to function as a resource for developing what Arjun Appadurai calls "counternodes of identity that youth can project against parental wishes or desires" (1990, 18–19). To be clear, heavy metal is not just about rebellion, the assertion of simplistically oppositional stances, or the adolescent rejection of parental values. It is also a constructive force, providing alternative cultural identities to those offered or projected by the cultural traditions, nationalisms, and religious movements that are influential in the locales where the music takes root. As in many (though certainly not all) social worlds, identity operates in the cultural performances of metal as an interpretive framework, a way of making sense of the conduct of others and guiding one's own acts. As Del Negro and Berger argue in "Identity Reconsidered, the World Doubled" (2004), to view any kind of performance as an expression of identity is to take some element of the meaning of that performance and project it onto one's vision of "society," a space of social individuals and social groups; the complexity of identity interpretations arises from the fact that the vision of identity that emerges in performance depends on the performers' and audiences' implicit social theory, which, across history and cultures, has an extraordinary diversity. It is certainly true that twentieth-century thinkers influential in American scholarship (such as the psychologist Erik Erikson and culture and personality school anthropologists like Margaret Mead and Ruth Benedict) proffered a narrow, culturally specific vision of identity and made it a preoccupation of both the U.S. academy and the broader society. However, a wealth of historical and anthropological work—by authors as diverse as Stuart Hall (1996), Philip Gleason (1983), Clifford Geertz (1983), Deborah Kapchan (1994), Judith Nagata (1974), Carol Silverman (1989), McKim Marriott (1976), and Norma Mendoza-Denton (1996)— shows that identity is indeed a live issue for the participants in many types of cultural performance, however differently notions of identity are constructed there. Viewing identity as an interpretive framework that can be flexibly applied by performers and fans and that is always contingent upon a culturally and historically situated social imagination, the chapters in this volume reveal the various ways in which metal in diverse locales serves as a medium for distinctive and specific forms of the performance of identity.

Scenes, the places where people make and celebrate music, provide the most important social contexts for specific performances of metalhead identity. Keeping this in mind, the chapters in this volume reveal the myriad ways in which larger social categories such as gender, ethnicity, and nationality play out in scenic performances. As Robert Walser has observed (1993b), much heavy metal is specifically about forging masculinity, and globally, the musicians and fans of heavy metal remain predominantly male (cf. Kahn-Harris 2007, 71). Certain metal subgenres, notably lite metal and nü-metal, attract more female fans, but these subgenres are considerably less globalized than others, such as thrash or black metal. Although Walser famously shows how androgyny is an effective strategy employed in European and American metal to explore gender issues, this phenomenon is considerably less common in the rest of the global heavy metal scene. At the time of this writing, gender constructions generally seem stable and unambiguous in heavy metal songs and videos outside Europe, North America, and Japan.

Inasmuch as heavy metal responds to feelings of frustration by offering thrilling experiences of transgressive empowerment, it appeals particularly to men who, by virtue of types of traditional gender socialization, expect themselves to be more powerful than modern society allows them to be. Initially, heavy metal tapped into ideas from the Western Romanticism of the late eighteenth and nineteenth centuries as an inspiration for the masculinities it enabled men to construct. Romantic themes included an emphasis on strong emotion as a basis of aesthetic experience, combined with a focus, carried over from the Enlightenment, on the individual as a relatively independent constructor of her or his social reality. Following this tradition, heavy metal thus invited constructions of the masculine as markedly individualistic, often rebellious or transgressive, powerful, and characterized by intense emotion (cf. Ascah 2003; Rafalovich 2006). As heavy metal globalized beyond Western contexts, such themes have largely been continued, carried along and developed in the songs themselves and in the discourses surrounding them. In some cases, however, globalized heavy metal has also begun to tap into local cultural ideals of masculinity. Wallach, in his chapter, finds that heavy metal circulates in Indonesia, Malaysia, and Singapore today through infrastructures that are rooted in preexisting patterns of male sociality. Wong's chapter shows how the band Tang Dynasty draws on the classical Chinese notion of the "ideal man" — a figure who displays equal measures of *wen* (cultural refinement) and *wu* (martial ability). The members of Tang Dynasty use traditional musical instruments and images from Chinese history to generate nostalgia for the Chinese imperial past and depict themselves as exemplifying the traditional gender ideal. Fans of the band use Tang Dynasty's music to forge a new form of masculine identity, one that has ties to the past and addresses the challenges offered by contemporary social life in China.

Global metal's relationships to the social categories of race and ethnicity are often highly complex, and it cannot be said that the music only has its audiences among ethnic majorities. For example, in Malaysia, Indonesia, and Singapore, the music appeals primarily to people identified as "Malay." In Singapore, Malays are a small "racial" minority, they are barely a majority in Malaysia, and they form a vast majority in Indonesia. While white power groups have attempted to co-opt metal music as a vehicle for their fantasy of a pure racial identity (see Hochhauser, this volume), heavy metal on a worldwide scale is, in fact, an exceedingly multicultural phenomenon. In the United States alone there have been well-known Latino, African American, Native American, and Asian American participants in the scene alongside Irish Americans, Italian Americans, Jewish Americans, Polish Americans, and those from other "white" American ethnicities. Some may explain the lack of a metal audience in, say, most of sub-Saharan Africa as resulting from a racial divide, but it is more likely that

26 the industrial and technological infrastructure necessary for the appreciation of metal's affective overdrive is not sufficiently present in most sub-Saharan countries.[23] (Further, a racialist explanation for the apparent absence of metal would be unable to account for the enormous popularity of American country music in the same region.)

National identity is also constructed in the production and consumption of metal music. The chapter by Idelber Avelar examines the complex relationship of the extreme metal band Sepultura to the Brazilian nation-state. In Avelar's analysis, Sepultura's music is situated not only with regard to the narrative of heavy metal's globalization, but also to the history of Brazil's popular music, its military dictatorship, its dynamics of race/ethnicity, and its crushing inequities of wealth and poverty. In this context, Sepultura uses the "foreign" musical form of heavy metal to provide a critical distance for reading issues of power in Brazilian society and for developing a new kind of Brazilian identity.

As heavy metal rages against such local machines, it does not often promote or advance comprehensive new plans or social orders to replace them. But by tapping into and channeling discontent, the music opens these social formations up to critique and offers fans the opportunity to forge identities rooted in the music itself, its affective positions, and the global community of heavy metal musicians and fans. A voice for feelings of discontent and rage, metal calls into question the forces that dominate the lives of millions of young men and women around the world and offers them a community that stretches beyond the confines of their local cultures.

THE FUTURE OF HEAVY METAL

Heavy metal is, I believe, forever. — Rob Halford (1985, ix)

There are unavoidable limitations to a study like this one. Even a multivolume work could not possibly cover all the active, vibrant metal scenes around the world, and we do not harbor any illusions of comprehensiveness here. We hope, however, to suggest some of the variety and richness of global metal culture and illustrate how diverse methodologies can be productively employed to interpret metal phenomena across the planet, from detailed textual and musicological analyses (for example, the Avelar and Hagen chapters in this volume), to archival research (Hochhauser,

graphic participant-observation (Bendrups, Greene, Wallach, Wong), to a
combination of these methods (Bell, Kahn-Harris, Muršič). We have also
sought to illuminate the intimate connections between the dislocations
and rapid changes caused by the forces of modernity and the globally expanding popularity of heavy metal, a music culture that shows no sign of
slowing its conquest of hearts and minds of people around the world. Relying on technologies of sound recording, amplification, and mass communication, metal is clearly dependent upon the tools of modernity. At the
same time, though, metal musicians and their fans use this music to insist
that a set of values must be preserved outside the logic of the marketplace
and the pressures of social conformity. In this way, metal is also a critical
response to modernity, and it is within this paradox that the social life of
global heavy metal plays out. Using diverse methods and a range of case
studies, the chapters of this volume explore this space, shedding new light
on one of the richest and most vital of today's popular music cultures.

While scholars attempt to analyze its meanings and map its contours,
the global metal universe continues to grow and evolve, and with this, new
questions are raised. Will metal scenes eventually be found in every place
where economic relations are ruled by capitalism? Will other new genres
arise in formerly peripheral areas and attract a global constituency? How
will multinational corporations in the future attempt to profit from and
exploit metal music? Can metal hold onto its audiences in the places where
it originated?

Metal will continue to evolve, but its serious fans will likely maintain
their memory of the genre's history. New metal subgenre labels continually emerge, but all metal bands are believed to share a common tradition: a history of classic metal groups and albums, which, while contested
and varying among genres and scenes, is understood as the metalhead's
musical and cultural heritage. The metal canon (the precise composition
of which depends on historical and regional factors) is more than a set of
musical masterpieces; to its fans, it anchors an alternative set of values to
the mainstream consumerism, parochial nationalism, and religious fun-
damentalism found in most contemporary globalizing societies. Metal
culture offers heroic individualism, in-group solidarity, nonconformity to
the majority culture, and the appreciation of "great art" to fans who often
receive little positive attention from the societies in which they live. For

these and other reasons, we believe that metal will be with us for a long time.

NOTES

1 See Wallach 2008b, 232, for a description of a strikingly similar metal show in Jakarta, Indonesia.

2 In the context of popular music, the word "metal" has a range of meanings. Usually a shortened version of "heavy metal," it can be used to refer to all variants of the genre (including those popular in mainstream media, such as the "lite metal" or "pop metal" of the United States in the 1980s), or it can be employed in a more restricted sense and refer only to "real," "underground," or "extreme" variants (genres that are not popular with mainstream audiences and are produced and consumed by members of localized scenes). This double meaning can be confusing, but the ambiguity it introduces is also instructive because the world's metal fans often disagree about which subgenres count as "true metal." It should also be noted that though Keith Kahn-Harris's important work (2007) uses the term "heavy metal" as a synonym for "trad metal" (traditional heavy metal that predates the emergence of thrash and post-thrash subgenres), in this volume we agree with Fabian Holt's use of the term (2007, 16) and regard "heavy metal" as an umbrella category that includes all metal styles.

3 See LeVine 2009 for a thorough overview of government repression and censorship of metal music in Egypt, Morocco, Iran, China, Indonesia, and Malaysia.

4 It is worth mentioning that three of this volume's contributors (Kahn-Harris, Walser, and Weinstein) appeared in the documentary film *Metal: A Headbanger's Journey* (2005). A critically acclaimed examination of the history and culture of heavy metal music in North America and Europe, the film had a wide theatrical release around the world and is now available on DVD. The filmmakers, Sam Dunn and Scot McFadyen, have produced a second documentary titled *Global Metal* (2008) that examines the spread of this music around the world, and they consulted Jeremy Wallach and Cynthia P. Wong about the metal scenes in Indonesia and China, respectively. The film also explores scenes in Brazil, India, Japan, and the Middle East and contains interviews with members of several bands discussed in this book, including Salem, Sepultura, Seringai, Tang Dynasty, and Tengkorak.

5 These include entries for Bow Wow, Cosmos Factory, 5x, Heavy Metal Army, Itakaski, Loudness, Mariner, Murasaki, Nokemono, Akira Takasaki, and Kyoji Yamamoto from Japan; Rene Arnell, Trevor Rabin, and Stingray from South Africa; and Dragon from New Zealand. Though the overwhelming majority of listings are for bands and solo artists originating in the United States or the United Kingdom, the *International Encyclopedia* also includes groups and artists from Belgium, Czechoslovakia, Denmark, France, Finland, Germany (East and West), Holland, Hungary, Iceland, Ireland, Italy, Norway, Spain, Sweden, Switzerland,

and Yugoslavia, as well as Canada and Australia. The encyclopedia also frequently mentions the importance of Japanese live appearances and "live" albums made in Japan for the careers of a number of international artists in the 1970s and early 1980s (see Waksman and also Kawano and Hosokawa, both this volume).

6 See Wilson 2008a for an intriguing argument that links 1990s rap and metal to American-style "supercapitalism."

7 Bushnell writes, "As of 1984, heavy metal sentiments were widely advertised on the walls [as graffiti], but not otherwise apparent. Within two years, the fans of heavy metal had coalesced into groups of *metallisty* who had their own loose organizations, hangouts, and distinctive dress" (1990, 87). As the essays in this book illustrate, this emergence of a full-fledged metal subculture in the mid-1980s parallels similar developments in other non-Anglophone countries, particularly in Eastern Europe, Asia, and Latin America.

8 For a thorough treatment of the complex relationships between aesthetic and ethical orientations, see Berger 2009.

9 Academic writing on heavy metal comes from a wide range of disciplines. For an excellent review of both the ethnographic and experiment-based literature, see Brunner 2006. Furthermore, a new interdisciplinary field called "metal studies" has taken shape in the past few years. A comprehensive and frequently updated metal studies bibliography once could be found on Keith Kahn-Harris's Web site (2008); the list is now managed by Brian Hickam of Benedictine University. In November 2008, the first academic conference on heavy metal music and culture was held in Salzburg, Austria. The participants were a diverse group of scholars, from ethnomusicologists to philosophers; more significant for this volume, those present also revealed the thoroughly international character of contemporary metal scholarship, with delegates from universities in Brazil, Canada, Denmark, Finland, Germany, Norway, Switzerland, Turkey, the United Kingdom, and the United States. In October 2009, an international conference on "Heavy Metal and Gender" was held at the University of Music and Dance in Cologne, Germany; it featured participation by both scholars and metal performers, including Doro Pesch, Angela Gossow, Sabina Classen of the German metal stalwarts Holy Moses, and Britta Görtz of the German extreme metal group Cripper. Another metal conference took place in Salzburg in November 2009 and a peer-reviewed journal, several edited volumes, and an international scholarly society of metal researchers are in the works at the time of this writing.

10 Setting the study in a wider context, we agree with Martin Stokes's observation (2004) that the present historical moment is a particularly fertile one for research in global musics. Increasingly over the last decade and a half, ethnomusicologists have examined popular musics; at the same time, the fields of popular music studies and cultural studies have started expanding beyond their focus on Western cultures to take on popular music phenomena on a global scale. Significant books at the intersection of these disciplines include those by Simon Frith (1989), Deanna Campbell Robinson, Elizabeth B. Buck, and Marlene Cuthbert (1991), Timothy Taylor (1997), Toru Mitsui and Shuhei Hosokawa (1998), Har-

ris M. Berger and Michael Thomas Carroll (2003), Paul D. Greene and Thomas Porcello (2005), Rupa Huq (2005), and Ignacio Corona and Alejandro Madrid (2008). Within this juncture of growing scholarly attention can be found a number of edited volumes published in the new century that, like *Metal Rules the Globe*, focus on a single music genre from a global, cross-cultural perspective. Examples include studies of hip hop (Mitchell 2001), salsa (Waxer 2002b), jazz (Atkins 2003), rock (Hernandez, L'Hoeste, and Zolov 2004), Indian film song (Gopal and Moorti 2008), and country (Fox and Yano forthcoming). The collective impact of these books attests to the growing interest in studies of world popular music genres in cross-cultural perspective. None of the edited volumes listed above, however, contains a sustained examination of metal, a genre that is arguably one of the most globalized of Western-originated popular musics.

11 Since its inception, heavy metal has developed an extremely broad range of subgenres, and their proliferation can be confusing, even for people firmly entrenched within the scene. To cite one example, the English-language version of Wikipedia, the Internet encyclopedia written by its users, lists twenty-seven metal subgenres or "fusion genres." The subgenres are avant-garde metal, black metal, classic metal, death metal, doom metal, folk metal, glam metal, gothic metal, groove metal, NWOBHM (New Wave of British Heavy Metal), post-metal, power metal, progressive metal, speed metal, symphonic metal, thrash metal, and Viking metal. Alternative metal, Christian metal, crossover thrash, funk metal, grindcore, industrial metal, metalcore, nü-metal, rapcore, and grunge are listed as "fusion genres." The subgenre of death metal has developed a more or less uniform sound around the world; black metal (a subgenre whose name refers to its focus on evil and the occult, not its racial makeup), however, often combines the musical style and imagery of Western extreme metal with that of the traditional cultures in the regions to which it has spread. For a discussion of metal's major subgenres, see Weinstein's chapter in this volume.

12 Metal's "loudness" is created in part by electronically boosting the upper and lower audible frequencies, not unlike the "loudness" button on a stereo system. This emphasis on aural extremes can be considered part of the oppositional stance of metal (Wallach 2003b, 47–48).

13 For another view of the complex relationship between heavy metal and amplification technology, see S. Kelly 2006. On extreme sensual experiences in performance, see Hahn 2006. For an early attempt to capture what we are calling "affective overdrive" in metal performance, see Breen 1991, which memorably describes a Metallica and Anthrax concert as creating "a moment of absolute identification with everything and nothing, a complete abstraction involving something untried and unknowable, and yet fully revealed in that moment of artistic, rock and rolling immediacy" (192).

14 Exploring related ideas, Mike Males concludes, "The biggest single theme of the metal groups I listened to was anti-victimization." He characterizes metal lyrics as expressing "enraged individualism" more than any explicit political ideology (1996, 125).

15   To an outsider, punk and metal—both rock-derived genres that emphasize distorted guitars, pounding drums, and a confrontational stance—might sound quite similar. However, subcultural insiders know that they are separate movements with significant differences in ideology, practice, fashion, and the musical devices they employ. Relations between these two styles are complex and historically variable (see Waksman 2009), and they shift considerably from place to place, depending on the history of exposure to these genres in the locale in question. Emerging in the United States in the 1980s, the genre of thrash metal was strongly influenced by hardcore punk, particularly in its use of fast tempos and driving ensemble passages. Differing dynamics played out in non-Western scenes. In Bali, Indonesia, metal fandom came to the island in the late 1980s, while punk did not arrive until the second half of the 1990s. At first, the Balinese punk scene was centered around Green Day, the popular group from California, but by the end of the decade it had mutated into a purist punk underground that preferred older, increasingly obscure punk bands and allied itself with a pan-Indonesian underground music movement that also included extreme metal (Baulch 2007; see also Pickles 2000 and Wallach 2003a, 2008a, 2008b). In general, punk's ethos of autonomous grassroots production, summed up by the slogan "Do It Yourself" (DIY), has been profoundly important to the development of underground metal scenes worldwide, while punk's tendency to reject musical virtuosity and its customary privileging of doctrine and lifestyle over musical quality have been rather less influential.

16   Surveying the world of extreme metal, Keith Kahn-Harris similarly concludes that "the [global metal] scene is oriented towards the mundane production of transgression" (2007, 66). In his view, scenic institutions make the experience of transgression repeatable and routinized by offering individuals the possibility of everyday forms of participation through activities such as music distribution, promotion, correspondence, and the purchasing of sound recordings and 'zines.

17   Metal bands in the United States and United Kingdom have long drawn on heroic images of the pre-modern past in their music, and such themes are found widely in global metal as well. For example, Cynthia P. Wong's chapter in this volume shows how the Beijing band Tang Dynasty deploys motifs from Chinese history and philosophy to evoke a nostalgic longing for imperial China. Likewise, Ross Hagen explains in his chapter how Norwegian black metal bands romanticized their country's pre-Christian past in forging their transgressive sound. Voicing both a frustrated desire for the benefits that modernity promises and a vitriolic critique of the ways in which modernity has actually played out, metal offers meanings that are complex and three-dimensional, and these examples represent a very specific moment in the music's complex, dialectical relationship to modernity. Clearly, the use of electric amplification and heavy distortion locate metal solidly in the contemporary world, and, as far as we know, no one in these scenes advocates for a Luddite renunciation of technology. Likewise, the music's strident themes of transgression and individual freedom make it implausible

that any band would support a submission to the strictures of pre-modern social mores. We would suggest that the celebration of the pre-modern here functions as a critique of modernity's unfulfilled promise, rather than the expression of a genuine desire to return to bygone days.

18 Beyond the world of white supremacist bands that Hochhauser documents, one place in global metal where racism has played a high-profile role is in the international black metal scene. Hagen notes in his chapter in this volume that some of the Norwegian founders of the genre in the early 1990s explicitly espoused racist views and celebrated a racist, anti-Christian, "pagan nationalism" (cf. Kahn-Harris 2007; Olson 2008). These bands tended to look for inspiration to an imagined Scandinavian "white warrior past" (L. Taylor 2008). However, the broader Scandinavian scene was far from uniform in its support of fascist or racist ideologies, and many scene members felt that the emphasis on politics drew attention away from the music or that the association of black metal and hate sullied the reputation of Paganism. See Hagen's chapter in this volume for further discussion of this issue.

The scholarly debate on the actual relationship between contemporary Paganism and Europe's pre-Christian past is complex, and we will not explore it here. It should be mentioned, however, that black metal did not draw solely on Norse Paganism, but also on Satanism, which many scene members preferred to call Devil Worship to distinguish their literal belief in Satan from the more philosophical writings of the twentieth-century American Satanist Anton LaVey (see Olson 2008).

19 Despite the emergence of hatecore metal, in most locales the music and its culture operate as an alternative to right-wing political and religious fundamentalist organizations, groups that aggressively recruit from the ranks of disenfranchised youth. As an anti-authoritarian music, metal generally serves as an antidote to the enforced conformity of fascist belief and practice.

20 To give just one illustration of the commitment that most metalheads have to the scene's global dimensions, we will mention an e-mail message that Wallach recently received from a member of Metakix, a thrash metal band from India, that—beneath the exclamation, "THIS IS FUCKING INSANE!!!!!!!"—contained links to jpeg images of the Brazilian Andreas Kisser, the American Derrick Green, and the German Mille Petrozza, each holding copies of Metakix's *Connect & Inspire* CD. Kisser and Green are both in the famed metal band Sepultura, while Petrozza is in Kreator, another internationally known metal act.

21 Examples of crossover between the metal scene and the mainstream music industry in non-Anglophone countries include the pop music career of Pablo Rosenberg, the former vocalist of the Israeli metal band Stella Maris; the co-writing of the 2003 Eurovision Song Contest winner "Everyway I Can" by the veteran Turkish metal guitarist Demir Demirkan (Ayik 2008); and the bizarre case of Lordi, a flamboyant, quasi-metal band from Finland that won the Eurovision Contest in 2006 (Wilson 2008b).

22 In subsequent decades, these two bands would be excised from the heavy metal

canon and treated as mere hard rock groups, as were many bands from that era. In the 1970s, though, both Kiss and Led Zeppelin were considered by many to be central to the genre.

23 While metal bands in this part of the world are rare, they are by no means unheard of. Notable groups from the region include Angola's Neblina and Botswana's Crackdust and Wrust. See Nilsson 2009 for a report on the scene in Gaborone, the capital of Botswana. The island nation of Madagascar is also home to a burgeoning heavy metal/hard rock scene that includes the internationally known group Sasamaso.

THE GLOBALIZATION OF METAL

Deena Weinstein

Bombs and bullet casings aren't the only forms of heavy metal in Iraq of late. The music that goes by that name is also there in force. But where bombs and bullets don't discriminate between people, heavy metal does so absolutely.

Most Iraqis have not encountered this style of music, but for those who have, it has had an extreme impact, positively or negatively. Heavy metal is used as a "soft-torture" technique by the American military on prisoners of war to demoralize them (Cusick 2008). Blaring metal is not a new tactic. The U.S. military has done this before, to the Panamanian dictator Manuel Noriega, when he took refuge in the Vatican embassy, and when Special Forces attempted to get al-Qaeda fighters out of caves in Afghanistan. "These people haven't heard metal before. They can't take it," the U.S. Psychological Operations Company Sergeant Mark Hadsell claimed to a *Newsweek* reporter (Borger 2003). The sergeant admits to personally liking the music, and there are a large number of American troops in Iraq, as there were in the Gulf War more than a decade earlier, listening to heavy metal in their tents. Detailing the torture techniques at the infamous Iraqi prison Abu Ghraib, a *New York Times* article explained how loud music was blasted into the cells of chained prisoners. One prisoner stated that he was forced to sit "naked, for 23 hours out of 24, with loud music blasting from a stereo. 'If they would have played for me good music, maybe I could have slept—boom, boom, boom!'" he said (Fisher 2004).

Other Iraqis not only have heard heavy metal before but also are ardent fans of the music. Bodybuilders working out at a Baghdad gym incorporate metal into their training routines. (Iraq dominated the Mr. Asia championships in the 1970s and 1980s.) The place was "buzzing with activity—huge men pump iron to the accompaniment of deafening heavy metal music" in preparation for international competition (Walker 2003).

Iraq also has had a couple of heavy metal bands. Foremost among them is Acrassicauda, which is named after a species of black scorpion native to the Iraqi desert. The band's sound is influenced by Slayer, Metallica, and Machine Head, and, according to its former frontman, the son of an Iraqi military officer, the band members learned their metal "through pirated CDs and videos smuggled in from Turkey and Jordan" (Freund 2003). The band's drummer told another reporter that they had seen heavy metal performances on television (Ghazal 2004). Before the fall of Saddam Hussein, the band would perform a song in his praise, while putting other songs into its set that slyly denounced him. The BBC reported on the band's January 5, 2004, concert in a community center "in an upmarket suburb of Baghdad." The venue was the Christian-run Hindiya Club in the Karrada district (Ghazal 2004). Because of the curfew, it was an afternoon show. "No one bats an eyelid," the reporter said, when "the dull thud of another bomb going off elsewhere in the city is hardly audible, but the glass doors of the building shake" (Hogg 2004). Acrassicauda's songs are all in English, even though its fans don't speak that language. One reason for this is the band's commercial aspirations; in English its recordings would sell better abroad. But another, more significant, motivation is the ideological significance of English. Muhammed, the band's drummer, says, "We want to sound educated. We want to prove to the outside world that our band can write and create music they can understand" (quoted in Ghazal 2004).

The members of Acrassicauda departed Iraq in the flood of refugees unleashed by the carnage there, finally making their way to Istanbul in 2007. Turkey's metal community, about 250 bands, helped them get equipment and a practice space. In November 2007, the band played at a multi-band concert to 350 people (Birch 2008).[1]

METAL'S GENEALOGY

Any discussion of the globalization of metal is faced with the problem of understanding what sorts of music are included under that category. As a genre, metal has been in existence for more than four decades, and in that time various subgenres have developed. But newer styles erase neither the styles from which they evolved nor any others, including the original. As a cultural formation metal prolongs its past into the future, maintaining older genres and adding diverse stylistic mutations as time goes on. It has no line of development with fixed stages; it is a cumulating archive. Complicating things further, styles of music that were once seen to be outside the genre become grandfathered into it years later. The music's fans add another level of complexity: those who consume mainstream media have a different understanding of metal than those who exclusively recur to specialized media, such as indie metal record labels.

Metal's geographical dissemination has both economic and cultural dimensions. Tracing the worldwide flow of a genre that was internationalized from its origin requires attention to the ways in which it was dispersed and appropriated, and why it resonates in any specific locale. General issues of metal's diffusion will be addressed in this chapter. The specific case studies that comprise the other chapters of this volume provide a clearer understanding of why metal (in general or one of its subgenres) becomes favored by some group somewhere in the world.

The genre of heavy metal emerged in the early 1970s. Determining the exact moment of metal's birth is difficult, if not impossible. The problem isn't the lack of historical research into the question, but the vagueness about what constitutes a genre and the condition that a genre cannot be known until sometime after it is in existence (see Weinstein 2000, 6–8). In other words, heavy metal, like other genres of popular music, existed before it had a name. By definition, a genre requires more than one band. One band's unique sound, or its earliest recordings that evince that unique sound, don't constitute a genre. At best, they constitute that band's signature sound.

Several approaches to the history of metal have been taken by those who have considered the subject. Ian Christe (2003) has taken a journalistic approach, stressing key bands and genres that were featured in major metal magazines. Robert Walser (1993a) has applied musicological methods to the topic. And I have treated the theme from the perspective of cultural sociology (Weinstein 2000). Although there are differences among the various interpretations (such as where subgenres begin and end, and how microscopically they are discriminated) the broad outlines traced by historians of metal are similar.

The genre's formative bands came from the United Kingdom and the United States. Many scholars of heavy metal point to Black Sabbath, emanating from the industrial British midlands at the start of the 1970s, as the first heavy metal band. However, if one were to give that distinction to the band whose music was first described in print by the term heavy metal, the honor would go to the more obscure American group, Sir Lord Baltimore. In a 1971 review of its album in *Creem* magazine, the critic Mike Saunders wrote: "Sir Lord Baltimore seems to have down pat most of all the best heavy metal tricks in the book." Saunders wasn't aware of his role in this naming process until a quarter century later. He, like many others, believed that his colleague Lester Bangs gave the genre its name.[2] (Bangs might have done so in conversation, but he wasn't the first to use it in print.)

In its formative years in the first half of the 1970s, heavy metal bands toured North America, the United Kingdom, and Western Europe. Black Sabbath's "initial impact was . . . on the Continent, where they toured continuously for seven months in 1969. By the late fall, they were well regarded by rock fans in Belgium, Holland, Denmark, Sweden, Germany, France, and Switzerland" (Clifford 1983, 57).

Like most genres, heavy metal became codified and crystallized after its formative period. I would nominate Judas Priest's second album, *Sad Wings of Destiny* (1976), as the first that embodies all of the genre's sonic, verbal, and visual codes.[3] Hearing *Sad Wings of Destiny* is like watching the first land creatures emerge from the primordial ooze. The music still has some vestiges of hard psychedelia, but it also has the unmistakable markings of earlier Black Sabbath and, less so, Led Zeppelin. Priest's powerful, emotional vocals, guitar virtuosity, driving heavy bass sound, and lyrics that speak of cosmic doom created the model for countless bands. The imagery of religious fantasy on the album's cover epitomizes metal's visual conceits: a grieving naked male angel, feathered wings outstretched, sits amid hellfire and brimstone. Around his neck he wears an upturned double-armed cross that became the band's icon.

Despite the genre's evolution, during which a variety of subgenres developed, heavy metal in both its formative and in its crystallized stages has not been erased. One reason for this is the metal subculture's demand over the past decades that new members learn the genre's history. Young fans collected the key works of defunct groups, bought their back catalogues, and went to shows of bands long in the tooth. Another reason for the persistence of metal's past is that many fans, themselves no longer young, maintain an allegiance to the bands that rocked their world during their youth. They may not keep up with newer styles, but they continue to enjoy the live and recorded music of their old favorites—and newer bands that play in that older mode.

At the same time that the genre was fragmenting and developing new subgenres, it was also enlarging its geographical domain. The means by which metal encircled the globe will be addressed after a brief discussion of the genealogy of metal styles.

Under the influence of the late 1970s British punk movement, the crystallized form that emerged in the heavy metal of Judas Priest used faster tempos than the earlier bands did. This new style, centered in the United Kingdom, became what is called the New Wave of British Heavy Metal (NWOBHM) and included bands such as Diamond Head and Iron Maiden. Starting in the late 1980s, metalheads began to refer to the crystallized form of 1970s heavy metal and the NWOBHM as "classic metal."

Fans of NWOBHM further increased the tempos in their own bands. By the start of the 1980s, this more aggressive and faster style of metal was gaining currency. First called "speed metal" and then "thrash metal," it was taken up by bands in the United States and Western Europe, including American groups Nuclear Assault, Anthrax, Metallica (the 1980s version), and Slayer, England's Venom, and Germany's Destruction. This punk-inflected subgenre, with its fast tempo and growly vocals, was played by musicians with straight long hair wearing black T-shirts and jeans— quite unlike their idols' costumed look. Thrash metal was the first style in what would later be called underground metal.

Thrash crystallized at the same time that the mainstream media, MTV especially, produced and promoted bands that took the hard rock elements of 1970s metal (particularly those associated with lyrics of love and lust) and the sounds and themes of 1970s hard rock bands like Aerosmith and developed what they, the media, marketed as "heavy metal." From the viewpoint of the fans of classic heavy metal, let alone those who championed the newer thrash metal, this MTV-made style wasn't "true" metal. They hurled terms like "poseur metal" and "false metal" at it. Another term used to describe this very popular form is "lite metal," which contrasts it to the heavy version. Lite metal is lighter in its sound and includes a tendency toward tenor-voiced and light-haired lead singers and lustful lyrics. "Hair metal" was another epithet for this commercial subgenre, alluding to the well-coiffed long hair of its performers. "True" metal hair was merely clean, long, and preferably straight; in contrast, "hair metal" hair was professionally cut in layers, often curled and teased, and held in a gravity-defying position with copious helpings of hairspray. Poison, Warrant, Twisted Sister, the more blues-based Cinderella, and the Springsteen-influenced Bon Jovi are examples of lite metal. Beyond MTV, mainstream media from glossy magazines to Top-40 radio stations embraced this style because it was selling so well. Of course, their promotion helped it to sell far better.

Lite metal's long and lucrative reign came to an end when the mainstream media embraced a new genre that they could deliver to a newer generation: grunge. The demise of lite metal coincides with the ascent of Nirvana's hit album *Nevermind* in late 1991. Metal was off the mainstream radar, especially in the United States, while grunge (packaged with some other styles by radio as the "alternative" format) reigned. When grunge played itself out, in part due to too many clones and too much heroin, the mainstream media promoted a new style that they dubbed "nü-metal" (also spelled "new metal"). Like the lite metal of a decade earlier, this mainstream metal descended from the hard rock of the 1970s, rather than classic or thrash metal. (Indeed, those hard rock bands that ruled the 1970s, such as Aerosmith and Kiss, were reinterpreted as metal in the 1980s.) Nü-metal bands, including Korn, Limp Bizkit, Slipknot, Linkin Park, and Disturbed, color their hard rock hues with elements of hip hop and coat them with grunge's angst-ridden aggression. Part of the style's initial mainstream recognition is exhibited by a feature in *Spin* magazine in 1998. The style was described as a "hybrid that takes as many cues from alternative rock, hip hop, and SoCal [Southern California] hardcore skate culture as it does from Black Sabbath and Slayer" (Ali 1998, 88).

Both lite metal and nü-metal were very much "made in the USA," where the vast majority of their bands and fans resided, and they did not spread far beyond their origins.[4] The reasons that those styles didn't globalize as extensively as classic metal and especially death metal are found in the fact that they are hybrids of metal with other forms of rock and, in some part, because they appeal to women. Where metal initially gains a foothold, it is usually as a form of male, working-class resistance. Non-Anglo-American cultures also have their own forms of popular music, which makes an American hard rock/metal hybrid less likely to receive an audience. Finally, in many societies outside the West, the cultural divides between gender roles are wider, making it less probable that a basically "male" style of music can be readily diffused to women, even in a hybridized form.

Other metal styles had emerged and competed with commercial American metal bands. One of them is doom metal, rooted in the early heavy psychedelia of Black Sabbath. Early bands like Pentagram, St. Vitus, Candlemass, and Trouble developed the subgenre. Melancholy themes pervade their lyrics and are reflected in the atmospheric gloom of their sound. Some doom bands such as My Dying Bride and Avernus encase their sound in synthesizers, adding goth flavoring to their mix, especially in the vocals and visuals. Another variety of this "slow 'n' heavy" sound draws on metal's psychedelic roots (that is, Kyuss, Sleep, Slo-Burn). At the turn of the twenty-first century, this style blossomed anew with festivals of its own, often under the label "stoner rock." It is represented by bands like High on Fire, Queens of the Stone Age, Spirit Caravan, and Sheavy (for more on doom metal, please see Bell, this volume).

Power metal, which was begun in the mid-1980s by the German band Helloween, takes the NWOBHM sound and exaggerates its powerful tenor vocals and melodicism, while continuing the mystical/mythical/sci-fi themes. Currently, this form is proliferating with key bands like Hammerfall (Sweden) and Iced Earth (United States), as well as worldwide festivals of its own, such as the one held in Atlanta, Georgia, in 2002. Referencing the progressive rock of the 1970s, progmetal is similar to power metal. (The Brazilian band Angra is claimed by both subgenres.) With significant practitioners like Dream Theater (United States), it stresses elements of avant-garde music, especially nontraditional time signatures, and emphasizes virtuosity even more than does classic heavy metal.

Thrash metal, neglected by the mainstream media during lite metal's prominence, gave rise to a wide variety of styles that collectively have been called "extreme metal." This includes death metal and black metal, two of the most globalized and the most intense of the music's subgenres. "These

forms," Keith Harris (2000b, 14) writes, "eschewed melody and clear singing in favour of speed, downtuned guitars and growled or screamed vocals.
Whilst each style has distinctive features and distinct networks of fans and
musicians, they share enough to be frequently referred to by fans and musicians as 'extreme metal.'" Rejecting pop-star posturing, the various fla-
vors of extreme metal's lyrics are devoid of romantic sentimentality, hippie
hopefulness, or wallowing in one's weakness. Their obsession is good and
evil, or—more precisely—evil.

Mapping metal, especially its active "underground," is a messy task at
best. No laws or sharpshooting border guards keep bands playing within
one style, nor are there any official music guardians or academic gatekeepers enforcing the standardized usage of terminology by critics, publicists,
or fans. Moreover, styles are not watertight containers: they leak, bleed
into others. Musicians borrow and steal, and styles constantly evolve and
transform into new styles. With borders more porous than those between
Mexico and the United States, or Pakistan and Afghanistan, not even fans
or critics know where to draw the lines. The following discussion describes
only the better-known varieties of extreme metal.

Metalcore, played by bands including Machine Head and Biohazard
(both from the United States), combines thrash metal with hardcore punk.
The style has grown as hardcore punk bands have metalized their sound,
fusing the once feuding genres. While metalcore tends to be American,
grindcore, initiated by Napalm Death and Carcass in the late 1980s, originated in the United Kingdom. This small subgenre includes Brutal Truth
and Extreme Noise Terror, and noisily combines death metal with hardcore
punk, including the political thrust of the latter's lyrics.

Death metal rules underground metal; the subgenre has the largest
contingent of bands and the most extensive global reach. It is found in
every part of the world where there is an industrial working class and is
more ubiquitous than McDonald's. Thrash metal bands like Slayer (United
States) and Venom (United Kingdom) stimulated the formation of innumerable death metal bands. Its distinctive style combines a variety of
features, such as downtuned guitars and the heavy use of double-kick
drums. Vocalists growl as if gargling with razor blades and acid, emitting
probably the lowest pitch of any form of vocal music. In concert, or with a
stereo played at a volume sure to annoy neighbors, it delivers a tactile as
well as a sonic experience. Inspired especially by Cronos (the vocalist from
Venom) and Switzerland's Celtic Frost, Chuck Schuldiner's band Death

(United States) fully defined the subgenre in its classic release, *Scream Bloody Gore* (1986).

Death metal could well serve as the soundtrack to the movie version of Dante's *Inferno* or at least as hell's Muzak. Its lyrics are fixated on death, disease, decay, and diabolism. Band names faithfully reflect these themes, as a sampling of a few of the thousands of practitioners demonstrates: Entombed, Morbid Angel, Obituary, Cannibal Corpse, Six Feet Under, Suffocation, Dismember, Malevolent Creation, Atheist, Eyehategod, Angelcorpse, and Deicide.[5]

The other major form of underground/extreme metal is black metal, which erupted in Norway in the late 1980s out of thrash and death metal. Both death and black metal share distorted and ferocious electric guitars, rapid tempos, and an insistent and prominent rhythm with emphasis on bass drums. Black metal vocalists have a taste for rasped screams, rather than growling. Most black metal bands, especially the earlier ones, "tune in E, are concerned to create an aggressive atmosphere and are not unfamiliar with either keyboards or sampling. The melodies develop logically, the lyrics are more or less audible and the harmonies are sad, dark and almost beautiful in their minor keys" (Pedersen 2000, 7).

The driving force behind the first crystallized black metal band, Mayhem, and behind black metal in general, was Euronymous (b. Øystein Aarseth). He played guitar in Mayhem, released recordings by other black metal groups on his own label, and ran a metal record shop called Helvete (Hell) in Oslo. In 1993 a musician in another black metal band murdered Euronymous, stabbing him twenty-three times. Far more than the previous sensational actions of Norwegian black metal musicians (such as cemetery desecrations and church burnings) or the earlier gory suicide of Dead, the singer in Mayhem, the news of this crime gave black metal worldwide notoriety.[6]

The first wave of black metal lyrics focused on Satanism but then became suffused with allusions to pre-Christian religions and ancient warriors. While the musical form and lyrics of death metal are fairly consistent in their various manifestations around the world, black metal has incorporated elements from local musics and cultures as it has globalized, including traditional instruments, themes that engage traditional folk tales, and local dialects or dead languages (for more on black metal, please see chapters by Hagen and Kahn-Harris, this volume).[7]

Apart from the forms of metal endogenous to its development, an ideological subgenre resisting satanic imagery emerged. Initially called "white metal," it became better known as "Christian metal" in the 1990s. Bands so labeled are found in every subgenre, from classical and thrash to death and black metal. Mainly confined to America (although recently European Christian black metal bands have come into existence), Christian metal bands are most often explicit about their message: "they are primarily [Christian] evangelists—metal missionaries" (Hart 1988, 19). But others, like Kings X, are wary of the label. That band's singer, Doug Pinnick, argued that "Christian metal bands want to be preachers to save the world. We want to relate to people, not to preach" (Dasein 1991, 46). Tourniquet, a death metal band based in Los Angeles, is hardly preachy, as it adheres to one of the subgenre's thematics—gore. In "Theodicy on Trial," a song from *Pathogenic Ocular Dissonance* (1992), the band describes Job's trials in terms of the black boils erupting all over his skin. What's more, "his breath was super roached, stomach caving in." With bands touring the country to testify and witness, a metal ministry was begun in the 1990s by the evangelical minister Bob Beeman, as an expansion of his heavy metal church in California (Glanzer 2003).

Since the beginning of the current century, the task of charting metal's nether regions has been made even messier by the mixing and matching of all forms of extreme metal: blends such as black death, doom death, and death thrash have proliferated. These extreme forms should be understood in the larger context of the heavy metal genre as a whole. If Dante were to map metal's genealogy—and having him do so would be a nod to the medievalism that permeates the genre—*Paradiso* would contain the lite metal and nü-metal bands that top sales charts and receive exposure on TV and commercial radio. *Purgatorio* is where there is a possibility of entering *Paradiso* (mainstream media and its financial rewards), after working off one's sins; styles like power metal would fall into such a limbo. Musical styles classified as extreme metal would be confined to *Inferno*, damned forever to marginal-to-the-mainstream media status, never to see the light. But as AC/DC famously sang, "Hell ain't a bad place to be."

THE PROCESS OF METAL'S GLOBALIZATION

The diffusion of metal around the world has two distinctive phases. In the first, ending in the late 1980s, metal gradually spread outward from its original sites in Britain and the United States. In the middle of the 1970s, it was found throughout Western Europe, Australia, and Canada, and, by the end of the decade, in Japan. By the middle of the next decade, metal had spread behind the Iron Curtain (aboveground in some areas, like Poland, underground in others, like the Soviet Union) and to the more affluent and urbanized areas of Latin America, particularly in Brazil and Argentina.

Like the spread of McDonald's, television, and indoor plumbing, the direction of the first phase of metal's diffusion was from more economically and technologically developed areas to less developed ones. The second phase of metal's globalization, which was well underway by the start of the 1990s, increased the international reach of the genre, penetrating Asia's Pacific Rim, many of the major cities in Latin America, and the secular sectors in the Middle East. Even Saudi Arabia has metal bands, including Wasted Land, which has played in Jeddah, Saudi Arabia, as well as at EgyptFest in Cairo and the Shamal Battle of the Bands in Dubai (El Evil Emperor 2007). While initially lagging behind, the sub-Saharan African metal scene, which is dominated by but not exclusive to descendents of European immigrants, has grown recently, with bands appearing in South Africa, Botswana, Namibia, Tanzania, Zimbabwe, and Madagascar. In great part, this is merely a continuation of metal's phase-one march. What marks it as a distinctive period of development, though, are a number of factors, including but not restricted to changes in metal's subgenres and the introduction of new media (particularly the Internet). With these factors, the music no longer moved only from developed countries to less developed ones; to the contrary, metal began to move in the opposite direction and also circulated among scenes in the developing world. The worldwide metal scene is still firmly within this second phase.

Despite the marked differences between the two phases of metal's globalization, the processes by which it becomes established in a new area follow the same general pattern. In many respects, this path resembles the way in which plants and animals have diffused geographically from the areas of their origin to other locales.

The first step along the path is merely to arrive at the new location. When flora and fauna become established in areas far from their origins, some get there through intentional human intervention, like the rabbits of Australia or the kudzu of the American South. Others migrate through unintentional human action, like the zebra mussels overtaking the Great Lakes, which arrived via ship ballast discharge, or the smallpox virus that decimated Native Americans, at first unwittingly introduced by the more resistant Europeans. But most globe-trotting species travel without humans, as when coconuts are carried by ocean currents to newly formed islands or when birds, blown off course to new places, deposit seeds that they had ingested at earlier ports of call. Metal, as a cultural form, gets to previously metal-free areas only with human intercession.

Unlike so many other forms of globalized music, metal's globalization is not due to the movement of diasporic communities that took their culture with them when they migrated. Instead, metal diffuses through the efforts of one or more of the following three social actors: musicians, fans, and mediators. In contrast, popular cultural forms such as reggae and Bollywood movies were disseminated as part of the cultural baggage of Jamaican and Indian immigrant communities, respectively.

Despite metal's Anglo-American origins, the genre has not been seen as belonging to any specific culture. Like hell and paradise, one cannot point to a place on a realistic map of the world to show where metal is rooted. It is instructive in this regard to compare metal with the mid-1970s British punk movement, which was specifically national. Those bands composed songs about British issues, like the Sex Pistols' "God Save the Queen" and the Clash's "White Riot." Vocals were delivered in a distinctive (often newly acquired) Cockney accent. Visually, bands, fans, and album covers sported a despoiled British Union Jack or pictures of the Queen.

Like transnational capitalism, with corporations located in the metropole but active in sites far afield, metal was always deterritorialized. It did not speak from any country or culture. Even in the 1970s the Scorpions from Hamburg, Germany, whose members spoke in highly accented and rather fractured English, sang in English; when asked why, the singer said that German was inadequate to express metal feelings and themes.[8] During this period, English was the global language for metal.[9] Most bands that were well-known in their country and all that were known internationally sang in English.[10]

With the exception of some recent black metal, what has been said about rave music holds for metal in general: "New musics of the nineties, such as dance and rave . . . have not only crossed but even eradicated previous cultural, conceptual and national boundaries, replacing them with shifting patterns of taste and 'alliance.' These alliances and rapidly evolving 'scenes' . . . are replacing loyalties of place and class among the young, as well as of culture and nationality" (Llewellyn 1998). Metal has constituted itself as a set of communities of fans, bands, and mediators — virtual diasporic cultural groups that feel alienated from and disdainful of their various host nations, or class or ethnic enclaves. Fans of classic metal were especially proud of their worldwide "Denim and Leather" wearing "Brothers of Metal" (to quote song titles by Saxon and Manowar, respectively).

"[W]orld music artists and fans, it is argued, cannot be defined by national borders nor shared language, but rather as an imagined community in which 'one can claim citizenship by listening to and borrowing from others' musics'" (Guilbault 1996). Metal artists and fans also lay claim to citizenship in an "imagined community," but, in metal, they are listening to their *own* music. Metal is transcultural, not cross-cultural. In other words, metal is not a music tied to a particular culture, which people in other cultures happen to enjoy as outsiders; rather, metal is the music of a group of people that transcends other, preexisting cultural and national boundaries. As Martin Hooker, the founder of the British label Music for Nations, has observed, metal "might not always be trendy, but it's always there and it's the one kind of music that you can always sell in every territory throughout the world—which is why I called the company Music for Nations" (Hunt 1987, 36). Another metal label, Black Mark, employs the slogan, "Metal for the World" in its logo.

Metal's transnationalism and its transcultural community are evinced in the songs and visual iconography of the classic heavy metal band, Manowar. Formed in the early 1980s by New Yorkers, the band is still actively touring and releasing new material today. Each of the sixteen cuts on Manowar's double live album *Hell on Stage Live* (1999) was recorded in a different venue in Europe and South America. Fan Web sites for the band come from over twenty countries. Its albums contain songs about Viking, ancient Greek, and Native American warriors. There are also allusions to J. R. R. Tolkien's Middle Earth, the fictional medieval world that many metal bands embrace.[11] The cover of Manowar's *Kings of Metal* (1988) album depicts metal (personified as a muscular male warrior) defeating nation-states, whose flags lie in ruins beneath his feet. As these few examples illustrate, metal has not only been transnational, but has valorized its transnationalism.

The audience for lite metal and nü-metal is a mass fan base. Fans learn about the music via the mass media, especially major radio stations and MTV. But fans of metal's other styles have been anything but mass audiences, even though they experience solidarity across diverse subgenres and localities. Addressing the German metal scene of the late 1990s, Bettina Roccor (2000, 87) concludes that fans "feel themselves to be members of one family because all heavy metal styles are based on the same basic musical patterns, the values supporting their culture have remained predominantly the same and the music's negative image has unified the fans in their indignation."

Rarely aired in major media outlets or covered in general rock magazines, thrash metal and its descendents gained adherents mainly through interpersonal contacts—friends, older relatives, or pen-pals linked via imported metal magazines. This underground/extreme metal took root around the world despite, rather than through, the offices of hegemonic mediators. Amardeep Singh's (2000, 92) analysis of punk also applies to metal: "They have 'globalized' *without* evident channel-based transmission, without being manipulated or exploited by the broadcast system of the 'difference-making machine' (Lawrence Grossberg's term) of transnational media capitalism." The spread of extreme metal among Indonesian fans is typical for that music's penetration elsewhere: "Indonesian fans learned about non-mainstream rock genres, first from commercial crossovers promoted in the global media, and later from their own forays into the direct-mail-order world of small independent recording labels and low-budget fanzines" (Wallach 2003a, 58).

Among the many channels of metal's diffusion are U.S. armed services radio and interactions between U.S. military personnel overseas and locals living near the bases. Given metal's strong appeal to young lower-middle-class and working-class males (the same demographic that is found in troops stationed abroad), the genre was effectively disseminated. Travel by individuals, including return visits by immigrants and students who had studied abroad, also enables the circulation of metal, as it does for so many other forms of music.[12] Then, too, general rock music media, such as magazines, movies with musical soundtracks, and MTV, may include stories about metal or songs that lead potential fans to explore the style.

Widely popular rock bands of the 1970s, like Deep Purple, whose music bordered on metal (listen, for example, to its song "Highway Star"), served as a gateway to metal; like entry-level drug users, some of their fans developed a taste for the harder stuff. Further, when Deep Purple's virtuosic lead guitarist Ritchie Blackmore left to form the heavy metal band Rainbow, some of Deep Purple's fans followed him into the genre. Given Deep Purple's vast popularity, it was able to bring its tours to areas previously virgin to arena hard rock. In 1975, for example, Deep Purple played in Yugoslavia (Zagreb and Belgrade), Indonesia (Jakarta), and Hong Kong (see Young [1997] 2000).

In the 1980s some major classic metal bands also traveled to the "periphery" (the term that globalization scholars use to refer to the area outside the dominant currents of power in the world economy); notable among these was the most popular of the New Wave of British Heavy Metal groups, Iron Maiden. In Rio de Janeiro, Brazil in 1985, Iron Maiden, Ozzy Osbourne, the Scorpions, and various other groups played to an audience numbering in the tens of thousands (see Avelar 2003). Fans who attended these concerts experienced the vast popularity of the style and felt a sense of community with those attending, strengthening their commitment.

At the start of the second phase of metal's globalization, in the late 1980s, Sepultura brought its made-in-Brazil thrash metal to non-Western arenas. The band's impact was significant, in part because its members themselves came from the periphery, which resonated with non-Western audiences and minority audiences, such as Latinos in the United States, showing them that metal could be made, and made well, by "peripheral" peoples. Although 1970s-era metal had some following in Brazil, Sepultura and its contemporaries were influenced by bands like Slayer and Venom. It was not only their thrash metal but also their punk-based do-it-yourself ethic that generated innumerable bands "among working and lower-middle classes in the Belo Horizonte—with some presence in Sao Paulo, Porto Alegre, and other metropolises" (Avelar 2001, 127–28). Sepultura's impact coincided with one of the pivotal factors for the second phase of metal's diffusion, the maturing of economic markets in many areas of Southeast Asia and Latin America.

MAGAZINES AND 'ZINES

It was magazines and recordings that were most responsible for creating fans in the periphery, which only then led promoters to book the tours of international metal bands. Coinciding with the New Wave of British Heavy Metal and the growth spurt in the heavy metal audience throughout the West, specialized heavy metal magazines began to appear. *Kerrang!*, which started in the United Kingdom in 1981, was joined a few years later by *Metal Forces*, *Metal Hammer* (subtitled *The International Hard Rock and Heavy Metal Magazine*), and *RAW* ("Rock Action Worldwide"). These publications were read by fans from many countries. In the latter part of the 1980s, other magazines included *R.I.P.* (United States), *Hard Rock* (France), *Metallion* (Canada), *Heavy Rock* (Spain), *Livewire* (Germany), *Morbid* (Norway), *Revenge* (Brazil), *Madhouse* (Argentina), *F.E.T.U.* (Japan), and *Grim Death* (New Zealand). Introduced to one another through the pen-pal section of magazines, fans traded letters and tapes, strengthening the ties among them.

Punk not only influenced metal's increased tempos but also provided the model for fanzines. These modest efforts, written by one or sometimes several intense fans, form one pole of an axis on which the glossy magazines, which cover the more popular bands and have more pictures than words, anchor the other.

Metal's transnational links and its globalization are fully displayed in an issue of the Malaysian magazine *G.O.D.* from 1995. There, a black metal musician from Lithuania is interviewed in a rough-and-ready form of English. Toward the end of the piece, he is asked: "What are you know about my country Malaysia, especially about Black Metal bands?" The Lithuanian replies: "About Malaysia I know very little, sorry. About bands? I know Aradia, Bazzah, Misanthrope, Nebiras—fine Black band. Death Metal I know Brain Dead, Suffocation [*sic*], Sil-khannaz, Kitanai Chi, Silent Death. Yeah! Nothing more!"[13]

RECORDED MUSIC

Major labels based in the United States and Western Europe released much of the work of the classic metal bands, the lite metal that MTV featured, and the nü-metal that came into prominence toward the end of the century. But the bulk of the metal canon, especially those styles categorized as "underground" and "extreme," has, with a handful of exceptions, been confined to independent labels. "Indies" like Music for Nations initially emerged in Britain, where the metal subculture was strongest.

Indies in the United States began by re-licensing British imports for U.S. distribution, as well as producing records by U.S. bands. One of the more successful, Metal Blade, began in this manner in 1983. Its list focused heavily on the new speed/thrash subgenre, with bands such as Slayer, Satan, Nasty Savage, Sodom, Malice, and Tyrant. Both in terms of the number of bands it handled and the complexity of its organization, Metal Blade's growth is somewhat typical. Indie labels in one area began signing bands from other countries with underdeveloped metal industries. For example, in 1987, Roadrunner, located in New York, signed the Brazilian band Sepultura.

Until the second phase of metal's globalization, fans from the periphery could obtain recordings only via mail-order companies such as Wild Rags and Relapse, or from travel abroad. By the 1990s indie record companies were well established outside the West. Developments in recording technology made production far less expensive—as Jeremy Wallach (2005a) describes for Indonesia—and allowed for the proliferation of small labels. "The lower cost of production," another analyst argues, "enable[s] small-scale producers to emerge around the world, recording and marketing music aimed at specialized, local grassroots audiences rather than at a homogeneous mass market" (Frith 2000, 314).

Licensing distribution deals also greatly expanded the ability of fans to buy metal recordings globally. For example, the Indonesian extreme label THT has distribution deals in its home country and in Japan, Slovakia, Latvia, Italy, Czech Republic, Romania, Ukraine, Bulgaria, Australia, Norway, France, Mexico, Brazil, and the United States. *The Painful Experience* (2001), an album by THT's band Kekal, was released by three independent labels: Clenchedfist Records (United States) for the North American territory, Fear Dark (the Netherlands) for the European territory, and THT Productions for the Southeast Asian territory.

As the number of metal fans increases in any area, retail record stores begin to serve them. Imported and local metal can now be found in mainstream record stores and mega-chains. Some cities even support metal-only retail stores, like those in Stockholm and Chicago.

ELECTRONIC MEDIA

The economics of magazines and recordings allow for intensive specialization. Electronic media, especially radio and TV, require larger and less segmented audiences. Just as the pop varieties of metal have filled the shelves of mass retail stores, they are staples of radio and television, mainly MTV. In contrast (and by definition), underground and extreme metal have been ignored by these mainstream media. Non-commercial radio is an exception. In the United States, for example, many college radio stations have had a weekly specialty program devoted to underground metal. In a 1998 e-mail message to me, an executive from an independent U.S. record label wrote that he tallied about five hundred such shows, and in Poland in the 1980s, when it was a Communist country, the state radio aired a specialty metal show.

In a few countries even extreme metal is integrated into some commercial radio fare, typically in the later hours. In the United States, the satellite station Z-Rock uploaded a metal show from Dallas and broadcast it to dozens of local market radio stations around the country from 1986 through the early 1990s.

After its first two years, MTV restricted its initially broad playlist to resemble that of commercial radio. The cable network aired videos by lite metal and, later on, nü-metal bands, excluding underground/extreme metal. For several years, starting in the late 1980s, MTV had a late night metal program called *Headbanger's Ball* that included videos by the more popular underground metal bands. In Latin America, Europe, and Asia, MTV was more open to metal, in part because the extreme forms are more popular in those regions than in the United States.[14]

THE INTERNET

In contrast to radio and television, the Internet's global reach, low cost, and ease of use allows for incredible specialization, at the same time that it aggregates the contents of diverse media such as magazines, recordings, radio, and television.

The advent of widespread Internet use is one of the defining features of the second phase of metal's globalization. Established magazines maintain Web sites augmenting their paper editions, but more significant is a proliferation of Web-zines (or "e-zines") with no connection to printed publications.[15] These sites offer current news, provide archives of past interviews and reviews, give dates for upcoming concerts, have contests, allow interactive discussion boards and chat rooms, display numerous — expensive to print — pictures, and let users hear music via streaming audio or downloadable MP3s. Without the cost constraints of paper, printing, and postage, Web-zines can offer far more information than magazines.

Some sites focus on a single metal style, either globally, regionally, or nationally. Others exhibit the fans' obsessions with one or a few favorite bands, and as in every popular music style, bands have their own official Web sites. In addition to magazine, fan, and band sites, indie metal labels maintain sites with links to their bands' homepages and often with full or partial songs from new releases. These sites include news of new recordings and tours, band biographies, photos, reviews and interviews, discussion boards, and numerous links. All metal Web pages tend toward a highly graphic visual format, with dark colors, and they often sport moving visuals of fire, skulls, and dripping blood.

The Internet serves as a virtual medium for retail stores, jukeboxes, radio stations, and music video TV, allowing one to hear or acquire the widest variety of music. Those who make and maintain the various sites, as well as their visitors, come from all parts of the world that have metal fans and Internet access. Most sites, including those that host discussion groups, are in English, but an increasing number offer language options: Russian or English, Spanish or English, Chinese or English.

Simon Frith's (2000, 315) general statement that "technology makes for a new music culture, organized around neither local traditions nor global corporate trends" is especially true for the Internet's impact on metal. The Internet supplements and reduces the influence of traditional media and interpersonal communication. Also, it more effectively enables extreme metal styles to take root around the world, since they had never been dispersed by hegemonic mediators. The globalization of metal received enhanced momentum when the rise of the Internet coincided with the economic boom that increased the standard of living in "peripheral" areas, especially in the metropolitan centers of Southeast Asia and Latin America.

LOCAL BANDS

The various mediators of metal provided the initial fan base that then allowed promoters to book tours of international metal bands. The initial establishment of a fan base of metalheads in a country is only one step in the process of incorporating that country in metal's globalization, and some nations do not go beyond the fandom stage. The second and more complicated step is the indigenous production of the diffused style.

In a given country, the exchanging of air guitars for real ones requires a sufficient fan base with both the financial wherewithal to purchase musical equipment and the leisure time to practice and rehearse. The proliferation of metal fans around the world has led to a profusion of metal bands. Once there are enough fans, some begin to make their own music, first covering their idols' songs and then writing their own. "All our friends would just hang out and listen to heavy metal albums every day, and eventually we had to do something besides that, perhaps we could do something our-

selves," the singer for Dark Tranquility, a Swedish black metal band, relates. "Then we formed a band" (Pizek 2003, 5).

Over time, bands break up or at least play a version of musical chairs,
rarely keeping all of their founding members. Some musicians quit because
of family obligations or outside career opportunities; others are dismissed
because their musical skills haven't advanced to the same degree as their
bandmates, or they are seriously impaired by drug use; and, of course,
there are all sorts of disagreements and disagreeable personalities that
split up bands. Thus, there is need for a pool of potential musicians and
others who can help with the concerts and the recording process.

Further, there must be a scene that sustains these fledgling bands.
Venues in which to play and recording studios can be difficult to find in
areas that do not have an infrastructure in place for rock music. Even if
studios exist, each style of music is best handled by producers who are
knowledgeable in that genre.[16] As local scenes grow and bands play international dates, it is only a matter of time before some bands have an international membership based on the worldwide language of metal.[17]

TOURS AND FESTIVALS

Another site of metal's globalization is international festivals, many
purely metal, which draw an international set of bands and fans. One
of the earliest was England's Reading Festival in 1980; performers included British bands like UFO, Def Leppard, and Iron Maiden, the Anglo-
American group Ozzy Osbourne, the Swiss band Krokus, Germany's Scorpions, and Australia's Angel City. The Monsters of Rock was a touring
festival held in several countries. In 1988 it played in England, Germany,
Holland, Italy, Spain, and France, showcasing U.S. and European bands
playing thrash metal (Anthrax), power metal (Helloween), and classic
metal (Iron Maiden). In the United States, the annual Milwaukee Metal-
fest began in 1987 with fifteen thrash and death metal bands. Growing
larger each year, the event had gathered over one hundred fifty (mainly extreme metal) bands from sixteen countries, including the Czech Republic,
Poland, Mexico, and Japan in 2000.

There are now dozens of annual metal festivals, most of them in Europe
but some on other continents. The largest, Wacken in Germany, sold over
sixty thousand tickets five months before the three-day event was to take
place in August 2008 (Blabbermouth 2008).

CONCLUSION

In 1997 the punk elder statesman Jello Biafra said, "Isn't it ironic that death metal is the first form of rock music that has caught on with poor people over the world. . . . Death metal is popular from Moldavia to Cuba. [No rock subculture is] as tight culturally as the death metal community[,] where you have people in Norway swapping tapes with people in Malaysia, and all the bands sound more than a little bit alike" (quoted in Grad 1997).

Ironic? Only if we fail to look more closely at the meaning of the term "poor." The vast majority of the world's peasants in the villages of Africa, Asia, the Indian subcontinent, and Latin America, who live without electricity and indoor plumbing, are not, even if adolescent and male, fans of metal. Access to and appreciation of the music requires being in an industrial society. Metal's audience is generally adolescent males from working-class backgrounds. The more "underground" the audience is, the more this demographic generalization holds true. If there is an irony, it is that the proletarian internationalism that is dear to Marxists finds its most conspicuous cultural expression in underground metal, a style most music critics outside of metal, Marxist and otherwise, tend to despise.

In many places, death metal or black metal is the music of choice for members of subordinate ethnic groups (but that may also be a factor of class). What most of the audience seems to share is an alienation from the post-industrial world, their parents, and the future. Discussing the background of Sepultura and countless similar bands in Brazil, Idelber Avelar (2001, 132) comments that they "originated primarily in a milieu fully exposed to modernization but excluded from its fruits." Working-class values of craftsmanship and muscularity, and a disdain for schooling, have little benefit in a world dominated by computers and high-tech global capitalism. The morbid themes that run through extreme metal may reflect the situation of a group of people with the vitality of youth who are locked into a hopeless situation as members of a declining class. On the flip side, the glorification of those values would reflect the sublimation of lost power.

Although death metal and black metal are rooted in a common structural situation, they differ in the ways in which they have globalized. The older form, death metal, has a worldwide uniformity of sounds, themes, visuals, and language, and English tends to be its lingua franca. In contrast, much of the newer black metal tends toward a *glocalized* model,[18] in which the broadly diffused style is combined with elements of a local group's pre-modern culture, such as melodic approaches and scalar materials, musical instruments, allusions to glorious ethnic myths, and the indigenous language (in this volume, see chapters by Idelber Avelar, Paul D. Greene, Ross Hagen, and Cynthia P. Wong for diverse examples of metal's glocalization). This shift may reflect a rising nationalism, a resistance to the oppressive force of economic globalization.

Extreme metal's fervent fans constitute, by their common demographics, what George Lipsitz (1994, 27) calls "aggrieved communities." He would interpret their musical culture as a new kind of politics that "takes commodity culture for granted," but that produces "an immanent critique of contemporary social relations." Kean Wong (1993, 21) shows how this process occurred in Southeast Asia:

> The heavy metal subculture becomes a home, a refuge for those dislocated in urban migration, caught between stereotypical racial politics and often fluid urban space divisions brought on by rapacious property development. [It] might seem like ham-strung vaudeville from a media-saturated Western outlook, but this internationalized language of stock rebellion and theatrical posturing clearly resonates for youth in Indonesia, Malaysia or Singapore, and offers comfort and identity to those still ambivalent about buying into the post-feudal/colonial capitalist environment that's being rapidly constructed around them.

Wong is right that metal might "seem like ham-strung vaudeville" to some Western onlookers, but certainly not to all—not to metal's fans in North America, Europe, and Australia, where the style started. Perhaps there are shades of difference, sometimes marked, among the ways that metal is appropriated and appreciated around the world, but Wong's point about Southeast Asia has general application: the reception of metal globally is rooted in an "ambivalence" about buying into the "post-feudal/colonial capitalist environment." Audiences in, for example, Buddhist cultures may interpret satanic images metaphorically, audiences acculturated to rock music will hear metal in terms of a wider sonic and symbolic context than those who have grown up with other forms of music, and audiences in countries where metal is legally banned will endow it with added elements of underground resistance; yet, they all share a common class position in their societies and are bound to the same transcultural metal community.

Wherever a global entertainment culture is being rapidly diffused to a new market through many, highly impersonal, channels, reception

THE GLOBALIZATION OF METAL

will tend to be eclectic. In the case of metal, the personal and localized chains of appropriation will be supplemented and supplanted by generalized points of access, such as the Internet. In 2004, Brad Warren, whose doctoral thesis analyzed the Australian metal scene, reported to me in an e-mail message that in Guangzhou Province in southern China, there is increasing interest in metal among the youth, manifest through their growing music collections and the appearance of stores specializing in metal recordings and related items. The new audience does not have distinctive loyalties to subgenres but experiments with many forms of metal and, indeed, with related rock styles. One of Warren's students sent him a mobile phone message at the start of 2004 that read: "I have many records about [sic] heavy metal: Sinister, Avulsed, Tristania, Opprobrium, Slayer, 12 Rounds, Pearl Jam, Fear Factory."[19]

Metal is not just a name for a set of unrelated musical styles. It is a cultural form that continues to generate varieties and hybrids while maintaining a continuity of code and a self-conscious tradition that remains determinative wherever it travels. From a sociological standpoint, this indicates that metal is a recurrent cultural response to common structural tensions in capitalist economies. This fits, I would argue, with Lipsitz's notion of taking commodity culture for granted and generating an immanent critique of it—of metal as an ambivalent response to the predicament of being a member of a declining class.

It is impressive that without the assistance of hegemonic cultural institutions, and even facing hostility from them, working-class youth created an oppositional subculture of genuinely global reach and content. Death metal croaks the same damning message around the world—that all human decencies and fantasies of comfort will be subverted and overwhelmed by the forces of evil and chaos (sublimated and displaced revolutionary destruction). Black metal screeches the praises of heroes and demons who are always the same warriors, whatever local tradition the band in question is appropriating to sublimate and displace revolutionary heroism. Common to many death and black metal songs is a strong anti-Christian stance. This direct attack on Christianity resonates with Marx's famous notion that "religion is the opium of the people," although, in this case, Nietzsche's idea that Christianity is a "slave morality" might be more to the point.[20]

Metal has globalized effectively because it responds to the psycho-social needs of an audience that remains much the same in its structural situation throughout the world. Economic globalization and its handmaiden, industrial and post-industrial technology, create their casualties and resistances. Metal was thought by the Soviet Communists to be "one of the cleverest ideological diversions yet invented by capitalist imperialists" (Sarkitov 1987, 93). Far from it—metal is a symbolic rebellion of a compromised class, proletarian internationalism in a most imposing and surprising form.

NOTES

1 *Editors' Note*: For the interested reader, the story of Acrassicauda is depicted in the documentary film *Heavy Metal in Baghdad* (Moretti and Alvi 2007).

2 Mike Saunders, in a personal e-mail message to me in December 1999, wrote:
   "1971 was definitely the first year the term 'heavy metal' was ever used in print in the rock press (in either reviews or articles). During spring 1971 I sent Dave Marsh a review of the 1st SIR LORD BALTIMORE lp . . . and I recall the review itself kicked out/wondered out loud which term you would label that album . . . Anyway, by Fall 1971 everyone was using the term, which would have consisted of a bunch of fanzine people/fanzines, and the only two reviewers reviewing metal albums in Rolling Stone (Lester Bangs, myself) and other mags."

   "PARANOID," he wrote, "was all over the few cool FM radio stations via 'Iron Man' and 'War Pigs' (like the infamous zillion-watt latenight KAAY 'Bleecker Street' out of our hometown Little Rock) in Summer 1971, which is where I first heard said tracks and was instantly converted. BEFORE the Paranoid LP, definitely no use of the term anywhere, so that album would be the closest to the nomenclature switch . . . (from 'heavy' rock a la Cream, Blue Cheer, etc). ALSO, since there was a lot of correspondence between that era's rock writers, it's possible Lester Bangs started using it on paper preceding [its] actual use in reviews . . . again, only my files know for sure . . . but for sure between May day and Labor Day 1971, the term became the official label overnight (well, in 90 days or less)."

3 The band's first album, *Rocka Rolla*, is not metal; it is a clear example of psychedelia.

4 *Editors' Note*: There are some notable exceptions to this, such as the global success of Linkin Park, whose album *Hybrid Theory* (2000) had a particularly profound cultural impact among youth in mainland China (Liu n.d.). That same year, Indonesian metalheads had a passing infatuation with what they called the "hip metal" of Korn, Limp Bizkit, and their ilk; a number of tribute bands formed around that time. One member of a Korn tribute band even spent a prodigious sum to import a set of bagpipes into the country in order to better emulate the group!

5 Most death metal bands tend to focus on one of the two distinctive themes of the subgenre: gore or Satanism. In the United States, according to SoundScan figures, both of these sell well. Since 1991, when SoundScan began collecting data, the best-selling death metal band has been Cannibal Corpse, and Deicide has been a close second. The names of these bands express their subject matter. For details on the SoundScan sales figures, see Blabbermouth 2003.

6 For a fine description of the first wave of this subgenre, see Moynihan and Søderlind 1998. See also Hagen, this volume.

7 One of the reasons for this hybridity is the widespread practice among Scandinavian metal musicians in recent years of actively participating in more than one band at a time. This adds to the proliferation of bands in a concentrated geographical area—bands that need to distinguish their sounds from one another. It is a move that Charles Darwin would well understand.

8 The validity of such a claim is highly suspect; one only needs to hear later German metal bands or read German literature, which addresses the same themes, to realize that it isn't true.

9 Now that many, particularly black metal, bands sing in local languages, their lyrics are translated into English on their CDs and Web sites when there are international sales prospects.

10 The early work of Trust (France), Loudness (Japan), and Baron Rojo (Spain) are some of the very few exceptions.

11 For a discussion of Tolkien's influence in metal, see Melzer 2002.

12 Van Wyck Brooks (1947, 86) describes the effects of travelers globalizing music in the mid-nineteenth century: a traveler to Syria in 1853 sang a "Negro minstrel tune" and the Arabs there appropriated it; in Spain, local boatmen were heard singing "Carry Me Back to Ol' Virginny"; in Delhi, a "Hindu minstrel" performed "Oh Susanna," a song that he had learned from English soldiers, who had learned it from Americans.

13 *Suffocation* is an American death metal band; the veteran Malaysian thrash metal band is *Suffercation*. See Wallach, this volume, for more on Malaysia's long-standing metal scene.

14 Compilations (by label, genre, or band) of videos that could have been shown on MTV in the United States were sold in record stores and by mail. Since 2002, MTV2 has begun to broadcast *Headbanger's Ball* in the United States again.

15 For links to numerous metal e-zines see the Web site Metal Underground.

16 For a discussion of the significance of studio technology and knowledgeable producers in "peripheral" areas, see Wallach 2005a.

17 For example, Opeth, based in Sweden, is comprised of Swedish and Uruguayan musicians.

18 The term "glocalized" is used differently here than in its original sense. It was first employed in the 1980s to refer to international businesses adapting their products and marketing to local cultures. (Think of McDonald's outlets in India selling curry.) Since that time, the term has been expanded to describe alterations in cultural forms as they are disseminated from their points of origins.

See, for example, Bauman 1998, Robertson 1992, Giulianotti and Robertson 2004, and MacDougall 2003. The distribution of extreme metal is anything but centralized, and the modifications are done only at the local level.

19 In a 2004 e-mail to me, Warren also notes that the metal scene, "still an underground, niche market thing[,] . . . is more organised and homogeneous than it was in '01."

20 For a detailed discussion of Satanism, Christianity, and metal, see Weinstein 2000, 258–63.

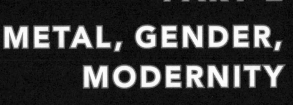

PART 2 METAL, GENDER, MODERNITY

"A DREAM RETURN TO TANG DYNASTY"

Masculinity, Male Camaraderie, and Chinese Heavy Metal in the 1990s

Cynthia P. Wong

*(Dalian City, July 1997.) It's 9:50 P.M., twenty minutes past the time adver-
tised for Tang Dynasty—Mainland China's original longhaired, leather-clad,
distortion-heavy, guitar-driven headbangers—to take the stage at Sun City.
Throngs of young men and women (teens to early twenty-somethings) are
crowded in the entranceway. Inside, the audience is growing anxious. Although
the area in front of the stage is roped off, some audience members continue trying to push closer to the stage, so the police order the first few rows to sit down
on the floor, creating a human barrier between the mob and the stage. Finally,
the house lights go down, and the stage is flooded with red light. The crowd begins to scream, and a couple of the seated fans try to stand up, but the police
quickly step forward, sternly warning them to sit or be removed.*

*Without ceremony, a door behind the stage opens and four tall, strapping
men in black mount the stage, taking their positions without even glancing at
the audience. With one unified nod, they strike the first power chord to their
concert opener, "A Dream Return to Tang Dynasty." The sustained chords slowly*

melt into waves of sonic distortion that overwhelm the crowd's roar. The per-
formers bear a look of fierce determination as they anchor themselves with
each new chord, the unrestrained volume increasing the physical strength and
potency of each man as every chord summons with renewed urgency the spirit
of warrior-heroes from China's glorious past.

Suddenly, the waves of distortion subside, replaced by a clipped guitar
melody. In a low, growling voice, the lead singer begins his cryptic incantation:

> Chrysanthemum, ancient sword, and wine,
> Coffee steeped into the hubbub of the courtyard
> Different races worship the moon of the ancients at the
>   Temple of the Sun
> The flourishing age of Kaiyuan is enrapturing.[1]

Tang Dynasty (*tangchao*), a band founded in 1988 by two Chinese locals
and a Chinese American overseas student, is the first in the People's Republic of China (PRC) to consistently incorporate the musical conventions
of Western heavy metal performance. To foreigners who follow rock in
China, the combination of the band's appearance, on-stage deportment,
and sound distinguished them throughout the 1990s as the most artisti-
cally consistent Chinese heavy metal band in the PRC. Among Chinese rock
fans, Tang Dynasty was a point of Chinese pride and an emblem of native
masculinity.[2]

The band's success was due in part to the consistency of the musical concept it crafted, that of a "heavy metal band with Chinese characteristics."
These characteristics were drawn from a historical Chinese conception of
the ideal man espoused by ancient thinkers. This conception called for a
man to possess a balance of cultural refinement (*wen*) and martial ability
(*wu*), as in the axioms "*Wen* and *wu* together complete" (*wenwu shuang-
quan*) or "*Wen* and *wu* form the complete set of talents" (*wenwu quancai*).[3]
Recognizing that both *wen* and *wu* are specific Chinese male prototypes,
Sinologist Kam Louie explains that "in practice, *wen* can refer to a whole
range of cultural attributes such as literary excellence, civilized behaviour,
and general education, while *wu* can refer to just as many different sets
of descriptors, including a powerful physique, fearlessness and fighting
skills" (Louie 2002, 161).

Each Tang Dynasty band member stood nearly six feet tall with broad
shoulders, a lean muscular physique, and a flowing mane. In concert, they
would headbang to the powerful, relentless rhythm of the drums and bass,

which was accompanied by screaming vocals and wailing virtuosic guitar solos—all amplified to a near-deafening volume. But if one listens closely to its recordings, one is also struck by the literary qualities of many of the band's lyrics, which are modeled after classical poetry from the Tang Dynasty (618–907 A.D.). The refined sounds of zithers (*qin* and *zheng*), instruments commonly associated with the literati and genteel urban teahouse culture of ages past, are audibly present in quieter sections, as is marked pentatonicism in particular riffs and scalar passages.[4] The band's use of classical poetry and particular musical devices reminiscent of ancient China evokes the soundscape of a genteel Middle Kingdom as idealized through poetic remembrances of the past. These wen attributes, exhibited through the lyrics and timbre, are juxtaposed with the wu masculinity of Tang Dynasty's aggressive distorted guitar sound, onstage behavior, and use of martial themes.

In the 1990s modern PRC men, having emerged from the Great Proletarian Cultural Revolution (1966–76), a politically tumultuous time when public discourse on gender and sexuality was repressed, continued to search for viable gender ideals and ways to relate those ideals to their senses of self.[5] Bolstered by images from foreign popular cultural products (Hollywood blockbusters, American and European music videos, Hong Kong and Japanese action films, etc.), young urban Chinese naturalized a mode of masculinity that placed great value on strength, power, and aggression as desirable attributes for men. These images, which directly confronted the asexual ethos of the Cultural Revolution era, produced a surge of intense interest in gender differentiation and expressions of individuality beginning in the 1980s, just as Western heavy metal and rock first arrived in the PRC. Furthermore, the PRC's economic reforms, launched after the end of the Cultural Revolution, initiated a host of dramatic social changes, including explosive urban growth, demographic upheaval, increasing disparity in distribution of wealth, and the rise of consumer culture. These changes had many consequences for modern PRC society, chiefly the promotion of intense competition for capital and resources and the breakdown of traditional social networks—both of which had a damaging impact on the urbanites' value structure, social relationships, and senses of self.

This chapter explores the use of heavy metal music in redefining local cultural ideals of Chinese masculinity and in forging new modes of sociality among male PRC heavy metal fans in the 1990s. As we shall see, the

Chinese American and the local Chinese band members had very different formative experiences and thus different engagements with their Chinese heritage. The dynamic this created is important to understanding their collaborative construction of an alternative masculine ideal. The evocation of China's genteel past, while consistent with Western heavy metal's tendency to construct fantastical worlds in the medieval past, also proved conducive to the joint excavation of the band members' cultural heritages, albeit from very different points of departure.

The concept of heavy metal as an expressive culture providing a social space for young white males to perform and observe rituals of masculinity-in-community has been thoroughly explored in English-language literature by Berger (1999a), Walser (1993a), and Weinstein (1991). In terms of heavy metal songs and performance, Walser identifies some of the attributes of this Western masculinity, such as a need for freedom and adventure, a tendency to display "spectacles of male potency," and a strong inclination toward male-bonding behaviors that demonstrate an independence from, or deliberate exclusion of, women.[6] These attributes identified by Walser resonate with the Chinese conception of wu masculinity. But while it seems to present one clear model of masculinity, Western heavy metal only touches on one half of the Chinese masculine ideal as reconstructed by Tang Dynasty.

In the whirlwind of social change brought about by the forces of modernity in the PRC, Tang Dynasty provides an interesting glimpse into how some Chinese (and Chinese American) men crafted specific modes of gender identification by taking cues from their own cultural history. By reaching back into selected moments of the historical past and referencing particular images and icons, the band and its fans were tapping into a specific image of the male hero, recovering a native sense of masculinity.

HEAVY METAL IN BEIJING

The story of heavy metal in China began in the early 1980s, when a small group of young urbanites (primarily artists and musicians) encountered Western rock and pop music through foreign students and expatriates in Beijing. Although it is difficult to say whether there was ever a cohesive metal scene, there was a strong metal contingent within the initial circle of people who were interested in rock music, more broadly defined. The available Western popular music in Beijing at that time ran the gamut from

Elvis Presley to Metallica, and interested musicians became enamored of different sounds and styles, picking up playing techniques on whatever instruments they liked best. Because they were introduced to three decades of foreign rock music all at once, in no particular order, and by sometimes unreliable sources (that is, amateur musicians and fans), early understanding of rock genres tended to be very idiosyncratic.[7]

The PRC's pioneer rockers unanimously agree that American and British rock from the 1960s and 1970s was important to their early musical development. Bands such as Pink Floyd, Jefferson Airplane (later Jefferson Starship), King Crimson, Deep Purple, and Led Zeppelin often came up in conversations about early influences. Jimi Hendrix, Eric Clapton, and Yngwie Malmsteen were also named as important figures by guitar players.[8] According to many musicians, what initially attracted them to metal was the music's "sound," which was full of distortion (*yinxiang shizhen*) and feedback (*fankui*). And, despite the fact that they may not have understood the meaning of the English-language lyrics, they could feel that the music was "hard" (*yin*) and "noisy" (*zao*)—completely antithetical to the patriotic revolutionary songs they had learned as children, with their simple, sing-along melodies and strophic form.

Li Tong, a guitar player in the band Black Panther, remembered, "When [our] band first started, we played heavy metal. At the time that Chinese rock first began, there were people who thought that only heavy metal could be rock" (interview, April 4, 1998). Other early Beijing bands such as Again, Breathing, 1989, and Overload also initially billed themselves as heavy metal bands. The Chinese music critic You Zhou describes heavy metal as liberating and enabling catharsis for Chinese performers and fans in the post-Cultural Revolution era (Zhou 1994, 10). He suggests that many young people began growing long hair, learning to play guitar, and forming bands in attempts to reproduce the feelings and sensations they experienced when listening to this music. And, whether or not they played metal, many of the pioneer rockers adopted a dress code consistent with that of hard rock and heavy metal performers in the West: long or teased-out hair; T-shirts with logos of famous bands, images of album covers, or motorcycle iconography; and leather or denim wear.

In the early 1990s, as musician and audience knowledge about rock styles increased and musical tastes grew more diverse, the noisiness (that is, distortion and volume) of many early metal bands gave way to a broader variety of sounds and styles. Some bands incorporated elements of funk,

The seminal Chinese band Tang Dynasty in 1990. Musicians (L to R): Zhao Nian (drums), Ding Wu (lead vocals and guitar), Liu Yijun (guitar), Zhang Ju (bass). Photo by Wang Di. Used with permission.

reggae, folk, and softer styles of rock into their music, while others simply changed altogether to more accessible (meaning more "pop") styles. Black Panther, for instance, altered its style to include more singable melodies and softer, romantic ballads, earning it the label "China's Bon Jovi" for a period during the 1990s.[9]

Unlike its peers, Tang Dynasty remained stylistically consistent throughout its career. The band combined howling vocals and long instrumental sections with memorable choruses that encouraged audiences to sing along. Moreover, the band's goal to combine Chinese elements with Western rock aesthetics was received enthusiastically by audiences and read by their fans as exalting China's glorious past. The music critic Zui Dao, for example, said "They express in their own way a longing for a strong and influential China: a return to Tang Dynasty" (quoted in de Kloet 2001, 67). Some others identified with the image of masculinity conveyed by both the band's physical presentation and its lyrical evocation of knights in the ancient world. According to a nineteen-year-old male college student I met in a local record shop:

[The musicians of] Tang Dynasty are the Chinese heroes of our time. They take the glory of our country's past and translate it into a language that we young people can relate to. Their lyrics have a Chinese literary component (*zhongguowenxue defenliang*) and the musicians all have long hair and strong physique, just like the knights (*xiake*) of the past. They look so strong and brave, and their music is so powerful. . . . I listen to their tape every day. (Interview, February 7, 1998) [10]

In expressing his admiration for the band, this young man pinpointed the essence of Tang Dynasty's self-presentation—erudition and brawn—and, through this, achieved his own identification with the wen-wu masculinity from China's ancient past.

TANG DYNASTY: THE GENESIS OF A CHINESE HEAVY METAL BAND

Tang Dynasty is among the survivors of the original crop of rock bands formed at the end of the 1980s. Chinese rock fans often name this band as one of their first experiences with *yaogun* (rock) or *zhong jinshu* (heavy metal). In the early history of the PRC rock scene, there were handfuls of foreigners involved with founding bands, promoting underground rock parties, and setting up the infrastructure for an industry of locally produced rock. Tang Dynasty was no exception. The band's co-founder and guitarist, Kaiser Kuo, then an American overseas student at the Beijing Language Institute, recounted the story of how the band came together:

> One day, in October of 1988, I wandered into a music store at Liulichang [an open-air antique market] with an American friend of mine, Sean Andrews. We plugged in some guitars and started playing around and drew a little crowd in off the street. The manager of the place . . . came out and we were sure we were going to be scolded and asked to leave. Instead he insisted on taking us into the back room and pouring us expensive liquor and handing us expensive cigarettes. And with this sort of pompous silence, he looked at us and said, "How would you like to be on stage next Saturday night?"

The owner paged a local musician named Ding Wu, who was a member of the newly formed band Black Panther. "He showed up pretty promptly, wearing a stylish trench coat," Kuo recalled. "He was a real tall, thin guy with long beautiful hair, an exceptionally large nose, and he was also wearing a '40s detective hat. In his ear was dangling a brass house key as an earring. I was looking at him and thinking, 'Wow!' I mean, this was 1988 and you just didn't see characters like this in Beijing often, so we instantly bonded" (interview, June 8, 1997).

Soon after the meeting, Kuo and Andrews started a band with Ding and another musician, Zhang Ju.[11] Even before meeting the two Americans, Ding and Zhang were already fans of heavy metal, but Kuo introduced them to more progressive bands like Rush, Yes, and Genesis (of the Peter Gabriel era), which provided the foundation on which the group began crafting its musical identity. According to Sun Hao, the band's manager from the mid- to late 1990s, "They stirred up a lot of excitement within the rock circle, especially with the kind of heavy metal they played. It allowed people to see that Chinese can also play this kind of crazy, intoxicating music" (interview, April 17, 1999).

FORGING A PATH INTO THE PAST: NAMING THE BAND

In the spring of 1989, when the musicians were ready to embark on their first tour, the band needed a name, so Kuo suggested naming the band "Tang Dynasty," recalling a period when "outside ideas were freely incorporated into Chinese culture without threat to its own Han identity."[12] For the English version of the band's Web site, he elaborated: "The Tang was such an open and cosmopolitan time. Without any lack of confidence in its own native Han culture, [the] Chinese during the Tang absorbed the best of what the whole known world of the day had to offer, opening its doors to all forms of cultural expression."[13]

Kuo grew up listening to stories from Chinese history told by his grandfather and his parents.[14] As Chinese expatriates, Kuo's parents encouraged their children to study Chinese language and history. Ironically, his bandmates, raised in the PRC, had less of a connection to their own history because of their formative experiences. Education was disrupted during the Cultural Revolution when the Red Guards (mostly high school students) were incited to take up the revolutionary cause and traveled the country fighting enemies of the Communist Party. The disruptions were most severe in the urban areas where all schools were shut down from 1966 to 1969—the period when many of this generation of rockers were just entering elementary school. When schools reopened, the teaching of history centered on exalting the PRC's (recent) revolutionary past and the Chinese

Communist Party's accomplishments. Discussions about China's dynastic past were only used to criticize the reactionary, feudal thinking of the past and to justify the need for class struggle. As a result of this negative representation of the dynastic past and the lack of formal education on the subject, a generation grew up with little connection to China's extended history.

As it turned out, Chinese history ended up providing both inspiration for the identity of the band and an important point of connection for Kuo, Ding, and Zhang. "When we named the band, we didn't think too much about its meaning. We just thought it was a good name," said Ding. "Then, little by little, we started to understand more about the history of the Tang Dynasty, and started paying attention to the connotation of these two words. Naturally, over time, this deeply influenced our music. We began to include more things from our own culture in order to evoke a certain feeling" (interview, August 3, 1997). Motivated initially by their goal of forming a viable professional band, the three men eventually found a joint connection to their own roots, exploring their own history and its cultural forms as material for their music.

CONTEMPORARY CHINESE MASCULINITY

During the Cultural Revolution, the Chinese masses were conditioned to view one another as only proletarians and revolutionaries. The anthropologist Mayfair Yang observes, "Collective identifications other than class and nation were discouraged. . . . Thus, gender relations in China in this period were not so much transformed as gender itself declined as a salient category of discourse." The repression of dialogue on gender and sexual relations resulted in what urban intellectuals later deemed the "erasure of gender and sexuality" (*xingbie mousha*). Yang continues, "Revolutionary asceticism imprinted young people's aspirations with lofty ideals of nation building, so that love and sexuality were relegated to petty personal matters of a sordid and lowly nature" (Yang 1999, 44). The erasure of sexual desire and the resulting loss of gender identity left many men of this era feeling powerless and emasculated, as evidenced by many of the literary and dramatic works produced in the decades following the end of the revolution that feature male protagonists lamenting their loss of manhood or indulging in sexually promiscuous lifestyles and erotic adventures.[15]

Beginning in the 1980s, as urban youth were developing an appreciation of *wu* masculinity from foreign films and magazines, there was also a revival of interest in Chinese literary epics. These epics exposed their readers to two highly specific modes of masculinity in their protagonists. Martial tales, such as *Romance of the Three Kingdoms* and *Tales of the Water Margin*, featured the rough-and-ready warrior-type such as Guan Yu (from *Three Kingdoms*), who was described as being extremely tall, strong, principled, loyal, and a skilled sword fighter. Romance novels, such as *Peony Pavilion* and *Story of the West Wing*, featured the elegant scholar-type, such as Scholar Zhang, who was described as delicately beautiful, sensitive, romantic, and learned. There are certainly other modes of masculinity portrayed through characters wielding political and economic power, but the archetypes of the martial warrior and refined scholar are arguably the most prominent.

While it is difficult to ascertain how much of Ding and Zhang's conception of masculinity was inflected by these foreign and historic cultural forms, we can be certain that they came in contact with Kuo's ideals of masculinity, which were informed by a combination of his family upbringing, his personal formative experiences growing up Asian American, and his fantasy of the rocker lifestyle. "In the early days," he marveled, "young rocker wannabes would come and watch me play and then mimic what I did on stage. But, the best part [about being a rocker here] is the women. In the States, I'm just an ordinary guy; here, women just throw themselves as us. It's amazing!" (interview, June 13, 1997). Theodore Gracyk observes that "easy sex could be a powerful incentive to becoming a rock musician" (Gracyk 1996, 189). Kuo's pursuit, then, puts him in the company of many other young male rock musicians. However, when we factor in the typical experience of Asian males growing up in white American suburbia, the possibility of a deeper motivation emerges.

In a research project on Asian American male identity conducted in the mid-1990s, my data indicated that many men of Asian descent (especially those who grew up in predominantly white suburban neighborhoods) experienced a conflict during their formative years between the literary and screen images of Asian men and how they saw themselves. One Chinese American recalled, "When I was growing up, I had a really strange self-image of what it was to be an Asian American man. I saw all the stereotypes on television and realized I [didn't] fit [them]" (quoted in C. Wong 1996). These stereotypes were identified as being on two ends of a spectrum. On one was the bumbling, asexual Charlie Chan and on the other was the evil and cunning Dr. Fu Manchu.[16] In the absence of acceptable Chinese mas-

Tang Dynasty's Kaiser Kuo
strikes a pose during a guitar
solo, Dalian City, 1997.
Photo by C. Wong.

culine role models, many Asian American men were motivated (often unconsciously) to break from these caricature-like representations.

By the time I met Kuo, he had cultivated notoriety within the rock scene as an avid womanizer. He reveled in his "womanizing rock star" persona, which, one can argue, allowed him to prevail in China in a way he could not in the United States. In China, he felt like anything but an ordinary guy. He was the standard by which young rock wannabes crafted their own rock musicianship and on-stage deportment. He was a great rock guitar player and, to top it all off, he was a sexually attractive man. In short, Kuo was able to live out an American man's rock 'n' roll fantasy. And, whether he was aware of it or not, by publicly embracing this persona, he disinherited a battery of negative American stereotypes about Chinese men from his formative years. Kuo's comportment highlights many of the attributes often stereotyped as important components of the Western male's sense of self. However, having been raised in an overseas Chinese family where he was made acutely aware of his heritage, Kuo also internalized the values

"A DREAM RETURN TO TANG DYNASTY"

Kuo playing onstage while sinking to his knees and head-banging as the audience looks on. Photo by C. Wong.

of traditional Chinese wen-wu masculinity and may have been searching for a way to negotiate the values of masculinity from both sides of his bicultural identity.

MARTIAL EPIC AS INSPIRATION

The events of the Cultural Revolution and the subsequent era of economic reforms also had an enduring impact on the social landscape and interpersonal relationships within the PRC. One legacy of this period was the lack of trust between people. During the Cultural Revolution, individuals, especially those categorized as politically problematic, were encouraged—and at times compelled by desperation and survival instincts—to single out others for purported disloyalties to the revolution. In the politics of the era, loyalty to family and friends was superseded by loyalty to the Communist Party. This breakdown of traditional social relationships led to the loss of important modes of sociality. Later, during the era of economic reforms, the social turbulence reinforced people's instinct for self-preservation and wariness of others, often creating a sense of profound alienation and isolation.

Describing his friendship with Ding and Zhang, Kuo recalled, "The three of us were inseparable. All day, we would listen to and play music. At night we'd go out to eat or go out drinking. That was some of the best times of my life. We were like the three blood brothers in *Romance of the Three Kingdoms*." Although the novel features the heroic deeds of hundreds of men, the bond forged among three in particular (Liu Bei, Guan Yu, and Zhang Fei) epitomizes the ancient *xiake* chivalric code of fealty, honor, courage, and brotherly love.[17] Their character and bravery created enduring images of the male hero, providing a *wu* model of masculinity for centuries of young Chinese men. The representation of the ancient hero in this epic inspired some playful moments between the band members and served as a model of masculinity that influenced the self-image of each individual. Kuo described a fond memory with Ding and Zhang from the spring of 1989: "We all had long hair and we were big, tall guys. One day, we got the idea that it would be cool to pull our hair up in topknots, like men used to in the ancient days, so we got these strips of leather and tied it up. We walked around the city like that all day. We joked that we were the three blood brothers [in *Romance of the Three Kingdoms*]" (interview, July 16, 1989).

The sacred oath of brotherhood and the rewards that come from that kind of male bonding are important themes that pervade *Romance of the Three Kingdoms*. Throughout the novel, there are episodes that underscore the sworn brothers' mutual trust in and fidelity toward one another. Given the repressive climate of the Cultural Revolution, where trust and fidelity could not be taken for granted, even among family members, and considering the alienating effect of the rapidly changing social environment of the post–Cultural Revolution era, we can see how the notion of blood brothers might have been appealing to Ding and Zhang.[18] This notion of an unalterable bond between friends opened up a mode of sociality that allowed for feelings of mutual trust between brothers, creating an emotional and social connection that was otherwise elusive.

The epic nature of this novel also appealed to Kuo's childhood love of stories with fantasy, war, and martial arts themes. But, he added, "This is all natural for a kid growing up reading English-language fantasy novels like Tolkien and always imagining that there was this whole East Asian counterpart to that" (personal correspondence, August 13, 2004). Since the themes found within the genre of Chinese epic tales—historical events, battles between good and evil, internal turmoil, death, and power struggles—lend themselves well to heavy metal, it was natural for the band to realize this in heavy metal's "East Asian counterpart."

IDEALIZING THE PAST IN SONG

Instrumental prelude to Tang Dynasty's song "Epic": A moment of silence gives way to howling winds. Tall grasses bow in hypnotic waves as each new gust blows across the wide, open land. The hero stands above the scene survey-ing his territory. Without word, he draws his sword and raises it high to heaven, signaling his troops. The battle begins with a thunderous crash of cymbals and a martial riff. With each repetition, the battle cry becomes louder, stronger, and then gives way to a long series of two-measure riffs; the lead guitar delivers a haunting melody over this relentless galloping of the rhythm guitar, steadily driving the momentum forward.[19]

This song is a particularly strong example of how Tang Dynasty uses heavy metal musical devices to carry the listener into a fantasy world, evok-ing images of the heroes of times past. When the band first began work-ing on this song during the summer of 1997, Kuo described in rehearsal the mood and image he wanted to create: "Going into battle in ancient times, I see warriors with swords drawn and in full armor racing toward the battlefield on horseback. In the distance, battle flags are waving in the wind and military drums signal the beginning of the battle" (fieldnotes, August 3, 1997). This song, the title track on the band's second album, is a heavy metal nod to the literary genre of heroic epic tales, specifically *Romance of the Three Kingdoms*.[20] The song is conceived in two parts. The first, already described above, is a standard extended heavy metal instru-mental prelude. The second part begins with a sudden shift in mood and instrumentation, setting up a different narrative frame for the listener. The thunderous sounds give way to the delicate timbres of woodblocks, finger cymbals, and zithers, opening a dreamscape that signals a shift from wu to wen.[21] The episode continues with a *zheng* solo before the shimmering of the cymbals eases the listener back to reality. The electric instruments enter again softly as Ding Wu's falsetto delivers the entire text from the introductory song to the story:

Surge over surge, the Long River passes east away,
White blooming waves sweep all heroes on

Ding reciting the text to "Epic" in his signature falsetto, Dalian City, 1997. Photo by C. Wong.

As right and wrong, triumph and defeat all turn unreal
But ever the green hills stay to blush in the west-waning day.
The woodcutters and fishermen, white-headed, they've seen enough
Spring air and autumn moon
To make good company over the wine jars,
Where many a famed event provides their merriment.

This passage ends with a hypnotic guitar riff that is interrupted again by the shimmering of the cymbals. Suddenly, a power crash of cymbals brings back the martial riff that opened the song, but only for a moment because it all abruptly ends. As in many of Tang Dynasty's songs, the presence of wen and wu are intertwined in performance. While the wu is easy to identify through the musicians' on-stage deportment and aggressive sound, the wen is more subtly suggested by the poetic style of the lyrics and the imagery used.

Many of the band's lyrics are loosely patterned on Tang poetry in theme

78   and style, particularly their use of couplets and meter, demonstrating the erudition required of the learned man. The art of poetry flourished in court and literati cultures of past dynasties.[22] Composing poetry was a greatly prized skill, demanding intellectual sophistication, and was even incorporated during the Tang period as part of the imperial exams for anyone wishing to advance in the national civil service system. The choice to deliver their fantastical narratives in Tang poetic form serves to highlight the wen attributes of the men of Tang Dynasty.

Occasionally, one will come across the use of stock phrases and images (such as flowing rivers, falling snow, and the moon reflecting in water) or quotations from well-known literary and heroic figures.[23] Since the narratives are often cast in dream state, the time frames are ambiguous, disconnecting engaged listeners from the here and now, and transporting them to a more ethereal place and time:

> Moon dream, deep and silent
> An expanse of shimmering frost
> Jade spirits scatter and disappear
> How miserable they are! . . .
> Clear drops of pearl fragments
> Jade-blue water by the riverbank
> The moon shatters in pieces as numerous as fish scales
> Shaking the wellspring of my heart. (from "Moon Dream")

In the conjuring of fantastical places, there is a clear identification with the heroes of times past. For example, in "Epic," two couplets speak to the duties of a hero:

> Hero of the world
> Through the tempest the valiant warrior is without equal
> Righteous courage and lofty ideals — he should be fearless
> Hero of the world
> The loyal and upright hero's words are honest
> His life's goal is to protect the rivers and mountains.

With a little imagination, listeners can journey vicariously through the singer's narratives to distant, mystical lands, venturing into ancient battles. Or, they can immerse themselves in the plots of the epic tales, where one can still be a hero in a time when honor and loyalty among friends were held sacred:

I recall the old days when Kaiyuan flourished
When friends in the world all stuck together
The world was so wide you couldn't see its end
Oh, for a great mansion with thousands of rooms!
(from "Dream Return to Tang Dynasty")

Nostalgia for a time lost is a pervading theme in both Tang poetry and Tang Dynasty lyrics. Consistent with Tang poetry, the band's lyrics tend to be filled with a sense of loss and longing for the idyllic in an imagined, idealized past. Both writings seem to suggest that gone are the days when righteous and courageous heroes protected the rivers and mountains—the borders of the land; gone are the days "when friends in the world all stuck together." In Tang Dynasty's narratives of the past, heroes stuck together, swearing blood oaths to protect the land and to watch over one another to the death. This kind of loyalty, notably absent in the post–Cultural Revolution era, could apparently still be found by returning in dreams to the Tang Dynasty.

RESURRECTING TANG DYNASTY: PAYING TRIBUTE TO A FALLEN HERO

During the band's first tour in the spring of 1989, violence broke out in Beijing between the army and student protestors in Tiananmen Square, and Kuo left the country at the urging of the American consulate. "I didn't even have a chance to go back to Beijing to get my stuff," Kuo said. "I had to take the nearest flight out of the country. It was scary. No one really knew what was happening" (interview, July 7, 1997).[24] Though Kuo helped set the band on its musical course, his departure came soon after the band's formation.[25] So while one can argue that Kuo gave the band its initial artistic direction, the Chinese members were largely left to their own devices to realize Tang Dynasty's particular conception of a heavy metal band with Chinese characteristics. After a brief hiatus, they resurrected the band with a local drummer, Zhao Nian, and a gifted guitar player named Liu Yijun (known within the circle as Lao Wu).

The band's first album, *Tang Dynasty* (1992), was an unprecedented success. Unofficial estimates place legitimate sales of *Tang Dynasty* upward of 900,000 copies.[26] However, almost as quickly as the band rose to fame, it vanished just three years later. In the whirlwind of concerts and parties after the release of *Tang Dynasty*, the two founding members, Ding and

Zhang, became addicted to heroin. In May 1995, Zhang was killed in a high-speed motorcycle accident. He apparently lost control of his bike and was crushed by the wheels of a cargo truck. Rumors circulated that he was intoxicated from heroin at the time of the accident. The uncertainty following his death was compounded by personal and artistic conflicts within the band. The strain proved too much and the group disintegrated.

In 1996, Kuo returned to Beijing to work in a family business. Soon after his arrival, he and several other local rockers who were close to Tang Dynasty's late bassist were invited to contribute material for a Zhang tribute album.[27] Working alongside other musicians inspired Kuo and the remaining members of Tang Dynasty to pull the band back together. As they made plans to reunite, Kuo replaced Liu as guitarist, and Gu Zhong, who had been a temporary replacement for Zhang because of his "look" (matching height and build), was made the permanent bassist. After several months of long, intensive rehearsals and songwriting sessions, the band Tang Dynasty was resurrected.

GENERATING NOSTALGIA IN PERFORMANCE

(Beijing, July 12, 1997.) *Tang Dynasty's comeback concert is staged at the Keep in Touch Bar. Tonight's concert has been eagerly anticipated by fans and members of the rock scene. The air in the room is practically tingling with anticipation as the band steps onto the stage to begin the haunting introduction to its signature piece "Dream Return to Tang Dynasty." The audience, overwhelmingly male and Chinese, crowds shoulder to shoulder in front of the stage, each person maneuvering to get closer. The sound of the opening chords is punctuated by people yelling the name of the song in recognition. The room feels alive with cameras flashing, fists pumping, and heads bobbing in rhythm to the music. The bodily movements of both the band (posturing during showy guitar solos, headbanging, coordinated stage antics) and the audience (headbanging, singing along, arms physically reaching out toward the stage) seem to elicit an almost palpable communication between them, driving up the energy in the room. The physical impact of the volume of sound booming from the huge amplifiers combined with Ding's ghostlike falsetto serve to transport the listener's mind and body into another place and time. The entire room erupts with the words of the chorus as the audience sings in unison with the band, some screaming the lyrics at the top of their lungs, others feeling the music with their eyes closed. The text, offering a point of connection, allows each individual to actively engage with and contribute to a voice larger than his own—a performance of amassing and*

Kuo singing "Your Vision" in tribute to the late Zhang Ju, Beijing, 1997. Pictured left to right: Kuo, Ding, and Gu. Photo by C. Wong.

expressing power in unity. After a few short moments of singing the same lines together, strangers around the room suddenly feel more familiar, and at least in that fleeting moment there is a connectedness that links everyone through a common knowledge of the band and of the songs.

All through the night, fans would occasionally yell out Zhang Ju's name, as if to conjure his presence. In the middle of the first set, Ding makes a comment about Zhang's spirit being with all of them that night and a hush falls over the room. Quietly, Kuo steps up to the microphone to introduce a song he wrote in memory of Zhang called "Your Vision." Since the text is in English, he explains briefly in Chinese the meaning behind the lyrics: "Zhang Ju used to love to talk to Ding Wu and me about how we were all going to be great friends when we were old men, still wearing our hair long and watching our grandkids playing together and starting their own rock bands. . . . He imagined them as children climbing around on the piles of drums and amps we'd have amassed by then, fighting with drumstick swords while we looked on, drinking, smoking, and reminiscing."[28] After the introduction, the audience is silent, the air somber, as Kuo begins the slow, melancholy tune. Even though the majority of the audience cannot understand the lyrics, no one moves and I observe each person listening in respectful silence. During the instrumental bridge, a few of them flick on their cigarette lighters and begin swaying their arms in the air; soon after, rows

"A DREAM RETURN TO TANG DYNASTY"

of bodies are swaying in synch with the music. When the song ends, the room is perfectly still for a moment before the audience responds with claps and cheers.

CREATING BONDS OF BROTHERHOOD

Between sets, I asked a few male Chinese audience members about their reaction to the song. One young man answered that he felt a profound sadness; that the tragic death of the bassist Zhang Ju was, to him and to many young Chinese rock fans, similar to the loss of Nirvana's Kurt Cobain to the American grunge scene. Although Cobain and Zhang died under very different circumstances and lived very different lives, Chinese rock fans recognized some things in common: the unexpected, violent, and premature death of an artist in his prime. In Zhang Ju, they mourned a lost hero, and perhaps had a point of local pride, too, for they now had a tragic figure for their own developing Chinese rock lore.

Rallying around Zhang's tragic figure, scene participants were drawn into camaraderie with one another. During the performance of "Your Vision" the collective pathos in the room seemed to translate into nostalgia for the dead bassist, no longer in the mortal world but transformed into a hero occupying the dream world so often evoked by his bandmates in song. The agony of death, loss, and regret created, through no effort of the band's, a community of fans (mostly strangers to one another) with a profound psychological and emotional attachment to it. Even though many in the room were not able to understand the English text of the song, the context of the fallen hero, a lost brother, was powerful enough to bind them into brotherhood. That night, everyone was able to share in this new mode of sociality, extending the camaraderie among the band members to all in the performance space.

FORGING A NATIVE MASCULINITY IN CHINESE HEAVY METAL

By hearkening back to the historical past, Tang Dynasty attempted to re-animate a particular image of the Chinese hero, one exhibiting both wen and wu qualities. On stage, the band members' wu qualities were clearly exhibited through their powerful, aggressive sound and body language. At the same time, their more cultivated, introspective wen side emerged through their lyrics as they incorporated historical texts and poetry, producing a sense of camaraderie with listeners as they together idealized a valiant moment in their collective past.

The strategy of constructing a musical male fantasy world where pleasures, power, freedom, and camaraderie reign is fairly commonplace in Western heavy metal performance. Not unlike the fantastical worlds constructed by Black Sabbath or Iron Maiden, Tang Dynasty reconstructed a world from a historical past where heroes roamed the earth and the codes of honor and loyalty were binding for life. As Walser observes, the fantastical quality of metal allows for real social needs and desires to be "addressed and temporarily resolved in unreal ways. These unreal solutions," he suggests, "are attractive and effective precisely because they seem to step outside the normal and social categories that construct the conflicts in the first place" (Walser 1993a, 134). Considering the continuing and, arguably, increasing, social and economic turmoil that plagued the PRC in the post–Cultural Revolution era, Walser's insight may shed some light on the impulse to generate a utopic past, where human values and relationships are more pure and binding, and life is simpler and clearer. For the band members and their fans, the ideal of the wen-wu masculinity addressed more than just the need to redefine masculinity on their own terms; it also addressed the alienation and lack of moral code induced by the massive social changes within the PRC. In the make-believe world created during performances, the shared knowledge of the music provides temporary relief, for musicians and fans, from the everyday reality of social alienation. The heroes conjured up in Tang Dynasty's lyrics have a strong sense of purpose and a moral mandate to remain true to themselves and to one another. This construction brought into stark relief the contrast between the men of the past as empowered beings and modern Chinese (and Chinese American) men still struggling to find themselves. The band's construction of an essentialized masculinity from an idealized representation enabled a continuing exploration of its members' gendered selves. By distancing themselves from the present moment, they sought to understand and take control of their own gender representation and to find their way forward.

NOTES

1 "Dream Return to Tang Dynasty" (*Tang Dynasty* 1992). Kaiyuan is the third flourishing of the Tang Dynasty (ca. 713–42 A.D.). All lyrics in this chapter are translated by Christopher Rae.

2 This essay is based on field research conducted between May 1997 and April 1999 when the band membership consisted of Ding Wu, Kaiser Kuo, Gu Zhong, and

Zhao Nian. During this time, Kuo was the driving force behind the band's artistic vision. He and the band parted ways in May 1999 over a political disagreement (and friction with Ding's then girlfriend).

3 Etymologically, the written Chinese characters *wen* and *wu* derive from the names of two venerated rulers of the ancient Zhou period (ca. 1027–221 B.C.), King Wen and King Wu. Allusions to these two men can be found in classical texts as early as the *Analects* and the *Book of Rites*, where King Wen is said to have ruled with his learned intellect and King Wu, with his military might. Hence, the terms *wen* and *wu* have come to designate two prototypes of the estimable man: one possessing great intellectual prowess and the other great martial abilities.

4 The *qin* is a symbol of high culture. It is closely identified with Confucius, who regarded the instrument as an important tool for cultivating one's conduct and enriching the human spirit. In iconography, the instrument is commonly depicted on the lap of a contemplative scholar in the serenity of his garden courtyard, alone or in the company of his fellow thinkers.

5 But while these issues were not openly discussed at the time, they were negotiated in more subtle and complex ways in the public arena (see, for example, Honig 2002; Perry and Dillon 2002). For more information on the history and experiences of the Cultural Revolution, see Barnouin and Yu 1993, and Feng 1996.

6 Walser terms this last attribute "'exscription' of the feminine—that is, total denial of gender anxieties through the articulation of fantastic worlds without women—supported by male, sometimes homoerotic, bonding" (1993a, 110).

7 However, since the mid- to late 1990s, especially with access to satellite music television and Internet music sites, genre differences have become much more distinct. For an interesting cross-cultural comparison, see Greene 2001 and in this volume on the development of heavy metal in Nepal over a similar period of time.

8 Malmsteen is actually Swedish, but he lived in California and played with a few bands there in the early 1980s.

9 Chinese rockers acknowledge that songs with singable tunes and easily discernible lyrics are vastly more popular with fans than songs with a good rhythm or short melodic riffs. Some use this audience preference as a way of explaining the popularity of karaoke throughout China.

10 A *xiake* is a martial arts warrior of ancient times who was bound to a chivalrous code of conduct.

11 Biographies of the Tang Dynasty band members are provided in C. Wong 2005, 151–206.

12 The Tang Dynasty is regarded as one of China's greatest periods for the development of arts, religion, and culture. It was the longest and arguably most stable dynastic reign, spanning the years 618–907. During this period, China achieved unprecedented levels of prosperity, political stability, foreign relations and trade, and military power.

13 This quote was taken from Tang Dynasty's English-language Web site, which is no

longer active (http://balls.hypermart.net/Tang/band.html, last accessed October 29, 2003).

14 Kuo's grandfather was the eminent historian Kuo Ting-yee, who was the director of the Modern History Bureau of the Academia Sinica in Taiwan until his death in 1976.

15 Some notable examples of this body of work include Zhang Xianliang's novel *Half of Man Is Woman* (1986) and Jia Pingwa's novel *The Abandoned Capital* (1993), as well as Jia's film *In the Heat of the Sun* (1994), based on Wang Shuo's earlier novel *Wild Beasts* (1991).

16 Bruce Lee was one exception and many Asian American men admitted to taking martial arts lessons as boys to emulate Lee.

17 In the first chapter of the novel, Liu, Guan, and Zhang swear a blood oath of brotherhood to fight together to defeat the Yellow Turbans and to restore peace to their lands.

18 It is worth noting that, about this same time, the notion of a brotherly bond between men, the "gang of brothers (*gemer bang*)," had re-emerged as a theme in popular Chinese fiction.

19 "Epic" (Tang Dynasty 1999).

20 In fact, the name "Epic" (*yanyi*) is taken from the title of that book, *Sanguo Yanyi*.

21 The timbre of the *qin* is replicated by the bass guitar. In live performance, the lead guitar plays the *zheng* part, but on the recording, the real instrument is used.

22 Classical poetry tends to be highly structured with regard to the number of characters per line, accurate symmetry—meaning and (speech) tone—between lines, which lines of text should rhyme, and rhetorical cadence.

23 For example, a couplet used in "Epic": "Let me but leave a loyal heart, Shining in the pages of history," is attributed to a Sung dynasty hero, Wen Tianxiang.

24 The violence culminated in what became known as the 1989 Democracy Movement or the Tiananmen Square Massacre. For details about this incident, see Ding and Chan 1999; Han and Sheng 1990; Yu and Harrison 1990.

25 Between 1989 and 1996, he visited only intermittently but remained in close contact with the band.

26 In the People's Republic of China, because of the piracy problem, sales of two hundred thousand legitimate copies are considered impressive. As of 1997, the band members had collected twenty-seven different pirated versions of or bootleg compilations including songs from their first album sent to them by fans or picked up while traveling on tour. These versions were mostly reproduced and sold outside Beijing.

27 *Goodbye Zhang Ju (Zaijian Zhangju)*, released by Scorpion Culture in June 1997.

28 This excerpt, similar to the introduction used that night, was taken from Kuo's tribute to Zhang Ju on the fifth anniversary of his death (Kuo 2000).

UNLEASHED IN THE EAST

Metal Music, Masculinity, and "Malayness" in Indonesia, Malaysia, and Singapore

Jeremy Wallach

PROLOGUE: BANGI, SELANGOR, MALAYSIA, 1998

On a humid August evening on the campus of the Malaysian National University (UKM), I attended a rehearsal by a student *dikir barat* ensemble. *Dikir barat* is an Islamic musical tradition from Kelantan, the northernmost state in peninsular Malaysia; in its contemporary manifestation it is performed by a circle of men striking variably sized gongs, hand drums, and other percussion instruments while singing overlapping call-and-response chants. It is also high on the list of government-approved performance genres representing "traditional Malay culture" (cf. Ahmad, Zaiton, and Zakaria 1996). My presence, as an American foreign observer, appeared to change the dynamics of the rehearsal somewhat, particularly after I was invited to join the circle and play along with the ensemble. After singing through some standard dikir barat compositions, the performers decided to do something different. "Metallica!" they shouted, seemingly all at once, and before long we were all singing "Fade to Black" and "Master of

Puppets," draping the vocal melodies over the constant, hypnotic rhythm of interlocking gongs and drums. Several minutes later, the ensemble switched to the familiar melody of "Apa Nak Di Kata," a song recorded by XPDC, a popular Malaysian heavy metal group whose sound owes an obvious debt to Metallica.[1] At the time, I was struck by how natural and unforced this musical transition from "traditional" to "global" to "national" seemed for the participants in the performance, and I suggest in the following essay that the performative ease of that shift illustrates a curious and potent intersection of male sociality, ethnic identity, and heavy metal rock music characteristic of contemporary youth culture in this region of Southeast Asia.

METAL IN THE "MALAY WORLD"

This chapter investigates the remarkable development of indigenous metal music scenes in three neighboring Southeast Asian nations, Malaysia, Singapore, and Indonesia, over the last twenty-five years. The enormous popularity of metal music in these countries, independently produced extreme metal in particular, has been sufficiently conspicuous over this time span to attract the attention of several observers of Southeast Asian music and culture.[2] Even *Time Asia* magazine has noted the ascendance of metal and other "underground" rock genres in the largest of these three nations, proclaiming in a 2003 article, "Long the preserve of *dangdut* and gamelan, Indonesia now has a rock scene that actually rocks" (Tedjasukmana 2003).[3] The Malaysian ethnomusicologist Tan Sooi Beng writes of the emergence of a recognizable heavy metal Malay subculture in the late 1980s despite attempts by the Malaysian government to censor the music and limit its influence:

> In fact, since the banning of open-air rock concerts in 1986, a type of rock community comprising mainly male, Malay youths has been formed. The youths hang around shopping complexes and record shops, and attend rock concerts. They can be distinguished by their long frizzy hair, corduroy or leather pants, T-shirts, leather jackets, boots, and big motorbikes.... "Heavy metal" rock music, with its loud drums and electric guitar [and] bass pounding, provides an outlet for youth increasingly alienated from the materialist society. (1989/1990, 158; see also Lockard 1998, 256–57)

UNLEASHED IN THE EAST

During the same period, Singaporean metal bands, again comprised largely of ethnic Malay youths, began to attract enthusiastic audiences throughout the country for the music that became known as "Mat Rock" and have secured a recognized, if marginal, space in their own national music-scape (cf. Kong 1996; Fu Su Yin and Liew Kai Khiun 2008).

A comprehensive social history of the ascendance of domestically produced heavy metal music in Indonesia, Malaysia, and Singapore has not yet been written and will not be attempted here. Instead, in the following brief exploration I seek to move beyond general descriptive accounts and suggest three specific but overlapping arguments regarding the contemporary cultural significance of metal music in this part of the world:

1   While metal in Malaysia and Singapore is primarily associated with working-class Malay ethnonationalism, in Indonesia the national metal movement forges ties across boundaries of religion, ethnicity, and class.

2   Metal in the region constitutes a response to the dislocations caused by uneven development and rapid industrialization. These are parts of the same macro-socioeconomic process that has disempowered the traditional industrial working class of Western countries, including places where metal first began (in part as a working-class response to *de*industrialization). It is secondarily a response to the dramatic political turmoil in the region over the past quarter century.

3   Extreme metal music in particular has thrived in the region due to the establishment of scenic infrastructures anchored in preexisting patterns of male sociality. These scenic infrastructures sustain regionwide networks of cultural and musical exchange involving touring musicians and the wide circulation of musical and textual artifacts.

While the following discussion relies on cassettes, magazine articles, Internet sites, lyrics, and other musical, visual, and textual artifacts, as this essay's opening vignette suggests, it is primarily based on my ethnographic experiences — on knowledge obtained from attending performance events, observing recording sessions, and simply hanging out with local metal musicians and fans around the region. In choosing this focus, I hope to introduce readers to some of the actual places, events, practices, and personalities that collectively constitute the extreme metal movement in the three nations.[4] Moreover, the ethnographic vignettes below illustrate the reach of Malay metal music and culture in the region, from the remote Indonesian countryside to the cosmopolitan city-state of Singapore outward to the larger metal universe.

At first glance, the countries of Indonesia, Malaysia, and Singapore do not appear to constitute particularly hospitable environments for transgressive heavy metal rock music to take root. Their best-known indigenous aesthetic traditions, such as gamelan, foreground delicate beauty and refinement; their national cultures place great emphasis on the maintenance of social harmony and peaceful coexistence; religious piety is prevalent among people from all walks of life; and for most of their collective existence as nations, they have been ruled by authoritarian bureaucratic states that sought to censor and restrict all cultural expressions, including musical performances and the mass media, that threatened to cause a disturbance to public order. Moreover, in each nation's history, anti-imperialist nationalist movements of various sorts played a central role in the struggle for independence from European colonial rule and in the subsequent formation of a national culture. Accordingly, the need to reject the values and products of Western capitalist culture was, and occasionally still is, emphasized in nationalist discourses.

Nevertheless, despite these apparent obstacles to the acceptance of a mass-marketed, Western, secular, brutally unsubtle, and transgressive musical genre by people of the region, Indonesia, Singapore, and Malaysia are home to some of the largest metal scenes found anywhere in the world—a direct result of what Deena Weinstein (this volume) terms the "second phase" of metal music's globalization, in which the arrival of new forms of production, dissemination, and communication changed the simple center-to-periphery movement of metal music phenomena, adding moves from the periphery to the center and eddies confined to peripheral regions. Arguably one reason that globalized metal music has been so successful in Southeast Asia is the need felt by Southeast Asian youths facing massive political, social, and economic dislocations to rebel against conservative and reified traditional cultures, compulsory religiosity, and government restrictions on free expression. Notable among the freedoms for which Southeast Asian metal fans struggle is the right to define their own relationship to globally dominant popular culture forms, and to seek out alternatives to the dogmatic rejection of or neocolonial subjection to global capitalist culture and its expectation of uncritical, continual consumption of its mass-produced goods.

UNLEASHED IN THE EAST

METAL AND "MALAYNESS" (*KEMELAYUAN*)

In the authoritarian multiethnic societies of Malaysia and Singapore, musical taste is strongly correlated with "racial" categories. For example, J-pop (pop music from Japan) is wildly popular among contemporary young Chinese Singaporeans, but not among Indian or Malay Singaporeans. Southeast Asian editions of J-pop albums usually only contain Chinese translations, and Mandarin- or Cantonese-language remakes of J-pop songs are often top sellers (Ng 2002/2003, 9). Another example: Kuala Lumpur, Malaysia is home to a parallel industry of homegrown Tamil-language popular music recordings. These albums, by artists such as Nesam and Salanam Tamarai, are sold alongside filmsong cassettes and other musical imports from the Indian subcontinent at specialized music retail outlets targeting Malaysian Indian consumers. Heavy metal music, for its part, is inextricably associated with members of the ethnic Malay population. This is the case in Singapore, where Malays are a small minority (14 percent of the population [Quah 2000, 71]), and also in Malaysia (where they are approximately 55 percent of the population [Mariappan 2002, 203]). The fact that in the latter country metal's largest contingent is composed of disgruntled, economically marginalized members of the dominant "racial" group resembles the situation in Western metal scenes with regard to the stereotypical working-class affinities and the assumed "whiteness" of the music's fan base. (It should be added, however, here and *not* in a footnote, that like all assumptions of ethnic homogeneity [especially where metal is concerned], the exclusive Malayness of metal is entirely illusory. Non-Malays have played and continue to play key roles in the regional scene despite their minority status. Notable examples include Shyaithan, the Indian Singaporean frontman of Impiety [which will be discussed more later], and Eric Cheah, the Chinese Malaysian record producer and founder of Psychic Scream Entertainment, an esteemed Kuala Lumpur–based extreme metal label with an extensive international roster of bands.)

The Malaysian metal group FTG (which stands for "Freedom That's Gone," or, according to some of the group's fans, "Fuck the Government") includes a song that explicitly brings together metal music and the rhetoric of Malay nationalism on its 1998 album *Aku Tak Peduli* [I Don't Care] (1998), the band's first album recorded in the Malay language (the quartet's previous releases were sung entirely in English). The song, "Anak Melayu," contains the lines:

Jangan lupa negeri	Don't forget your country
Biar bumi jadi saksi	Let the earth be a witness
Tanya-tanya dalam hati	Ask in your heart
Jangan lupa mana asalmu	Do not forget your origins
Kita ini anak Melayu.	We are Malay sons.

With lyrics such as these, I would argue that FTG makes explicit the ethno-nationalism that is implicit but palpable in Malay metal fandom. This is magnified by the fact that while dangdut, a hybrid national genre with an infectious Bollywood-derived dance rhythm, is without a doubt the music of choice of the urban working class in Indonesia (see Wallach 2008b), the majority of young men from the Malay working classes in Malaysian cities and in Singapore have preferred hard rock and heavy metal for at least a quarter century. It is therefore no exaggeration to assert that heavy metal is the music of the Malay masses, which is why questioning the appropriateness of using an "imported" musical form as a vehicle for Malay nationalism only reveals the ignorance and naiveté of the questioner (see Thompson 2002).

Lian Kwen Fee notes, "Malay nationalism in the [Malay] Peninsula was exclusivist, being confined to a particular ethnic group. In Indonesia, by contrast, nationalist aspirations were broadly shared by a number of groups" (2001, 871). Nevertheless, the Indonesian nationalist movement did frequently exclude Indonesians of Chinese descent, who were marked as "non-indigenous" (*non-pribumi*) and occasionally branded unfairly as traitors to the nationalist cause (Suryadinata 2000, 42–44). Many Indonesian metal fans and artists, inspired by the militant anti-racist stance of Sepultura, Biohazard, Rage Against the Machine, and other foreign groups, have protested against the persistence of anti-Chinese sentiment in Indonesia and decry in their music racist acts against the Indonesian Chinese minority—especially those that took place during the bloody urban riots of May 13–14, 1998, when hundreds of citizens thought to be of Chinese descent were beaten, burned, raped, and murdered by rampaging pribumi mobs (and, it is suspected, hired thugs as well).[5] "Buried Conscience," a 1998 song by the Indonesian death metal band Excision, provides an unflinching analysis of the catastrophe (English in original, lyrics taken from Excision's now-defunct homepage):

A man cried,
His wife and two daughters were killed during riots

"Why they murdered my family? What's my fault?"
Nobody could answer his questions
Picture of life
Painted by unending bitterness throughout history
Yet few people are still showing their kindness and morality
When others are just gone ignorant.

"*We live in a racist world*," one Jakartan death metal musician told me in English, in the middle of an otherwise Indonesian conversation. He continued, asserting that while many pribumi Indonesians disliked Chinese, he himself had Chinese friends and had no problem with them at all. But whether Southeast Asian metal is used as a vehicle of anti-racist messages or ethnonationalist rhetoric, I would argue that the most crucial context for understanding it is the wrenching socioeconomic changes that over the last three decades have dramatically transformed everyday life in the region.

METAL, GLOBALIZATION, AND RELATIVE DEPRIVATION

Scholars of metal in the West (for example, Weinstein 1991; Walser 1993a; Gaines 1991; Berger 1999a; Wilson 2008a) have argued that metal music provides its largely male fans with a source of empowerment and mastery as they confront economic and social marginalization in mainstream society. Deindustrialization, with its concomitant disempowering effects on the traditional working class, has thus been identified as a significant social factor contributing to the development of the heavy metal genre and its audience in the West.[6] In Southeast Asia, the rise of indigenous heavy metal has occurred in a context of *industrialization*, a large-scale social and economic process with disempowering and disorienting effects on certain segments of the societies subjected to it.

During the same interval of time, from roughly 1973 to 1997 (the year the Asian currency crisis started), manufacturing jobs fled the United States and Western Europe and workers' real wages there decreased or stagnated while the economies of Indonesia, Malaysia, and (especially) Singapore expanded at a staggering rate, primarily as a result of high levels of foreign capital investment.[7] The concomitant inflows of wealth, technologies, ideologies, and cultural forms gave rise to massive social changes, particularly in urban areas. While some sectors of society experienced rising prosperity through hard work, education, and/or rentierism, corruption, and connections, many others were left behind. Among the demographic segments most adversely affected by these changes have been undereducated young men who lacked the means to attain the affluent, consumerist, hedonistic lifestyle they increasingly saw celebrated in the mass media all around them. This situation of inequality was further complicated in Malaysia, which before and after its independence has struggled with demands to grant special treatment to the indigenous, politically dominant Malays while at the same time participating in a competitive global economy as a multiethnic, rapidly industrializing nation-state (Mariappan 2002, 222). "Using government power, Malay leaders suppressed the opposition and critics of Malay political dominance, but globalization brought new challenges. Malay nationalism became focused on economic pursuits and created a culture of aggressive wealth accumulation, with a tendency for it to be concentrated within a closed circle of wealthy Malays. The Malay masses, on the other hand, are still relatively deprived and this has given rise to charges of UMNO [United Malays National Organization][8] being irresponsible and betraying Malay nationalist causes" (Salleh 2000, 167).

While shaped by the opposite ends, as it were, of the same macro-socioeconomic processes, metal in both Southeast Asia and the West thus can be said to appeal to disenfranchised and socially alienated members of society. Moreover, in Southeast Asia, where many disenfranchised Malay men, particularly in rural areas, choose to embrace militant Islam, metal fans opt for a musical form of resistance to the status quo instead of adhering to fundamentalist religion. The Malaysian cultural critic Sheryll Stothard suggests that the embrace of Islamism actually has something in common with the cultural resistance of urban metal fans: "When it comes down to it, very little separates the rural Malay youth—sullen and unrelenting in his *kain pelakat* [traditional men's sarong], armed with morality and religion, and the urban Malay youth—sullen and unrelenting in low-slung skintight jeans, armed with the anarchy of his rock music. Both are angry with development and wealth because they have been alienated from the Malaysian Dream reserved for the urban monied classes and their children" (1998, 156).

There remains an important distinction, however: while both identity choices can be interpreted as responses to the experience of class resentment, heavy metal music, rather than rejecting the heteroglossic cultural modernity made possible by globalization, seeks to redefine it on its own terms with a political outlook that, in most cases, is emphatically secular.

METAL AND POLITICS

The metal scene in Southeast Asia tends to remain aloof from formal politics, with a few notable exceptions. Emma Baulch (2003, 201–2) and the anthropologist Steve Ferzacca (1996, 41–53) describe the use of heavy metal imagery by the opposition Indonesian Democratic Party (PDI) during the Indonesian election campaign season in 1992, in which the two-fingered "devil horn" salute familiar to metalheads everywhere was appropriated as a representation of the party's water buffalo emblem and was flashed by longhaired, leather-clad motorcyclists parading down the street during rallies. The battle cry of these campaigners was "*Metal!*," which in this particular context was glossed as an acronym for *merah total*, or "totally red" (red was the PDI's official color).

While instances like the above are somewhat rare, political themes—including specific references to national issues—have often been present in heavy metal song lyrics in the region, even when censorship of controversial subjects was the norm (Wallach 2003a, 2005b; see also LeVine 2009). In 2000, after it was relatively safe to use the Indonesian language to criticize the former regime, the Malang-based underground metal band Sekarat (Death Throes) independently released the song "Rezim Dosomuko,"[9] a scathing indictment of the authoritarian New Order government of former Indonesian president Soeharto.

Sistem politik ego penguasa	A political system ruled by egotism
Rapuh dan sengsara rakyat	The people brittle and suffering
Panik dalam ketakutan	Panicking in fear
Hidup dalam ketidakadilan	Life under injustice
Tragis tak berpengharapan	Tragedy with no hope
Hilang . . .	Lost . . .
Rezim orde baru	The New Order regime
Daulat rakyat dirampas	The fortunes of the people confiscated.

Explicitly political lyrics such as these are fairly typical in Indonesian metal songs, particularly since the country's successful democratization in 1998, which led to the rapid dismantling of government-imposed restrictions on freedom of expression (Human Rights Watch 1998). Politically charged

MASCULINE HANGOUTS

Studies of heavy metal in the West tend to emphasize the genre's association with "exaggerated male techno-power" as well as the blatant misogyny
of some of the genre's offshoots (Denski and Sholle 1992, 53). In societies
such as those of Malaysia, Singapore, and Indonesia, a certain prudishness
regarding sexualized display combined with a relative lack of mainstream
media representations of overt violence toward women (at least compared
to Western societies) has perhaps led to the popularity of metal styles that
tend toward what Robert Walser (1993a, 114–16) famously termed "exscription" of women rather than those that celebrate male sexual potency
or heterosexual romance (this preference is the norm in global metal; see
the essay by Wallach, Berger, and Greene in this volume). An additional
factor is likely the importance of homosocial male bonding in the male
adolescent cultures of all three societies. This masculine culture of "hanging out" (*nongkrong* in Indonesian, *lepak* in Malay) provides a key context
for the development of social networks devoted to the production, reception, and evaluation of metal music.

An essential prerequisite for the growth of a local metal scene in Malaysia, Singapore, and Indonesia has been the existence of physical spaces
where likeminded metal enthusiasts can gather in person. In her landmark
study of the Balinese metal scene, Baulch notes the early importance of
the local radio station Radio Yudha not only as the source of the island's
most celebrated metal radio show, but also as a physical hangout space for
metal fans that helped "territorialize" the globally oriented Balinese metal
scene (2003, 196–97). Among the most important of the local institutions
that sustain grass-roots metal scenes is the band rehearsal studio, which
usually doubles as an informal hangout space where scene members and
newcomers meet and interact. These studios are often owned and operated
by local metal musicians who have outgrown their student years and are in
need of a source of income to support themselves and their families. Two
studios I visited, one in the Malaysian city of Kajang, the other in the Indonesian city of Surabaya, exemplify this phenomenon.

Located on the second floor of a shopping plaza in Kajang, a small city near Kuala Lumpur primarily known for its delicious satay, Studio Kemolorg was a focal point for the local metal underground scene in Selangor province, Malaysia. When I visited the studio in the summer of 1998, I met its proprietor, Matt, a longhaired twenty-seven-year-old Malay man. Matt played lead guitar in a metal band also called Kemolorg, which he explained was the name of a demon in Malay mythology. Like many rehearsal studio owners, he was also married, with two children, aged two and five. His wife didn't like to come to the studio, he told me—not surprising considering the studio's almost exclusively male environment—though his children liked to visit and try their hands at playing the instruments. Matt boasted that they could already play "hard metal" music. Matt proudly revealed that FTG and Suffercation, two of Malaysia's most successful metal bands, both regularly used the rehearsal studio for practices, although most of the groups that rehearsed in the inexpensive space were amateur cover bands composed of young Malay students. Such groups paid a quite reasonable fee of 20 ringgit per hour (at the time, around US$5.30; the rate had been recently raised from 18 ringgit in response to the national currency crisis) plus three additional ringgit an hour to use the studio's double bass drum pedal. There was also an additional charge of two ringgit for each additional person over the seven person maximum. (Few metal bands had more than seven members, but in Southeast Asia rock band rehearsals tend to be social events, with a number of non-members in attendance, there just to hang out.) A band did not need to own much musical equipment: the studio provided a PA system and microphone, three large amplifiers (two guitar, one bass), a complete Paiste drum kit, cables, and a number of guitar effects pedals: digital delay, distortion, phaser, and so on. The only major items not provided were drumsticks.

Kemolorg's rehearsal schedule ran from 11 AM to 1 AM. After closing time, a large group of young men from the local area, all Malays and friends of Matt, would hang out at the picnic tables in the deserted plaza courtyard outside the studio until the early morning hours, playing music on an old boombox, smoking, inventing plays on words, and joking around. This was their space, away from the responsibilities of the domestic sphere.

The scene following a long night of hanging out (*tongkrongan*) at Inferno Very
Noise Studio in Surabaya. Most of the stickers on the glass panel on the left are for
Indonesian underground metal bands. Photo by J. Wallach, 2000.

STUDIO INFERNO

When I visited in the summer of 2000, Inferno Very Noise Studio, located
in Surabaya, East Java, had existed for over three years. It was owned by
Samir, then the lead guitarist of the local death metal group Slowdeath.
The studio was used by bands for rehearsals (six two-hour shifts a day) and
at night was a central hangout spot for members of the Surabaya underground music scene, where young men stayed up talking and smoking until
dawn or until they dozed off on one of the several old mats scattered on the
floor. The studio complex also included an Internet café and its wall décor
consisted of flyers advertising past concert events around Indonesia (many
featuring Slowdeath), band posters, and scores of stickers containing logos
of bands from all over Indonesia (and of a few international artists as well)
affixed to the glass panels surrounding the practice space. There was also
a glass display counter by the front entrance containing independently
produced underground cassettes (primarily consisting of music by fellow
bands from East Java), fanzines, and, of course, lots of stickers.

A final crucial hangout spot is the recording studio, which is usually just
a rehearsal studio that has been wired for recording with modest sound
recording apparatus of some sort. Reporting on the Balinese underground

rock scene circa 1994–96, Emma Baulch writes, "There are no locally based recording studios, and few bands have enough original music in their repertoire to record an album" (1996, 4). This changed dramatically in subsequent years: by the late 1990s, underground music rehearsal studios, including Underdog State in Denpasar, Bali and Reverse Outfits in Bandung, West Java, among many others, offered onsite recording facilities featuring four- or eight-track cassette recorders, mixing decks, effects processors, and other equipment at the semiprofessional "home studio" level.[10] Such facilities spread rapidly throughout the region and were used to produce hundreds of independently released cassettes representing a variety of underground genres, black and death metal prominently among them.

EXTREME METAL IN THE HINTERLAND: NGAWI'S TROOPS OF THE UNDERGROUND

Heavy metal in Asia is often assumed to be a predominantly or exclusively urban phenomenon in the academic literature, but this outlook ignores the fact of rural-urban migration for many young Asians, and there is evidence that this characterization no longer applies in Indonesia and Malaysia, where networks of masculine sociality can extend to the remote countryside. One example: Ngawi is a small town surrounded by farmland located in the province of East Java, far away from Surabaya. The town does not have a movie theater, but it does have an underground metal scene, even if it consists of only two bands.

While in Ngawi I met a young metal guitarist who played in both of them. The first, called Leax—named after the *leak*, a malevolent and terrifying spirit in local mythology—was a "brutal death" group; the second group played black metal music and had two names, one in English (Inquisition Symphony), the other in Indonesian (Sinfoni Kubur, literally "Symphony of the Tomb"). Both bands regularly rehearsed in a small room with egg crates on the walls (for soundproofing) located in the guitarist's parents' house. However, according to the guitarist they seldom played concerts in the town of Ngawi itself, since their variety of music "was not accepted" (*tidak diterima*) by the local residents, who preferred Javanese music and dangdut. Instead the two bands played occasional shows in the nearby mid-sized East Javanese city of Madiun—home to an active, punk-dominated underground music scene—and also played (somewhat less frequently) in the more distant cities of Malang and Surabaya. While the guitarist did not have any Leax or Sinfoni Kubur cassettes he could play for me during my visit, he did show me some of the many stickers he created featuring the two bands' logos. One of the Leax stickers displayed the English caption, *"The Troops Underground of Ngawi"* — even in a two-band scene, local pride was apparently still important! I was also shown an impressive trophy collection — prizes won by one of the two groups at band competitions all over East Java. A typical inscription read: *Group Band Favorite, Parade Musik* (Favorite Band, Music Parade) . . . *Malang, 5 September 1999.*

The above example illustrates how even relatively isolated parts of the region under discussion are connected to the international network of metal fans. These connections include commodity flows, but more importantly, they also provide access to the social infrastructure of organized concert events and other institutions and practices that support local underground scenes and foster opportunities to acquire "subcultural capital" (Kahn-Harris, this volume). Indeed, as more groups sign with major labels and their albums become more widely available, the rural fan base for extreme metal in Indonesia and Malaysia is likely to further increase. Even in Kelantan and Terengganu, two largely agrarian Malaysian provinces under the control of PAS, Malaysia's strict Islamist party, underground bands fight to exist despite harsh governmental restrictions on their music (Ranawana 2000).

INTRAREGIONAL EXCHANGES

Although the Malay and Indonesian languages are quite distinct in their everyday, spoken forms, the elevated literary register conventionally used in songtexts is quite similar. Thus Malay lyrics are intelligible to Indonesian listeners, and vice versa. Furthermore, much of what became Indonesian rock and metal culture first passed through Malaysia. Heavy metal cassettes manufactured in Malaysia and brought to Indonesia by returning migrant workers provided an important early point of access to international metal culture (cf. Baulch 2003, 200). One Malaysian music distributor, Valentine Sound Productions, appears to have been almost singlehandedly responsible for introducing many of the most influential indie label metal albums of the 1980s and 1990s into both the Malaysian and Indonesian domestic markets (cf. Baulch 2003, 201). Youth in both countries consequently had access to cassettes by seminal groups like Germany's

Destruction and America's Death Angel, as well as by less seminal artists like the American hardcore-metal-novelty band Apple Maggot Quarantine Area (AMQA), which as a result of its being picked up for distribution by Valentine Sound Productions quite possibly had more fans in Indonesia than in its country of origin.[11]

Even during the repressive years of the Soeharto regime, greater opportunities for live musical performance by metal bands have existed in Indonesia than in the highly regulated societies of Singapore and Malaysia (cf. Tan 1989/1990, 139–41). In Indonesia's local metal scenes, even relatively inexperienced bands have the opportunity to perform before an audience during all-day concert events organized by student committees (*panitia*). These festivals, which may take place in rock clubs, soccer fields, or concert arenas, have titles like Jakarta Meraung (Jakarta Roars), Millenium Brisik (Noisy Millennium), and Nocturnis Orgasm, and many have sequels. A major extreme metal concert event organized by Nino Aspiranto's Morbid Noise Productions, Jakarta Bawah Tanah (Underground Jakarta) took place in Jakarta on September 27, 1997. Its successor, Jakarta Bawah Tanah 2 ("Total More Than 8 Hours [of] Sicknees [sic] & Brutality," according to the concert poster), took place on February 6, 2000, followed by Jakarta Bawah Tanah 3 (billed as an "Underground/Brutal Death/Gore/Grindcore/Black Metal/Noise Fest") on April 30, 2000. As a member of the audience at all three events, I was impressed with both the rabid enthusiasm of the crowds (each event attracted well over a thousand spectators) and the continuity between the three concerts, the first and last of which were separated by two and a half eventful years, straddling the downfall of the New Order regime. Indeed, what is particularly striking about these three festivals is the number of bands that were scheduled to perform both in 1997 at JBT1 and in 2000 at JBT2 or JBT3: Anti Septic, Betrayer, Corporation of Bleeding, Dirty Edge, Homicide, Purgatory, Trauma (Nino Aspiranto's death metal group), and Vindictive Emperor. Tengkorak (Skull), the highly acclaimed Jakarta grindcore band, played all three events, as did the lesser-known Gibraltar. By 2000, these bands—many with their original lineups still intact—were scene veterans, and most had released cassettes of original material either independently or on large commercial labels. (In April 2005, Tengkorak, with a modified lineup that included the Slowdeath guitarist Samir, opened for the legendary British grindcore group Napalm Death when it played a rare concert in Jakarta and the band is still going strong in 2011).

Most major underground concert events in Indonesia feature "guest stars" (*bintang tamu*) from other cities. These bands' home scenes are usually printed in parentheses after their names on concert flyers.[12] The most prestigious guest stars of all are from Singapore or Malaysia. Often these honored guests fail to materialize on the day of the actual event due to the logistical vagaries of international travel, but in any case they tend to attract the largest crowds. Thus, in the symbolic and material exchanges that characterize relations between the underground metal movements in Malaysia, Singapore, and Indonesia, Indonesia provides both "cultural" resources (in the form of its traditional and popular musics [see Zach 2002]) and a less-regulated performance environment, while the metal scenes in Malaysia and Singapore provide their Indonesian counterparts with sources of economic and subcultural capital important for building scenic infrastructures.

Singaporean and Malaysian bands can often perform before much larger crowds in Indonesia than in their own countries. In addition, bands from Singapore can take advantage of that nation's relative affluence and tour other locations as well. The Singaporean "black death" (black metal and death metal) band Impiety has not only played concerts in Indonesia, but has performed in Thailand, Spain, Germany, and Belgium. "Impiety might not be a household name in Singapore," explains a reporter in the Singaporean *Straits Times*, "but in the global underground metal scene, they are the Republic's most famous export" (Eddino 2008). With obvious pleasure, in 2000 Zul (XXXUL), the Malay Singaporean who was then one of the guitarists in Impiety, told me how his band had convinced neo-Nazi audience members in Germany that Southeast Asian people really could play metal, after the band was first mistaken for a group from Japan and then from somewhere in Latin America. Thus Impiety and other Singaporean groups that can afford to tour internationally act as ambassadors not only of Singapore, but of the entire Southeast Asian metal movement.

CONCLUDING THOUGHTS: METAL FORMATIONS AND REGIONAL CONSCIOUSNESS

When I visited in mid 2000, the enormous Tower Records store located in Singapore's gleaming Orchard Road shopping district carefully categorized its impressive selection of non-Anglo-American popular music products by language and nationality: Malay, Japanese, Chinese (subdivided into Mandarin- and Cantonese-language recordings), Korean, Indonesian. By contrast, the recordings in sections labeled only with musical genres (rock/pop, R&B, jazz, and so forth) invariably originated from the Anglo-American world. The store also included a large section that lacked a label but was clearly intended for all manner of extreme metal, with labeled sub-sections like "doom/sludge" and "grindcore."

Significantly, this unmarked section was the *only* part of the store where albums by Indonesian, Malaysian, Singaporean, and Western recording artists were displayed side-by-side without regard for nationality. For the most part, these recordings appeared indistinguishable from one another, unless one noted the significant differences in price between them. I found that this willingness to mix together metal artists of different nations was also apparent in Malaysian record stores and in the cassette display prac-tices of itinerant underground metal cassette vendors who sold their wares at student-organized concert events in Indonesia (Wallach 2002, 98–99). There is a sense, then, that metal does not transcend nationality so much as it dissolves the hegemonic ontological barrier that separates global (read Western) and national musics so that they can occupy the same space and, in so doing, acknowledge a shared history.

The extensive and ever expanding network of metal-related activities in Indonesia, Malaysia, and Singapore analyzed in this chapter could even-tually form the foundation of a regionwide "Malay"-focused metal move-ment that crosses national boundaries as well as confounds normally non-negotiable differences between domestic and foreign musics.[13] Pan-Malay nationalist movements have a long and uneven history in the region. For the most part, however, sentiments of solidarity between "Malay" peoples that cross national borders have historically been attenuated by territori-ally based nationalisms and governmental policies circumscribed by the borders of particular nation-states (Lian 2001; Barnard 2004). Nonethe-less, the brief sketch above hopefully demonstrates how metal music in Southeast Asia provides an avenue for intragenerational solidarity based on shared affinity, unburdened by the pious platitudes and authoritarian conformism of official nationalism, the puritanical and exclusivist ten-dencies of fundamentalist religious movements, and the transparent phoniness of market-driven mainstream youth culture, which threatens to supplant the sovereign (but not solitary) male subject with the poly-morphously perverse, narcissistic, and ambiguously gendered figure of the consumer. In the grip of these forces, metal offers its fans in Malaysia,

Indonesia, and Singapore not only compelling music, but also a source of masculine and cultural pride and connection to a far-flung network of fellow "proud pariahs" (Weinstein 1991) discontented in similar ways with the injustices of modern life.

1 Though this song was popularized by XPDC's version, it was originally recorded by Blues Gang, an older Malaysian pop/rock group with Malay folk influences. The title of that original song is "Apo Nak Di Kato," and it is in the Minang dialect of Malay spoken in the Malaysian province of Negeri Sembilan. The title phrase can be loosely translated as "What is meant to be said?," but in colloquial Minang speech also can mean "Like it or not" (Lockard 1991, 74).

2 Examples include Tan Sooi Beng 1989/1990, 158–59; Lockard 1991, 1998; Baulch 1996, 2003, and 2007; Kong 1996; Sutton 1996, 254; Perlman 1999; Pickles 2000; Sen and Hill 2000; Barendregt and van Zanten 2002; Thompson 2002; Fu Su Yin and Liew Kai Khiun 2008; and Wallach 2003a, 2005b, 2008b. Heavy metal fans are also ubiquitous figures in the popular culture of the three countries, appearing in comics, movies, television, and other mass media as stock character types. To cite just one example, in a bestselling Malaysian-Singaporean joke book, a cover for a fictional magazine called *Mat Rok* [Malay Metal] *Monthly* advertises columns about guitars, jeans, motorcycles, and hair salons, and references Iron Maiden (Mathews 1995, 129).

3 While this passage might seem to imply the existence of wide chasms between the genres, see Wallach 2008b for numerous examples of creative musical experiments that combine elements of gamelan, dangdut (a national popular music with Malay, Indian, Arabic, and Western influences), and underground rock (including metal) in contemporary Indonesia.

4 Some important bands in the region during the fieldwork period on which this chapter is based (1997–2000) include Betrayer, Corporation of Bleeding, Cromok, Cryptical Death, Death Vomit, Delirium Tremens, Doxomedon, Eternal Madness, FTG, Grausig, Grind Buto, Impiety, Infectious Maggots, Puppen, Purgatory, Rudra, Sadistis, Sil Khannaz, Slowdeath, Suckerhead, Suffercation, Tengkorak, Trauma, Urbankarma, Vile, and XPDC. Three representative compilation albums from that time are, for Malaysia, *From Heaven to Hell* (1998); for Indonesia, *Metalik Klinik 3* (2000); and for all three countries, *Panggilan Pulau Puaka II* (Call of the Haunted Island II; 1999). Since 2000 the regional scene has grown dramatically and received increasing attention from the global metal scene. While a large proportion of the older bands are still extant, scores of younger groups and "supergroups" made up of scene veterans (such as the Indonesian bands Seringai and Dead Squad) have also risen to prominence in recent years.

5 For a discussion of the myriad cultural responses to these traumatic events by Chinese and *pribumi* Jakartans as manifested in architecture, literature, and cul-

tural performance, see Kusno 2003. By pure coincidence, the 1998 riots took place during the twenty-ninth anniversary of the worst interethnic rioting in Malaysian history, the aftermath of which saw the implementation of legally mandated preferential treatment for those citizens defined as Malays (see Goh 1971).

6 Harris Berger's ethnographic portrait of the death metal scene in Akron, Ohio (1999a), part of the postindustrial "rust belt" of the Midwestern United States, remains the best developed and most nuanced study of the existential link between the experience of deindustrialization and the cultural practices of North American metal fans and musicians. Donna Gaines's powerful ethnography of "burnout" teens in a New Jersey turnpike town (1991) explores similar issues from the perspective of an engaged, activist sociology of youth, examining the impact of the social dislocations and shrunken life chances caused by the decline of the manufacturing sector on the lives of the young working-class metalheads she encountered.

7 Singapore's dramatic rate of economic growth since its withdrawal in 1965 from then newly independent Malaysia is widely regarded as one of Asia's greatest economic success stories. Between 1960 and 1997, Singapore's per capita GNP increased seventy-four-fold, from US$443 to US$32,940 (Quah 2000, 75), and the city-state now enjoys a comfortable standard of living comparable to that in industrialized nations in North America, Europe, and East Asia. In 2007, Singapore had a gross national income per capita of US$48,520, compared with $13,570 for Malaysia and $3,580 for Indonesia (UN Data 2010).

8 Founded in 1946 by Malay nationalist leaders, UMNO is Malaysia's dominant political party.

9 The title means "Dosomuko Regime." Dosomuko is the name of the demonic villain of the Hindu Mahabharata epic, familiar to many Indonesians through its dramatization in performances of *wayang*, traditional Javanese and Balinese shadow puppet theater.

10 These "Do-It-Yourself" recording studios relied on the new availability of high quality, relatively inexpensive recording equipment designed for the burgeoning "home studio" market in developed countries (Théberge 1997, 231–35). For more information about Denpasar's Underdog State and its recording activities, see Wallach 2005a.

11 I remember the shock of recognition I felt when witnessing an Indonesian underground band cover a song by Apple Maggot Quarantine Area in 1997. Although I had expected to hear songs by Metallica, Sepultura, and other platinum selling metal acts "covered" at local concert events, it was quite a surprise to hear songs by an obscure band whose album had just happened to find its way into the holdings of my college radio station! Arian13, singer and lyricist of the bands Puppen and Seringai, told me that one of his early groups used to cover "Bowling Balls," one of AMQA's more amusing songs.

12 For example, the venerable Balinese death metal band Eternal Madness (see Wallach 2005a) was supposed to headline JBT3 but didn't end up making it.

13 See Nagata 1974; Shamsul 2001; Barnard 2004; and Kahn 2006 for valuable discussions of the historical evolution of Malay identity. Malay is also the official language of Brunei Darussalam, the oil-rich kingdom on the northern coast of Borneo; also, southern Thailand is home to a sizable Malay-speaking minority. More research is necessary in order to assess the cultural significance of heavy metal music, if any, in these areas. The native inhabitants of the Philippines are also considered to be of "Malay stock" but due to significant differences in colonial history (Spain and the United States rather than Britain and the Netherlands), religious leanings (Catholicism, not Islam, is the dominant faith), and linguistic profile (a variety of Austronesian languages are spoken, but not Malay), they are often not included in discussions of the "Malay World." Nonetheless, heavy metal is a vitally important genre in the Philippines. Furthermore, American musicians with Filipino ancestry, such as Kirk Hammett of Metallica and the members of Death Angel, have made significant contributions to heavy metal music in the United States, the Philippines' former colonizer.

Is there some kind of transhistorical affinity between "Malay culture" and metal? Highly unlikely, though in faraway Madagascar (which was settled by peoples from the Malay archipelago centuries ago), Malagasy musicians and fans in that country's nascent metal scene describe their attraction to the music as a consequence of their "Indonesian" heritage (Markus Verne, personal correspondence, January 2, 2011)!

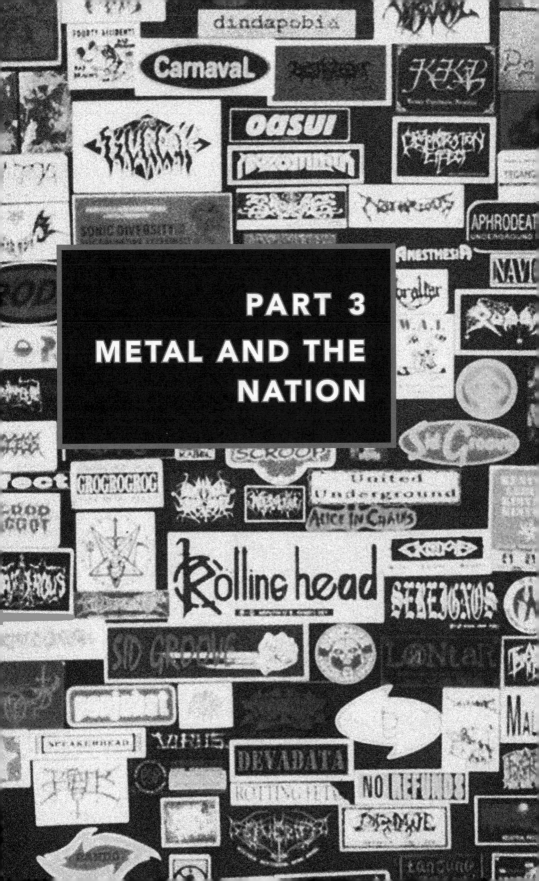

PART 3

METAL AND THE NATION

ELECTRONIC AND AFFECTIVE OVERDRIVE

Tropes of Transgression in Nepal's Heavy Metal Scene

Paul D. Greene

This chapter is a study of tropes of transgression in the heavy metal scene of Kathmandu, Nepal, from 1999 to 2003, a period of social and political turmoil in the country.[1] A distinctive and perhaps definitive feature of heavy metal in the many scenes in which it has emerged worldwide is that it symbolically rebels against or transgresses aesthetic, cultural, and religious norms, boundaries, and limitations. The power that many fans experience in heavy metal is a power to break out of confining musical and cultural expectations and limitations. The channel overflow that produces the hallmark heavy metal sound of the heavily distorted electric guitar, together with other sonic distortions due to singing styles and overall volume, index an expressive force so powerful that it transgresses the limitations of the means of its own transmission (Walser 1993a). In addition, as Western heavy metal has appropriated the figuration, chords, and virtuosity of baroque and Viennese-period classical music, it has transgressed what many listeners feel are the "sacrosanct boundaries" of classical music, "reworking what is now the most prestigious of musical discourses to serve the interests of what is now the least prestigious of musical communities" (Walser 1993a, xv). In the dazzling speeds of solos and the broad band-widths of timbres, heavy metal guitarists exceed the boundaries of earlier conventions of musical style. As some heavy metal songs symbolically attack religious norms and practices, they open up religion for critique (see Berger 1999a, 264). Heavy metal around the world operates as a vehicle by which fans who have adopted a modern sense of the individuated self can become symbolically rebellious against their families and cultures (Weinstein, this volume).

At the same time as heavy metal sounds, album art, and lyrics effect symbolic transgressions, heavy metal culture as a whole strains, in some ways transgressively, beyond the geographical and cultural boundaries of its many situated contexts toward the global and the translocal. One of the more striking aspects of the global transmission of heavy metal music is that it frequently comes to function as a resource for developing "counter-nodes of identity which youth can project against parental wishes or desires" (Appadurai 1990, 18–19). In Nepal of 1999–2003, heavy metal musicians and fans listened avidly to metal from around the world through recordings and satellite television; their musical experience was perhaps as translocal as it was Nepal-based: "In Nepal, listeners normally start out with Western heavy metal music, and then they get into Nepali heavy metal as well. In my opinion, not even one single person listens only to Nepali heavy metal: always also Western" (a member of UgraKarma, a Nepali thrash metal band, in an interview I conducted on December 31, 2002). Nepali fans and musicians also actively participated in e-discourses with metal musicians and fans in Singapore, Malaysia, Indonesia, Thailand, China, Brazil, Germany, and elsewhere. Arguably no other music-based subculture in Nepal involved such a deep and focused immersion in and allegiance to such a specific, translocal culture. The practice of allying oneself so deeply with translocal—rather than local—cultural values was certainly experienced by Nepali parents as an act of rebellion and defiance of cultural expectations: one parent I met voiced the common complaint that her son, who was involved in Nepal's heavy metal scene, was more dedicated to his television set and Internet connection than to his family. Heavy metal's globalization thus involves both critiquing local cultural expectations and the forging of identities that take shape beyond the traditional confines of the local culture: in this sense, it is a process of transgressing traditional cultural boundaries. Metal is experienced by many fans as a globally based response to local constraints and limitations; it is a culture that strains transgressively outward toward the translocal and the global.

Because heavy metal has become a global phenomenon, with scenes forming throughout the whole world, several scholars have developed theories to explain its emergence and spread as resulting from broad-based social forces. Walser (1993a) theorizes that heavy metal emerges as a response to working-class frustrations caused by processes of deindustrialization in Western cities. Wallach (this volume) argues that processes of industrialization in Indonesia, Malaysia, and Singapore are every bit as disruptive and frustration-inducing as Western deindustrialization. Weinstein (this volume) theorizes that processes of globalization and modernization leave many people in the world marginalized, frustrated, or at least ambivalent about the new and changing world in which they are expected to participate. Clearly all these theories accurately reflect powerful processes that motivate the emergence of heavy metal today. Yet in my ethnographic study I found that Nepali listeners and musicians perceived themselves as turning to heavy metal as a rebellion against specifically local phenomena. Both fans and musicians said that they participated in Nepal's heavy metal scene because of frustrations with Nepali family obligations, frustrations with traditional duties of Hindu praxis, and anxieties due to Nepal's uncertain political circumstances: all local, Nepali causes. Although broader social processes were undoubtedly at work behind the scenes, it is important to note that, in the experiences of my informants, Nepali metal raged against a machine that was distinctly local.

Because symbolic rebellion is, for many, central to heavy metal, notions of rebellion and conformity must be explored ethnographically in the immediate cultural setting in which the music acquires cultural force. What may be experienced as transgressive in one context may be normative in another. For example, whereas Walser (1993a) finds that the loud sound and broad bandwidth of the heavily distorted electric guitar of heavy metal are experienced as new and unsettling sound qualities in Western contexts, it is important to note that these sound qualities are not experienced as particularly unsettling in Himalayan experience. Many alpine horns, such as the Gorkha *narsingha*, the Newar *neku*, or the Tibetan *dung chen*, also produce loud sounds with broad bandwidths. In addition, Nepali sound systems are generally not adequate to produce shockingly loud musical sounds in live concerts (which is a matter of considerable regret for some contemporary metal fans). In Nepal, metal's transgressive "edge" lies along other dimensions.

Because tropes of rebellion and transgression are common, perhaps even definitive features of heavy metal, then paradoxically the genre may be said to depend for its character—perhaps for its very existence—on local boundaries and limitations to transgress. Although metal is a highly translocal, rapidly globalizing subculture, it is in many ways rooted in frustrations against social and aesthetic limitations that are very local. In the absence of such locally situated frustrations, my informants told me, they would not have turned to heavy metal: "If we are happy, then we would not play this heavy metal because we are not angry. The angry person gets peace when [one] gets a loud voice. Make a loud voice so that all the things in the mind come out" (a twenty-year-old male concertgoer).[2]

In this chapter I investigate the local limitations, constraints, and anxieties that caused the frustrations felt by young Nepali metal fans. As Nepali heavy metal transgressed against local constraints it raged outward, reaching toward a perceived global heavy metal subculture that would transcend all local constraints. And this global heavy metal culture continues to emerge through countless locally situated acts of self-differentiation and symbolic rebellion against local expectations, acts that are also, quite often, moments of intense affective experience.

NEPALI POPULAR MUSIC AND THE EMERGENCE OF HEAVY METAL

In Nepal, the appearance and evolution of heavy metal must be heard against the backdrop of Nepal's popular aesthetics. For five decades, a pervasive aesthetic emerged in Nepali popular music in which primary emphasis was placed on the clarity and expressive power of the lyrics and on a beautiful vocal line. This aesthetic emerged alongside (and, in some ways, in support of) Nepali nationalism. The entrenched aesthetic became a foil against which heavy metal transgressively rebelled, particularly starting in 1999, as Nepali musicians began to place much more emphasis on the musical instruments rather than the vocal line, and as vocalists sang in a deep, growling style such that it was difficult for listeners to understand the words.

In Nepal, as in Malaysia (Chopyak 1987) and in many other Asian countries, the initial development of popular music was directly linked to nationalist aims. Popular music in Nepal may be said to have begun in 1950 with the broadcasts of the country's first radio station, the state-run Radio Nepal. Two genres of popular music were cultivated at Radio Nepal: *adhunik git* ("modern song"; see Grandin 1989, 116–19) and *lok git* (literally "folk song"; see Henderson 2003). These genres drew together elements of Indian light classical music, Nepali folk songs, and Western harmonies. Adhunik git and lok git were, in many ways, self-consciously developed to serve as sonic emblems of the Nepali nation: they at once embodied both modernity in their Western instrumentation and chords and the nation of Nepal through the incorporation of distinctively Nepali and South Asian instruments and musical features of Nepali folksongs. Particularly important for the nationalist agenda was the fact that songs were sung in the national language of Nepali, rather than Hindi, English, or any of the languages spoken by Nepal's various ethnic groups. Further, the music of these two genres was carefully designed so that the Nepali-language lyrics and vocal lines were very clear and prominent, which undoubtedly helped to promote the national language. To be sure, the development of this aesthetic could not be traced exclusively to the nationalist efforts of Radio Nepal: many genres of Nepali folksong likewise placed emphasis on the vocal line, as did Hindi filmsong, which has been an ongoing influence on Nepali popular musics. But it is safe to say that a mainstream aesthetic emerged in Nepal's popular music, starting with adhunik git and lok git, such that the words were the root of the expressive form and they must be clearly understood. This aesthetic, which is compatible with nationalist aims, became an entrenched aspect of mainstream Nepali popular music; it was continued in Nepali pop—a genre of popular music developed by young Nepalis in the 1980s and 1990s (see Greene and Rajkarnikar 2001); and it remained part of the musical expectations of Nepali listeners during the period of my field study.

As David Henderson shows in our co-authored article (Greene and Henderson 2000, 104), most Nepali listeners considered lyrics to be paramount in Nepali popular music. Whereas in Western popular music it is not uncommon for listeners to mishear or disregard the lyrics (for example, in Jimi Hendrix's "Purple Haze"), Nepali listeners placed a greater priority on accurately apprehending the lyrics. As a result, vocalists came to be valued for their skill in bringing out the emotions of the lyrics through musical aspects of their performance, and the accompanying instruments were expected to help the vocalist to achieve this aim. The priority of the vocal line affected the creative process significantly in Nepal: in adhunik git and lok git, as in North Indian filmsong (Manuel 1988), the lyrics and melodies were composed first and chords were added later in order to embellish melodic lines. This reversed common compositional practice in Western popular and classical music, in which melodies are commonly invented to fit into a preexisting framework of chords. In adhunik git and lok git, Western triads and other chords merely embellished the melodic line and brought to it a Western, modern touch. With heavy metal after 1999, Nepali musicians turned to a more common Western practice, as they typically composed the chords, rhythms, and melodies before the lyrics.

Although the musical influences that merged to form Nepal's popular music were initially all funneled through media that were controlled and influenced by the state (initially Radio Nepal; Ratna Recording Trust began to produce recordings in 1961; and the Royal Nepal Film Corporation emerged in 1973), Nepalis were increasingly influenced by other popular musics reaching them through other channels. It was through such nonmainstream channels that heavy metal entered Nepali awareness. Starting in the 1960s, Nepal has been a magnet for European, American, and Australian trekkers and tourists, who have brought with them all varieties of Western popular music, including hard rock and eventually also heavy metal. In Kathmandu, shrewd vendors in the marketplaces of Freak Street and later the Thamel area not only listened to Western pop, but also created a healthy business selling inexpensive bootlegged copies of all forms of Western popular music to tourists. In time, Nepalis also began to purchase and listen to Western music, and this was the means by which heavy metal first substantially reached Nepal. With the advent of satellite and cable television, Western popular music entered middle- and upper-class homes and also some hotels and restaurants in Nepal. FM radio stations began to broadcast a wider variety of music, including European and American heavy metal. Although adhunik git and lok git retained their dominant position in Nepali popular music, listeners increasingly had access to a wide variety of popular music sounds — including heavy metal — through these additional media channels.

At the end of the 1980s and the beginning of the 1990s, many Nepali high school and university students began to pick up Western instruments themselves, form bands, and play their favorite Western pop songs. Electronic keyboards, electric guitars, and rock 'n' roll drumsets were marketed in the Kathmandu Valley. One of the first genres to be performed by Nepalis was heavy metal (Greene and Rajkarnikar 2001, 15). Nepali bands such as Wrathchild, Crisscross, and Prism covered the heavy metal of Iron Maiden, Anthrax, and Metallica, and also the hard rock of Aerosmith and the Rolling Stones, singing in English. The new bands performed in school auditoriums, hotels, restaurants, and public spaces such as Kathmandu Durbar Square on the occasion of Nepal Sambat, the Newar New Year. These performances, which often attracted huge audiences, offered a specifically youth-oriented alternative to the popular music dominating the media, which in contrast came to be cast as "old-fashioned" or music of an "older generation."

Some musicians also began to compose their own songs. And within the resulting genre, which came to be known as Nepali pop, some bands, most notably Cobweb, began to compose and record new heavy metal songs in Nepali (for a history of Nepali pop, see Greene and Rajkarnikar 2001). Starting in 1993, Cobweb formed and self-consciously marked itself as a heavy metal group. Although it incorporated the heavy metal distorted guitar timbre, rapid guitar figuration, and sinister album art, Cobweb continued the traditional aesthetic — which was pervasive in the public soundscape — of ensuring that the vocal line was well-constructed and clearly heard. As I argue in "Mixed Messages" (2001, 173–77), the distinctive sound elements of heavy metal entered Nepali popular music as underdetermined signifiers. That is, heavy metal sound qualities took on a much wider range of meanings for Nepali listeners than they did for Western ones. Nepali listeners heard the music variously as happy, energetic, dance-inspiring, and sad; for many the music had no transgressive or dangerous force at all. The distinctively Nepali form of heavy metal cultivated by Cobweb eventually came to function, for many young Nepalis, as a doorway to appreciation of the more extreme forms of Nepali heavy metal that were cultivated a few years later.

SYMBOLIC TRANSGRESSIONS IN NEPAL'S EMERGING THRASH METAL SCENE

While the sounds of Western and Nepali heavy metal were taking on a wide variety of meanings, becoming broadly popular, and in many ways conforming to established aesthetics of the Nepali public sphere, some young Nepalis were listening to more extreme versions of metal (Greene and Rajkarnikar 2001, 17). Around the turn of the millennium a small but dedicated fan base emerged for thrash metal and other darker variants of the genre. Influential bands included Metallica, Iron Maiden, Anthrax, Megadeth, Slayer, Sepultura, Cannibal Corpse, Carcass, and King Diamond. Nepalis also listened avidly to some of the heavier songs of nü-metal bands such as Limp Bizkit and Slipknot. Some of these listeners formed their own bands and began to write their own music, in both Nepali and English. Starting in late 1999 with Drishty,[3] and at an accelerating pace over the ensuing years, a small number of Nepali musicians began to produce new, more extreme forms of heavy metal, with sound qualities and lyrics that shocked mainstream Nepali listeners, including those who had become fans of Cobweb.

A scene emerged around this new, more extreme heavy metal. Bands performed at restaurants, parks, and concert halls, and local distributors began to market their recordings. Most listeners and musicians were middle-class Nepalis in their teens or twenties, mostly male, in school or university programs. The scene attracted many mainstream Nepali pop listeners who listened with some interest, as well as a numerically small core of very enthusiastic fans.

The new metal sounds, performed by Iman and Sharad, Stash, X-Mantra, UgraKarma, and also to a lesser extent in some songs by Matrix, Grease, Mile Stone, and Robin N' Looza, have a more transgressive "edge" in terms of qualities of music and lyrics. Starting in 1999 with Drishty, Nepali metal songs were deliberately produced with distorted and often incomprehensible lyrics, often rendered with a thrash-fashioned, deep, growling vocal quality.

The fact that it was difficult to understand the words proved to be one of the most shocking—even transgressive—aspects of the new metal music. "Almost half of the song is non-understandable," declared one rather exasperated Nepali, listening to Drishty's "Jeewan" on cassette. "Anyway the song is trying to show the contrast of good and bad side of life." Of Drishty's "Program #3": "This song is not understandable at all. One can hear only music and the growling voice of the singers." After a heavy metal concert one teenage girl said simply, "Heavy metal lyrics *bujhdina* [I do not understand]." The aesthetic emphasis on the lyrics and on the vocal line as a whole—an aesthetic carefully cultivated at Radio Nepal, pervading Nepal's public sphere for five decades, and entrenched in Nepal's popular music—was challenged, creating an almost shocking effect. Nepali extreme metal after 1999 may be seen as rebelling against what is perceived as an "official" or "mainstream" aesthetic, much as many American and European heavy metal listeners and musicians see themselves as rebelling against commercially manufactured pop aesthetics. This is why, when Drishty first began producing songs with distorted lyrics in late 1999, the musicians were interviewed by Nepal's leading popular culture magazine and had to explain themselves (*Wave* 1999). In my interviews with heavy metal fans in their teens and twenties, it was evident that listeners were keenly aware of the fact that this music placed priority on the instrumental sounds over the vocal line, as they explained its value to me:

PAUL GREENE: Why is it difficult to understand the lyrics?

FAN: Because all the musicians are making high [here referring to quality] sound. And the lyric should be in soft. . . . From the music, they can attract the audience, because the music part is the best. First of all I prefer this. If the musical instruments are good and if they perform better, then automatically the lyrics will be appreciated. If they perform well, then automatically whatever the lyrics are, it will be good. In school when I listen to heavy metal, the whole time the words cannot be understood.

PG: Why is it difficult to understand the words?

FAN: They just want to give the heavy musics to the people more than the words.

PG: Why write music in which it is difficult to hear words? Is it because of violent lyrics?

FAN: That's not it actually. I think they just want to express musical beats more than lyrics.

Musically, a strong influence specifically from thrash metal (and to a lesser extent death metal) was evident in post-1999 Nepali metal. This was audible in the distinctive use of low-pitched, growling vocals; downtuned and heavily distorted guitar sounds; rapid guitar figuration; and, with Ugra-Karma, the use of double bass kick drums. Guitar solos, cultivated in the earlier stages of Nepali metal, were considerably shorter or dispensed with altogether. As one fan put it: "Thrash metal is what it is called when we cannot understand the words. It is very fast." Most fans identified their Nepali metal music with thrash metal or death metal. Although Nepali fans often characterize UgraKarma and other Nepali bands as "death metal," their

musical characteristics were more typical of thrash metal as defined by
Weinstein (this volume). UgraKarma introduced the term "blood metal" to
describe its music: "We are a death metal band. . . . We call it 'blood metal.'
We wanted to create something new. These days 'death metal' is thrown
around for any kind of music. Even nü-metal. So we created this name
'blood metal' for ourselves" (interview, December 31, 2002).

With its lyrics of violence and mayhem, UgraKarma's "blood metal"
could perhaps be considered a form of "gore metal": a metal subcate-
gory identified by Berger (1999a, 57) in his ethnographic study in Akron,
Ohio, although the term was not in currency in Nepal. Also, the sacrilegious and blasphemous lyrics of some bands suggested something akin
to black metal in Nepal, although it is important to note that the symbolic religious transgressions were against Hinduism rather than Christianity. Musically, Nepali metal more closely resembled thrash metal than
black metal, because the tempos of the songs were generally quite fast and
the lyrics growled. Paralleling the emergence and development of thrash
metal in Europe and America (Gaines 1991, 194–204), a constructive synergy emerged between thrash metal bands and punk bands in Nepal; Ugra-
Karma and members of Drishty performed and worked with Nepali punk
bands such as Nastik, Nusil, and Inside Two Stupid Triangles.[4] Inspired
by punk, thrash metal bands cultivated new extremes of frenetic energy
and speed in their guitar and drum rhythms, and they also adopted punk's
do-it-yourself posture of resistance to the commercial pressures of music
producers with whom they worked, and to their record companies. Other
underground metal strains, such as doom metal or power metal, seemed
to be less influential in the Nepali metal of 1999–2003.

Lyrics increasingly recounted "dark" themes: descriptions of death and
corpses; the angry, and despairing emotional world of a suicide; and images
of bloody warfare from the Bhagavad Gita. Some bands even introduced
sacrilegious elements into their lyrics, suggesting that Hindu deities were
"following the bad things." When listening to the Drishty song "Mriga-
trishna" (Illusion), one listener declared: "This song is partly understandable, but does not make any meaning. In this song the singer is expressing
the feeling of frustration. He expresses this toward the God, and he says
that all his wishes and aims are an illusion." Drishty combined Sanskrit
slokas (passages traditionally chanted) from the Bhagavad Gita concerning war with heavy metal. To be sure, there were precedents: despairing

songs of heartbreak have been prevalent in Nepali pop since the 1980s; and Nepali folk culture, like that of India (for example, in Shulman 1986), has long been rife with accounts of warfare, often set to music. Further, it was not unheard of for Hindu devotional songs to include passages in which a singer momentarily expresses what could be considered almost a criticism of a deity: an occasional devotional song might include phrases such as "after I have honored You so faithfully how could You ignore me?" as part of a broader devotional strategy of drawing a deity's attention to one's acts of devotion and also one's requests of the deity (Greene 1995, 276 ff.). But the lyrics of Drishty and especially UgraKarma departed from all precedents in the intensity of emotional expression, in the vividness of descriptions of dark feelings and of violence, and in their pointedly blasphemous and nihilistic statements. The cover art of UgraKarma's album *Blood Metal Initiator* was a graphic image of self-dismemberment that horrified and puzzled most Nepalis who saw it.

While older Nepalis and mainstream Nepali pop listeners heard the sounds and lyrics with bewilderment and shock, many students and people in their twenties listened to the music with respect and interest, but not active involvement. "Heavy metal is not bad," a teenage male heavy metal concertgoer told me. "Even the very normal people listen to heavy metal. Teenagers are not bad who listen to heavy metal. They listen not because they are a junkie [*sic*], but because they are angry at this society." A young woman in her twenties dining with friends at a restaurant in a shopping complex said, "Yes, I think [some of the new Nepali metal] is against religion. Still it does not particularly mean it should be stopped. If you enjoy doing it, you should keep it." When I asked what was the meaning of the new heavy metal music, one young listener in his twenties said, "It is a new interest. It is for younger people, for those who are [a] little angrier than the others. It is also about creating new music, and good melodies." Many of the audience members I met at Rubber Soul, a Nepali heavy metal/hard rock concert in Kathmandu in December 2002, said they were only occasional heavy metal listeners. They came in order to enjoy and dance to a hip, contemporary musical experience with their friends. For many, heavy metal was simply a good dance music that attracted large crowds because of its fast, high-energy beat. Because the lyrics were difficult to understand, some concluded that heavy metal was about melody, and good, danceable beats: "If a singer sings a sentimental song, [the] crowd will be silent. When music is a little heavy, [the] crowd starts to dance themselves. . . . It is just for the time being, just for entertainment. It keeps the body fresh. When we listen to sentimental music it does not help the whole body, but we can dance to the rhythm of heavy metal. . . . With heavy metal people dance fast. . . . Disco is also heavy."

To a small but enthusiastic minority of young Nepalis, the new heavy metal resonated on a deeper, more personal level. These listeners were mostly middle-class males in the fifteen to twenty-two age bracket. For these Nepalis the new sound inspired powerful affective experiences that helped them grapple with intense personal frustrations: "We want to scold the family, scold the politicians. . . . Love tragedy is also a problem. If your love partner betrays you then that will make you angry for your whole life. . . . We have deep feelings. If you feel this way how you can do it [sing] in a soft voice? Such emotion should be loud. In loud voice we want to lose control, just say anything and not have a fear." Many enthusiastic listeners brought up such personal frustrations. Through interviews I found that the leading causes of frustration were religious obligations, family pressures, romantic rejections, and Nepali politics. Frustrations were often described in very personal terms: heavy metal listeners and musicians typically expressed frustrations with specific family members in their lives, with specific religious obligations they were expected to fulfill, and with certain professional lines of employment their families expected them to undertake.

PG: What is the source of anger or frustration?

FAN: It could be anything. Unsuccess. You want to do something but are not able to do it. You are not what you are, or who you want to be. That can cause frustration. That feeling is turned into music, and that is known as heavy metal . . .

Always family wants me to do this, do that. But no, I have my own desire. It is not that education can make me good.

PG: What is the source of frustration?

FAN: Lots of sources. Everyone's parents are not [the] same. Not all parents are good. Environment in the family is not always good. . . . Here we have to stick to the family. Now I am twenty-four years old but still stuck with the family. I can't go my own way. . . . I know they mean good, but they want to make us doctors or engineers, like that. We want to make music. It's not about earning

money. They relentlessly hamper us by saying things—emotional **121**
blackmail by parents. Say: how can you do this to me, I am your
mom, uncle—like that. It pretty much frustrates us.

It is important to note that the frustrations articulated by Nepali heavy
metal listeners and musicians were in every case highly localized, framed
in terms of the Nepali family, religious, and political condition, and not in
terms of global or translocal conditions or problems. Nepalis were frustrated with ways in which their personal freedoms were curtailed by family
and by religion, and also with local Nepali politics. Frustration was not directed toward broader entities or processes, such as globalization or modernization. Scholars often theorize that heavy metal operates as a cathar-
tic release from frustrations and ambivalences caused by large-scale social
processes such as deindustrialization or marginalization within the global
cultural economy, yet it is also worth noting that this was *not* the experience of Nepalis. Instead, Nepali metal fans described themselves as forming global allegiances in response to frustrations with local, specifically
Nepali conditions. In other words, heavy metal is often modeled as a local
response to global conditions, yet paradoxically, it was experienced by Nepalis as a globally based response to local conditions. This point is developed further below.

For Nepali fans, heavy metal was a specific kind of response to these
frustrations: a response of affective saturation, as is evident in these three
excerpts from my interviews:

Heavy metal should be so much louder that every corner of the mind is
music and you can hear nothing but the music. It should blast your ears
and go to your brain. Heavy metal is like that . . . you don't just listen
from the outside. . . . I used to be angry, so I listened to heavy metal.
When I listen to other songs, my mind would still think about anger.
But when I listen to heavy metal, my whole mind is in the heavy metal
song. . . . I want to spend my whole life in music.

I used to be angry . . . When I listen to other songs, my mind will still
think about anger. But when I listen to that heavy metal my whole mind
is in the heavy metal song.

I listen to death metal and it totally occupies my mind. I cannot think
of anything else. It makes a person mad.

These listeners departed from more mainstream Nepali experiences of metal in the intensity of the affective experiences they sought, and in the way they sought to saturate their whole awareness and even their lives with the experience. They were unlike their classmates in school who listened to a rich variety of musical sounds in the contemporary mix of Nepali pop music in order to "journey toward professional identities" in the new, cosmopolitan Nepal (Greene 2001, 182–83). In this vein, the manager of Kath Shop, a music store specializing in recordings for the emerging thrash metal underground, likened the new music to a particular (somewhat idiosyncratic) branch of Osho meditation, a spiritual practice based in India that has been growing in popularity in Kathmandu's middle class:

> There is a sort of meditation by screaming: Osho meditation. People cry out in all sorts of ways, as each one wants. It sounds like a madhouse. If someone doesn't know the program [purpose], he would assume it is a madhouse. There are different ways to exit the emotions. Some people try to reduce anger by punching a door or something. This is a way of expressing or exiting the emotions in a different way. In Osho, people have different ways of relaxing. So it is also the songs [of heavy metal] that will relax.

Because of this desired affective response, several of my informants reasoned, the new, more extreme Nepali heavy metal had the distinctive qualities of highly distorted electric guitar, exceptional speed sustained throughout by guitar and drums, and lyrics that were difficult to apprehend:

> PG: Why are the words difficult to understand?
>
> FAN: If one is frustrated, one cannot sing in a clear way. They are expressing, not so we can always understand. . . . If they are not angry they would sing in a well manner. If they are angry they cannot sing in a small voice, or an understandable voice.
>
> For sentimental type of music, the vocal must be good. And next the lyrics must be good. But for metal the main thing is the music. When they hear the rough, heavy music, listeners will feel excited, so they dance along with the music.
>
> PG: What is the meaning of the distorted guitar sound?
>
> FAN: Screaming, that is the cry. If you are disturbed, that is the cry. We want to make the world to be disturbed. So we play in distortion, because we want to disturb.

BAND MEMBER 1: We don't want to make it complex or anything like that. You need some skills. Need relentless and fast strumming. Need damn good stamina. As far as guitar skills goes it is apparent in metal you have to know how to strum in metallic manner. Not like rock but endlessly with power, stamina.

BAND MEMBER 2: Yes, as far as technical skill goes, we are pretty good at it. But we don't want to be too technical. It would lessen the power in the music. We want power with a bit of technicality. Our songs are pretty much technical but with power. Power is from old school death metal, but technicality is from brutal death metal.

BAND MEMBER 1: What skill you need on guitar is speed: strumming fast and relentless.

BAND MEMBER 2: We play no guitar solos at all. We can play them but don't want to. When you can speak pretty loud with music and lyrics, you don't need solos. We don't want to show the world our great guitar skill.

BAND MEMBER 1: Speed, aggression, and power: these things are most important. Technicality is there but is not important; relentless speed [is].

Listeners who become fans of extreme metal developed and voiced deeply felt allegiances to their heavy metal subgenre and to the metal scene. Many young Nepalis made new, lasting friendships through shared interest in this new aesthetic: "Metal makes lasting friendships in the sense that very few people do it and once you find someone who is in it it starts. I have friends who I know solely because they are into same kind of music" (a member of UgraKarma). Fans found themselves united in their indignation toward metal's critics (cf. Roccor 2000), and they praised heavy metal musicians as more talented and less stilted than mainstream Nepali pop musicians:

All the pop and classical musicians say that heavy metal is bad music. But heavy metal people do not say these other musics are bad. I have found that this heavy metal musician is much more talented than this

124   pop musician. So it is a true thing. I like this thing. Not about who is
beautiful. No, heavy metal musicians are like their fans. Dress like their
fans, don't act better than their fans. The pop singer is not so. I used to
be a fan of a pop singer. I used to call them but they say they are not at
home. Like that. If we like their music, they should like us too.

   These heavy metal musicians do not want money. If they wanted
money they could be doctors. You can judge them: they are very talented
persons.

   Heavy metal is good music. It is more difficult than this pop. You
have to work very hard, all the time training on guitar. Unfortunately
[the] pop star cannot play music like that. The timings are so fast, very
difficult to make the timing.

For fans, Nepali thrash metal thus occupied a kind of moral high ground,
in that the musicians did not seek money or personal prestige or stand-
ing over their fans. Also, much as Walser found of Western heavy metal
(1993a), Nepali thrash metal made claims to the prestige of superior musical talent over other popular music.

NEPALI THRASH METAL AND HINDUISM

Drishty's song "Antya Satya" (Truth of Death) includes sacrilegious statements:

   What happened to the God today?
   The God is also following the bad things,
   As the opposite knowledge occurs in the time of destruction.
   The world is becoming dark.
   What else is there to take with you when you die?
   One day, this whole body must be mixed into the soil.

These lyrics, about a deity pursuing bad or evil aims, were intended to be
shocking. And indeed, several Nepalis I met did take offense at such songs.
In the Nepali context, "the God" could be taken to be either a Hindu or a
Buddhist deity; the two religions have long been mixed in complex ways in
the Kathmandu Valley, and several well-known deities have become associated with both religions. But in my interviews, I found that musicians
and fans were much more critical of Hinduism than Buddhism. Hinduism
was the dominant religion in Nepal, and its praxis involved many obliga-

The logo of the Nepali thrash
metal band UgraKarma.

tions and ritual observances (see Gellner 1992, 137 ff.) that young Nepalis
increasingly found frustrating. Frustrations with Buddhist ritual obligations were less in evidence among my informants.

Sacrilegious statements were considerably more prominent in the
lyrics, album art, and statements of UgraKarma, Nepal's leading thrash
metal band, than those of other groups. UgraKarma saw itself as revital-
izing thrash metal from the past. Inspired by Slayer, Cannibal Corpse, and
Carcass, UgraKarma combined lyrics of violence with the power and musical intensity of 1980s thrash metal. The band's logo included an inverted
trident. "The trident is the weapon of Lord Shiva. It's upside down. This
means we are against religion: that's what we are trying to say through
symbol. . . . Also this [inverted trident] is Shiva when he is angry: the *ugra*
version, extreme version." When asked for clarification, members of the
band explained that they were actually against certain aspects of Hindu
religious praxis rather than Hinduism itself.

The name UgraKarma, which band members translated as "Extreme
Deeds,"[5] seemed to hint at the violent and sacrilegious acts described in
the group's lyrics. The lyrics of songs in their English-language album,
Blood Metal Initiator, drew together images of graphic violence, suicide,
bloodlust, desecration of shrines, and assertions of atheism and nihilism.
The opening song, "Nihilism . . . Shall Remain," was a kind of proclamation
of their project:

> We have been unleashed
> Armed with the power of the metal of death

ELECTRONIC AND AFFECTIVE OVERDRIVE

Religions and all moral values dismembered
Battle against society and morality we declare
. . . our morbid proclamation of nihilism shall remain.

UgraKarma performed and sang in English rather than Nepali (for more on patterns of language use in world popular musics, see Berger and Carroll 2003; Greene 2003). One of the unexpected results of this was that the band received e-mails from fans complaining that they could not understand the lyrics, even when they were printed in the album liner materials; listeners actually had to refer to dictionaries to discover the precise meanings of the descriptions of violence in the songs.

In an interview, the band members collectively clarified their position on religion:

BAND MEMBER 1: So much in our society, everything is so much controlled by religion.

PG: So you want freedom?

BAND MEMBER 1: Yes! That is the most important thing. I miss that. Freedom from temptations, traditions, dogmatisms.

BAND MEMBER 2: Actually, we are not against Hinduism. It is a great philosophy. We admire it. We are against worshipping God. In Hinduism there is even a place for atheists and cannibals. We are also Hindus even if we do not believe in God. But we have to do such ceremonies.

There is this death ritual *shraddha* [ancestor worship]. My father died one year ago. I have to do the ritual. I don't believe, but it's for my mom. She wants me to do it, why disappoint her? . . . The pundits [clergymen] just want the money. They don't care what happens. Hindu philosophy is great, but . . . those pundits change Hindu philosophy into religion. Even if I don't believe, I have to do it for the family. I have to do the death ritual for my mom to make her happy. She says at least do it for me.

The fans of Nepali thrash metal also frequently brought up criticisms of Hindu religion in interviews:

FAN: Yes, it is a great problem. Nepali religion is not good. We have to do this and that. In our religion we have rice-based alcohol. So drink is our religion: to kill our pain. In Dasaiñ we have to sacrifice goats and buffalos. We cut them in [the] neck, and they bleed slowly. That is not religion; it never can be religion.

Hindu religion is conservative. We have to cut animals in sacrifice, hurt them. . . . The animal is still alive, the blood is spilled on various things [ritual objects]. Still alive. But object [to which the offering is made] is not a living thing; it does not need the blood. Sometimes they do it on a Honda vehicle, to make it safe from accident. We must eliminate these bad things. Religion is not bad, but conservative people are not good. I try to convert my family in this way, but they are not agreeing.

The tropes of transgression against Hinduism, evident in lyrics, album art, and in the accounts of listeners, were not a mere "translation" of the critiques of Christianity found in some European and American heavy metal. Rather, the frustration that motivated the symbolic transgressions seems to be very locally motivated: musicians and listeners were raging specifically against local, Nepali religious constraints and obligations. In this vein it is worth noting that the very UgraKarma fans who appreciated lyrics of violence and gore were actually opposed to animal sacrifice, and also to Hindu death rituals. Therefore, it would be too simple to conclude that these metalheads were merely obsessed with death or violence. I would suggest that violent lyrics in Nepali thrash metal actually constituted a symbolic attack on specific, local norms and obligations of moral and religious behavior—norms and obligations that they perceived as restricting their freedoms. The fact that they appreciated themes of dismemberment in lyrics but criticized it in acts of religious sacrifice indicates that death and dismemberment imagery in Nepali heavy metal was actually subservient to a specific agenda of symbolic rebellion: that is, against local Hindu religious obligations. Likewise, many metal musicians, including those in UgraKarma, took pro-peace positions and were horrified at the rising death toll of the ongoing struggle between the government and Maoist insurgents in Nepal at the time.

The symbolic transgression against moral and religious norms was a form of critique that served specific affective aims but did not seek to project or construct a coherent model or vision for an ideal society. Nor did it idealize death or violence. The music, imagery, and lyrics critiqued and symbolically attacked the norms of moral behavior of Hinduism but did not propose a new religious order to take its place. Fans and musicians were forming a community around shared frustrations and shared affective responses, but the community did not project shared social solutions or agendas. In this regard, Nepali thrash metal paralleled black metal in Euro-America, in which anti-Christian imagery and themes were sometimes voiced, but the majority of musicians and fans (with the famous exception of a few zealots, mostly Norwegian) did not actually aspire to overturn Christianity or establish a new religious order.

THRASH METAL AND POLITICAL ANXIETY

One of the most tumultuous and anxiety-producing aspects of contemporary life for young urban Nepalis lies in the fact that, from the late 1990s to 2006, Nepal was transformed from a peaceful country remarkably free of violence to one of ongoing political strife and an uncertain future. Nepal, following an arduous and lengthy struggle by a movement for democracy, became a constitutional monarchy in 1990 when the late King Birendra relinquished official powers to a democratic national government. A multiparty parliamentary system took hold. Successive administrations have been thwarted by numerous problems, however, including scandals, accusations of corruption, and persistent economic and cultural problems in rural Nepal. The nation was deeply shaken when ten members of Nepal's royal family—including King Birendra—met their deaths on the evening of June 1, 2001, or in the ensuing days following their hospitalizations. While the precise details of this tragedy remain unknown, an official report issued on June 14, 2001, states that Crown Prince Dipendra, under the influence of drugs, shot and killed members of his family and finally himself. In addition, a Maoist insurgency that began in 1996 had increased in intensity and violence, particularly since November 2001, resulting in several armed conflicts and bombings of government and private institutions. The Maoists' strength grew as they promised to meet the cultural and economic needs of alpine communities, and they continually enlisted new followers from these communities. In 2003, the Maoists exercised tangible influence throughout rural Nepal. An additional change took place when King Gyanendra (crowned on June 4, 2001) declared that the government had failed to function effectively and, on February 1, 2005, dissolved the elected government, suspended freedom of the press, and appointed a cabinet to assume direct executive powers over the country. Subsequent to my field research, the king, following widespread protests, returned power to elected officials, who in 2006 negotiated a peace accord with the Maoists. The country reorganized itself as the Federal Democratic Republic of Nepal, and despite a number of setbacks it has seen a general reduction of violence and made significant political progress toward lasting peace and stability. These developments have been accompanied by changes in popular music and in the metal scene (see Greene forthcoming); however, the focus of this chapter is on the heavy metal scene during 1999–2003, when the country was in the grip of deep and growing political and social anxieties.

My Nepali informants voiced regrets that the once peaceful Kingdom of Nepal had become a place of strife, violence, and uncertainty. As bombings continually took the lives of citizens and officials, the military became an increasingly tangible presence. Armed guards patrolled urban and rural streets, and armed checkpoints were set up at all roads entering the Kathmandu Valley, and also at the points of entry to the city of Kathmandu itself. The activities and dreams of young Nepalis were further constrained by repeated *bandhs* — "strikes" in the Kathmandu Valley: the Maoists used their influence and the threat of violence to order a complete shutdown of all businesses, schools, universities, and institutions, and also a stop to all motor traffic throughout the Kathmandu Valley for periods of several days or even weeks at a time. Anyone who violated a bandh was threatened with punishment at the hands of the Maoists. During this period, the end of the ongoing conflict and political uncertainty was not in sight, and the precise roles of the royal family, a multi-party democratic government, and the Maoists in shaping Nepal's future remained very uncertain.

While the lyrics of Nepali heavy metal songs rarely concerned politics, either directly or indirectly, many Nepali heavy metal fans and concert-goers told me that, in their experience, Nepali heavy metal was often, in some sense, "about" the disappointment with corrupt politicians and the ongoing conflicts with the Maoists:

> The political situation? That's true. The situation is bad in Nepal. So we would like to scold these politicians, and tell everyone what they

ELECTRONIC AND AFFECTIVE OVERDRIVE

are like. They are corrupted. It is about corruption. We cannot say in simple language, so in heavy metal we express and scold and just use bad words.

Most of the heavy metal singers are singing about terrorism [referring to Maoist bombings]. . . . Nepal used to be known as a peace[ful] country. But killing, war everywhere: why is it so? Let's be together and get peace.

Much as UgraKarma waged a symbolic attack on Hindu religious praxis but did not propose a new religious order, so too the Nepali thrash metal group X-Mantra symbolically lashed out at Nepal's political troubles but did not articulate a specific political vision or plan. X-Mantra's album art, music, and lyrics invoked key symbols of the Nepali nation. The cover of its first album, *Crying for Peace*, presented a familiar Nepali symbol: the all-seeing eyes of Lord Buddha, which were painted on the pinnacles of Swayambhu and Bodhnath Stupas and were prominent emblems of both Nepali Buddhism and of Nepal itself. But here the eyes were pictured crying red tears, which suggested blood. Swayambhu Stupa is perched on a mount that overlooks the city of Kathmandu, and many Nepalis say that the watchful eyes painted in the pinnacle can see everyone in the city. The eyes are believed by many to be a comforting, protective, watchful presence. The album cover therefore brought a suggestion of injury to a well-known Nepali symbol, suggesting that perhaps the Buddha was saddened or even injured by witnessing the tragedy of Nepal during this period. Incorporation of blood in album imagery was, of course, a standard trope in heavy metal of the sort introduced into Nepali album art in 1993 by the mainstream metal band Cobweb. But here the image resonated with the disappointment and frustration many Nepalis experienced with the ongoing strife, violence, and uncertainty in their country.

While sounding politically charged frustrations, X-Mantra did not articulate a political plan. For one thing, X-Mantra cultivated a standard thrash metal sound, with growled lyrics that were difficult to understand. The lyrics were largely drowned out by the guitar and drums. In fact, members of X-Mantra told me that they estimated that only 5 percent of their listeners could understand their lyrics.

In their songtexts X-Mantra symbolically attacked or deconstructed the prized symbols of Nepali nationalism, the democracy movement, and democratic politics. "Shaheed" (Martyr) is a good example:

Hey, Mom! Mom, I am just dead.

Why a martyr, why [did I] become a martyr?

First of all, a [political] game has been played on my dead body,

They have created a big "issue" [English word] in the name of
    my corpse.

About a meter of shroud is needed to cover my corpse.

[And] the Nepali heart is needed for performing the last ritual
    [before burning the corpse].

But on my dead body,

The shroud is put of some political party.

Hey, Mom! Mom, I am just dead.

Why a martyr, why [did I] become a martyr?

With the image of a martyr, X-Mantra invoked the Nepali listener's rec-
ollection of the many revered martyrs of Nepal's democracy movement,
whose arduous struggles and sacrifices gradually led to the establishment
of a democratic constitutional monarchy in 1990. But the martyr in this
song surveys the contemporary Nepal, in which politicians use the martyrs of the past for their own personal political games, and asks in exas-
peration, "Why did I become a martyr?" The singer adopted the persona of
a freedom fighter from the past in order to voice frustration with Nepal's
contemporary political situation.

Although UgraKarma and X-Mantra both employed religious symbolism, they did so to quite different effects. Whereas UgraKarma symbolically attacked Hinduism, X-Mantra used shocking religious symbolism to
sound frustration or disappointment with the political situation, without
criticizing religion itself. Although Nepalis did say the cover art of *Crying
for Peace* was a bit shocking, few considered it to be as sacrilegious as the
work of UgraKarma. Similarly, the image of a political flag being substi-
tuted for the traditional funeral shroud in "Shaheed" was not interpreted
as a critique of the obligations and observances required in the elaborate
Hindu death ritual: obligations that were pointedly criticized by Ugra-
Karma's members in their interview with me (see above).

Although there was no political plan in X-Mantra's songs, heavy metal
listeners did indicate that the songs imparted a general sense of urgency
and purpose:

Heavy metal will have a good impact on Nepal. We have to be angry.
[We] have to make others angry. In the angry person there is more

power than the other [that is, non-angry] person. This is the time to be angry. We are still sleeping. [We should not always] listen to the love song. This is not the time to love. This is time to do something for [the] country. Country is in [a] great dilemma. We must wake up. But we are not, we are just listening to music.

If we listen to Nepali heavy metal, what we gain is: we have to do something for our country, for the world. . . . [There is] some kind of message, more or less.

Some heavy metal musicians encountered difficulties in writing songs about politics. In the shifting and uncertain conditions of Nepali politics, there was considerable danger that political songs would be censored by the government, and possibly even result in legal entanglements for band members. Understandably, in some cases musicians decided to pursue different artistic directions: "I wrote one song named 'War.' Half of the lyrics concern the American Afghanistan war. . . . But our producer will not let us do that. We're pretty much okay with that" (Nepali heavy metal singer).

NEPALI METAL WITHIN THE GLOBAL CONTEXT

Nepali heavy metal musicians and fans saw themselves as rebelling against constraints and limitations they perceived as local in nature: family, religion, and local (Nepali) political turmoil. In their experience, they were not raging against such processes as global capitalist restructuring, economic marginalization, Westernization, or modernization. To be sure, it is possible for a social scientist to link the frustrations voiced by Nepalis to broad social factors and transformations. For example, the pressure young Nepalis felt to pursue educational degrees and professional employment may have taken the form of edicts from their parents, but may actually have been due to broader social processes. That is, although young Nepalis voiced frustration with their parents, the actual cause may have been the rising bar of professional credentials and accomplishments required to maintain middle-class lifestyles in twenty-first-century Nepal. But because the constraints and frustrations were perceived in localized terms, the songtexts, imagery, and other tropes of symbolic transgression in Nepali heavy metal were crafted in local terms as well.

Because their limitations and constraints were construed as local, Nepali metal listeners sometimes developed unexpected imaginings of America:

If I love someone deeply and she betrays me it affects me my whole life. I am angry my whole life. Especially true in Nepal. In America people are busy and do not have enough time. Can forget things easily. Not possible in Nepal. We think. Use the brains. [Do] not forget. In America you have to forget. You get busy, have to do work. In Nepal most people are unemployed. We fall in love and just spend days with girlfriends just talking and dating. After betrayal I have time to remember. The result is heavy metal.

Here, America was imagined as a place free of the specific Nepali conditions that caused this heavy metal listener so much frustration: Americans were busy and Nepalis were not. This focus on the local nature of all limitations and sources of frustration led to an imagining of an America that was free of the conditions that would motivate heavy metal. This is, of course, not the case.

If heavy metal in Nepal of 1999–2003, as well as in other settings, is experienced by its musicians and fans as raging against local cultural constraints rather than broad social processes, then it is important to ask the following questions: What might the world's multiplying heavy metal scenes share? How is it possible for a global heavy metal culture to emerge with the cohesiveness that is evident today, if (or to the extent that) each scene grows out of distinctly local frustrations, and voices frustrations framed in local terms and symbols? Perhaps part of the answer lies in the affective position cultivated by heavy metal and evident in the accounts of my informants. Heavy metal, in Nepal as elsewhere, seems to inspire for its most dedicated fans experiences of intense, life-saturating, transgressive empowerment. Nepali listeners repeatedly reported that they sought to fill their minds and their lives with heavy metal music to such an extent that it was not possible to think about anything else. Thus, listening to heavy metal is at once an act of self-differentiation from one's local aesthetic and cultural context, and also a sustained practice of intense affective experience. Perhaps it is this affective experience that metalheads share around the world, even though they may rage against markedly different social and cultural limitations and circumstances.

As understood from the Nepali metalhead perspective, the notion that Nepali metal was a subculture—whether local or global—would be inside-out. Heavy metal is, by virtue of its transgressive character, that which is limitless and boundless; in this sense it is not accurately modeled as a

134   subculture. Instead, it declares itself to be an ultraculture ("ultra," Latin, meaning "beyond" or "on the other side of"). And unlike a superculture ("super," Latin, meaning "above"), as modeled by Slobin (1993), heavy metal does not construct or even gesture toward a cohesive, overarching cultural logic. That is, a supercultural music (such as Indian film music) offers a broad, shared basis of experience whereby diverse peoples can experience a coming together as a nation, or other large cultural formation (see Gopal and Moorti 2008). Heavy metal does not offer such a broad basis of experience, but rather a *very specific affective experience*: the thrill of liberation and empowerment that comes with transgressing all limitations of the local. It is this powerful, affective experience that drew together enthusiasts in the small scene located in Nepal, and perhaps it also draws together those in other metal scenes around the world.

NOTES

1 The period of the field research that informs this chapter is 1998–2003, so this chapter does not address developments in heavy metal or Nepali social history after 2003. During subsequent years, the insurgency intensified, and the King of Nepal declared a state of emergency allowing him to assume direct political power. In time, the political parties came to work together with the Maoists to form a new government together. Subsequent developments in Nepali history and Nepali metal are documented elsewhere (Greene forthcoming). Also, in addition to the Kathmandu metal scene, there is a smaller heavy metal scene based in the Nepali city of Pokhara to the west. This chapter takes as its primary focus the larger scene that has formed in the greater Kathmandu area.

2 Unless otherwise indicated, quotations in this chapter are from interviews I have conducted with young Nepali heavy metal fans in their late teens or early twenties. Interviews were conducted at concerts, restaurants, shopping complexes, and homes in the Kathmandu Valley. For this project, interviews were conducted in English unless otherwise indicated.

3 Drishty means "vision" in Nepali; the band's first album cover prominently pictured two eyes.

4 The name Inside Two Stupid Triangles refers to the Nepali flag, which consists of two red and white triangles.

5 The members of UgraKarma translated their band name into English as "Extreme Deeds," translating karma as "deeds." But karma, a complex and multifaceted concept in Indian philosophy, is more often understood to refer to destiny caused by deeds.

OTHERWISE NATIONAL

Locality and Power in the Art of Sepultura

Idelber Avelar

Heavy metal is a post-dictatorial genre in Brazil, one whose significance is best grasped by mapping the meanings acquired by metal music among urban youth during the decline of Brazil's military regime in the mid-1980s. As in most countries, speed, thrash, and death metal evolved in Brazil primarily as working-class urban youth genres. Unlike their Anglo-American and continental counterparts, however, Brazil's pioneer metal bands began to craft their art in a context of intense censorship and repression, courtesy of a long dictatorship (1964–85). Brazilian metal not only had to face the usual aesthetic and moral reprimands flung against it in the North, but also a political accusation that as a form of protest it was not socially aware enough. Never mind that bands or fans themselves rarely phrased their own agenda in such crude terms as "protest" or "resistance." Once a certain orthodoxy defined that such was the function to be attributed to popular music, the debate was already framed as a no-win situation for the genre. In order to establish itself heavy metal had to implode the terms of that debate and show their inadequacy in accounting for the genre's sound, compositions, and iconography. The band I will follow here, Sepultura, has been for over two decades (1985–2008) largely responsible for the genre's victory in that national cultural battle, one that the band could only win by rephrasing it as an *international* debate.

As stated above, in Brazil headbangers did not only have to prove to the usual guardians of musical standards that theirs was genuine music and not sheer noise; nor did they only have to prove to the usual guardians of morality that their message was not immoral and did not incite violence; they also had to prove to then influential guardians of political meaning that theirs was not a futile and alienated form of protest against the country's still grim reality. As Deena Weinstein shows, detractors of metal come from left and right alike: "Metal's ecstasy is seen as mindless and gross sensation by the progressives. Its play is viewed as a malign will to corrupt by conservatives" (Weinstein 2000, 239). Both positions are predicated on misreadings of the genre, as religious right-wingers blame it for teenage suicide and alcoholism, and progressives attack it for being politically alienated music. In peripheral post-dictatorial countries like Brazil, the latter critique was particularly ferocious and damning when metal fandom was contrasted with "good taste" in more acceptable styles of popular music. In Brazil, that style was *música popular brasileira* (MPB), that heterogeneous ensemble of harmonically and lyrically "sophisticated" acoustic musics centered on the singer/songwriter, which enjoyed a large audience among members of Brazil's middle class.[1]

Squeezed between the moral/aesthetic right and the cultural/political left, heavy metal was always intensely challenged by contradictory demands from several sides at the same time. The history of the genre's elaborations, responses, and parodies of those attacks in Brazil remains to be written. It is true, however, that the genre fared quite well in those cultural battles—thanks solely to its musicians and fans, as the music industry, academia, and rock journalism cannot take any credit for the genre's successful response to those challenges. Forced into a corner between the demand for positive morality or aesthetics and the demand for cultural or political criticism, heavy metal crossed both avenues and parked nowhere. It took a line of flight and did it its own way.

In his mapping of the logics that organize popular music, Simon Frith has pointed out that there is no reason to suppose that "the accumulated knowledge and discriminatory skill" (1996, 9) underlying value judgments in popular forms differ in any significant way from those sanctioned by elite culture. As anyone who has devoted attention to heavy metal can confirm, the genre's value-laden acts of self-definition include a myriad of subtle and complex distinctions that have evolved for well over thirty years. Although all metal fans will produce positive statements about which bands best represent the genre for them, they most commonly define heavy metal in opposition to what it is not. Heavy metal fans generally agree, for example, in defining the genre against one particular neighbor: For most fans, metal is *that which is not hard rock*—where one thing starts and the other ends being always a heated point of contention. Ask a Metallica fan, and chances are that he or she will not consider Poison a metal band, although Poison fans might think otherwise. Likewise, Metallica's later, more melodic work may not qualify as metal to the ears of Sodom or Slayer fans. I point this out not to set up a search for "objective" criteria that would allow us to define where the genre starts and ends, but to approach the genre's language within the discursive battles through which it is constituted. Critical, theoretically inflected ethnomusicology reminds us of the primary point here: It is precisely *because* boundaries are socially contingent that the rigorous musicological analysis of melody, harmony, volume, mode, rhythm, and pitch is strictly necessary. As Susan McClary points out, "given the tendency in cultural studies to stress the radical idiosyncrasy of each listener's musical perception, we need to find ways of understanding the socially grounded rhetorical devices by means of which music creates its *intersubjective* effects; otherwise the medium remains privatized and mystified, impervious to cultural criticism" (1994, 32). In other words, the socially contested nature of meaning cannot function as excuse to give up formal analysis.

Heavy metal as a genre takes the will to rupture, break, negate that underlies all rock music to its ultimate conclusion. In metal, more than in most rock genres, self-definition takes the form of an opposition (what the music is not) accompanied by a claim that a faster and louder brand is in fact heir to rock music's true spirit. It therefore denies elements in the tradition perceived as pop or commercial betrayals of the radical spirit of rock music. Harris Berger's ethnomusicological research explains the genre's fans' preference for the depiction of "the history of their music in a progressive fashion" (1999a, 56). This preference is often organized in narrative form around tropes of *radicalization* (associated with changes in volume, tempo, and pitch as well as with darkened iconography, stripped-down performance, and anguished, aggressive, or apocalyptic lyrics) and tropes of *negation* (what heavy metal *is not* being a crucial component, for most fans, in any explanation of what *it is*). What Emma Baulch has shown for Balinese metal applies also to the early Brazilian scene: "authenticity appeared to lay in an absent elsewhere which could only be reached by diligently rehearsing foreign repertoires" (2003, 203).[2] In that rabid rejection of locality that characterized much early extreme metal in various parts of the globe, Sepultura's uniqueness lies, as Keith Kahn-Harris has shown, in the most interesting leap it took from being a Brazilian-based band performing non-Brazilianness to ultimately becoming an American-based "global" band that consistently explores Brazilianness (Harris 2000b, 14). In a further irony, its name was a translation *not from but into Portuguese*. Unlike other local groups such as Vulcano, Viper, and Witchhammer, which chose English names, the name "Sepultura" emerged thanks to one band member's habit of rewriting Anglo-American metal songs in Portuguese. Max Cavalera, one of the Cavalera brothers in the band, translated the title of Motörhead's song "Dancing on Your Grave," using the Portuguese *sepultura* for "grave," unaware that he was creating the moniker for a group that arguably would match Motörhead in its accomplishments as a heavy metal band.

Metalheads ground their value judgments about their favorite bands and the non-metal traditions they inherit primarily in a vocabulary that stresses negativity and superlatives—fastest, loudest, dirtiest. Although their syntax is relatively simple, the codes governing such judgments can acquire considerable complexity. Most Brazilian metal fans would claim that Bahian rocker Raul Seixas's juxtapositions of Northeastern accordion music (*baião*) and Elvis-inflected, 1950s-style rock 'n' roll are "heavier" and "more authentically true to the spirit of rock music" than all the theatrical electrified "hard rock" that circulated in Brazil until the mid-1980s, some of which was even classified as "heavy metal" in the specialized press at the time.[3] In metal's intensely contested terrain, the Brazilian band Sepultura combines two unique accomplishments: for twenty years its music has *been changing constantly*, yet it is universally recognized by metal fans as a premier and uncompromising *death/thrash metal* band. This has allowed the band continually to redefine its relation to its national origins as well as to the industry and to its multinational fan base. Sepultura has methodically invented ways to introduce difference within the genre's strict codes, a move made possible by its understanding of the dialectic of negation/radicalization that underlies heavy metal music. I will not only make an argument about Sepultura's music, but also suggest that its casting of this tension can help us further unsettle a few oppositions that still plague cultural studies. These oppositions include the celebration of globalization versus the eulogy of the local, the championing of authenticity versus its debunking, and the defense of "resistance" in popular culture versus the affirmation of its ultimate futility. Sepultura's music and performance provide us with elements to move beyond these binaries.

Many of the formal traits mapped by Harris Berger's analysis of death metal apply to Sepultura's early music, and to some degree to its later albums as well: experimentations with "extremes of tempo" (Berger 1999a, 59), efforts "to avoid the diatonic or blues-based harmony" in favor of "unexpected half steps or tritones" (62), distinctive "noisy, unpitched vocals" that replicate the distorted guitar timbres (57), and "variations of the harmonic vocabulary that break up the minor tonality and obscure the tonal center" (58) that move away from the vocabulary of minor chord progressions typical of earlier metal. These musical operations go hand in hand with a new performative ethic/aesthetic, as metal acts opted for "stripped-down stage moves" (70) as a reaction against what many fans and musicians perceived as the phony, artificial theatricality of commercial hard rock. In Sepultura the sheer intensity of its sound establishes a strong contrast to that contained style of performance. As with most heavy metal, and especially its faster, speed/thrash varieties, the art of Sepultura depends on a careful balance between energy, that is, power and intensity, and control, that is, containment and enclosure. In the past decade the band's music has often juxtaposed the suggestion of enclosed territories (an "oppressive" wall of guitars, loud and fast drumming) to the evocation of lines of flight away from that enclosure, be it through abrupt variations of rhythmic patterns or specific influences from Afro-Brazilian percussion or native South American singing.

Founded in 1984 in the early days of a national heavy metal boom particularly strong in the band members' hometown, the southeastern state capital of Belo Horizonte, Sepultura's first lineup consisted of the brothers Max and Igor Cavalera (guitar/vocals and drums), Paulo Jr. (bass), and Jairo T (guitar). Picked up by the emerging metal label Cogumelo Records, they recorded *Bestial Devastation* (1985) and *Morbid Visions* (1986), still grounded in a quite traditional death metal recipe. In 1987 Jairo T left the band and was replaced by Andreas Kisser. A superior guitarist, steeped in the blues and in traditional metal, Kisser brought an entirely new texture to their sound. The Cavalera brothers, Paulo Jr., and Andreas Kisser continued to be the lineup from their qualitative leap *Schizophrenia* (1987), through the international breakthrough *Beneath the Remains* (1989), the unorthodox yet unmistakably metallic *Arise* (1991), the enraged experimental protest record *Chaos A.D.* (1993), to the metal-Afro-diasporic sound feast of *Roots* (1996). After *Roots* a disagreement over the role of Gloria Bujnowski (Max's wife), the band's manager for the previous five years, caused Max's departure from the band. He was later replaced by Derrick Green, the African-American lead singer (and former pianist!) heard on *Against* (1998), *Nation* (2001), and *Roorback* (2003). Green, later called "Predator" due to his six-feet-plus figure, was increasingly welcomed by the Sepultura fan base as he passed tests of heaviness as well as Brazilianness of spirit, detected in his passion for national cultural markers such as soccer. Max Cavalera went on to form Soulfly and record the albums *Soulfly* (1998) and *Primitive* (2000). With excursions into reggae, hip hop, and Afro-Brazilian rhythms, his band also expanded upon the cross-genre experiments of Sepultura's *Roots*.

For over twenty years Sepultura's uniqueness has resided less in the maintenance of a presumably pure and original "authenticity"—the band changes its music constantly—than in the ability to *think ahead and act accordingly*. The band's members understand that the coding of their music by journalists, record companies, academics, and moralists has always tended to be one step behind the music itself. Before the defenders of territories can stake these territories out, Sepultura's music has crossed into an elsewhere. By the time the detractors of "heavy metal Satanism" discovered Sepultura's *Morbid Visions* (1986), the band no longer offered satanic imagery, but rather an anguished critique of social alienation, as in *Schizophrenia* (1987) and *Beneath the Remains* (1989). Before moralists could misunderstand that and accuse the band of "inciting violence or suicide," Sepultura was somewhere else again, putting forth *Arise* (1991) and *Chaos A.D.* (1993), records that offered a powerful metal recipe of radical, internationalist social critique sprinkled with a number of incursions into Brazilian rhythms. When the band reached worldwide success, the defenders of national purity did not have much time to condemn it, as Sepultura effected a political and musical rediscovery of Brazil in the cross-genre experiments of *Roots* (1996). The success of *Roots*, especially given the album's incorporation of a host of non-metal references, led many metal purists to discard the band as irrevocably crossover and lost to the genre. They did not have much time to formulate their attack either, as Sepultura returned with a new vocalist, Derrick Green, and recorded two fast, heavy, and unmistakably metal records, *Against* (1998) and *Nation* (2001).[4] In the early 2000s, the band faced attacks from people who argued that combining internationalization with references to Brazilianness would inevitably lead to the band's exoticization and eventual sellout. They arrived late again, as this essay will demonstrate.

As the Brazilian military regime ceded power to the first civilian government, albeit still an undemocratically elected one, in 1985, heavy metal bands in Belo Horizonte, Santos, São Paulo, Rio de Janeiro, and other metropolises began to brew a cultural phenomenon of considerable proportion. Influenced by Motörhead, Iron Maiden, Slayer, Metallica, and Megadeth, they took the genre known in the 1970s as *rock pauleira* (hard rock) to a new level of distortion, loudness, and aggressiveness. Out of the most unlikely Amazonian state of Pará, far removed from the country's cultural centers, a band named Stress traveled to Rio in 1982 to record the eponymous album that fans would later acknowledge as a foundational moment for national metal (Dolabela 1987, 158). In Belo Horizonte bands such as Sepultura, Sarcófago, Sagrado Inferno, Morg, Armaggeddon, Holocausto, Chakal, and Overdose (in addition to Minotauro from São Paulo), participated in either one or both editions of the BH Metal Festival, events that led to most of those bands recording singles, EPs, and/or LPs. The city's intense metal scene congregated around Cogumelo Records, a store founded in 1980 that evolved into an independent label in 1985, the year of the Sepultura/Overdose split album *Bestial Devastation/Século XX*. This album is an underground legend that helped turn Cogumelo into Brazil's first successful metal label. In São Paulo a compilation entitled *Metal SP*, released by the independent rock label Baratos Afins, featured Salário Mínimo, Avenger, Vírus, and Centuria. In the neighboring coastal city of Santos, the pioneers of Vulcano climbed from the "Om Pushne Namah" single (1982) to their *Live* LP (1985) on their way to the landmark *Bloody Vengeance* (1986) that is still a cult object among Brazilian fans. In Rio de Janeiro, for interesting reasons, heavy metal always had a smaller following than other international youth genres like funk and hip hop, but the city is home to one of the country's most respected metal bands, Dorsal Atlântica, which has been around since its *Ultimatum* EP (1985) and its debut LP *Antes do Fim* [Before the End] (1986).

The national scene was given greater impetus by the mega-festival Rock in Rio (1985), a ten-day event where all the metal acts were international: Iron Maiden, Ozzy Osbourne, Whitesnake, Scorpions, and AC/DC. The latter four were packed together twice, on a couple of long metal nights, unfortunately opened for by melodious rock artists from Brazil, who surely paid the price (Alexandre 2002, 190–205). Speed and thrash metal giants such as Metallica, Slayer, and Venom soon began to include Brazil in their tours. Magazines such as *Heavy* or national editions of international fanzines such as *Rock Brigade* began to pop up. Following Belo Horizonte's Cogumelo, other stores invested in low-budget, independent record producing. Among those that consistently put out metal records are São Paulo's Baratos Afins and Devil Discos as well as Rio's Heavy and Point Rock. A few stations lifted the blockade against metal on radio for one hour with the emergence of weekly metal shows such as *Comando Metal* on São Paulo's 89 FM, *Metal Massacre* on Belo Horizonte's Liberdade FM, and *Guitarras para o Povo* (Guitars to/for the People, certainly a deliberate Lennon reference) on Rio's Fluminense FM. All of this contributed to a scene that a critic later described as an "anthill of black shirts exchanging information all over Brazil" (Alexandre 2002, 349).

By the late 1980s metal was as important a cultural phenomenon in Brazil as it was misunderstood by rock journalists, moralists, and popular music stars alike. Wasn't heavy metal music invariably repetitive, noisy, and bereft of any artistic merit? Weren't metal bands copying a foreign genre and doing a disservice to Brazilian popular music? Weren't they involved in strange satanic rituals? Weren't they renouncing the most important task of popular music, the conscious political protest? Didn't their music convey a nihilistic and negative message that could dangerously influence youth? Never mind that such questions often contradict one another, all of them betraying ignorance about the genre. Given the context of Brazil in the 1980s, these hostile interrogations had a highly politicized spin that continually besieged the genre. As late as 1995, when Sepultura was already one of the world's most successful metal bands, the Hollywood Rock festival that brought Megadeth, Judas Priest, Slayer, and Queensrÿche to Brazil had to face an intense letter-writing campaign from metal's ever loyal fans to be convinced that Sepultura should be included on the bill. As often happens, the marketing-oriented organizers were more in tune with statistics of radio airplay than with the social reality of concert-going and failed to understand that even *Slayer* or *Metallica* would have been shocked if the metal night of a rock mega-concert in Brazil in 1995 were held *without* Sepultura.

Outside the English-speaking world heavy metal bands patiently concocted vocabulary through translation. One can find metal sung in other European languages, but heavy metal music means, to an extent unparalleled in most other youth genres, music sung primarily in English, even when composed in Brazil, Sweden, or Germany. Latin American criticism still needs to understand these acts of translation in terms more complex than either the simple lament for the adoption of foreign models or the tired, facile celebration of the "subversive" or "resistant" hybridity of peripheral appropriations of metropolitan languages. The choice of language for Brazilian metal bands in the mid-1980s was not casual and was discussed by musicians and fans. The Rio de Janeiro power trio Dorsal Atlântica was one of the genre's few acts singing only in Portuguese, on *Ultimatum* (1985), *Antes do Fim* (1986), and *Dividir e Conquistar* [Divide and Conquer] (1988), before the band's definitive switch to English on *Searching for the Light* (1990). On the historic Sepultura/Overdose *Bestial Devastation/Século XX* shared LP (1985), Sepultura filled its side with songs in English, while Overdose preferred Portuguese. By Overdose's first full-length LP *Conscience* (1987), the band had adopted mostly English lyrics. Although most metal bands choose English, Witchhammer (*Mirror, My Mirror*, 1990) and other examples show that Portuguese lyrics were sometimes preferred on punk/hardcore collaborations, or cross-genre experiments with other youth music. In regard to language—and in many other respects—Sepultura defined early on what would later become a standard choice for the genre—momentary flights from Portuguese that would allow for both a critique of the nation and a very particular entrance into the international market.

Sepultura's lyrics on its first albums feature apocalyptic theaters on *Bestial Devastation* and *Morbid Visions*, schizo-paranoid dismantling of societal hypocrisy on *Schizophrenia*, and images of ruins that synthesize its earlier, anguished work on *Beneath the Remains*—the international breakthrough album produced in Brazil by Tampa-based producer Scott Burns, "who played a crucial part in developing the 'clean,' precise guitar sounds that dominated Death Metal in that era" (Harris 2000b, 19). Sepultura's album covers and liner art are often in dialogue with music and lyrics, as covers evolved from an aesthetic of darkened, nightmarish monstrosity to a focus on individual psychic pain, expressed by drawings rather than photographs or paintings (*Schizophrenia*, 1987). *Beneath the Remains* (1989) featured a reddish skull set on a dark background; the close-up orientation from below humanized the skull and made it into an allegory of the caging and suffering embodied in the lyrics and music. Over the years these references to enclosure evolved to depict a gadget that looks like a torture device from which a dehumanized and strapped-up body hangs upside down, on the blue-ish cover of *Chaos A.D.* (1993), or an Orwellian, role-playing-game type of monster like the one-eyed tentacular creature on the brownish cover of *Arise* (1991). Accompanying transformations in the music, the cover art would later increasingly highlight a focus on politics, as in the painted Indian face on the cover of *Roots* (1996) or the return of symbolic political statements such as the raised dark fists against the bright orange background of *Nation* (2001). The raised fist (known in much of the world as the code gesture of the "Internationale") enters into dialogue with the back cover of the liner notes, where the image of a red flag with a star at the center overlooks a darkened, reddish urban scenario. The jewel case includes a powerful photograph of an inner-city parking lot against the background of a moving bus and an apartment building under the CD. A certain hardcore punk sensibility links Sepultura's cover art from 1985 to 2004, but the band's covers became more eloquently political as the 1990s evolved.

As Sepultura became more aware of the workings of violence in Brazil and abroad, *Arise* and *Chaos A.D.* established the band as a worldwide reference for vigorous, socially aware heavy metal. Sepultura then initiated a decade-long history of collaboration with Brazil's foremost punk band, Ratos de Porão. Sepultura's turn to radical internationalist politics — inspired by both punk and reggae — included videos where the fast tempo of metal is in dialogue with the fast montage of images of violence (shot with a low, handheld camera) from places such as Palestine, Northern Ireland, and Brazil. The video for "Territory," the winner of Brazil's MTV Music Video Awards in 1994, is an excellent example of this aesthetic.

Much like Brazilian Cinema Novo's "aesthetics of hunger" — which turned the poverty of technical means into an auteurist and politicized statement about filmmaking in the Third World — Sepultura's first records use the lack of technological resources to intensify the raw and harsh character of its sound. Through 1983–84 Igor Cavalera developed his playing while counting on no more than a snare drum, a floor tom, and a cymbal. *Bestial Devastation* (1985) was recorded without bass drums, as he did not own drum pedals and had never used any. At that time Cavalera's broom sticks were often enlisted as support for the cymbals. By then, however, Igor had enjoyed long percussive training in jams with *charangas*, the poly-rhythmic, thirty-plus-member percussion combos that lead fan chanting in major Brazilian soccer games.[5] *Bestial Devastation* and *Morbid Visions* were recorded in an 8-track studio with overdriven amplifiers. Having self-produced their three first records on Cogumelo Records, for *Beneath the Remains* (1989), Sepultura's first album with the international label Road-runner, members of the band had to be convinced that a producer could enhance their sound. *Beneath the Remains* was recorded in nine days in a studio in Rio de Janeiro, or better said nine nights, as Sepultura still needed to use nightly studio time, at cheaper rates, and sleep during the day in the stifling, 100-degree Rio summer. *Beneath the Remains* circulated as a cult object in Europe and was chosen by several fanzines as the best thrash/death metal album of 1989. By the following year Sepultura was playing in front of twenty-six thousand fans in Holland's Dynamo Open Air Festival and mesmerizing metal and non-metal fans alike at Rock in Rio II. By the early 1990s the band was playing shoulder-to-shoulder with bands that inspired them, such as Metallica and Kreator, as well as open-ing for heavy metal legend Ozzy Osbourne. With *Arise* and *Chaos A.D.* the band established a routine of gold or platinum records and legendary tours, not only in Europe and the United States but also in places like Indo-nesia and Japan. By the time the band traveled to the occupied territories of Palestine to shoot the video for "Territory," Sepultura had achieved feats hitherto unthinkable for a thrash metal band. Its members had become the most widely, globally known Brazilian musicians ever, overtaking a certain Antônio Carlos Jobim, who, although still alive back then, was not fully equipped to understand what was going on (perhaps unable to see the striking analogies between the irruption of his own music into American jazz in the early 1960s and Sepultura's trajectory in the 1990s).

Throughout its history Sepultura has increased the speed of the already fast tempo it inherited from influences like Slayer, Metallica, Motörhead, and Venom. Sepultura's sound is directly indebted to Igor Cavalera's power-ful drumming style, developed over a career marked by increasing use of unexpected variations and syncopation learned in the polyrhythms of *charanga* percussion combos. Distortion on Max Cavalera's and Andreas Kisser's guitar is likewise raised to the limit. Following Igor's lead in the rhythm section, Paulo Jr.'s bass lines have evolved from the "louder and faster" aesthetic of death metal to variations of Brazilian/Afro-diasporic inspiration. Early on Max Cavalera developed a hoarse, low-note style of vocalization that would become one of the band's trademarks and inaugurate a distinctive style in Brazilian heavy metal. The syncopated syllables growled by Cavalera into the intervals of his brother Igor's aggressive drumbeats made the lyrics minimally intelligible, a trait of the genre that Robert Walser shows was established by Anglo-American metal vocalists singing in their native language. Sung in low notes, but in as high a volume as possible, Cavalera's vocals battled with the "wall of sound" created by highly distorted guitars.

If, as Walser has pointed out, the dialectic of freedom and control is an apt metaphor to describe metal (1993a), in the early art of Sepultura (and in most metal bands in post-dictatorial Brazil) that dialectic perennially tilted away from freedom toward the pole of control, asphyxia, enclosure. For this reason it is hard to find anything resembling a drum solo in early Sepultura songs, a feature not uncommon in other brands of heavy metal. The drum solo (with its own dialectic of freedom and control) would not have fit the asphyxiating atmosphere that Sepultura wanted to create on its first albums, where the metaphor of *enclosure* was the dominant one. Drum solos, funky bass lines, and instrumental syncopation increasingly appear in their later work, as collaborations with other genres developed.

On "Territory" and "Propaganda," two powerful protest songs on *Chaos A.D.*, Andreas Kisser provides the listener with longer guitar solos, lines of flight that offer some breathing room away from the enclosure suggested by the oppressive and suffocating wall of sound. Likewise, "Territory" features one of Igor Cavalera's first studio drum solos, in dialogue with Andreas's as yet another line of flight offering escape. As a whole, *Chaos A.D.* was the first Sepultura album to truly register Igor's experiments with unexpected tempo variations inspired by Brazilian/Afro-diasporic polyrhythms. This would lead to the "explosion of sounds" heard on *Roots*, where the band enlisted the collaboration of Brazilian percussionist Carlinhos Brown and relied on recordings from the Amazonian Xavante, collected by the band during a visit to the Xavante reservation in the midwestern state of Mato Grosso. National content that earlier had represented a cage, a suffocating territory for the band, was now being incorporated on the band's own terms, as the nation became a source that would allow the band to tilt its musical dialectic back toward freedom. The evolution of Sepultura's music is, then, consistent with an interesting transformation: The nation is initially a hostile territory, coded in ways that by definition excluded the genre. It was thus a territory to be traversed and transgressed. Thanks to the band's intelligent thinking and incessant musical learning—as well as to an international success that allowed it to rediscover Brazil from another angle—the nation progressively becomes a source for musical and cultural lines of flight, unexpected experiments and collaborations. Sepultura continually redefines the metal genre's very boundaries at the same time as it refines what had hitherto been understood as *Brazilian* music.

I will illustrate this movement with an analysis of the fourth track of Sepultura's *Roots*, "Ratamahatta," the song that most powerfully evokes Sepultura's rediscovery of Brazil. The song features not only the usual metal rhythm section, distorted guitars, and hoarse loud vocals but also a percussion ensemble made up of large bass drums (the *surdo*, used in samba and other Brazilian/Afro-diasporic genres), cans, *djembes*, water tanks, and rattles, all played by the Bahian percussion wizard Carlinhos Brown. The song also makes use of material recorded by Sepultura during its visit to the Xavante. The track opens with Xavante vocals over drumming in 2/4 time, accompanied by the metallic sound of a shaker. Performed in low notes, the singing privileges the closed vowels /ô/ and /ê/. Collective performances of song and dance are known among the Xavante as *da-ño* [glottal stop] *re*, and can be of three types according to their content, the movements of the dance step, and time of day when they are performed (Graham 1995, 79). As made clear by Laura Graham's extensive ethnographic research among the Xavante, song and dance performances are a crucial part of the community's relation to its surroundings.[6] The visit to the Xavante nation had a profound impact upon Sepultura, and *Roots* makes use of the material recorded there on several tracks.

The presence of the drumming and mournful Xavante chanting in the introduction to a Sepultura song produces anticipation for the entrance of the distorted guitars and the loud, fast rhythm section. The listener's feeling of anticipation is again produced and frustrated at 0:12, as the Xavante chant and drumming is interrupted not by a metal rhythm section, but by an introductory *maracatu* phrase, performed on the bass drum by Carlinhos Brown. The maracatu line barely remains long enough to establish a tempo and is immediately cut short, this time by silence.[7] Following Brown's "one, two, three" call, the metallic expectation is again created and denied, as the maracatu phrasing on the drums picks up where silence had left off. Only at 0:31 do Max's and Andreas's distorted guitars come in, with a melody harmonized in power chords. The bass and snare drums continue dictating the rhythm, as for 10 seconds the song combines the time of maracatu and the guitar phrasing of heavy metal. At 0:41 Max begins to intersperse hoarse growled vowels in the intervals of the beat, announcing that the metal ensemble will gather in its totality soon, as Igor's 4/4 drumming comes in as loud as ever.

The metal ensemble is in place at full speed, but the maracatu rhythm continues underneath, on Brown's surdo and snare drums, in dialogue with Igor's rock drumming and producing a polyrhythmic effect that is not only original but full of cultural and political meaning in Brazil (given the social distance between maracatu and metal). By the fifty second mark, two of Brazil's loudest and richest percussive machines—Brown's unique synthesis of Brazilian/Afro-diasporic rhythms and Sepultura's fast thrash metal—dialogue to great effect. Brown accompanies his drumming with vocal effects that recall the hip hop art of scratching, while Max continues to build up the vocals with a high-pitched "o" at intervals between the beats. After a full minute of buildup, Brown's and Max's syncopated and grave vocals storm in with lyrics that are in dialogue with Brazilian minimalist, "dirty" poetry, shouted in the form of call and response:

> biboca/garagem/favela [shithole/garage/slumtown]
> fubanga/maloca/bocada [hodgepodge/hut/hideout]

This call and response pattern in a vocal duo was unknown in Sepultura's previous work, and further connects the song with an Afro-diasporic sensibility. More than simply summoned for their meanings, the words are used for their *rhythmic power*. They are all highly vocalic words where every consonant is followed by a vowel, thereby creating the "typical" Portuguese sequence of two-letter syllables. All words in the stanza are trisyllables accented on the second-to-last vowel, which is also the "default" accentuation pattern in Portuguese. The stanza features an alternation of voiced and voiceless bilabial stops—[b] and [p]—and an alternation of voiced and voiceless velar stops—[g] and [k]. Building on these four highly percussive sounds, Max's and Brown's vocal art dialogue replicates the instrumental syncopation going on between Brown's ensemble and Igor's metal drumming.

Much like the Amazonian chanting and Brown's maracatu drum phrasing in the introduction, the lyrics in Portuguese (uncommon in Sepultura's earlier work) come in *to signify Brazil*. Not only are their phonology and rhythm quite typical of the Portuguese language, their semantics are un-mistakably Brazilian, as most words are of indigenous origin. Of these six words *garagem* is probably the only one comprehensible to a non-Brazilian speaker of Portuguese. *Biboca* comes from the Tupi and its original mean-ing of "excavation" or "valley" was first expanded to designate a poorly built shack, before becoming urban slang for "shithole." *Favela* is an inter-nationally known term for the urban Brazilian slums. *Fubanga*, a word still not found in dictionaries, suggests to most youth a rag, a worthless piece. *Maloca* is an Araucanian word that reached Portuguese through Spanish and means "indigenous hut." Over time it also came to designate urban shacks, and among urban youth tribes in Brazil the noun gave birth to the verb *malocar*, meaning to hide, especially drugs or an illicit object. *Malocar* is an art invariably associated with oppressed groups and always alludes to the hiding of something from the eyes of a repressive authority. *Bocada*, coming from *boca* (mouth), designates a faraway, hidden, and dangerous place often associated with drug dealing. The chorus's overall effect is a pan-national youth-inflected portrayal of Brazil from the jungle to the city, one that emphasizes oppression and struggle.

The symmetrical accentuation pattern (as all words are composed of three consonant-vowel pairs, and all stressed on the second-to-last syl-lable) allows the lyrics to follow neatly the beat of Igor Cavalera's drums, forcing the usually soft-singing Carlinhos Brown to a volume he probably had never before attempted. At 1:13 Max's and Andreas's short and fast phrases on the guitar return. Although one can hear Carlinhos Brown's Northeastern-inflected percussion in the background, Paulo Jr.'s metal bass and Igor Cavalera's metal drumming come to the forefront. Accom-panying the return of metal-style distorted guitars, Brown's vocals fade and give way to Max's hoarsened [ô]s, growled in the intervals to the beats. By the time they reach the bridge, Igor's furious drumming has turned to syncopated beats, announcing the return of the call and response pattern in the vocals, this time devoted to Brazilian folk legends and anti-heroes:

Zé do Caixão/Zumbi/Lampião
[repeat two times]

Zumbi, the leader of the largest American Maroon state in the seventeenth century (the Quilombo dos Palmares in Northeastern Brazil), has become a symbol of black struggle for freedom and a national hero widely respected among whites as well. It is not surprising that his name would be invoked

150   in "Ratamahatta," a song devoted to rescuing sounds associated with oppressed populations. Neither is it surprising to see his name in a genealogy continued by Lampião, the Northeastern outlaw hero who became a
Robin-Hood-type legend in the backlands, until the police and the army
concluded a decades-long drive to destroy his gang in the 1930s. Zumbi and
Lampião are two of the foremost names in a long tradition of popular figures who took up arms to struggle against slave masters or land-owning
oligarchs. The illustrious pair of underground heroes is joined by Zé do
Caixão (Coffin Joe), a horror film director who endured ridicule in Brazil
from the 1950s to the 1970s before seeing his horror cinema revered internationally as cult favorites. His most celebrated films, *At Midnight I Will
Take Your Soul* (1964) and *Tonight I Will Incarnate in Your Corpse* (1966) combine cartoonish, parodic horror with a disturbing aestheticization of violence, as they tell the story of a demented gravedigger who terrorizes his
small town while looking for a woman to bear him a son and "reproduce his
breed." Unlike most horror directors, who opt to set their stories in imaginary lands, Coffin Joe is firmly rooted in the violent and socially unjust
reality of urban Brazil. His films make, for example, abundant reference
to syncretism and Afro-Brazilian religious practices. By referencing him
along with Zumbi and Lampião, Sepultura establishes a lineage of national
figures united in a struggle against official—racist, oligarchic, colonized—
versions of the country.[8]

Nationality is also foregrounded in the chorus inasmuch as these three
highly vocalic words contain the nasal sound [ão], the phonological trademark of the Portuguese language. At 1:48 Brown's percussion again becomes the predominant element in the musical texture, with the guitar
sound being suspended for a while. This time the beat is a loud funk led
by bass, drums, and Brazilian percussion instruments. In the background
the snare drums continue phrasing in recognizable samba rhythm. Brown
now shouts English lyrics, breaking the words in autonomous syllables
("hello up/town, hello down/town, hello trench/town"). By now the song
has established a dialectic that it will follow until the end: metal and Afro-
Brazilian rhythms coexist, act in dialogue with each other, and take turns
leading the way. The alternation generates diverse sets of expectations and
is coded differently depending on the listener's genre of preference. When
the guitars return Igor's drums return as well, and on top of their aggressive, heavy metal rhythmic patterns Carlinhos Brown and Max Cavalera
take turns playing gutturally with the sounds of the chorus word. "Ratama-

hatta" is not a Portuguese word, in fact, but a suggestive sound combo full of associations, as "*rata*" means rat, and "*mahatta*" cannot but evoke, given the song's themes, Mahatma Gandhi, after whom is named one of the famous squares in Rio de Janeiro—among the places Rio's punks first called home. Furthermore, Cavalera and Brown play with the word also to make it suggest "*mata*," the familiar command form for the Portuguese verb "to kill" and at the same time a noun meaning "the woods" or "jungle." Overall, the chorus crowns the themes of violence, struggle, and oppression constructed musically and lyrically by the song. The call and response pattern, initially limited to vocals, takes over also in the dialogue between Brown's Afro-Brazilian percussion ensemble and Cavalera's and Kisser's guitars.

The song "Ratamahatta" made use of material recorded during Sepultura's stay with the Xavante nation in Mato Grosso, but for the video the band opted for stop-motion puppet animation designed by Fred Stern. Images of drunkenness, visits to Afro-Brazilian *candomblé* priestesses, flirtation in the slums, and incarcerations are all portrayed in fast succession amid an atmosphere that evokes black magic, voodoo, and tribal ceremonies. Featuring "little creatures" coming out of jungles and urban slums at a faster and faster pace to accompany the music, the animation quite deliberately suggests a complete loss of consciousness in its frenetic pace and dark, surrealistic settings. Masked beings descend first upon the jungle and the ghettos. In the jungle a tribal ceremony honors a tycoon type clad in a tuxedo, while in the city a collective ceremony foregrounds a passive multitude moving their heads to a leader. The video concludes with the masked beings appropriating some of the behavior they find (such as the drinking), as the metal and Afro-diasporic rhythms slowly fade to give way to the Xavante healing chant that returns as a coda to the song. "Ratamahatta," then, can be conceived *as a totality*: its use of rhythm, melody, harmony, pitch, and volume, its minimalist lyrics, its unique form of production, its featuring of a highly symbolic partnership, and finally its innovative and caustic video, are all elements that help ground our final reflections devoted to Sepultura's revolutionizing of the representation of nationality in sound.

Reflecting back on the band's early days in the 1980s, Andreas Kisser, Sepultura's lead guitarist, recounted, "We listened to heavy and black metal and found everything made in Brazil to be shitty. We didn't like *samba*, we didn't like national rock, we didn't like any of that crap" (quoted in Alexandre 2002, 347). For large sectors of the urban youth of post-dictatorial

Brazil, heavy metal became at the same time a metaphor for the absence of a nation with which they could identify *and* an antidote against that exclusion. Unlike metropolitan bands that emerged in opposition to and negation of other *genres*, Sepultura arose by initially negating the *totality* of the nation's music—quite a courageous gesture if you are playing in musically rich Brazil. It was not by chance that it was national music that had to be negated for metal to establish itself. The array of musics coded as "Brazilian" by the 1980s included several varieties of the national genre, samba, traditional instrumental genres such as *choro*, rhythmic verbal arts such as *embolada*, percussion-based maracatu or *coco*, piano- or guitar-based *bossa* and post-*bossa* sounds, accordion-based musics such as *baião* and *xaxado*, and even what was then beginning to be called "national rock."[9] The codification of nationality in sound was not only actualized through discourses that linked one or more of these genres with the authentically national. Paralleling these discourses was the remarkable operation by which certain musics (evolving either out of samba or fusion with regional musics) ascended to a status increasingly identified with good taste in music: the malleable category of MPB (*Música Popular Brasileira*), a term that does not designate the totality of the country's popular music, but rather certain forms associated with sophistication. The sociocultural category MPB projected the fable of exceptionality of one particular social class. Theoretically, music of any kind can become MPB by erasing its regional origins if it derives from a regional genre, by trimming its rough edges if it is too electric or too percussive, by complexifying its harmonies or arrangements if it draws on popular forms. When the heavy metal revolution was initiated in the mid-1980s, the elastic throat of MPB had already engulfed and neutralized rock music's outsider aura, as Brazilian rock bands such as Titãs, Paralamas do Sucesso, Legião Urbana, and Blitz were slowly ushered into the MPB pantheon of middle-class good taste.

Regardless of how the young members of Sepultura phrased their antinational cry back then, their conscious gesture of refusing national music as such *called attention to the exclusionary practices governing the coding of nationality in sound*. Long after the debates in the 1960s against folkloric and mythical conceptions of nationhood in music had been won, "national" music—though no longer coded in terms of authenticity—was still produced through mechanisms that left unrepresented a large portion of youth not identified with either MPB or "Brazilian rock." Instead of struggling for a particular position within the universal concept at stake

("Brazilian music"), Sepultura denounced the concept in its totality. In refusing the term *tout court*, the band exposed its false universality, its dependence on a previous exclusion, its reliance on a constitutive abjection. These musical traits of nationality only started to be pursued in conscious fashion much later, however, as Sepultura's *internationalization* allowed it to refract to Brazil's musical establishment an image of the nation that this establishment was not ready to recognize. The band's internationalization also allowed it to carry out the "rediscovery" of Brazilian rhythms that led to the sound feast of *Roots*, in the process unsettling the codes by which the nation had learned to project itself in sound.

As the *Arise* and *Chaos A.D.* tours drew multitudes of people everywhere from Holland to Japan, Sepultura began to be known among European fans as "the jungle boys." The great irony is that they were from a metropolis, Belo Horizonte, and most certainly got to see London and Amsterdam before they ever saw an Amazonian parrot. In ascending to the international market Sepultura was led to *become* a Brazilian band, and its national origin was increasingly highlighted in its concerts and records. Of course, the international music market also coded the nation in ways that members of Sepultura did not recognize as their own: "Jungle? What jungle? It's easier to get to New York than to the Amazon from here." In this broken mirror where internal and external images of the nation get reflected, it is to Sepultura's credit that its journey into its nation's sounds was never phrased in the tired vocabulary of authenticity.[10]

One may question as voluntaristic or politically naïve the terms in which Sepultura (most frequently by the eventually departing Max Cavalera) presented the Sepultura-Xavante collaboration. One may ask legitimate questions about royalties. It seems clear to me, however, that this particular encounter differs considerably from a whole set of engagements by world-famous pop artists with Third World musicians everywhere, from South Africa to Brazil. The most illustrious pattern, epitomized by Paul Simon teaming with South African musicians on *Graceland* in 1986, is fraught with ambiguities that have not escaped the attention of ethnomusicologists. As Louise Meintjes has noted, "despite the deliberate effort to convey a sense of mutual cooperation and benefit in the composition and production of *Graceland*" (Meintjes 1990, 40) and the true cooperation, say, in the crafting of a song such as "Homeless," the relationship established by Paul Simon with South African musicians can be said to have been one of exploitation. Meintjes mentions a few cases in point: "Simon profits financially from the project over and above everyone else. Music and arrangements are co-credited in some songs . . . but Simon holds the copyright on the album. Additionally, as producer, principal vocalist, and songwriter he dominates the music making process. . . . In the *Graceland* case, however, the split also replicates and expresses the differentials in sociopolitical and economic power represented by Simon and the Black South Africans" (Meintjes 1990, 47). The paradigm represented by *Graceland* is replicated in real relations of exploitation in the industry, which assigns wage laborer status to band musicians and elite art status to the star, as Steven Feld points out in one of the pioneering scholarly critiques of that practice (1988, 34). There is, for example, an interesting discrepancy in the composer credits of *Graceland*: Simon shares the credits to "Homeless" with Joseph Shabalala, the leader of Ladysmith Black Mambazo, but not the credits to "That Was Your Mother" with Good Rockin' Dopsie, the black New Orleans zydeco artist, even though the latter's musical input into the final product was just as great. Steven Feld has suggested that one of the answers to this lies in the more overt otherness of South African blacks vis-à-vis American minorities (1988, 34–43).

Although Sepultura looked to the Xavante for symbology, musical exchange, and ethical-political inspiration, members of the band never phrased their visit to the Xavante nation as a "recovery" of something presumably lost or in need of redemption. That sets it apart not only from Paul Simon's *Graceland*, but also from other cross-cultural collaborative projects by artists that one would need to differentiate from Simon's, such as those by Peter Gabriel, Ry Cooder, or David Byrne, whose endeavors on that front are, in my view, far more defensible ethically and musically. Sepultura phrased its collaboration with the Xavante in political terms, first and foremost as an alliance between two marginalized sectors, the urban working-class youth and the country's isolated indigenous groups. After the collaboration with the Xavante nation on *Roots*, Igor Cavalera stated, "We did not want to do a world music record" (*Folha de São Paulo* 1996, 5). His insistence that "everything is mixed and distorted" was not only an attempt to highlight the album's heaviness, but most importantly to set the band's collaboration with the Xavante nation in terms irreducible to the Paul-Simon-type recourse to South African or Afro-Brazilian indigenous musics, marked by an exoticizing that in practice denies those musics any coeval status with the artist doing the gathering. In contrast, Igor Cavalera stresses upfront the work of mixing, and thereby removes the discussion from the terrain of preservation, authenticity, recovery, that is to say he removes it from the language of world music. Implicitly asked to become "boys" of a "jungle" they had never known, the members of Sepultura indeed went Amazonian, attempting not to bring back an "anthropological document" but a politicized and polyrhythmic counterethnography.

In addition to their upfront account of how the music was actually produced, recorded, and mixed, Sepultura visited the Xavante as fellow Brazilian citizens. While that in itself does not for a minute guarantee a truly collaborative or non-exploitative relationship, the Xavante have been one of the most active indigenous nations when it comes to intervening in the larger Brazilian public sphere (Graham 1995, 44–63). Perhaps it appeared to many Xavante—a nation not exactly oblivious to the workings of Brazilian politics, as Graham's ethnography shows—that Sepultura's journey into the culture and music of the inland was indeed to forge an alliance against the same oligarchic structure that has been oppressing the Xavante for five hundred years. In short, the Sepultura-Xavante dialogue breaks with the world music paradigm precisely by taking place on the terrain of a common critique of dominant representations and practices of nationhood in Brazil. These dominant representations do not affect indigenous groups in the North and working-class youth in the urban South in the same fashion, but these two and other oppressed populations do share a common ground of opposition to that order. This is a collaborative critique that was unavailable to Paul Simon in South Africa as well as to Ry Cooder in Cuba, no matter how truly sympathetic they were with the African and Cuban subjects with whom they interacted. While it would be risky to assume one knows what the various Xavante responses to the collaboration with Sepultura have been, we can make some judgments from what we do know about the process from the production of *Roots* until the appearances of members of the Xavante nation in concerts leading up to Sepultura's twentieth-anniversary bash. It does seem that the band and many in the Xavante leadership agree as to their understanding of the collaborative process far more than, say, the rather discrepant perceptions of the *Graceland* process that separate Paul Simon from many South African musicians.

Anthropologist Hermano Vianna has noted the irony that Sepultura, Brazil's most international band, should release a record entitled *Roots* (Vianna 1996, 5). He is quick to add that the Xavante-Sepultura alliance makes sense, as it is "the encounter of tribes inimical to an ideal of national homogenization that determines that 'whoever doesn't like *samba/*

156 can't be a good type'" (5).[11] The most "primitive" and the most "international" are both excluded from the dominant coding of nationality in sound. They would find in their musical kinship (especially in the strong percussive energy of both) the key to cracking open an exclusionary definition of national identity in music. In the process, they also challenged the international market's labeling of "Third World" musical nations, and such coding was not unaffected by their intervention. It is not a question of assuming they can romantically subvert the production of exoticism in the world music arena.[12] Sepultura's awareness of the terrain on which it operates suggests, however, that it is framing these debates in terms that fit neither the preservationist paradigm of authenticity nor rock music's tired dialectic of self-marginalization versus sellout. Constantly engaging international references in debates around nationhood (and conversely reframing the nation in ways unexpected by the global arena), Sepultura turned the Brazilian musical nation into something previously unknown. As it rediscovered the nation it was transforming, the rediscovery would not leave the metal genre unchanged. After this encounter neither the place nor the sound would remain the same. The complexity of this clash forces us to rethink not only previous conceptions about heavy metal and about constructions of Brazilianness through music. It can also help us rethink a number of frozen oppositions that still plague the cultural studies of popular music.

NOTES

1 Best grasped as a sociocultural category rather than a musical genre, MPB began to circulate circa 1966 as a term to designate a set of acoustic musics, based primarily on the guitar/voice duo (mediated or not by the bossa nova revolution), and developed as nationalist alternatives to the first experiments with rock 'n' roll. In the 1970s, somewhat freed from the constraints of that opposition, MPB became the acronym for a spectrum of "sophisticated" popular music in Brazil, associated with figures such as Gilberto Gil, Caetano Veloso, Chico Buarque de Hollanda and Mílton Nascimento—all known for complex harmonic progressions, multiple operations with rhythm, innovative melodies, and highly poetic, "literary" lyric writing. For an indispensable English-language study of MPB, see Perrone 1989.

2 The notion of "elsewhere" displays a curious oscillation in Emma Baulch's "Gesturing Elsewhere" (2003), a study of Balinese metal's relation to locality and globality. On the one hand she uses it as a synonym for rootlessness or the absence of place, as when she notes that death thrashers in Bali gestured elsewhere

by refraining "from associating 'core values' with specific geographies" (Baulch 2003, 205). On the other hand she uses the term as a shorthand for the Anglo-dominated "global scene" (195, 210), a phenomenon that is ubiquitous (if differently inserted into various local contexts) but that cannot be simply equated with placelessness. This ambiguity, far from being a weakness of Baulch's article, accurately reflects a real oscillation in the understanding of place by heavy metal fans in peripheral societies. What does beg correction in her article is the statement that Sepultura's *Chaos A.D.* and *Roots* "contain several tracks in Portuguese" (201)—for the latter contains one, "Ratamahatta," and the former contains none except for the bonus track "Polícia" included in the Brazilian and the tin box European releases, but not in the more widely circulated "worldwide" edition of the CD. As I argue in this piece, Sepultura's trajectory is a sequence of multiple appeals both to locality and to globality, rather than a linear process of "lyrical and linguistic indigenization" as Baulch claims (202).

3 For a full discography and indispensable information on these bands and on Brazilian rock until 1986, see Dolabela 1987.

4 Sepultura later added a polemical—among hardcore metalheads—album of covers, *Roorback* (2003).

5 About the powerful soccer *charangas*, Max Cavalera would respectfully say on an interview on British radio: "They can get louder than a metal band."

6 See Laura Graham's work for an invaluable account of the symbolic role of performance in the Xavante nation. Her account includes their first appearances in colonial documents of the late eighteenth century, later attempts to force them into settlements, the traumatic crossing of the Araguaia River in the latter half of the nineteenth century, and later struggles over land demarcation (Graham 1995, 22–61). See also, most importantly for music scholars, her discussion of Xavante performance of dreams (103–36).

7 Particularly popular in Northeastern Brazil (especially in the state of Pernambuco), *maracatu* is an Afro-Atlantic dramatic dance that relates the crowning of a king and a queen. It is performed over percussion (large bass drums called *alfaias*), uses quite stylized costumes, and features a host of characters and several plot lines. Relying on percussion ensembles and utilizing a variety of tempos, maracatu has evolved from a semi-folkloric regional dance to a fundamental component and inspiration for a variety of new hybrid genres in Brazil.

8 Coffin Joe graciously returned the homage in a newspaper piece where he affirms, in his typically grandiose terms, that Sepultura's music "transports us to Armaggedon, to chaos, to the darkest pathways of Dante's Inferno, all the while updating the spirit of Wagner's music" (Coffin Joe 1996, 4). For a detailed biography of Coffin Joe, see Barcinski and Finotti 1998.

9 The Portuguese bibliography on most of these genres is relatively abundant, and quite daunting, in fact, in the case of samba. For an English-language introduction to these genres, see Olsen and Sheehy 2000 and McGowen and Pessanha 1998.

10 One of the important tasks of popular music criticism is to understand "authen-

ticity" for what it is, namely a fable, a narrative that, in the case of rock music, provides a "reenchantment of the world mediated by the grand apparatuses of mass media and technology" (Ochoa 1999, 174). See Ochoa 1999 for an insightful critique of the ways in which the fable of authenticity has been appropriated in the "simultaneous movement of transnationalization and regionalization of the record industry" coded circa 1987 and incorporated into the Billboard charts in 1991 as "world music" (176). For a perceptive account of the consolidation of "world music," see T. Taylor 1997.

11 The original lines (*quem não gosta de samba/bom sujeito não é*) appear in a song that celebrates *samba* as the national genre and have since then become part of the *vox populi* in the country. The song was composed by Dorival Caymmi, since the 1930s a key figure in the canonization of *samba* as well as in the irruption of his Afro-Brazilian state of Bahia into the center of national music. On Dorival Caymmi the indispensable reference is Risério 1993.

12 For a forceful reflection on how "world music" has become a terrain where even the most seemingly "horizontal" collaborations are traversed by a multinational corporate establishment of considerable power—one in which even concepts of "oral tradition" are instrumentalized for further exploitation and production of profit—see Feld 2000b.

PART 4
METAL AND EXTREMIST IDEOLOGIES

THE MARKETING OF ANGLO-IDENTITY IN THE NORTH AMERICAN HATECORE METAL INDUSTRY

Sharon Hochhauser

It goes by many different names, including National Socialist Black Metal and Odinist metal; however, a current fringe metal scene based in the United States and Canada also goes by a more accurate and revealing name—hatecore metal. This underground form of heavy metal music is based around a far more dangerous theme than rebellion against paren-tal authority, and it carries with it an incitement to violence in the name of the white power/Anglo-identity movement. While themes of anarchy and social disorder are fundamental to much of underground metal, in the North American hatecore metal scene they are matched with a deeply rooted fear and loathing of ethnic minorities, those adhering to religions other than Christianity, "world governments," and gay, lesbian, bisexual, and transgender populations. The resulting style combines the musical characteristics of other forms of metal that do not have a single, overt po-litical orientation (such as speed, death, and goth metal) with lyrics that promote the agenda of its far-right-leaning listeners and musicians. As a

162   vast majority of hatecore metal bands have strong personal and business connections to established racist and separatist groups, such as the World Church of the Creator, the National Alliance, the Aryan Nation, and the Michigan Militia, their influence in the underground metal market has very real and dangerous implications.

The combination of popular music with ideologies of hate is not a new development by any means, nor is it unique to the United States and Canada; however, the North American hatecore (often spelled H8core) metal scene has distinguished itself from its European equivalent by adopting a clearly focused, well-defined plan for marketing this music and drawing adherents into its movement. By downplaying explicit racism in their lyrics and advertising, hatecore metal bands are promoting their music not as a fringe style created by a politically radical subculture but as a home-grown, grassroots alternative to current musical trends. Beginning in the 1990s and continuing to the present day, hatecore metal bands have directed their attention to a more discriminating but otherwise unsuspecting music consumer—the underground heavy metal fan. Motivated by profit and a desire to spread their doctrine beyond the established Aryanist boundaries, hatecore metal bands and record companies are partaking in a particularly sinister form of consumer fraud.

This chapter discusses how the hatecore metal industry's alteration of media images, marketing techniques, and distribution methods in the late 1990s and early 2000s created an entirely new, media savvy sector of the underground metal industry, one that even today exploits listeners' dissatisfaction with the mainstream music industry and cleverly disguises the fact that its product involves more than just music. Through careful analysis of lyrics, iconography, and direct marketing materials, this chapter will explore the ways in which the hatecore metal industry in North America has been able to exploit the underground metal scene to serve its agenda. The consequence of this exploitation is a hatecore metal industry that functions not only as a moneymaker for the white power movement in the United States and Canada but also as a powerful and subversive recruiting tool.

As is to be expected when working with groups of people that prefer to operate on the fringes of society, the names of groups and movements involved in hatecore metal can become confusing. Because regionally, nationally, and internationally based hate organizations thrive on a reputation of secrecy and exclusivity, imprecise terminology helps to perpetuate their mystique. To clear the ground, it will be necessary to discuss this issue briefly.

The term most often used by the media to describe members of the hatecore metal subculture, "skinheads," is fraught with problems. The media has inaccurately used this term to describe everyone who exhibits the dress code adopted by German hate groups. In reality, the term "skinheads" refers to several different groups with diametrically opposed ideologies, rituals, and dynamics.[1] The original skinheads were English working-class youths who did not practice ethnic bigotry but whose favored clothing style was later appropriated by their German imitators. This is where the similarity ends. The English skinhead subculture and its music are based in principle around the idea of racial equality, reflecting its integrated, working-class origins. Ironically, skinheads, by their original definition, actively promote events designed to educate others about the benefits of racial and religious integration. That is not to say that the lines separating skinheads with anti-racist views from far-right skinheads, such as those belonging to the National Front, are always clear. There is a measure of fluidity in membership between the groups, but all skinheads, racist or not, embrace violence, excessive drinking, hyper-masculine gender performance, and blue-collar toughness. Because the different kinds of skinheads have similar styles of dress, the media often conflates them.

In contrast, neo-Nazis are those that claim to adhere to the principles devised by Adolf Hitler and the German National Socialist Party of the 1930s and 1940s. Their principal goal is the resurrection of a "purified" Europe led by what they see as the racially superior Aryans. While the media has focused on those neo-Nazis who wear skinhead regalia, they only represent a small number of neo-Nazis. The term "Aryan separatists" refers to people who aspire to rid their countries of ethnic and religious minorities and any other people deemed impure. Their focus is on the distillation of global society into separate, racially based nations, occupying distinct regions of the world. "National separatists," found primarily in North America, commonly claim membership in racially motivated hate groups as well, but the impetus behind their activities is based on overthrowing current governments whose principles they feel have been compromised. National separatists believe that the American and Canadian governments have been corrupted by minorities, liberal activists, and women's rights groups, and are under the control of a Zionist conspiracy bent on the destruction of the white race, one country at a time. They be-

164 lieve that they must defy their governments in order to establish a new country in which to practice their way of life.[2] As I discuss below, the philosophies that fuel these fringe groups, as well as extremist Christian and Anglo-identity movements, are closely related and overlap on many crucial issues, reinforcing the social ties between their members.

To accurately evaluate hatecore metal's unique place in the broader world of heavy metal, it is necessary to first examine its musical and ideological predecessors. While Aryanist popular songs can be traced back to the 1920s, it was during the Nazi era that popular music was most effectively employed to promote a racial and political agenda in Germany. As a propaganda and marketing tool for the Nazi party, patriotic songs such as "Tirol du Bist Mein Heimatland," "Jubelklänge,"[3] and "Wir standen für Deutschland" served not only to spread its rhetoric and recruit party members but also to foster a sense of "German-ness" (von Kuehnelt-Leddihn 1993, 268). The establishment of a singular German identity was crucial to the concept of German superiority and was fully exploited to serve the Nazi cause.[4] In the postwar years, neo-Nazis continued to focus on national cohesion and methods of purifying the population by eliminating undesirables. Today, openly nationalistic acts such as Frank Rennicke, Deutsche Patrioten, and Edelweiss weave stories of national heroes and Germanic mythological figures into their lyrics, creating a central point around which to express their justification for national identity. All their works involve a singular focus—renewed national pride.

Direct incorporations of Nazi doctrine into the German pop music scene waned until the late 1980s, when severe economic difficulties triggered by German reunification once again brought nationalist sympathies to the forefront of media debate. As is common during times of economic depression, the usual scapegoats—non-Germans—were blamed for economic and social unrest. During the same period in England, a sharp economic downturn gave strength to a nationalist movement based in the working and underclasses of London.[5] The musical expression of these nationalist sympathies developed from a West Indian ska and punk hybrid style called "oi," the name taken from a common English working-class greeting. While oi expressed the dissatisfaction and angst of working-class and underclass English youths, it also rejoiced in the expression of racial cooperation. The combination of West Indian musics, which were brought by immigrants to London's East End neighborhoods, with the punk style of their white neighbors created an independent music industry alternately called "oi" or "two-tone." This celebration of racial and cultural unity was evident in the album cover iconography, and its fans adopted the characteristic clothing styles of the white, English working class—workman's boots, suspenders, pork pie hats, and above all, very short or completely shaved hair. This visual style was originally a marker for ethnic and racial harmony and cultural cohesion. The original skinheads' German counterparts mimicked these clothing and hair styles, but early German oi bands expanded the themes beyond national unity to national superiority. Old themes of purification and violence began appearing in the music. Songs by Kahlkopf, Endsieg, and Werewolf became the background for typically violent neo-Nazi skinhead activities.

While pop songs filled with Aryan imagery were sanctioned and promoted by the National Socialist government, Aryanist sentiments were and still are subject to harsh scrutiny by postwar German governments. To help curb the destructive influence of neo-Nazi music, the German government took action against both oi distributors and fans. Beginning in 1985, new anti-hate laws made the production, distribution, and possession of music deemed harmful by the Office for the Protection of the Constitution a crime punishable by substantial prison time and a hefty fine.[6] In the years that followed, some skinhead activities, including concerts, rallies, and the distribution of CDs, were conducted in secret. Despite the law, however, German skinhead bands such as Störkraft, Endsieg, Kahlkopf, Volkszorn, Enstüfe, and Tonstörung proudly exhibited Nazi-era regalia and symbols on their clothing, promotional posters, and album covers. For example, the cover of Störkraft's album *Das Waren Noch Zeiten* (2003) features a photograph of a man wearing a T-shirt emblazoned with a swastika and the words "Who Needs Niggers"; Schwarzer Orden's album *Kamaraden* (2002) shows a drawing of brown-shirted soldiers flying the Nazi flag. Even though such displays were clearly illegal, most neo-Nazi bands explicitly advocated hate. In "Kampfhund," a song from the album *Mann für Mann*, Störkraft sang, "We are the power that cleanses Germany," and "Fighting dogs of German blood, do not fear but be careful. There will be bad times for the scum in the land. The fighting dog of Germany has them in its grip. Trembling with fear they will stand with their backs to the wall. The dog is stalking without mercy or morals" (Störkraft 1991a, translated from the German by the author). In the band's most successful song "Kraft Für Deutschland" the lead singer Jörg Petrisch shouts, "We fight shaved, our fists are as hard as steel. Our heart beats true for our Fatherland.

THE MARKETING OF ANGLO-IDENTITY

166   Whatever may happen, we will never leave you. We will stand true for our Germany, because we are the strength that makes Germany clean" (Störkraft 1991b, translated by the author). "Deutchland" by Die Böhse Onkelz (The evil uncles) contains lyrics such as "Our loyalty to you will not be destroyed. There's no land free of filth and splinters. We were born here and we don't want to die. German women, German beer, black and red we'll stand by you. Germany, Germany the fatherland" (Die Böhse Onkelz 1984, translated by the author). In "Bloodsucker," No Remorse proclaimed (in English), "One day the world will know that Adolf Hitler was right." (No Remorse quoted in Masland, Breslau, and Foote 1992, 53), while Endsieg's biggest hit, "Kanakensong" contains the line, "When you see a Turk in a tram, and he is looking at you annoyingly, you have the right to just stand up, and give him a strong punch and stab him seventeen times" (Endsieg quoted in Masland, Breslau, and Foote 1992, 53). Such sentiments were often couched in nationalist rhetoric. Lyrics emphasizing the elimination of religious and ethnic "impurities" highlighted the bands' desire to restore the nation to a pure, strong, unified state, a national utopia, if you will. It was a German ethnonationalist agenda set to an oi soundtrack.

The Office for the Protection of the Constitution monitored the activities of neo-Nazi skinheads and assisted the police in the prosecution of cases by transcribing and analyzing tapes and CDs confiscated in raids. Within the first month of crackdowns, police confiscated over fifteen hundred vinyl records and two hundred fifty CDs from businesses and private homes (Jacobs 1993, 18). The following month, the government shut down Rock-O-Rama Records, a former punk label that had evolved into Germany's most successful publisher of fascist music. Ironically, police raids such as these seem to have turned neo-Nazi band members into folk heroes among neo-Nazis. Industry sources claim that the sales of Störkraft records had multiplied tenfold to fifty thousand annually since the raids began (Jacobs 1993, 18).

Despite the government's efforts during the 1980s and 1990s to control the spread of hate music, there were a few bands that not only transcended the gap between the skinheads and the average rock fan but even enjoyed an astounding amount of sales success in the "legitimate" record arena. A Frankfurt band, Die Böhse Onkelz, scored its biggest hit with the album *Holy Songs* (1986). Fueled by the hit single "Türken Raus" (Turks get out) *Holy Songs* reached number five on Germany's pop music chart (Kemper 1992, 30).

Although the underground oi industry flourished in Europe between 1980 and 1992, its core consumers consisted of fans who already had strong ties to racist groups and it was only moderately successful in forwarding its cause. Due to harsh enforcement of hate crime laws, the industry did not have nearly the impact on the general public that it might have. Albums were distributed primarily through mail order catalogs or at outlets set up at concert venues—methods easily monitored and undermined by the authorities. The illegal status of neo-Nazi materials such as oi tapes or posters, T-shirts, or cloth patches with Nazi symbols helped suppress the spread of oi music. This is not to say that existing hate crime laws have been entirely effective in eradicating these materials. Experts hired by the German government, including educators, sociologists, and officials from Germany's internal intelligence service determined that the real problem facing lawmakers was a group within the skinhead culture that was concerned with overthrowing the government. This more radical faction was particularly strong in the former East Germany. Police raids of eleven known separatist compounds in Saxony-Anhalt yielded seventy-five hundred CDs, computers with mailing lists of customers, and videos and posters of swastikas and other neo-Nazi paraphernalia (Hooper 2000).

By 2001, enforcement of hate crime laws had been expanded from those who merely possessed and sold oi CDs and tapes to include the bands who made the music. On September 29, 2002, three members of the German oi band Landser were charged with inciting violence and spreading hate through songs. Identified by prosecutors only as Michael R. (age thirty-seven), Andre M. (thirty-five), and Christian W. (twenty-seven), these men were accused of conspiring to set up distribution channels in order to circulate anti-Semitic CDs throughout Germany. Landser's CDs include *Ran an den Feind* (Get the enemy), whose title song calls for the bombing of Israel. Other tunes glorify one of Adolf Hitler's top aides, Rudolf Hess, or, in "Sturmführer," pay tribute to a grandfather who was a Nazi SS officer (Eddy 2002, 22).

Despite the best efforts of the European oi industry, German hate music appears to have had far less of an influence in North America, even among members of avowed racist groups. Due in no small part to language barriers and a disorganized underground industry, German bands experienced great difficulty in reaching their target audience, despite the fact that their albums thrived in underground cassette-trading circles in Europe. A similar situation had existed in the United States with long-standing hate groups. For example, the old guard of the KKK resisted using rock music as part of its recruiting plans because of the music's African American roots. Klan leaders argued that rock-and-roll was nothing more than a plot by Jews to drag white youths into the "jungle music of the Negro" (Burghart 1999, 10). Adding to the general disinterest towards German oi, neither the racially integrated English oi nor the German version had achieved the same level of acceptance or sales as they had in Europe, making most North American racist music fans less familiar with the genre and leaving them to search for some other sound that better fit with their lifestyle.

The popularity of oi faded by the end of the 1980s, but it was soon replaced by a more familiar and media friendly genre, heavy metal. When American and Canadian neo-Nazis participated in tape trading, it was limited to English-speaking racist bands such as No Remorse and Skrewdriver, whose songs "White Power" and "Nigger Nigger" made their way to the underground market in the United States in 1986. The latter ensemble has the unique distinction of being among the first English hate bands to deviate from the oi musical style favored by non-English speaking groups. For the most part, Skrewdriver, and its notoriously racist lead singer Ian Stuart Donaldson, retained the racially charged lyrics of German oi, but its musical style was far more reminiscent of Black Sabbath and Motörhead. In North America, the incorporation of such themes into metal, a style that appealed to a primarily white audience, appeared to neo-Nazis to be a far more potent and accessible amalgamation. The union of inflammatory lyrics with a familiar metal sound created a product that could be exported to the previously untapped North American market.

During the 1980s and early 1990s, the hate music scene in the United States and Canada was limited to a group of fringe bands. Despite the fact that their music and lyrics were protected by the First Amendment of the U.S. Constitution, their influence outside the neo-Nazi subculture was severely restricted by a distribution system that was weaker and more disorganized than its European counterpart. Bands worked independently from one another, and barring a small number of regional underground record labels, few had either recording or distribution contracts. Regardless of the protections that make even hate speech legal, hate bands were still subject to the scrutiny of the major record labels. To date, not a single hate band has ever been signed to a major label record deal. This is not to say that national or international audiences did not have access to the music of these bands. With the rise of the Internet came the opportunity to spread the music of North American hate bands to an international audience of racists and non-racists alike. The Internet not only created a new forum for expressing hate but also a worldwide audience for it. Over the last decade, the internationalization of the neo-Nazi movement—what is often called pan-Aryanism—has broadened the range of hate-music listeners from those on the extreme fringes of society to a wider audience.

The musical and business transition from oi to hatecore metal can be traced back to 1993, when George Hawthorne (also known as George Burdi), an avowed Canadian neo-Nazi and a member of the World Church of the Creator, founded Resistance Records in Detroit. Working out of his parents' basement in Windsor, Ontario, Hawthorne signed and promoted bands that he felt were not getting their fair share of the white power music market, including his own band RAHOWA.[7] His own musical tastes ran not to German oi bands but to the English metal pioneer Skrewdriver. In promoting its records and those of other English-language hate metal bands, Hawthorne created a musical and business focus for the previously fragmented hate-music industry in North America. In the years since its inception, Resistance Records has become a clearinghouse for all manner of hate metal and has influenced many white supremacist groups in North America. By establishing the definitive direct-order Internet music business, Resistance Records has distributed an increasingly large catalogue of hate music without the help of major record companies, which by law are regulated by the Federal Communications Commission. In utilizing this completely unregulated method of distribution and advertising, Resistance Records has been able to bypass every hate speech law in the world. The explosion in exposure for such music has given even the most marginally successful hatecore metal band a worldwide forum for selling its particular brand of racist, homophobic, and anti-Semitic recordings. According to Hawthorne, who has since left the hate movement and now works to educate music fans about the dangers of white supremacist groups, the Internet made it possible for Resistance Records to sell over fifty thousand CDs in the label's first eighteen months of business. The label's newsletter, entitled *Resistance Magazine*, boasted a circulation of over nineteen thousand and growing. According to Mark Wilson, the co-founder of Resistance Records and the son of a former German Wehrmacht officer, as early as 1996 the company had a distributor or champion in every "white" country in the world (Talty 1996, 42).

Although its base of operations was in Windsor, Ontario, Canadian anti-hate laws made it illegal for Resistance Records to conduct business there. Consequently, the record company offices and warehouses were and still are located in Detroit, where such activities are protected by U.S. law. It was not until 1996, when U.S. authorities in Detroit began investigating Resistance Records on suspicion of tax evasion that they realized how widespread the problem of hatecore metal had become. In 1997, during a raid on the company's main offices and Hawthorne's home, authorities confiscated over one hundred thousand CDs boxed and ready for shipment, as well as the Resistance mailing list, consisting of over five thousand contacts worldwide; these figures were once proudly displayed on the label's Web site (Resistance Records 2003a).

Aided by the widespread availability of what is sometimes called the "world white power web," the anonymity it provides to "net-Nazis" (Back 2002, 124), and the proven financial success of Resistance Records, the racist music industry mushroomed between 1992 and 1999. Resistance and its imitators began to sponsor all-day concerts and festivals, and their success in the United States and Canada helped to revitalize the white power music industry in Europe. In Sweden, for instance, only one white power concert was held in 1992. By 1995 there were twenty. New labels dedicated solely to hate music began sprouting up in many European nations, most significantly MSR Productions in Germany and Ragnarok and Nordland Records in Sweden.[8] According to Hawthorne, Resistance sold between sixty thousand and one hundred thousand CDs and tapes in the three years ending in early 1997, with sales virtually doubling every quarter. He has said that he could often pre-sell an album's entire first pressing to European distributors before a single CD had been produced (White Pride World Wide 2001).

Four years after the raids by the IRS and after Hawthorne served time in prison for assaulting a female protester, Resistance found itself besieged by tax problems and was sold to William Pierce, the leader of the National Alliance, based in Hillsboro, West Virginia. Pierce, who wrote *The Turner Diaries* in 1978 under the penname Andrew McDonald,[9] bought Resistance for a mere $250,000 with the intent of making it the primary marketing tool for the anti-government movement in America. Although his personal tastes ran more toward Wagner, hatecore metal proved to be a more widely accepted style and therefore offered a better means of worldwide recruitment. Pierce's plans for the label included expanding into other musical genres, including country. "All too often we turn [our anger] against ourselves. We need to give a proper direction to that anger. . . . [Resistance Records will distribute] music of defiance and rage against the enemies of our people. . . . It will be the music of the great, cleansing revolution which is coming" (White Pride World Wide 2001).

As part of his efforts to recruit young people and generate revenue, Pierce expanded his influence in the hatecore metal industry over the next several years and took control of a number of smaller white power record labels. One addition to the growing musical empire was Cymophane LLC, the U.S. arm of Misanthropy Records, a Norwegian music label specializing in National Socialist black metal (NSBM). Through the purchase of Cymophane, Pierce sought to make inroads into the white power music scene in Scandinavia (Cressy 2008). Expanding his holdings in this way, Pierce was consistent in his vision of a New World Order, based not on national identities scattered throughout the world, but on a singular, international Aryan racial identity. Starting in the 1990s, previously fragmented and isolated supremacist and Christian identity organizations such as the American Front, the Fourth Reich, the Center for Action, Police against the New World Order, the Anglo-Saxon Christian Congregation, and the Aryan Nation began to see their movements increase in strength and visibility under the banner of racial, not national or religious, cohesion (Simon Wiesenthal Center n.d.).

Increasingly, white supremacists around the world began marketing their movement in international terms, and hatecore metal music contributed to this process. One 2003 article posted on the Web site of *Blood & Honour* (an online white power music fanzine founded in 1987 by Ian Stuart Donaldson) seemed to sum up these developments when it suggested that whites needed to "scrap the whole idea of nationalism for the sake of White racialism. . . . The term 'No more brother wars' [a white supremacist reference to wars between white people] can only be achieved through international cooperation and understanding between White people." "The ideal," he adds, "is naturally a pan-Aryan army with divisions wherever White people dwell. The days of pure patriotic xenophobia and imperialism are over. They have spilt enough Aryan blood" (Blood & Honour 2003).

Whereas contemporary European bands such as Svastika and Division S are still more inclined to address issues of national identity, basing their song titles, band names, stage clothes, and album covers on local myths and war heroes,[10] the shift of focus of North American hatecore metal, prompted by Pierce, is showing signs of international influence in

THE MARKETING OF ANGLO-IDENTITY

the 2000s. The common enemy has been redefined not just as Jews and other minorities who occupy whites' "homelands" but as the perceived Zionist-controlled media, the United Nations, and the American government (often referred to as the Zionist Occupied Government or ZOG). It is a variation on the familiar "Jewish world conspiracy" theory. These ideas have played a decisive role in the hatecore metal industry's assault on the otherwise politically unaffiliated metal market.

In this view, the American government is controlled by Zionists, seeks to undermine the country's racial and moral purity, and must be stopped at all costs. Zionists control the media as well and have the final say over what records can be bought and sold through retail outlets. Such a perspective depicts underground hatecore metal music as more real, organic, and uncensored. By flaunting their connections to the aforementioned independent record companies, and their rejection by all major labels, hatecore metal bands are offering themselves as alternatives not only to the music that is being played on the radio but also to the propaganda-laced music that the ZOG is forcing on the public. Under this theory, the record industry, which is regulated by the FCC, under the direction of the ZOG, curtails the flow of information given to Americans and limits the types of music available to consumers. Purchasing from non-mainstream outlets sends a statement that not only will consumers seek out new and alternative musics, they will do so in order to subvert the control that the government supposedly has on the minds of consumers.

The leaders of hate groups use the ideology of pan-Aryanism and their construction of racial enemies to increase their memberships, but for the North American hatecore metal industry and the subculture that it supports, the pan-Aryanist ideology also serves to internationalize the groups' appeal and their demographics. Although hatecore metal is the genre of choice among fringe groups, circulation of the music among only their members defeats the recruitment purpose set by Pierce. To achieve this, the Internet savvy hatecore metal industry has begun to use cross-marketing techniques in an attempt to influence a generation of metal fans.

With the Internet's potential of providing a worldwide audience for hatecore metal, Resistance Records has begun to depict its groups as disturbingly similar to those of politically unaffiliated metal bands. Like the differences in iconography, lyrics, and music that exist between thrash and death metal (as well as multiple other metal subgenres), the differences between avowed white supremacist music and non-politically inclined metal music continue to be deceptively subtle. To appeal to a mass audience, Resistance Records is careful to promote its bands as the next wave of "authentic" metal, not a fringe style created by radical upstarts. For example, in a 2003 press release, Resistance describes RAHOWA's sound not as oi or skinhead music, but as "neo-classical gothic metal" (Resistance Records 2003b), thus referencing terms common in the broader extreme metal scenes. By marking its artists' work as "artistic terrorism," Resistance represents them as cultural freedom fighters, working to free listeners from the artistic reins imposed by the mainstream recording industry.

Like underground metal labels unaffiliated with hate, Resistance and its American and Canadian competitors (including Panzerfaust, NGS Records, North X, Midgaard Records, Diehard Records, and Ancestral Research Records) strive for credibility within the global metal scene. All underground metal bands seek to distance themselves from mainstream music and, to a certain degree, mainstream society, and any implication of nonconformity contributes to that distancing. This is where the visual and thematic trappings of non-hate-based, underground metal become integral to the hatecore metal industry. The iconography associated with much underground metal music has traditionally involved pagan, mythological, quasi-gothic, or satanic imagery. As Deena Weinstein notes:

> Whereas the code for pop and country albums mandates photographs of the faces of the performers, the fronts of heavy metal albums are not graced with close-ups of band members. The heavy metal code specifies that what is depicted must be somewhat ominous, threatening, and unsettling, suggesting chaos and bordering on the grotesque. This metatheme was expressed in many ways until the late 1970s, when the code narrowed to include the iconography of horror movies, gothic horror tales, and heroic fantasies; technological science fiction imagery; and impressions of studded, black leather-clad biker types. (Weinstein 2000, 29)

Such imagery contributes greatly to the anti-establishment, rebellious appeal of these artists, but it rarely reflects a desire to cause violence and social upheaval. For example, satanic imagery is often (although not exclusively) used in metal to critique mainstream Christianity, or as a sanitized form of social deviance, rather than a call to actual satanic religious practice. There is a novelty, almost campy quality to metal's iconography. For example, songs such as Hellhammer's "Massacra" and "Revelations of Doom" from the black metal album *Apocalyptic Raids* (1990) highlight pagan, anti-Christian, and anti-social sentiments but are devoid of any real incitements to politically motivated violence.[11]

Whereas blatantly inflammatory images such as swastikas and other Nazi-era symbols are prominently displayed on CD and cassette covers of contemporary European bands, North American hatecore metal groups downplay or even eliminate such imagery in order to attract the attention of a wider audience. In downplaying imagery traditionally linked with racism, narrow-mindedness, and bigotry, the stigma associated with hate is reduced. Take for example this self-analysis anonymously posted on the official National Socialist Black Metal Web site in 2003.

> Most [fans of the music] accept to some degree all of the major beliefs of National Socialism, including ethnic nationalism, a rigid ethos of honor, environmentalism and anti-Semitism. Speaking for those behind this site, we believe that the modern republics, inspired by Christian and Humanist ideals of individualism and material comfort, have led us into a manipulative society. Our manly values have become passive, and in passivity, we have rejected natural law and nature, replacing it with a human creation of signals and social custom for which there is no natural precedent. Further, our society is currently on a hellbound stampede to eliminate these older ideas, unnaturally so (if they were truly obsolete, they would simply die out) and in the United States at least, people of Jewish and radical right-wing Christian heritage have disproportionate power. We reject the notion of "God" and of Judean morality; we embrace the ideals of naturalism, paganism, honor, blood and soil. Our goal is to create within society a group where these ideals can be practiced, in which we can begin to repair the damage done to our environment by industry and can have more meaningful lives than the technological drones and their convenience-based, product-oriented lifestyles. (National Socialist Black Metal 2003)

While the anonymous authors of the quote explicitly reference anti-Semitism, they spend more time advocating mainstream values of honor, patriotic nationalism, traditionally conceived masculinity, and environmentalism, thus making their message more palatable. In addressing how their music is used by the public, the same authors state:

It exists first to be music and as such an expression of beauty in the NS [National Socialist] style: all being is joined in the reaching forth of hope as found in doing anything to its fullest. It is our great pride that this music is first art and then expression of power. NS is not political; it is about bringing an end to politics through the focused power of a race. NS is not about politics and making people obey. It is about destroying politics and setting the people free. People listen because the music is great. (National Socialist Black Metal 2003)

They go on to define NSBM or hatecore metal as a modern variant on black metal, distinguished only by ideology, not musical character. They see NSBM as an alternative to black metal, one that speaks to bands, industry insiders, and above all "free thinkers." For the convenience of their readers, bands listed on the Web site are divided into three categories, true NSBM bands, those influenced by NSBM, and those who inspired NSBM. The last category includes more mainstream metal bands such as Motörhead and Slayer.

Many within the movement feel that they are a force for positive change and that their negative image is the result of a massive liberal bias in the American media. To counteract the negative media attention, the NSBM Web site has devoted a page to pointing out the perceived inaccuracies in the widely distributed reports on NSBM, including one from the Southern Poverty Law Center (SPLC).

[The] SPLC tells us that Nazism and Fascism are dangerous "group think" which must be persecuted or we will catch them like a disease. Group-think by your definition would be an overwhelmingly popular, easy truth. By a look at society today, this is clearly not the case with National Socialism, which remains persecuted in a society more obsessed over [former Atlanta Braves pitcher] John Rocker's opinions of blacks than quality schooling in the inner city. Our guilt is obvious, and our frustration is great, so we look for a scapegoat. That is straight from SPLC doctrine about racists, but it applies to the SPLC. In many ways metal is similar: it will not tolerate group-think. And that to you is a warning sign that in your zealous drive against "evil" you are covering a desire for control, one that is insidious and respects no culture. Your culture is that of commerce and its moral justice. The current generations, and black metal, reject that idea and have named your lies. (National Socialist Black Metal 2008c)

THE MARKETING OF ANGLO-IDENTITY

To explain their motivations behind the advocating of genocide, the un-named authors give the following statement:

> We support natural selection, and ethnic nationalism, which means that each state supports an organic population defined by language, culture, values and genetics. In the course of establishing such states, other nationalities must be relocated, and some have chosen to use genocide as a method. While we have no moral prohibition against it, many of us question its utility, while others question the historical record of the Holocaust. Those who write this FAQ view both methods and historical questions as immaterial; what matters is doing what's right. (National Socialist Black Metal 2008b)

Even the page with links to suggested groups helps to obscure the group's agenda. It contains links to Resistance Records, the Hitler Historical Museum, and the Libertarian National Socialist Green Party, as well as Earth First and the Earth Liberation Front (National Socialist Black Metal 2008d). Among the most deceptive items are those that can be found on the merchandise page. Here, albums and T-shirts by European NSBM artists are described in flowing, almost poetic terms. A description of a Graveland CD reads, "The forces that divide both universe and human being in conflict and emotion are here in force, through hardcore-derived but majestic songs of rising melody in the midst of chaotic harmonizations toward the sweeter side of darkly dissonant" (National Socialist Black Metal 2008a).

Hatecore metal record companies have capitalized on the wave of patriotism brought on by the events of September 11, 2001 and have skewed it to justify their goals. Many NSBM bands have begun to display military or military-associated images, downplaying the use of neo-Nazi imagery and its negative implications. A related rhetoric can be found in the music of specific hatecore metal bands as well. Songs such as Striking Distance's "Bullet for Every Enemy" and 25 Ta Life's "Wise to da Game" imply that the bands are rooted in patriotism and American camaraderie, not racism. Defending your way of life with military force is justified, the songs suggest, when personal rights and freedoms are threatened. Likewise, the front covers of both 25 Ta Life's album *Friendship, Loyalty, Commitment* (1999) and Better Red Than Dead's *The World Needs a Hero* (2002) feature white men supposedly engaging in armed resistance against unseen foes. Mention of the common enemy, Zionism, and the control it has over world governments is found only in the music. When compared to the swastika-

American bands becomes clear.

As is the case in the mainstream "legitimate" music industry, extra-musical merchandise also plays a role in defining a hatecore metal band's market appeal. The non-musical paraphernalia sold alongside CDs adds to the hatecore metal companies' incomes and also helps to legitimize the music for prospective consumers. Just as album covers obscure the visual cues, items like posters, stickers, flags, and other merchandise also serve to draw in listeners. For example, on the Resistance Web site, one can purchase an artist's rendering of a Celtic princess, cloth patches commemorating hatecore metal band members who have been imprisoned or martyred,[12] and flags emblazoned with pro–free speech messages, all featured right alongside lithographs of Hitler's watercolor paintings. Juxtaposing ideas from both ancient and modern mythologies, calls for hate speech and pro-democratic sentiments, and anti-American ideas as well as patriotic ones, the Web site's mixture of imagery creates conflicting information and obscures the group's hate agenda.

Even at live events, exploitation of metal fans' tendency toward anti-establishment leanings is a basic part of hatecore metal's rhetoric. A festival concert given in a restaurant in Scarborough, Ontario, on June 8, 2002, illustrates the diverse crowd that the music attracts.[13] The concert featured a number of hatecore metal bands, including the Angry Aryans and Blue-Eyed Devils, yet only a few attendees exhibited any visual cues as to their connections to supremacist groups. In an interview with Toronto's *NOW Magazine*, one of the audience members, a nineteen-year-old fan who gave his name only as Brad, said that this was not his first hatecore metal concert. "It's not really my thing," he said. "I'm more into hardcore. But the (racist) music doesn't offend me at all. I believe in free speech" (quoted in DiMatteo 2002). Even the Canadian Jewish Congress, which investigates activities like these, admitted that none of the people that it has identified as white power activists were involved with the organization or promotion of the concert in Scarborough (DiMatteo 2002). This mixing of audiences has found its way to Europe as well, most noticeably at the Ragnaröck Festival in Lichtenfels, Germany in 2007. Several NSBM bands performed at this previously all-pagan metal music festival, drawing the attention and criticism of the German press. According to Metalstorm, a Web site devoted to metal festivals worldwide, "After such negative coverage was aired nation-wide by a public broadcaster the organizer Ivo Raab didn't really have much of a choice other than abandoning the concept of an 'unpolitical festival' and had to take a stand against the kind of people who display their sympathy for national socialism in the course of the festival" (Metalstorm 2008).

The hatecore metal industry has found a viable and financially sound marketing niche for its far-from-mainstream artists. By offering signifiers both sonic and visual that speak not to racial motivations, but to patriotic sentiments, the hatecore metal industry capitalizes on already strong nationalistic feelings within the underground metal audience. In focusing on issues of free speech—and the purported efforts by governments to suppress such expressions—the hatecore metal industry represents itself as the champion of the people. Even to those who do not agree with Anglo-identity precepts, the hatecore metal labels and distributors seek to depict themselves as the last bastion of a free society, one in which everyone has the right to speak his mind. Songs envision a government conspiracy that seeks to control the actions of its citizens, yet the industry's very existence depends on that very same government's manifest commitment to free speech.

None of this is to imply that metalheads are as easily misled as the hatecore metal industry would hope. While such listeners constitute the primary target of their marketing campaigns, a majority of metal fans appear to be more politically aware and socially responsible than the hatecore metal industry would like. In fact there currently exist a variety of metal bands, including Napalm Death and Sepultura, that actively promote progressive causes. This ideological inverse indicates that metal fans are no more susceptible to racist propaganda than any other population and no more drawn in by its techniques. They are merely the demographic that the hatecore metal industry perceives as most vulnerable.

Those listeners who may or may not identify with the white power movement can still harbor a distrust of the media and the comparatively bland, processed, mass-marketed music that the major record companies offer. Hatecore metal offers an uncompromising alternative to the mainstream market, even if its overall message leans toward the destruction of the very government that affords it the right to do so. To listeners not already involved in the hatecore metal scene, this music is simply one of many viewpoints to be expressed through an uncensored, independent media. The effectiveness with which the hatecore metal industry has been able to capitalize on themes of authenticity, purity, and national pride indicates that its recruitment goals are potentially limitless, making its acceptance in the "legitimate" metal arena a very real and dangerous possibility.

1 For detailed discussions of skinhead rituals and culture, see, for example, Hebdige 1981 and Marshall 1991.

2 For further information on divisions within separatist movements, see Kaplan 1998.

3 This popular festival march dates back to 1938 and, ironically, is part of the standard repertoire for German military parades today.

4 For an analysis of the Nazi Party's use of post-Romantic music for the same purpose, see Levi 1990.

5 For excellent analyses of British youth culture during this time, see Gilroy and Lawrence 1988 and Brown 2004.

6 Among the laws that are specifically targeted toward skinheads are Law 130 of the German Federal Code (inciting crowds, which is punishable by a mandatory five-year jail term), Law 131 (inciting through racial hatred), Law 86 (the spreading of propaganda of illegal organizations), and Law 86A (the public display of National Socialist symbols).

7 The name is a shortened form of "Racial Holy War," a common expression in racist far-right discourse.

8 Note the revealing indicators found in the company names. The name of the North American company Resistance Records implies struggle for independence and autonomy from an unspecified enemy, while European labels like Ragnarok draw their names directly from local mythologies. Ragnarok is the name of the last great battle fought between the gods and the giants in Norse myth.

9 *The Turner Diaries* describes the destruction of an FBI building with a fertilizer-based bomb.

10 Particularly prevalent in Germany and Sweden are album covers featuring Nordic gods or fellow skinheads who are serving time in prison. Many bands also take their names from SS officers, including Dirlewanger, a band based in Göteburg named after Oscar Dirlewanger, the commander of the 101st Waffen SS division.

11 Hellhammer is the predecessor to one of the best-known bands within extreme metal, Celtic Frost.

12 Among the cloth patches offered on the Web site is the Hammer Joe patch which commemorates Joe Rowan, the lead singer of Nordic Thunder, who was beaten to death by three African American teenagers following a hatecore metal concert. The patch reads "We'll see you in Valhalla."

13 *Editors' Note*: Some may not even know what kind of festival they are attending until they show up. See the chapter by Hagen in this volume.

MUSICAL STYLE, IDEOLOGY, AND MYTHOLOGY IN NORWEGIAN BLACK METAL

Ross Hagen

At the 1998 Norwegian Grammy Awards, the black metal band Dimmu Borgir performed "Grotesquery Concealed," a song from its forthcoming album, *Spiritual Black Dimensions*. The singer, Shagrath, dressed in a long leather coat, white face paint, and stage-blood dripping from his mouth, screamed while flanked by pulsing jets of flame and female dancers in black leather. As the band stormed through the song, the camera offered glimpses of the rigid, tuxedo-clad audience. At the song's end, the audience applauded politely, offering a few whistles and a smattering of bemused "metal-horns." The attention then turned to the hostess, who joked about how evil Dimmu Borgir must be before continuing the show.

Black metal's introduction to the mainstream was hardly as controlled. In June 1992, the Fantoft stave church, a wooden building near Bergen dating from the twelfth century, burned to the ground in an arson attack, the first of several attacks against Scandinavian churches. The following January, Varg Vikernes, the sole member of the black metal band Burzum, claimed in an anonymous interview to run a network of satanic black metal terrorists who were responsible for the eight church arsons up to that point. By the year's end, Vikernes had been arrested for murdering Øystein "Euronymous" Aarseth, a fellow founder of the Norwegian black metal scene. Another prominent musician, the drummer Bård "Faust" Eithun of Emperor, was jailed for the slaying of a homosexual man near Lillehammer in August 1992. While in prison, Vikernes resurfaced in mainstream publications because of his increasing promotion of neo-Nazi ideologies.

With this notoriety and widespread media attention as a springboard, Norwegian black metal became perhaps the most profitable subgenre within extreme metal in the 1990s, inspiring hundreds of bands worldwide. The magazine *Terrorizer* placed Norway's Emperor at number fifteen in an end-of-the-millennium list of the most important metal bands, not far behind metal giants like Metallica, Slayer, and Black Sabbath. *Guitar World* magazine has recently published online video interviews and playing demonstrations by members of Emperor and Immortal. High recognition within the metal scene and increasing popularity in the mainstream are a testimony to black metal's lasting importance.

There have also been a number of recent publications about black metal, and extreme metal in general. The best-known publication by far is Moynihan and Søderlind's controversial work *Lords of Chaos* (1998), an investigation of the personae that drove the Norwegian black metal scene that includes extensive interviews and lurid anecdotes. The book is a valuable resource, even if it must be read as a product of the black metal scene itself, rather than an objective study, due to its apparent mythologizing agenda and co-author Moynihan's connections to Vikernes and other far-right ideologues, such as the industrial musician Boyd Rice (Coogan 1999).[1] Nevertheless, it provides a window into how certain key members of the Norwegian black metal scene view and articulate their history. Publications from Nicholas Goodrick-Clarke and Keith Kahn-Harris have further investigated the complex and often contradictory relationship between black metal, paganism, and far-right ideologies (Goodrick-Clarke 2002; Kahn-Harris 2004a).

Provocative as these works may be, they tend to avoid engaging the music beyond broadly descriptive terms such as "heavy" or "brutal." My intention here is to examine musical characteristics specific to Norwegian black metal, and investigate the relationships between these characteristics and the surrounding scene. In the course of investigating these re-lationships, other questions arise. What is to be made of the common as-sociation of black metal with heathen revivalists and neotraditionalists seeking to resurrect idealized ancient Norse and Germanic cultures and belief systems? Although heavy metal is produced in every industrialized society on the planet, why did a segment of Norway's underground metal scene become a haven for murder and domestic terrorism?

It should be noted that much of the research in this study stems from my own long association with the extreme metal scene as a fan and occa-sional performer rather than through formalized fieldwork. Given the fre-quently isolated and decentered nature of extreme metal fan communities, online fan culture became a crucial asset as did archives of interviews at Web-zines and band Web pages. Essentially, I continued my role as a scene member and contributor, while sometimes posing more direct questions to the online communities with which I am acquainted.

HISTORY AND CONTEXT

Black metal began as an offshoot of thrash metal and death metal in the late 1980s and early 1990s, inspired by the raw, often minimalist thrash metal of European bands such as Hellhammer, Celtic Frost, Venom, and Bathory. The term "black metal" initially referred simply to any extreme metal that was explicitly "satanic" in nature, but by the late 1980s a scene had begun to emerge that self-consciously used the term as both a descrip-tion of its music and as an essential identity (Kahn-Harris 2004a). The early black metal scene in Norway began to coalesce around a small circle of bands, but the two dominant personalities that emerged were Aarseth, the guitarist for Mayhem, and Vikernes.

Aarseth became a focal person in the black metal scene in the early 1990s, largely through his metal record store Helvete in Oslo. He is often credited with the codification of black metal's sonic imprint as well as its distinctively nihilistic worldview (Moynihan and Søderlind 1998, 63–76). Aarseth and Helvete gave focus to the fledgling scene, with nearly every band in the early scene becoming involved with him at some point. These bands formed a network often referred to as the "Black Circle" (Moynihan and Søderlind 1998, 65) even though their ties were fairly informal. Aar-seth also disseminated his aesthetic throughout the extreme metal press, presenting himself and the scene as the ultimate in evil. When Mayhem's singer, Per Yngve Ohlin, alias "Dead," committed suicide with a shotgun in 1991, Aarseth furthered his "evil" aura by stating that he had eaten part of Dead's brain and made necklaces from pieces of his skull (Moynihan and Søderlind 1998, 59; Steinke 1996, 65). He also stated that Dead had committed suicide because "trendy" new followers were destroying the old death and black metal scene. As shocking and nihilistic as these statements may be, there is also evidence that Aarseth, like many in the black metal scene, approached his evil image as a persona from which he could disengage (Moynihan and Søderlind 1998, 116).

Vikernes, who was a protégé of Aarseth, became the scene's other focal persona largely through his extreme actions, which culminated in several church arsons and Aarseth's murder. The actual motive of the murder remains sketchy, with common hypotheses involving money issues and jealousy over Aarseth's prominence in the scene. Another possibility is that Vikernes may have become disenchanted with what he saw as a lack of commitment on Aarseth's part. Vikernes himself has claimed that Aarseth was plotting to kill him and that the murder was preemptive. After the murder, the legend around Vikernes grew immensely due to his increasingly outrageous statements as well as rumors circulated by the tabloids.

The criminality of the Norwegian black metal scene in the early 1990s was an aberration as far as metal in Scandinavia and elsewhere is concerned. With a few exceptions, such as the assault conviction in 2007 of Gorgoroth's singer Gaahl, the overt criminality of the early black metal scene has not continued. Most of the violence in Norway had ceased by 1994 as the sociopathic element was either incarcerated or had simply outgrown such criminal activities (Kahn-Harris 2004a, 105). The Norwegian black metal scene also gained its fame largely as an exported product. As with the wider extreme metal scene, the black metal scene is decentered, with fans and bands communicating largely through 'zines and tape-trading in the 1980s and 1990s and more recently via bulletin boards and chat groups on the Internet. The Norwegian-ness of the bands also added an exotic appeal to their music for foreign consumers.

MUSICAL STYLE AND PRODUCTION

The musical style and production values of black metal as forged in Norway and pursued around the globe display several key stylistic components that differentiate them from other styles of heavy metal. For example, many black metal bands rely heavily on synthesizers, which are ignored or maligned by artists in most other heavy metal genres. The keyboard's synthetic choirs, strings, and pianos sometimes play such a prominent role that they challenge the guitar's primacy in the overall sound. The acceptance of keyboards also allows a wide variety of other textures and instruments to exist within the black metal genre. However, some black metal bands, such as Darkthrone, resisted the introduction of keyboards and influences from outside the metal scene, preferring a simpler and rawer sound.

The mid-to-high-pitched scream of black metal vocals is one of its more immediate identifying characteristics. While this vocal timbre is not exclusive to black metal, singers of this genre rarely, if ever, utilize the extremely low, guttural, and indecipherable vocals of death metal or the gruff tough-guy yell of punk. Black metal also occasionally utilizes "clean" vocals as well, usually favoring a forceful baritone timbre.

Norwegian black metal is also marked by an aesthetic of guitar playing that sets it apart from other forms of heavy metal. In particular, black metal makes relatively infrequent use of the "power chord" consisting of a root note, its upper fifth, and an octave. This musical device is so pervasive in most heavy metal that Walser terms it the "one feature that underpins heavy metal as a genre" (Walser 1993a, 2). One of the cardinal attributes of the power chord is that it creates a relatively "open" sound; its "power" is derived from the subharmonic resonance and overtones acquired through distortion. Black metal guitarists, in contrast, frequently use full chord voicings, which produce a denser and less clearly resonant timbre when played through heavy distortion. The Norwegian black metal band Emperor also has a predilection for augmenting the fifth in a power chord to create a chaotic and directionless sound that also serves to highlight the contour of the guitar part when played in parallel motion, as in the riff from the song "Ye Entrancemperium."

Black metal guitarists also rely on a technique known as "tremolo picking" or "buzz-picking," which refers to constant double-picking (striking the string with both up and down movements of the pick) at extremely fast tempos. In many cases, this technique precludes the ability to play more than one string simultaneously, adding a practical element to the dearth of power chords. As a result, chordal structures are often built from arpeggios or divided parts, as in "Ye Entrancemperium." In another example, the main riff of the song "Natassja in Eternal Sleep" by the Norwegian black metal band Darkthrone, a chord progression is built on a series

"Ye Entrancemperium" guitar riff. Written by Ihsahn and Samoth of the Norwegian black metal band Emperor, from *Anthems to the Welkin at Dusk* (1996). Author's transcription.

of three arpeggios. The first arpeggio is perhaps best understood less as a chord and more as a motion of B–E♭–D–E♭ over a B pedal in the bass. The second articulates a major third between D and F♮ while the final arpeggio outlines a D minor chord. The bass guitar, which simply repeats the first note of each bar, outlines a diminished triad, providing little sense of harmonic direction within the progression as a whole.

Finally, some Norwegian black metal bands demonstrate an affinity with traditional styles of Scandinavian folk music in their guitar parts, utilizing drones and modal melodic figures reminiscent of the style. Valfar, the late founder and main composer for the band Windir, opined that ancient Nordic folk music translates easily into the metal idiom because both have a similar "sad atmosphere" (A. 2001).[2]

The examples from Emperor and from Darkthrone lack significant harmonic direction and clear tonality, qualities that are not uncommon in extreme metal. Harrell describes the use of tritones and soloing techniques that obscure tonality in thrash metal bands such as Slayer (Harrell 1994, 94). Parallel harmonies and the tendency toward ambiguous tonality in American death metal are investigated in depth in Berger's extensive interviews with Dann Saladin of Sin-Eater (Berger 1997, 1999a, 1999b). Indeed, the augmented fifths in "Ye Entrancemperium" serve similar functions to the parallel thirds that Berger discusses in Sin-Eater's music (1999b, 216), as both are dynamically faint and serve to create a feeling of eeriness and to highlight the contour of the guitar part. The harmonic changes in black metal also generally move at a slower pace than in death metal, so speed alone does not obscure perceptions of tonality. Indeed, black metal often has a stronger sense of tonal center than thrash and death metal, if only because the harmonic changes are slower and frequently less complex, especially in more majestic or drone-based sections.

The relatively slow pace of harmonic change in black metal introduces a primary performance aspect that sets the Norwegian black metal style

Verse riff of "Natassja in Eternal Sleep." Darkthrone, *Under a Funeral Moon* (1993). Author's transcription.

apart from other styles of extreme heavy metal: its treatment of rhythm. Most styles of heavy metal have a propulsive rhythmic drive, intended to encourage moshing and headbanging, but black metal often deemphasizes this in favor of a swirling and indistinct atmosphere. Part of this effect is due to the production (about which more will be said shortly), but there are several key elements within the performance that create this sound.

One of the most common and idiomatic rhythmic devices in black metal is the "blast-beat" figure used extensively by black metal drummers. At its core, the blast-beat is an exercise in extreme subdivision and physical endurance. Rhythmically, the figure is usually not complicated and resembles a standard rock beat sped up to a frenetic tempo until the drums begin to bear an uncanny resemblance to a prolonged burst of machine-gun fire and become a sort of sonic blast.

The blast-beat figure serves several unique purposes within Norwegian black metal music that distinguish its use here from other metal subgenres. First, it is important to note that the rest of the music usually moves hypermetrically relative to the drummer, especially in passages based on chords rather than riffs. This hypermetric relationship creates a sense of suspended time, as the drummer no longer provides a primary source of rhythmic propulsion and metric structure. In contrast, death metal and grindcore drummers often use the blast beat to accompany fast riffs and create a pummeling sense of rhythmic drive. The perception of different temporal levels is of course not exclusive to black metal (Berger 1997), but the slower pace of harmonic change foregrounds the hypermetric relationship when compared to the frenetic pace of the drumming. As one black metal fan put it, "blast beats add to the atmosphere in that they become a sort of pulsating, throbbing sound rather than a truly percussive sound that serves as accentuations upon rhythm" (DJ 2004).

Black metal guitar techniques such as "buzz-picking" further contribute to the genre's frequent lack of significant rhythmic momentum. This picking technique is used for both melodic lines and underlying riffs, creating an overall droning quality and diminishing the rhythmic emphasis of the musical changes. Black metal guitarists also tend to avoid palm-muting, a technique in which the guitarist places the side of the picking hand's palm against the strings while playing, resulting in the heavy percussive sound of groups like Metallica and Pantera.[3] Another result of this rapid picking is that as the string remains in a constant state of wide vibration, the actual pitches produced are often slightly sharp of concert pitch, adding to the instability of the overall sound especially when combined with concert-pitched keyboards. The buzz-picking technique also differs from the aesthetic of most heavy metal, which generally emphasizes technical dexterity rather than rhythmic endurance.

The production values of black metal contribute significantly to the effect of these techniques. Rather than produce the recording in a way such that the individual voices are crisply defined and easily heard, black metal bands often blur the parts together to create an atmospheric wash of sound. As would be expected, this practice obscures the drummer somewhat and renders indistinct the rhythms of the other parts as well, sometimes drowning out the bass guitar entirely. Similarly, the vocals are often mixed quite low so that they become a part of the overall atmosphere rather than existing on a privileged plane within the recording.

If the history of heavy metal is considered as a "progressive quest for ever-heavier music" (Berger 1999b, 58), black metal is perhaps anomalous in that its sound runs contrary to what is considered "heavy" in metal. Although black metal guitarists certainly take advantage of the distorted electric guitar's noise and timbral expansion, the instrument's lower frequencies are rarely boosted to any significant degree, depriving the guitar of its rhythmic punch. Even on relatively "clear" recordings, the guitar sound often is thin and brittle when compared to the guitar timbres of other heavy metal subgenres. Obscuring the bass guitar and drummer produces similar results, denying the illusion of weight that creates musical "heaviness." It could be posited that the idea of "heaviness" in black metal has been divorced somewhat from its associations with low frequencies and has instead become associated with harshness and timbral density.

Black metal production quality is undoubtedly subject to financial pressures in many cases, but the primary aspects tend to remain constant even for some successful groups. This tendency is likely a result of early black metal's budget production becoming codified as the "true" black metal sound. The overall lack of clarity and definition then becomes an end unto itself rather than simply a byproduct of an "economy" recording. The muddled and often noisy production is also sometimes positioned as a mark of resistance to the mainstream music industry, as each recording has its own peculiar sound quality as opposed to the more homogenized sound of mainstream heavy metal.[4]

In the end, the esoteric qualities of a black metal recording are often confusing for an uninitiated listener. Even death metal devotees sometimes find black metal a little hard to swallow. In a quote that is a personal favorite of mine, a member of an extreme metal message board hosted by Relapse Records dismissed black metal as "just hissing."[5] Indeed, some black metal musicians realize that their devotion to "bad" sound borders on self-parody. When the band Ulver recorded the album *Nattens Madrigal*, its members purposely created one of the harshest recordings imaginable and then concocted an oft-repeated legend that the album was recorded in a snowy Norwegian forest.[6] One also begins to wonder if the chaotic and amorphous black metal sound is somewhat self-defeating, as a band such as Emperor thrives not only on its atmosphere but also on its technical proficiency. Emperor's last recordings, and those by more popular black metal bands such as Dimmu Borgir and Satyricon, are much clearer while still attempting to retain the aggression and atmosphere of their earlier work. This strategy often produces mixed results for black metal fans, however, as many regard gritty and "lo-fi" production to be a principal value of the subgenre.

IMAGE AND REPRESENTATION

In a subgenre as concerned with theatricality as black metal, any analysis of the music would be incomplete without examining the manner in which it is presented. Black metal musicians and fans use their images as signifiers that establish them as being simultaneously outside of normal society and a part of an exclusive inner subculture. This strategy is of course not unique to the black metal scene, as similar visual codes are present in everything from punk to country music and form a vital part of the scene's identity.

In extreme metal circles, the band logo serves as a visual symbol for the

Enslaved's band logo.

band and its music and often provides potential fans with their initial impression. The intricacy and even illegibility of many extreme metal logos adds exclusivity while providing a visual representation of the music's inscrutable and esoteric nature. Sometimes pagan or anti-Christian symbolism is quite overt in the logos, as is the case with those of the bands Enslaved and Mayhem. Enslaved's logo is centered over a Thor's hammer and its ornamentation is reminiscent of Viking carvings, while Mayhem turns the outside legs of the letter "M" into dual inverted crosses.

While most extreme metal bands avoid costuming, black metal bands often don chain mail, cloaks, medieval armor replete with spikes, and slightly anachronistic bullet-belts. They frequently pose with weaponry ranging from swords and axes to spiked clubs, torches, pikes, and the occasional revolver. Many of the bands wear white and black face paint, known in the scene as "corpse paint," often tracing narrow lines from the eyes and mouth, following the contours of the face. The eye socket is usually completely blackened in to appear sunken and skull-like. Even though the corpse paint is primarily a tool for performance, some musicians have noted that the masking also assists them in keeping their public personae separate from their private lives (Lystrup 2003).

Publicity photos are usually black and white shots taken outdoors, often at night, often in a forest, graveyard, or "medieval" setting. The band members pose menacingly in their costumes and sometimes give the appearance of being in a violent trance state, as if in the midst of a moonlit ritual. A band member spewing grain alcohol over a lit torch to create a giant fireball is also a popular and striking image.

These photos are often of poor quality, but they create a singular effect.

MUSICAL STYLE, IDEOLOGY, AND MYTHOLOGY

190   Since the pictures are shot at night and are usually printed in black and white, the members seem to exist in a murky void. This presentation also serves to accentuate the corpse paint and sometimes results in a picture that seems to be little more than a screaming face emerging from black nothingness.

Almost all black metal musicians around the world perform under stage names. In Norway, band members often adopt names derived from Norse or Germanic myth, such as Fenriz of Darkthrone. Tolkien is also a popular source, particularly with Vikernes, as both his band name, Burzum, and his initial stage name, Count Grishnackh, originate in Tolkien's writings.[7]

RITUAL AND MYTH

Vikernes provides a provocative entry into Norwegian black metal ideologies and their relationships to Germanic myth and legend. Although he remains controversial within the scene, his political and spiritual views often form a paradigm for younger black metal musicians and fans. Vikernes presented himself as a Satanist in the past, but now he considers himself to be a sort of right-wing Odinist or, in his words, a "pagan nationalist" (Moynihan and Søderlind 1998, 152–53). These two ideologies, Satanism and Paganism, form the backbone of much black metal philosophy and work together with the music in some striking ways, even in cases where the imagery is simply an affectation.

Of the two, Satanism is most often associated with extreme metal, and indeed with metal in general. For many practitioners, Satanism may not imply actual Devil Worship, but rather is a philosophy following the writings of Anton LaVey, the founder of the Church of Satan and author of *The Satanic Bible*. In LaVey's writings, Satan becomes a symbol for individual sovereignty, similar to the occultic libertinism espoused by Aleister Crowley (Medway 2001, 21). Some in the Norwegian black metal scene found this brand of Satanism to be overly humanistic and hedonistic and therefore antithetical to the dourness sought by early scene members.

However, some in the scene view Satan as a figure of pagan resistance and have moved toward a philosophy based more on ancient Norse and Germanic religions, a progression endorsed by Vikernes (Moynihan and Søderlind 1998, 152). Some bands, notably Enslaved and Einherjer, have left satanic imagery and some of black metal's more esoteric musical idioms behind entirely to focus on Norse or Viking themes, creating a new subgenre termed "Viking metal" in the process. An affinity for myth and legend can be found even in bands such as Emperor that don't explicitly refer to Norse mythology.

In addition to a simple fascination with the mythologies of ancient Europe, some black metal musicians and commentators have posited a more metaphysical connection between the black metal scene and these ancient religions. Moynihan and Søderlind present the idea that black metal represents a resurgence of an Odinist cultural archetype, taking inspiration from Carl Jung's 1936 essay "Wotan." They support this idea with the theories of "Kadmon," the editor of an Austrian 'zine named *Aorta*. Kadmon posits that the violence of Norwegian black metal devotees is a modern example of a Dionysian cult society called the *Oskorei* (Moynihan and Søderlind 1998, 172–75, 336–43). Although such mythologizing must be taken with several grains of salt, and Coogan demonstrates that Kadmon is a supporter of Vikernes and an artistic collaborator with Moynihan (Coogan 1999, 44), the parallels Kadmon explores are provocative. The Oskorei were allegedly made up of young men who rode through the countryside in winter, punishing those who violated rural traditions by playing pranks and causing mischief as a reenactment of the "Wild Hunt" of Odin's Valkyries in Norse myth. The raiders dressed in ghostly costumes and accompanied their revelries with screaming and noise, which Kadmon relates both to the theatricality and musical characteristics of black metal (Kadmon 1995; Johannessen 1967). The idea of punishment enters the rhetoric of black metal musicians who consider the church arsons as both revenge for the violent Christianizing of Scandinavia and as a way to, in the words of Vikernes, "show Odin to the people" (Moynihan and Søderlind 1998, 92). These fantasies of pagan retribution and resurgence are often acted out in lyrics and music, if rarely in reality.

The Oskorei legends introduce more to the black metal aesthetic than simple parallels and conveniently epic imagery. Masks and other sorts of disguises are not a new phenomenon in metal, as groups as diverse as GWAR, Slipknot, Marilyn Manson, and Kiss demonstrate. Masking also has a long history of association with unbound hedonism, religious ecstasy, and uncontrollable destruction (Segal 1982). Being disguised often creates a sense of anonymity and deindividuation, a sense of being outside of one's normal self. This effect can be noted in everything from sacred religious rituals to trick-or-treating at Halloween. Ultimately, and most importantly, the mask often serves to endow the wearer with the attributes of a god and helps the wearer to break through the barriers of social norms and enter into an ecstatic trance state (Segal 1982, 13, 215). Similarly, the costumes and pseudonyms common in black metal help the musicians get into a specific mindset for performance (Lystrup 2003).

Moynihan and Søderlind locate black metal's masked archetype in the Berserker figure of Norse myth (Moynihan and Søderlind 1998, 187). Clad in a magical wolf-skin, members of the Berserker warrior cult allegedly acquired an almost supernatural strength and resistance to pain in their ecstatic state. Beyond the myths, this thread perhaps articulates a parallel between ecstatic experiences and black metal music itself. The furious tempos certainly bear a resemblance to the Berserker ideal, as does the emphasis placed on rhythmic endurance. The blast-beat figure specifically seems to have a direct corollary in the ideal of superhuman strength and resistance to pain, as a drummer must possess an exceptional amount of stamina to be able to execute this device consistently and precisely, especially during a live concert. The rhythmic effects of blast beats and tremolo picking may also contribute to the feeling of transcendence and ecstasy by creating a sense of suspended time, much like drone-based religious chant traditions or the cyclical musical structures found in West African possession rites and electronic dance music (Sylvan 2002, 21–22, 127).

For black metal fans, and metal fans in general, the metal "experience," particularly the live concert setting, is often spoken of in quasi-religious terms. This fact has not escaped researchers. Robin Sylvan's chapter on heavy metal in *Traces of the Spirit* discusses the heavy metal concert as an experience of positive affirmation and psychological catharsis. However, Sylvan thinks that metal fans experience this feeling of catharsis because they have to "work through and release so much more negative emotion before they can arrive at the uplifting religious aspects of the experience" (Sylvan 2002, 167), reflecting the somewhat problematic image of the metalhead as essentially antisocial and depressive. Arnett has described the heavy metal concert as a type of manhood ritual, loaded with visceral sensations and physical tests (Arnett 1993, 313–31). Weinstein asserts that heavy metal's emphasis on forces of chaos and disorder allows for those forces to be confronted, at least in the listener's imagination (Weinstein 2000, 38).

Black metal musicians frequently draw on these mythologies as representing a romanticized heroic past, with Satanism often considered a part of the history of pagan resistance to the "weakening" influence of Christianity. Some in the scene also began to conceive of these mythologies as part of a national and cultural identity, often asserting it in racist and "elitist" terms (Kahn-Harris 2004a, 99). Vikernes in particular presented himself as a Viking chieftain mobilizing contemporary bands of Oskorei warriors to combat Christianity, even when he was in prison (Moynihan and Søderlind 1998, 166). Vikernes and others in the pagan white supremacy movement see their interest in the Norse pantheon as a Jungian archetype resurfacing from a collective Teutonic unconscious, with some individuals in the white supremacist movement taking this idea further into esoterica by mixing Nazism with occult mysticism or pagan religions (Goodrick-Clarke 2002).

Direct expressions of racism often find a conflicted audience in the black metal scene, as many fans worry that blatant politicization will detract from the music itself. Unequivocally neo-fascist black metal can be considered as an entirely separate scene, often known as NSBM (National Socialist black metal) (Kahn-Harris 2004a; Hochhauser, this volume). Kahn-Harris considers this elevation of the music itself above all its political associations as a sort of "reflexive anti-reflexivity" in that scene members are aware of the structure and politics in their scene, yet they purposely "exclude that awareness from scenic practice" (2004a, 106; see also Kahn-Harris, this volume). This insulation becomes problematic as expressions of racist or fascist sympathies in interviews are rarely challenged within the scene, as any ensuing controversy would undermine the importance of the music itself.

Even black metal bands that aren't part of the NSBM scene tend to share with it a worldview that considers Christianity to be a force that weakens and enslaves otherwise strong individuals. Often allied with this is a "law of the jungle" belief that is frequently expressed as a form of Social Darwinism, sometimes delving into critiques of liberalism and welfare states. In an interview with *Spin* magazine, Ihsahn from Emperor lamented that in Norway, "if you're weak everybody supports you. There are special centers, twelve-step programs. Everything is for the weak. Everything caters to people who are failures" (Steinke 1996, 69). Similarly, Vikernes claims that

MUSICAL STYLE, IDEOLOGY, AND MYTHOLOGY

if he is slain as revenge for murdering Aarseth, it will be his own fault for failing to be strong enough to survive (Moynihan and Søderlind 1998, 132).

National and cultural identities and mythologies are often important even for the majority of black metal bands that are not connected to right-wing political movements. Frequently, black metal lyrics reference myths of trolls and wizards and expound upon the natural beauty of Scandinavia, promoting an idealized existence as part of a mystical wilderness. Nature scenes are common in black metal cover art and inserts, as in the glacial fjord on the cover of Kampfar's album *Mellom Skogkledde Aaser*, and nature's rugged beauty and unforgiving brutality are often praised. Black metal's penchant for Nietzschean ideals is often couched in terms having to do with wilderness as well.

Curiously, the Norwegian black metal scene largely avoids the use of "Norwegian" texts, traditional instruments, or recognizable folk melodies, a common way in which concert hall composers have expressed national pride. This practice is also not an alien concept to extreme metal. For example, the Finnish death and progressive metal band Amorphis adapted Finnish epic poetry from the *Kalevala* and *Kanteletar* for its albums *Tales from the Thousand Lakes* and *Elegy*. Norwegian black metal bands, however nationalistic they may be, generally pursue a less immediately identifiable "local" sound, apart from the idiomatic musical characteristics detailed above.

However, a few bands in Norway have flirted with "traditional" music, such as Enslaved, whose 2002 album *Monumension* ends with a track that attempts to reproduce ancient Viking music. The band Storm, a "supergroup" including members of Satyricon and Darkthrone, recast traditional Norwegian tunes in a heavy metal idiom. Some in the press considered it a nationalistic record, an accusation the band denies by saying that it is instead a romantic recasting of music they love (Ulriksborg 2003). Similarly, the band Windir had an intense affinity for traditional music and Norwegian texts, drawing much of its lyrical content from local sagas, using traditional folk tunes in its music, and singing in an archaic rural dialect.

The use of nature and neotraditional themes in the service of national identity does not come without ideological baggage. Mythologized pastoral pasts and utopian community ideals played a large role in Nazi propaganda in the 1930s as part of a campaign designed to draw parallels between German blood and German land (Beckwith 2002). The neotraditional ideal of a homogenized tribal society at odds with urban multiculturalism is a frequent trope in "countercultural fascist" and racialist literature as well.

While the black metal scene's affinity for natural, neotraditional, and mystical rhetoric may not often extend beyond a certain romantic affectation, it can also allow neo-Nazi elements to be cloaked, and it blurs the boundaries between the black metal and NSBM scenes (see Hochhauser, this volume). One example from the United States is the outdoor "Gathering of Shadows" black metal festival in Colorado, which emphasizes spirituality and wilderness in its advertising but is organized by white supremacists, a fact I discovered when I attended the event in 2007.

Although the extreme actions and sensational nationalist rhetoric of individuals such as Vikernes have, for better or worse, undoubtedly provided the scene with massive publicity, support for his actions is often scarce in the current black metal scene. For example, Garm from Ulver sees little to be gained in actively attempting to "battle" Christianity. Garm says he has "much respect for [Vikernes's] conviction and courage, but not his sense of reality" (Moynihan and Søderlind 1998, 200–202). Many in the extreme metal scene also deride the scene's emphasis on being grim and "evil" and see the church burnings and costuming as a role-playing game gone awry.[8] Some that were a part of the scene also eventually found the atmosphere to be tiresome and slightly self-defeating as a way out of the blandness of everyday existence (Moynihan and Søderlind 1998, 196–97).

Even so, black metal musicians and labels still use the criminal element of the early Norwegian scene as a key ingredient in their marketing. In 1997 Century Black, a division of the Century Media label focused on black metal, produced a showcase compilation entitled *Firestarter*. The album's cover art shows a hooded figure holding a torch in a graveyard engulfed by flame, while the disc itself shows a steeple silhouetted by a full moon and surrounded by fire. The *pièce de résistance*, however, is a large match inserted into the spine of the jewel case. However, only two of the bands represented on the compilation, Emperor and Mayhem, had any involvement in the arson attacks in Norway, and several of the bands represented have only tenuous ties to the scene. Emperor's guitarist Samoth, who spent several months in prison for participating in one of the arsons, is credited with the concept for the compilation.[9]

That Century Media used the notorious aura of the early black metal scene as a marketing tool is significant, since many black metal bands that have gained international stature consider associations with criminals and far-right ideologies a liability. For example, Cradle of Filth from the United Kingdom, perhaps the most successful black metal band worldwide, culti-

MUSICAL STYLE, IDEOLOGY, AND MYTHOLOGY

vates a campy aesthetic of nineteenth-century libertinism and vampirism. Likewise, when I asked Shagrath of Dimmu Borgir a question about the lasting influence of the "Black Circle," he quickly disassociated his band from any of the Circle's criminal activities, emphasizing that "it's all about the music now" (Shagrath 2003).

CONCLUSION

The common thread that emerges throughout this investigation of black metal music and discourse is one of disaffection and alienation from the dominant society, apparent in lyrical content, in interviews, and in the esoteric qualities of the music. This is far from exceptional in underground music scenes, but where many would call for social change in their music, Norwegian black metal retreats to a world of fantasy and myth drawing on local cultural traditions. While some in the "Black Circle," especially Varg Vikernes, attempted to channel this dissatisfaction into an extended campaign to return Norway to an idealized pagan past through acts of destruction, the scene as a whole returned fairly quickly to a position of disengagement. Isolated acts of vandalism still occur, and some in the scene, like Gaahl of Gorgoroth, still engage in violence. Yet the incendiary rhetoric frequently leveled at Western urban society, multiculturalism, and Christianity has not produced the uprising and pagan resurgence that some in the scene claim to desire.

Ultimately, the apparent "failure" of black metal in this regard is not particularly surprising. Extreme metal in general does not lend itself well to inciting social change beyond its own scene, since the lyrics are frequently indecipherable and the musical characteristics are often confounding to the uninitiated listener. As noted by Shagrath and others, many black metal musicians are now attempting to focus on their actual music and do not want that to be overshadowed by social and political activism. While they may indulge in musical fantasies of destroying or rearranging society, all but an isolated few recognize that these are purely flights of imagination. Vikernes has stated that he began Burzum, along with an assortment of role-playing games, because of a lack of "magic" and fantasy in his otherwise boring adolescence (Moynihan and Søderlind 1998, 150). But when he and his circle attempted to realize these fantasies, they simultaneously exceeded the normal boundaries of the extreme metal scene and created a legend of sorts that continues to grow within the global metal in Norway began to act out their fantasies in such an extreme manner.

Moynihan and Søderlind advance several illuminating theories regarding Norwegian black metal's social origin, yet in the end none of them seem completely satisfactory in explaining its severe nature. As Norwegian black metal often positions itself in opposition to Christianity, it is pertinent that Norway still retains a Lutheran state church. However, an overwhelming majority of the populace, and especially the young, do not actively worship in it. Instead, evangelical congregations, many of which are extremely conservative and restricting, often fill the space. However, viewing black metal as a simple reaction against Norway's "official" religion and a conservative evangelical side of Norwegian society seems too facile, even if Vikernes and others surround the scene with militantly anti-Christian rhetoric.

Moynihan and Søderlind suggest that a media ban on televised violence and horror created a cultural barrier that left Norwegian youth unable to see through the campy posturing and imagery of bands such as Venom, causing them to take the product more literally than other fans (Moynihan and Søderlind 1998, 41). The rise of the black metal movement has also been tied to a series of lurid tabloid exposés during a "satanic panic" in Norway in the early 1990s (Moynihan and Søderlind 1998, 227).

Pål Mathiesen, a writer on theological issues for *Morgenbladet*, Norway's cultural newspaper, takes a different view in an interview given to Moynihan and Søderlind in *Lords of Chaos*. Responding to a question regarding the attraction of black metal for intelligent and charismatic individuals, Mathiesen states that Norwegian society suppresses individualism and holds down those with exceptional gifts. He sees the criminality of the black metal phenomenon as a reaction against the mediocrity that this situation seems to encourage (Moynihan and Søderlind 1998, 220–21). The frequent statements from black metal musicians that decry the "weakness" of Christianity and contemporary society in general address this perception, although in some ways they also demonstrate a need for excitement during an otherwise under-stimulating adolescence. Although black metal fans and musicians appear to value individualism and isolation, the scene itself provides a valuable social network in many cases.

If Moynihan and Søderlind's explanations seem incomplete, it is because they provide merely a backdrop for the rise of Norway's black metal scene without explaining why it became a staging ground for murder and domes-

tic terrorism. Moynihan in particular seems to favor the more romanticized and metaphysical explanations involving resurgent pagan and even
racial archetypes. Individualistic and anti-Christian rhetoric is common
across the American death metal scene, and metal bands worldwide look to
native traditions as a means to combat cultural hegemony (Harris 2000b),
yet nothing on the scale of the crimes in Norway has occurred elsewhere.
Cultural isolation and government censorship can perhaps be considered
tinder, but what is lacking is a significant cultural match to light the fire,
although Laura Wiebe Taylor's recent work argues that the ultranationalist
worldview of some black metallers is simply an amplified version of mainstream cultural nationalism in Norway (L. Taylor 2008). In looking for a
more specific catalyst, one invariably returns to the persons who initially
led the scene, especially Aarseth and Vikernes. In this case, the situation
may have simply required a core of charismatic leaders to mold the fledgling scene in their own image. However, we can concede to Moynihan and
Søderlind that Aarseth's and Vikernes's juvenile disaffection would likely
not have found such focus without inspiration from Scandinavia's pagan
history.

   In any case, this musical and social phenomenon has aged in a somewhat predictable fashion, becoming something of a fad. As evidenced by
Dimmu Borgir's Grammy performance (and later win in 2002), Norway
has latched onto black metal as something that can be sold to the mainstream now that the remaining criminal element has either been incarcerated or simply grown up. A cover story in the magazine *Listen to Norway*
considers black metal as part of a tradition of "devil's music" that traces
its lineage back to the Hardanger fiddle, an iconic folk instrument in Norway (Pedersen 2000). The Norwegian mainstream is also likely taking a
cue from the bands themselves, as many bands present themselves as distinctly Norse by writing lyrics in Norwegian, adorning their merchandise
with Norwegian flags or landscapes, and explicitly identifying their music
as "Norwegian black metal." In similar fashion to the rise of punk and rap
in the United States, the image and sound have been cleaned up slightly
and the music made more accessible in order to appeal to a wider audience. Dimmu Borgir's album *Death Cult Armageddon* (2003) shows this
change quite clearly, as the album's presentation and production are on a
par with anything from a major label and the music features orchestral arrangements recorded by the Prague Philharmonic. Following this release,
Dimmu Borgir toured as a main stage act for Ozzfest 2004. While some

fans feel, perhaps justifiably, that the black metal scene has been diluted beyond repair, the influence of the Norwegian black metal scene of the early 1990s remains strong even if bands in the current scene often use its extremity as simply another inspirational well as opposed to an essential identity.

NOTES

1 This article focuses on the first edition of *Lords of Chaos*. The second and third editions may have mitigated this problem somewhat.

2 Currently available on Windir's website, this piece was originally published on the *Majestia Webzine*.

3 In a recent video interview and demonstration with *Guitar World* magazine, the guitarists for Emperor noted that they later added in palm-muted accents for live performances (Ihsahn and Samoth 2007).

4 Angela Rodel (2004) notes that this strategy is also used by the hardcore punk scene.

5 Unfortunately, this quote is no longer available at the message board site.

6 When the possibility of a remixed reissue of *Nattens Madrigal* was mentioned on a Relapse Records message board, most of the community reacted negatively to the idea, as many fans had grown fond of the recording's esoteric charm. Unfortunately, this discussion has been deleted from the server.

7 *Editors' Note*: In Tolkien's Middle Earth, *burzum* means "darkness" in the Black Speech and "Grishnákh" (note original spelling) is the name of an Orc captain (see Olson 2008, 7). While his writings contain plenty of Romantic celebrations of nature and nation, Tolkien was a staunch foe of fascism and would likely have been repulsed by Vikernes's extreme political views.

8 An example of this can be found at http://www.antichristian.org/thoth/sparetime .htm. The site shows images of teens posing as members of a black metal band named Thoth and engaging in very "non-metal" activities, such as playing ping-pong and doing yard work. Tongue-in-cheek captions, such as "Pure Norwegian Yard-work Supremacy," accompany the images.

9 Reactions from non-Norwegian and arguably non-black metal bands, such as Katatonia or the Swedish progressive metal band Opeth, regarding their association with the church burners in this release, could not be found.

"YOU ARE FROM ISRAEL AND THAT IS ENOUGH TO HATE YOU FOREVER"

Racism, Globalization, and Play within the Global Extreme Metal Scene

Keith Kahn-Harris

In trying to understand the globalization of heavy metal, the accumulation of local case studies may not help us in identifying what binds global metal culture together. In particular it may obscure how the contemporary metal world may be held together by practices in which power is exercised. This chapter examines how the globalization of metal has been a process in which differentials of power and "capital" are reproduced and how this has been accompanied by the development of cores and peripheries within the global metal world. It concentrates on the extreme metal scene, perhaps the most globalized of metal cultures. Here, I show how the nature of the globalization of the extreme metal scene has changed over the years, looking at how racist practices have developed in the scene and how those practices have at times been conducted in a "playful" manner. The data come in part from my work on the global extreme metal scene in the 1990s and early 2000s, with case studies in Israel, Sweden, and the United Kingdom (Kahn-Harris 2007). The Israeli case study will be explored par-

ticularly closely in this chapter, with the addition of more recent material
pulled from my continuing engagement in the Israeli extreme metal scene.

THE ISRAELI EXTREME METAL SCENE CONFRONTS THE WORLD

Extreme metal, that is, a collection of related subgenres including thrash,
death, and black metal, emerged in the 1980s and early 1990s at a time
when heavy metal was a genre of great commercial importance. Traditional
heavy metal had a global audience, but its successful artists were mostly,
if not exclusively, American and British, as was the case in the music industry as a whole. In the case of extreme metal, while Anglo-American
artists have been important, they are in no way dominant. Extreme metal
developed in the early to mid-1980s through the efforts of small groups of
people across the globe who, as a reaction to what they saw as the effete nature of the heavy metal of the day, sought to create something that would
"restore" to metal its transgressive edge. This "pioneer generation" created
extreme metal through intensive networks of global communication.

One of the members of this pioneer generation was Zeev Tannenboim,
the founder of Salem, Israel's first extreme metal band, which played its
first gig in 1986 and is still going today. Tannenboim sent Salem's first
demo to *Kerrang!* magazine in 1986, and the brief review that followed led
to him receiving correspondence from throughout the world. Tannenboim
became an integral part of tape-trading networks that allowed the pioneers of extreme metal to share their work before there was enough of a
market to produce fully fledged recordings. Two widely circulated demos,
Destruction Till Death (1986) and *Millions Slaughtered* (1989), led to Salem
getting a record deal with Germany's Morbid Records in the early 1990s.
The band's latest albums are *Necessary Evil*, released on the French Season
of Mist record label in 2007, and *Playing God and Other Short Stories*, released by Singapore's Pulverised Records in 2010.

These networks of correspondence and musical sharing were characterized by its members as a "scene," a term that also has much to recommend
it for those seeking to understand the contexts within which musical production and consumption take place (Straw 1991, 2001). The key characteristic of the extreme metal scene in the 1980s was its global, decentralized
quality. Extreme metal was produced, consumed, and discussed by metalheads scattered across the globe within a scene that had no centralized institutions. Where strong local scenes did exist, such as in Tampa or Stock-

holm in the late 1980s, they did not institutionally dominate the scene. Bands, fanzines, record labels, and "distros" (distribution services) could be located anywhere within the global scene. The global postal system ensured that participation in the scene was possible in most places.

In the 1980s the Israeli scene consisted of little more than a handful of bands and a few people who, like Tannenboim, were plugged into global networks of trading and correspondence. The scene developed substantially in the 1990s. Although gauging the numbers involved in any scene is difficult, the biggest concerts attracted two thousand to three thousand people, suggesting that certainly less than five thousand were interested in extreme metal within the country. The scene overwhelmingly consisted of secular Israelis of Jewish origin, although there were a few exceptions, most notably the black metal band Melechesh, whose members were of Syrian, Armenian, and Palestinian Christian origin.

In the 1990s the Israeli scene developed a set of enduring institutions. By the end of the 1990s there were a number of distributors, one label (Raven) that regularly released CDs by Israeli bands, and a short-lived metal magazine. Regular concerts by Israeli bands took place, and a steady stream of prominent non-Israeli bands played in the country as well. Over a hundred bands released demos and CDs in the 1990s, although many of those had a short life. Compared to the scene in Norway—a similarly sized country—the Israeli scene might have appeared small and marginal. Certainly the impact of its bands was small outside the country, with the exception of Salem and another band, Orphaned Land, which released two CDs on the French label Holy Records in the 1990s.

It certainly seemed by the early 1990s that the global extreme metal scene was a fairly egalitarian space, in that musicians from countries traditionally marginal to the global music industry could participate fully in the creation of a new form of music. The Brazilian death metal band Sepultura, for example, was highly influential within the scene at that time (Harris 2000b; Avelar, this volume). Yet a dramatic event in 1991 cast doubt over just how egalitarian the early 1990s extreme metal scene really was. In that year, the Israeli police informed Zeev Tannenboim that they had intercepted a letter bomb that had been sent to him. The bomb turned out to have been sent by Varg Vikernes, the Norwegian black metal musician also known as Count Grishnackh who recorded under the name Burzum. Vikernes had previously sent Tannenboim anti-Semitic hate mail, and he eventually became notorious for his involvement in a series of church burnings and his eventual imprisonment in 1994 for the 1993 murder of Euronymous (born Øystein Aarseth) of the band Mayhem (Moynihan and Søderlind 1998). Today, having served his sentence, he espouses an unconventional but undeniably racist paganism.

The attempt to send a bomb to Tannenboim was not an isolated incidence of anti-Semitism, but a symptom of a notable rise in racism and anti-Semitism within sections of the black metal scene. The ideology of black metal as it developed in the early 1990s emphasized opposition to what was seen as Christian "weakness" and celebrated the metalheads' connection to the pre-Christian past. For a significant minority of the black metal scene, especially in Scandinavia, this ideology crossed over into an admiration for racist and fascist ideas, particular as expressed in occult versions of Nazism (Goodrick-Clarke 2002). Eventually, an overtly neo-Nazi black metal scene developed (Burghart 1999). While most black metal and extreme metal scene members are not neo-Nazi sympathizers, casual racism is far from uncommon within the scene.

Even in those countries with very small Jewish populations such as Norway, anti-Semitism has remained a mainstay of racist and neo-Nazi identity. The Israeli scene provides the major object for the expression of anti-Semitic abuse, as it is seen as a product of the Jewish state. Members of the Israeli extreme metal scene have experienced persistent, if low-level, prejudice since the early 1990s. For example, one Israeli group that had angered a Danish death metal band received a bar of soap in the mail along with a note asking if they could "find their ancestors in that." Another much more prominent instance of racist abuse, recounted to me on a number of occasions during fieldwork in Israel, began in 1996. The Israeli black metal band Bishop of Hexen received a bad review of its demo *Ancient Hymns of Legend and Lore* in the prominent Norwegian fanzine *Nordic Vision* (1996). In the following issue, Balzamon, the vocalist of Bishop of Hexen, wrote a letter furiously complaining about the bad review, concluding, "You hurt us really bad and we will never ever forget what you have done to us. We will never forget 'Nordic Vision.' Never!!" (Balzamon 1997, n.p.). The editor, Melankol X, printed the letter together with a heavily sarcastic and insulting reply, which began, "First of all you are from Israel and that alone is enough to hate you forever."

Whereas Salem and the few Israeli bands active in the 1980s interacted fairly comfortably within the global scene, in the 1990s Israeli scene members became persistently concerned with what was seen to be Israel's marginality. As I reported in an earlier article (Kahn-Harris 2002), there was intense concern by Israeli scene members that they were on the fringes of the global metal scene. As one Israeli scene member put it to me in an interview: "It's very very very frustrating here . . . you put more than a European band into what you are doing and you get a lot less response . . . it's like we're stuck in the edge of the world." In that article I showed how there was a common feeling that being in Israel was something significant within the scene. In other words, at least from the perspective of Israeli scene members, the global scene was one in which where you were from mattered.

At some point in the early 1990s then, the extreme metal scene changed so that location became an issue for both Israeli and non-Israeli scene members. How did this occur? What changed within the scene? What made racism possible there? To answer these questions, we have to examine the nature of the accumulation of "capital" within the global scene.

CAPITAL IN EXTREME METAL

In recent years, scholars in the humanities and social sciences have come to associate the notion of capital with the work of Pierre Bourdieu ([1979] 1984, 1991, 1993). Bourdieu saw the concept of economic capital as a powerful metaphor for any kind of resource that can be convertible into forms of power in particular settings. Human beings are fundamentally capital-maximizing creatures who struggle over the accumulation of capital. Such struggles occur within "fields" whose forms of capital and logics of capital accumulation are different from each other. Possession of particular sorts of capital within particular sorts of fields allows agents to have prestige and "symbolic power" (Bourdieu 1991) over the trajectories those fields follow. Fields have varying degrees of autonomy from each other, but, importantly, an overarching "field of power" has some kind of primacy in reproducing hierarchies of power throughout multiple fields. The field of power represents those forms of capital (economic, educational, and so forth) that have the most currency in society as a whole, possession of which allows for greater power and more flexible life chances. Capital in specific fields may or may not be "convertible" into capital within another, but the possession of capital within the field of power can often be "refracted" into forms of capital within multiple fields.

Contemporary works of popular music studies are routinely peppered with Bourdieuan concepts such as capital. Given that Bourdieu's analytical framework is a complex, interlocking whole, the eclectic use of Bourdieuan concepts can be more problematic than is sometimes recognized. There is a strong temptation to treat "scene" as a "field" by another name, but it is important to remember that the two concepts have very different gene-alogies. Bourdieu's own work, while it did consider forms of cultural pro-duction, did not apply the concept of field to anything that resembled the extreme metal scene; indeed he was more interested in "legitimate" culture than in "underground" phenomena.

Despite these issues, Bourdieu's analytical framework provides a valu-able tool for understanding how the dynamics of power work within the extreme metal scene and for investigating how hierarchies of power within the scene relate to hierarchies of power outside it. His framework directs our initial attention to the ways in which economic and other forms of capital drawn from the field of power circulate in extreme metal. In this respect, the development of the scene from the 1980s to the 1990s can be understood as a process in which economic capital became more concen-trated in certain hands within the global scene.

Metal in the early 1980s was a fairly egalitarian space that grew out of the global punk scene that had developed at the end of the 1970s. The scene essentially consisted of a small global circle of correspondents. As the scene developed in that decade, this network grew into a more established scene based on trading recordings. For much of the 1980s there were very few extreme metal records and labels; demos were the predominant mode of transmission for extreme metal music. They were either traded for other tapes, or bands sold them directly at cost. Trading facilitated an egalitarian scene with a high degree of autonomy from global flows of economic capi-tal. The accumulation of economic capital within the scene began in the 1980s, when some traders set up what became known as "distros" in order to distribute demos, fanzines, and, later, records and CDs. Initially, distros were little more than photocopied letters advertising a handful of items available either for sale at cost or to be traded for similar items. In the 1990s some of these distros developed into profitable firms such as House of Kicks in Sweden and Plastic Head Distribution in the United Kingdom. These companies developed sophisticated networks for the distribution of extreme metal to record shops, resulting in extreme metal becoming more widely available than it was in the 1980s. In the process, extreme metal has made use of capitalist processes by which transferable forms of economic capital are accumulated.

In the 1980s most extreme metal recordings were circulated through traded demo tapes, although a few recordings were also circulated via heavy metal record labels. By the end of the 1980s, this situation had begun to change with the rapid growth of previously tiny labels such as Earache in the United Kingdom. At the end of the 1980s, there was a sudden proliferation of extreme metal recordings and labels, as bands that had become established through tape trading began to release albums. The number of record companies within the scene grew exponentially in the 1990s. The most successful extreme metal releases now sold one hundred thousand to two hundred thousand copies. Dozens of small- and medium-size companies sold a few thousand or few hundred copies of each release. The proliferation of labels began to erode the institutions of demo tapes and trading.

The proliferation of labels and CDs has had consequences for the circulation of economic capital within the scene. Before the early 1990s, bands entered networks of economic capital circulation and accumulation very gradually, generally spending a considerable part of their early careers trading their demos and building up their reputations. By the mid to late 1990s, the erosion of tape trading meant that scenic activity involved an earlier and greater engagement with economic capital, with bands selling their recordings from an early stage. Bands and labels came to adopt business practices drawn from the wider music industry. The entry of economic capital into the scene increased the scope for conflict within the scene by raising the financial stakes of unsuccessful scenic relationships.

Economic capital also accumulated within the scene through the development of specialist extreme metal publications. Whereas initially the scene was served by small-circulation fanzines, the 1990s saw the development of profit-making extreme metal magazines such as the United Kingdom's *Terrorizer*. As with the growth of large distros, this development made it easier for members to access the scene but also provided further opportunities for economic capital to be accumulated. The importance of magazines has obliged labels and bands to utilize increasingly professional promotional strategies. In the 1980s, bands became known through letter writing, tape trading, and interviews with small fanzines. While these practices remained important, by the late 1990s even the smallest record labels had issued press releases and promotional photographs. CD releases came to be accompanied by huge "mail shots" of CDs to magazines and radio stations. Some labels employed publicity companies to ensure that releases were promoted effectively in as many countries as possible. Financial resources became increasingly important in the promotion of bands as large labels consolidated their position through their greater resources and smaller labels had to work increasingly hard to get noticed.

It might be thought that the rapid development of the Internet since the mid-1990s may have provided an antidote to the accumulation of economic capital within the scene. Theoretically, the Internet can enable a more egalitarian scene in which every band has a Web site and music can be obtained (legally or illegally) for free or for very little money. What is interesting, though, is that while extreme metal sites have existed almost from the Web's inception, it has only been since 2000 or later that the scene's institutions began to be significantly affected by the Internet. In the new century, the spread of broadband technology made sharing music for free easier. The Internet has all but killed off fanzines, most of which have migrated to Webzines or blogs, although a few still survive. Magazines continue to thrive, although they increasingly require a substantial complementary presence on the Web. The vast majority of extreme metal bands have Myspace pages, and file-swapping sites contain vast quantities of extreme metal MP3s. Myspace and other similar sites have almost completely eliminated demos. As in other areas of the music industry, record labels are struggling to come up with a viable economic model in response to these developments. Extreme metal is becoming ever more available on sites such as iTunes, as even the smallest labels become committed to a digital future. Yet there does not seem to have been a mass culling of labels or bands, and CDs are still released in the traditional manner.

The extreme metal scene, like other music scenes, is clearly in a transitional period, and it remains unclear what the future shape of the extreme metal industry will be. Promotional strategies have evolved to enable Internet-based marketing, but it remains the case that institutions with the greatest economic capital are able to ensure prominence and greater sales. The Internet certainly makes the scene far easier to access, as information that was once hard to find is now publicly available. While the Internet might be thought to democratize access to an audience for newer bands, it may simply bury them under an avalanche of information. Within this avalanche, the support of economically powerful institutions remains essential. Unknown bands tend to achieve prominence through traditional means such as touring and promotion, although exceptions—such as the rapid success achieved by the American band Job for a Cowboy, via Myspace in 2007—do occur and may become more common.

The still unfolding impact of the Internet notwithstanding, there has clearly been a historical shift in the way economic capital circulates within the extreme metal scene. In the 1980s the scene was small, fluid, and informal, with little economic capital circulating within it. In the 1990s and 2000s the scene became more formalized and types of economic capital accumulated within it. Once this capital became established within the scene, logics of capital accumulation began to influence scenic practices in certain directions. Once institutions make profits, allowing their owners and staff to be paid, such institutions must continue to make a profit and must orient their practices accordingly. The profit motive may come to dominate such institutions. Profitable bands may no longer have time to correspond with scene members. Profitable record labels cannot afford to sign and support bands that have little chance of providing some return on their investment. Profitable distros may not offer favorable terms for exchange or sale.

Inevitably, power relations and hierarchies within the scene began to emerge in the 1990s. Wealthier, more successful scenic institutions are able to promote their product more widely and so influence the overall direction of the scene. Once scenic production increased in the 1990s, promotion and marketing became even more important, giving greater power to "gatekeepers" within the scene. Inequalities in the possession of economic capital within the scene became intensified by preexisting inequalities resulting from scene members' relative positions within the field of power.

Despite the increased amounts of capital circulating within the scene, most bands are unable to make a living from their music. Most band members are amateurs who have other jobs or survive through social security or student grants. Those in developing countries or from poorer backgrounds within developed countries have fewer resources to bring to the scene. Members from richer backgrounds or who have better-paid jobs are able to put more money into bands, fanzines, and other institutions. In Scandinavian countries, for example, the social-security system allows some scene members to support themselves with state benefits while pursuing their musical activities. In Sweden, bands can hire well-equipped rehearsal studios for a minimal rent, obtain grants for the purchase of equipment, and participate in state-funded courses in popular musicianship. In poorer countries, even finding the money to buy musical instruments and CDs can be extremely difficult. In some countries with high import taxes, foreign CDs can be prohibitively expensive.

Economic capital is not the only form of capital that accumulated within the scene. Time is another resource that members use within the scene and that can be understood as a form of capital. This form of capital is less available to some scene members. For example, in countries such as Israel that have compulsory military service, members may be removed from the scene for considerable periods of time. Position within global fields of power endows or restricts access to other kinds of capital too, such as support from the state or the family.

Unsurprisingly, such inequalities fuel the emergence of cores and peripheries within the global scene. Countries such as Norway and Sweden, whose bands and institutions are highly influential, are unquestionably superpowers within the extreme metal scene. Compared to these countries, Israel appeared peripheral, at least in the 1990s: the country's relative economic weakness at the time compared to many European and American states, together with its compulsory military service and political instability, meant that scene members in Israel had fewer resources to bring to the scene. If they wished to participate within the scene, they had to work harder than scene members in other countries. But it would be unwise to overstate Israel's marginality and in any case the Israeli economy has boomed in recent years. Israel may be an unstable environment, but the barriers to participation in metal are far less than in much of the developing world. In any case, possession of economic or other forms of capital drawn from outside the scene does not automatically "explain" the scene's cores and peripheries. The scene's reciprocal networks of exchange remain strong. Irreconcilable splits have not emerged between more successful scenic institutions and others. The economic capital that has accumulated within the scene remains small; the personal incomes of even the most successful scenic entrepreneurs are modest compared to those achievable in other popular culture scenes.

Returning to the question of racism experienced by Israeli scene members, Israel's relative marginality and the difficulties of accumulating capital within the Israeli scene do not necessarily explain its vulnerability to racist attack. Nor is this necessarily explained by Israelis' Jewishness. Racism toward Muslims appears to be equally strong within metal, yet members of the nascent scenes emerging throughout the Middle East tend not to report racism as a major barrier to global participation (Hecker 2005). There are many marginal locations within the global scene, but few have faced the attacks that Israel has. To begin to understand this, we have to consider how Israel's marginality is reinforced, mitigated, or resisted by scene members. We need to consider how Israeli scene members are positioned with respect to forms of capital circulating exclusively *within* the scene. What hierarchies derive from such forms of capital?

THE ACCUMULATION OF SUBCULTURAL CAPITAL

According to Bourdieu ([1979] 1984), the specifically *cultural* forms of capital are accumulated through competence in various cultural practices and displayed through a kind of savoir-faire. Bourdieu was concerned with tracing the ways in which a dominant position within the field of power translates into the possession of cultural competence within multiple cultural fields, and vice versa. As such, there is a lacuna in his work concerning the applicability of concepts of capital to groups of fields where the translation of hierarchies between them is less straightforward, or where the hierarchies within the field of power are not fully unambiguous. Accordingly, the application of the concept of capital to music scenes requires further analytical work. In recognition of the problematics of adapting Bourdieu's ideas outside the sphere of dominant culture, Sarah Thornton (1995) developed the concept of "subcultural capital" in her analysis of dance music scenes in the United Kingdom. For Thornton, subcultural capital is a form of cultural capital that is far less readily convertible into economic capital and to positions within the field of power. Hierarchies resulting from disparities in the possession of subcultural capital can translate into hierarchies of power within society as a whole, but in very complicated ways.

Subcultural capital is "objectified," Thornton argues, "in the form of fashionable haircuts and well assembled record collections" and is "embodied," she continues "in the form of being 'in the know,' using (but not over-using) current slang and looking as if you were born to perform the latest dance styles" (1995, 11–12). The dance-music scene that she examines is obsessed with making distinctions and producing hierarchies of status. Subcultural capital rewards scene members with such intangibles as "prestige" and "status." When members have subcultural capital, they will be heard and will have influence over the trajectory of the scene. To possess subcultural capital is to have self-esteem and a real stake in the scene. No matter how it is claimed or rewarded, subcultural capital is *by definition* what everyone in the scene wants. Subcultural capital is thus something for which scene members strive and which they embody.

The implication of Thornton's reading of Bourdieu is that subcultural capital is always present within music scenes, but it takes unique forms there. Subcultural capital has become an increasingly important concept in the analysis of music scenes (see, for example, Hodkinson 2002), and I would argue that the extreme metal scene produces forms of subcultural capital that are unique to it. I want to briefly outline what I consider to be the principal forms of subcultural capital circulating within the extreme metal scene—mundane subcultural capital and transgressive subcultural capital—before looking at how these forms of subcultural capital relate to economic and other forms of capital.

MUNDANE SUBCULTURAL CAPITAL

It is through a plethora of "mundane" (Kahn-Harris 2007) everyday activities that the scene is produced—rehearsing, corresponding, trading, buying CDs. Such activities are often conducted alone or in small groups, and they may be tedious and routine (Kahn-Harris 2004b). However, in producing the scene they are oriented toward a collective practice: the imagined *telos* of such mundane practices is the collective. Mundane subcultural capital celebrates the scene as a space within which individuality is dissolved within the collective (Maffesoli [1988] 1996). The scene is a space of what Maffesoli calls "puissance," a mysterious power that emerges when people of similar interests gather together. It is through the myriad of everyday scenic activities that the possibility of this puissance is maintained. Mundane subcultural capital is oriented toward the possibilities of the collective puissance that is produced as a collective result of the mundane efforts of the totality of scene members.

Mundane subcultural capital is produced through a sustained investment in the myriad mundane practices through which the scene is produced as collective practice. It is claimed through self-sacrifice, commitment to the scene, and hard work. A crucial element of mundane subcultural capital, as in all forms of cultural capital, is the demonstration of savoir-faire within the scene. Scene members claim subcultural capital by knowing the complex histories of the scene and by having heard the music of its vast number of bands. Knowledge of the scene is something that scene members actively attempt to display. History is extremely important to scene members; they must know the obscure roots of extreme and heavy metal in the 1970s and 1980s, and the complexities of its development since then. Mundane subcultural capital is acquired and displayed through the ability to place bands within a network of differences among bands and locate those bands within the complex histories of scene personnel (Harris 1997). Take, for example, this extract from a review of a demo by the U.S. death metal band Incantation, taken from the Welsh fanzine *Mutilated Mag*:

> After leaving REVENANT, guitarist John McEntee joined up with Sal Seijo on guitar, Ronny Deo on bass, Peter Barnevic on drums and Will Rahmer of MORTICIAN on vocals, to form none other than INCANTA-TION.... Featuring four tracks, extreme stuff, in the vein of REVENANT, MORBID ANGEL, DERKETA and MASSACRE. Starting off with "Profinan-tion" through to "Devoured Death" which takes us onto side two for "Entrantment of Evil" and "Eternal Torture." Recorded in May 1990 at Stardust Studios with Ed Lotwis engineering (Of REVENANT fame!). (*Mutilated Mag* 1991, 11)

Subcultural capital can also be acquired through a detailed knowledge of the institutions and practices of the scene. This knowledge is considerably more difficult to acquire than a detailed knowledge of extreme metal music, since it requires an active experience of the scene. Mundane subcultural capital is produced through a commitment to work hard *for* the scene. Mundane scenic involvement is constructed as an altruistic, ethical commitment to the collective. This altruism is demonstrated in the following extract from an interview that I conducted with a British scene member who describes how he and a friend set up their own label: "sat around with [name] who's my partner in [name of label], we were round my house one night, and we just got talking about the way the metal scene was going. We decided that, you know, we could do something for the scene as such, the bands we believed in."

Given the geographic dispersion of metal, much of the ethics of the scene revolves around being a reliable correspondent. Since disputes are hard to resolve over long distances, reliability and honesty are crucial in avoiding intra-scenic conflict. Considerable discussion occurs within the scene over which institutions are most reliable in their transactions. Those that do have a good reputation gain subcultural capital.

The entry of economic capital from outside the scene that I discussed in the last section makes scene ethics considerably more complicated. Altruistic ethics are threatened when there is the potential for some members to make a profit. When money changes hands, the potential for being "ripped off" increases. However, making money from the scene does not automatically preclude the generation of mundane subcultural capital, as is the case in some punk scenes (O'Conner 2002). Profit and commerce are tolerated, *provided* that they are byproducts of scenic practice, rather than ends in themselves. As long as the scene "comes first" and an element of altruism is sustained, commercial imperatives are not necessarily problematic.

Long-standing scene members who have a reputation for ethical dealing and a commitment to the scene gain subcultural capital in the form of respect and fame. Respect translates into sales and increased attention paid to their respective institutions. Mundane subcultural capital is also acquired by musicians by refining and developing existing styles. The vast majority of musicians and bands are not innovators but refiners. Within a vast musical landscape of similar bands refining similar styles, it is hard for musicians to accrue mundane subcultural capital by musical means alone. Those bands that accrue the greatest amounts of mundane subcultural capital are generally those that are most adept at working within scenic institutions. They are the bands that write the most letters and are most skilled at forming relationships with a wide range of scene members. Accruing as much mundane subcultural capital as possible by these means maximizes a band's chances of having its music released by a prominent label with a high standard of production.

TRANSGRESSIVE SUBCULTURAL CAPITAL

A historically and culturally specific manifestation of the long-standing tension in capitalist societies between ideologies of individuality and those of group conformity, the interplay of mundane and transgressive subcultural capital is fundamental to the extreme metal scene. Mundane subcultural capital is accrued through an altruistic commitment to the collective. In contrast, transgressive subcultural capital is claimed through a radical individualism. The practice of transgression represents the desire to exceed, to cross boundaries and escape from the confines of society (Stallybrass and White 1986). Transgressive subcultural capital is accrued through displaying uniqueness and innovation. Transgressive subcultural capital is elitist and is not as freely available as mundane subcultural capital. It has to be fought for and is only selectively granted. It involves an attempt to be different, to challenge and transgress accepted norms within and beyond the scene. Indeed, transgressive subcultural capital can be claimed through a critique of the scene and its mundane subcultural capital. One of the strongest and most coherent critiques of metal's mundane subcultural capital can be found in a 1999 article in the Finnish fanzine *Isten 100* in which the authors discuss what they disparagingly call "Scene Metal." The authors argue that the contemporary scene is so supportive that it is killing "art." Supportive reviews and a plethora of labels ensure that most bands within the scene can produce, release, and circulate music with relative ease. The writers of *Isten 100* complain that there is no proper criticism of "boring," uncreative bands and that the scene is thus seen as undiscriminating, homogeneous, and bland:

> Look at you!
>
> You are cardboard people propped up in a scenery of a thousand years of greatness. Controlled by an industry that's only barely profitable but so deeply in love with itself it sups off its own excrement. You write, release and listen to songs about total war, but only brawl like a bunch of four-year-olds at best. And deep down inside, you're all in agreement, whatever you say.
>
> Which is exactly why you love "metal," probably. Friend Metal. Life Metal. Scene Metal.
>
> Consensus Metal.
>
> Yes-man Metal. Objective Metal. No Metal At All. (Mattila and Sarna 1999, n.p.)

The black metal scene—particularly the Norwegian black metal scene of the early 1990s (see Moynihan and Søderlind 1998 and Hagen, this volume)—is the section of the extreme metal scene in which members have claimed transgressive subcultural capital most assiduously. This scene was oriented toward transgressing boundaries within the extreme metal scene itself. Early black metal bands spent considerable energy in insulting other bands and scenic institutions in order to establish the notional existence of a tiny, "true" "elite." This tendency continues to this day. Black metal bands are far more vigorous in claiming transgressive subcultural capital than mundane subcultural capital. There is an assumption that the majority of people in the scene are mediocrities, with only a select few able to join the elite.

The activities and personalities of the early 1990s Norwegian black metal scene remain a source of fascination to this day. Characters like Varg Vikernes (the sender of the letter bomb to Tannenboim) are still revered for their total commitment to transgression. Similarly, those who are seen as musical innovators within the scene are endowed with transgressive subcultural capital. Bands that pioneered new styles, such as Bathory and Venom, are admired. Many pioneering bands were active in the 1980s, considered a time when the scene was at its most transgressive.

Transgressive subcultural capital has more in common with Bourdieu's idea of cultural capital than mundane subcultural capital has. Transgressive subcultural capital constructs art and individuality as the predominant ways of gaining capital. Potentially, at least, "great art" produces forms of capital that can be transferable into and out of other scenes. To a certain extent, transgressive subcultural capital is not subcultural at all. It is rather a particular version of a form of capital that exists wherever artists and other individuals seek to attack taboos and "the mainstream." Transgressive subcultural capital circulates within the extreme metal scene, but the attachment to the scene is contingent and pragmatic—to possess transgressive subcultural capital is to be *part of* the scene but not *of* the scene.

SUBCULTURAL CAPITAL AND SCENIC DEVELOPMENT

It is through the complex interrelationship of mechanisms for the production of mundane and transgressive subcultural capital that the extreme metal scene is maintained and developed. Both forms of capital are necessary for the scene's reproduction, but that is not to say that these twin forms of capital do not create tensions and fault lines within the scene. In particular, there is continual tension within the scene over the issue of change. Change threatens the mechanisms through which mundane subcultural capital is claimed. Those who invest most in mundane subcultural capital are most fearful of change and difference. In contrast, transgressive subcultural capital rewards individuality, unpredictability, and innovation. As Keith Negus (1999) points out, in all musical genres there are tensions between genre as "routine" and genre as "transformative." Genres are sites both of innovation and of stable creativity within strict limits. Within the extreme metal scene these very different views of creativity and innovation are negotiated in the context of the tension between the instability rewarded by transgressive subcultural capital and the homogeneity rewarded by mundane subcultural capital.

The development of the scene from the 1980s to the 1990s and beyond can be understood in terms of the complex interrelationship of transgressive and mundane subcultural capital. Mundane subcultural capital was the primary form of capital within the scene in the 1980s and resulted in the well-developed scenic institutions that had emerged by the early 1990s. The death metal music that dominated the scene had become extraordinarily uniform, and other forms of extreme metal had been pushed to the margins of the scene. At that time, scene members emphasized their "normality," wearing casual clothes and spending most of their time in correspondence with other scene members.

Yet, while the scene was musically and discursively at its most mundane, homogeneous, and static, in other respects it was able to incorporate difference and change. The early 1990s were the time of the scene's greatest growth. Coinciding with the commercial decline of traditional, melodic heavy metal, there was a rapid influx of new scene members. The scene grew throughout the world, extending to places where extreme metal had previously been unknown, with the influx of new members particularly marked in "marginal" countries, such as Israel.

By 1993 this situation had begun to change significantly. The black metal scene that developed in Norway and elsewhere was principally oriented toward claiming transgressive subcultural capital. The black metal scene produced dramatic musical and discursive innovation. Criminality, racism, and associations with the far right were new phenomena in metal. The black metal scene challenged the broader extreme metal scene, which was previously committed to mundane stability, to incorporate new sounds and practices that were highly disruptive and potentially dangerous. Yet at the same time, the black metal scene also claimed mundane subcultural capital. For one thing, most of its members were active in the institutions of the scene and were thus obliged to abide by its logic. But the black metal scene was also fearful of change and difference even as it introduced considerable disruption and diversity to the broader scene. Like many revolutionary movements, the black metal scene looked backward as much as it looked forward. Black metallers such as Euronymous and Vikernes were

METAL AND EXTREMIST IDEOLOGIES

not only critical of the scene in the early 1990s for being insufficiently transgressive, but also for having "betrayed" metal. The black metal scene looked backward to 1980s metal and, in particular, to German thrash metal.

The black metal scene of the early 1990s developed a logic of subcultural capital accumulation that has survived to this day. Whereas transgressive subcultural capital was formerly of lesser importance than mundane, the black metal scene ensured that the two now have equal importance. Although individual scene members do not necessarily have an equal commitment to both forms of subcultural capital, neither form of capital has come to dominate the scene.

Since the mid-1990s the scene has become a space both of difference and experimentation, and of nostalgia and stasis. The logic of mundane subcultural capital ensures that scene members have refined all existing extreme metal subgenres incrementally. However, there has also been a quite startling amount of radical experimentation within extreme metal. For example, stimulated by black metal's preoccupation with myths of nationality, a variety of bands from all extreme metal subgenres have incorporated "folk" musics into extreme metal, including Brazil's Sepultura (Harris 2000a), Finland's Korpiklaani, and Latvia's Skyforger.

What is remarkable about the contemporary extreme metal scene is the way in which reactionary and experimental versions of extreme metal coexist. That is not to say that all scene members embrace all styles of metal; there is a certain amount of suspicion between the most reactionary and the most experimental. Nonetheless, the scene has become a space that is conservative and yet, at the same time, one in which metal subgenres form the basis of wide-ranging musical explorations. The equal weight given to both mundane and transgressive subcultural capital endows scene members with a variety of musical and discursive means to gain capital. The scene maintains a delicate balance, which ensures that both transgressive and mundane subcultural capital are valuable in the scene and also that the means of gaining transgressive and mundane subcultural capital are not closely circumscribed. The "fulcrum" for this balance consists in the limits placed on musical and discursive experimentation and the continuing emphasis on the gaining and maintaining of scenic knowledge.

The balance maintained within the scene between transgressive and mundane subcultural capital since the mid-1990s has resulted in the development of new forms of power and hierarchy within the scene. Mundane subcultural capital is far easier to claim than transgressive, as all it requires is a dogged commitment to play by the rules within the scene. Scene members must be more creative and braver in order to claim transgressive subcultural capital, but its rewards may be greater than those offered by mundane subcultural capital. The most revered scene members are those who have committed themselves to transgressive individualism in some way. Those who are respected for their mundane commitment to the scene, such as label managers, can never quite achieve the same kind of admired notoriety. While mundane subcultural capital translates far more easily into economic capital, unlike transgressive subcultural capital it does not have the potential to be translated into cultural capital circulating in other fields and scenes.

THE FATE OF THE ISRAELI SCENE: POWER AND PLAY IN EXTREME METAL

Subcultural capital becomes more problematic when it builds on extra-scenic forms of capital. As I have argued, those who are endowed with subcultural capital may go on to gain other forms of capital. Conversely, for those for whom participation in the scene is already difficult, such as women and those from marginal locations, subcultural capital may be particularly difficult to claim. Mundane subcultural capital, for example, requires so much in-depth knowledge that those from marginal countries or poorer backgrounds may find it difficult to accrue. Thus, subcultural capital becomes concentrated in the hands of those who possess other kinds of capital.

An understanding of the forms of capital circulating within the scene helps us to understand the complex position of Israel within global metal. While Israelis can and do claim power and status in the scene through the accumulation of forms of subcultural capital, their position is much more tenuous than that of other scene members. The small size of the Israeli scene, its geographical isolation from larger scenes, and the smaller amounts of time and other forms of transferable capital available to its members create obstacles that are not encountered by members in other scenes, such as those of the United Kingdom or Sweden. The interaction of dozens of Israeli scene members within the global scene shows that these obstacles are far from insurmountable and indeed are less than in many other countries. But the crucial division between the Israeli scene and the core of the global scene has less to do with possession of transferable forms of capital *per se* than with less tangible feelings of security and insecurity. Israeli scene members are acutely aware of the conflict through which they are living and long for a "normal," secure experience of the scene and everyday life. Israeli scene members work hard to gain subcultural capital. However, it is not possession of subcultural capital alone that marks out the secure scene member; the ability to *play* within the scene, to move from the utilitarian, the "serious" into a more liberating kind of activity is also required (Huizinga 1955).

The early 1990s saw the development of racism as an oddly playful kind of practice. There were indeed a few outright neo-Nazis within the scene such as Vikernes, but most were not of his type. To understand this, consider how the confrontation I outlined earlier between Balzamon and Melankol X continued: Balzamon loudly complained about Melankol X in a number of scene publications. For example, in an interview in the fanzine *Mimes Brunn* (Smith 1997), Balzamon gave an impassioned defense of being a member of "the noble Jewish race" (n.p.). Clearly, he was deeply hurt by the anti-Semitic abuse he received and saw it as evidence of a threatening racism within the scene that he was obliged to confront. To the extent that a few scene members, such as Vikernes, have close ties to racist and fascist groups, Balzamon's analysis was not incorrect. Yet much of the racist practice aimed at Israeli scene members derives less from a consistently serious racist worldview than a desire to flirt with racism and "wind up" other scene members. Indeed, in a letter to me dated May 26, 1999, Melankol X described his response to Balzamon's letter as "just an overdone way of replying to his not so smart letter." Melankol X certainly takes pains to distance himself from overt neo-Nazis in his fanzine. Had he supported Bishop of Hexen's music, it is highly unlikely that the band's nationality would have received other than a passing mention. Since he did not, the apparent lack of taboos against racist language in the scene gave him ammunition in his humiliation of Balzamon. Melankol X, who has dealt unproblematically with Israelis within the scene at other times, chose to use racism as the most effective way of attacking someone he despised. Balzamon's attempted use of essentialist nationalism in his defense was of no value, since he failed to recognize that Melankol X had used racist discourses in a "playful" manner.

Other instances of the playful use of racist discourses within the scene abound. For example, the album *The Fire and the Wind* (1999), by the New

Zealand band Demoniac, features a song entitled "Myths of Metal," which contains the chorus:

> Hitler Metal want to bang my fucking head
> And fist the living dead in the middle of the night alright
> I really want to bang my head and fist the living dead in the middle
>   of the night my sign
> The Metal's in my blood and the power is here and now for you!
> HITLER METAL! SIEG HEIL!

Faced with its record being banned in Germany, the band released an apologetic statement explaining that the song was a tongue-in-cheek tribute to German thrash metal of the 1980s. Such instances, of bands playing with racism and fascism and then retreating when they are confronted, are common within the scene. They represent a paradoxical desire to use the scene as a transgressive space, but one that is safe from attacks by outsiders.

Extreme metal has playfully drawn on transgressive discourses for so long that it can be hard to tell when a band is making a "serious" racist statement. Metal has always used over-the-top imagery that often veers toward the camp and comic. Venom, generally considered to have "started" black metal with the album *Welcome to Hell*, used satanic imagery to an unprecedented degree, but within the scene there was, and is, a clear consensus that the band members were not "really" Satanists and had a tongue-in-cheek attitude to satanic imagery. Norwegian black metal bands are frequently contrasted with Venom, as in this interview I conducted with a member of the scene in the United Kingdom: "All the black metal bands in the 1980s, they used to sing a lot of the things that these Norwegian bands sing about, but you knew deep down that they never meant it. . . . Venom weren't Satanists, they were a rock-and-roll band, with these Norwegian bands, they were, I thought they were completely and utterly crazy and they were for real." So highly developed is the practice of reading elements of extreme metal in a playful way that some scene members initially had difficulty in reading Norwegian black metal as "serious." The following anecdote, from an interview that I conducted with the manager of a British label, is highly revealing:

> Vikernes came in this office, stayed at my house—this is before he did
> any murders or anything. . . . But he said a few comments like, when

we were having pizza and stuff at Pizzaland down there, it was like, little things like, just like out of the blue, he'd be telling like, "Oh yeah, I'm the mail-order party, mail-order branch of [the] Norwegian Nazi party." We were like, "Mmm, whatever, do you want garlic bread?" . . . Bullshit he was on about and he's like "No, no, no I've sold three flags, three swastika flags through my mail, that's my, I've sold three flags." And we're like, "Yeah, yeah, whatever, you know bollocks you're talking about" and um, you know, at that time it was like [inaudible] bravado crap he was talking about. But then it suddenly sunk in with us, it's like this guy, he's for real.

Varg Vikernes's claims to be a neo-Nazi were initially read as playful boasting. This turned to considerable shock when the interviewee eventually found out that Vikernes's activities simply could not be read in that way.

"Serious" and "play" racisms are both abhorrent, particularly to those such as Balzamon who are deeply hurt by either of them. Yet the latter kind of racism requires a very different response. As a "wind up" or a way of joking, overt and furious attempts at challenging them are likely to lead to more ridicule. This is a hard choice for some members to make. Those who are experienced within the scene and possess more subcultural capital are better able to cope with the problem. They are less likely to encounter it in the first place or be "wound up" by people who despise them. Further, they have the skills necessary either to ignore abuse or to play in return.

Significantly, Tannenboim's letter bomb incident was never widely publicized within the scene. Tannenboim knew enough about scene politics to keep a low profile, but he also used the incident as a resource in his creative work with his band, Salem. Salem's album *Kaddish* (1994) is named after the Jewish prayer for the dead and deals, both explicitly and implicitly, with the Holocaust. The album contains a version of "Ha'ayara Boeret" (The town is burning), the doleful Jewish partisan song of the Second World War. The album marked a striking change from Salem's previous output, which dealt with more generic extreme metal themes. The incident with Vikernes brutally showed Tannenboim and Salem that the non-scenic world could no longer be held back from the Israeli scene. Rather than rail at the injustice, Salem's *Kaddish* uses it to develop a new kind of music within the scene. Tannenboim and Salem have consistently attempted to gain subcultural capital through hard work and innovative recordings. This has not resulted in them becoming one of the scene's best-known acts, but it has ensured a long career in which they have had record deals with well-respected labels and have, since 2007, played concerts outside Israel.

It appears that, since the turn of the century, the insecurity and resentment expressed by Israeli scene members have started to abate. The Israeli scene has become ever more productive, with more bands being signed to foreign labels and touring abroad. Orphaned Land are now a major international act with two albums released since 2000 on the important metal label Century Media and have toured extensively worldwide. A younger generation of bands, such as Betzefer, which is signed to the giant metal label Roadrunner, had to struggle less to achieve success and interact within the global scene without expressions of insecurity. While anti-Semitic incidents continue, they are less likely to lead to the crippling insecurity of the kind expressed by Balzamon.

Furthermore, Israeli scene members have begun themselves to play within the global scene. In 2002 the Jerusalem-based black metal band Arallu released its second album, *Satanic War in Jerusalem*. The album makes a parallel between the war that was currently raging in and around Jerusalem and the prophecy that the apocalypse will culminate in the holy city. Far from refusing the mark of Jewishness, the album treats Jewishness as the highest level of Satanism. In a track entitled "Jewish Devil," Arallu embraces the old stereotype of the Jew as Satan:

> Here we are after the holocaust
> This is no nothing
> We are satan's [*sic*] sons
> And always we'll [*sic*] be!!!
>
> God is dead, we rule the earth
> Despite holocaust we are here
> Jews as Genii in the world of the dead. (Arallu 2002)

The liner notes to the album ridicule Scandinavian satanic bands for being too scared to play in Israel and for playing at war when Israeli bands actually live within it. They also ridicule the common Scandinavian preoccupation with the forest as a source of strength: "We spit in the face of those 'Virtual Warriors' bands, go back to your woods!! The devil came from the desert AND NOT from the forest . . . wake up and smell the flowers. . . . For we are the ones who smell the stench of blood." The Arallu album claims subcultural capital by claiming that Israeli black metal is more transgressive than other forms. It is not simply defensive about Israel's position within the global scene, but actively makes a virtue of it. Arallu does not defend Jews against racist abuse, but plays with racist stereotypes for its own ends.

The practice of play reveals much about power and capital within the extreme metal scene. Play is an activity for those who are comfortable and knowledgeable about the scene and possess enough subcultural, economic, and other forms of capital to feel secure within it. For those with less capital, it is very hard to engage in play, and participation within the scene requires serious effort. Cruelly, this serious effort may only make security within the scene even more difficult to achieve, as the example of Balzamon shows. Yet, as the example of Arallu illustrates, even those on the margins can play within the scene if they have a sophisticated enough knowledge of how the scene and extreme metal music works.

CONCLUSION

The extreme metal scene has been heavily globalized from its very inception. However, the nature of this globalization changed radically in the late 1980s and early 1990s. In tracing the transition from a scene where place was ignored to one where place was a major issue, one has to be careful not to underestimate the global inequalities in the scene in the 1980s nor to overestimate the inequalities in the scene after the 1990s. The examples of Arallu and Salem suggest that however forms of capital may have accumulated in global extreme metal since the early 1990s, they have not accumulated to the extent that participation within the scene is beyond the reach of those on its margins. Racism within the scene is never so great as to prevent those who suffer from it, such as Israeli Jews, from participation within the scene. The ability of those with more capital to play within the scene certainly disadvantages those with less capital, but play is possible even for those further down hierarchies of power.

It is certainly the case that the global scene is dominated by bands and labels from a limited range of locations, mostly Northern European, but there is still enough global interaction to allow one to talk of a global scene. The days when the extreme metal scene consisted of a few hundred scattered, letter-writing, tape-trading pioneers may be long gone, but their legacy has not been entirely forgotten.

PART 5
METAL AND THE MUSIC INDUSTRY

This "battle," howeve... the status of rock... expanded dra... described... 1970s... t...

ARENAS O

Global Tours and the Heavy M   ...ie 1970s

Steve Waksman

1973 was a record-breaking year for Led Zeppelin. The band's tour of the United States drew some of the largest concert audiences in recorded history, and its show at Tampa Stadium in Florida attracted over sixty thousand people, a number that broke the previous high set by the Beatles at their appearance at Shea Stadium in 1966 (Bloom 1973b, 68). Led Zeppelin bigger than the Beatles? Such was the claim made by the band's publicity department. Yet there was more immediate competition during the summer of 1973. As *Circus* magazine pointed out, Alice Cooper was staging his own epic tour that year, one that was expected to "blast" fifty-six U.S. cities as opposed to the thirty on the Zeppelin map. In what the magazine called a "Battle of the Bucks," *Circus* reported that Alice Cooper had the numbers on his side, but that Zeppelin had the rhetoric. The band was promoting its tour not only as the biggest in history, but as an endeavor that would "make Alice's look like a second class safari in Bechuanaland" (Bloom 1973a, 50).[1]

er much a media relations ploy, reveals much about in the 1970s. The average size of the rock concert had matically by the early 1970s.[2] While such large gatherings as above occurred during the 1960s and even earlier, during the they became more routine, more definitive of the economic and cultural context of live rock performance. A survey of the concert history of the Rolling Stones, one of the most successful live bands to make the transition from the performance environments of the 1960s to those of the 1970s, demonstrates this change in scale. Isolating the Stones' record of concerts in New York City, one can see that their first appearances in 1964 and 1965 were at the Academy of Music, a mid-sized venue that held a few thousand concertgoers. In 1966 the band played the Forest Hills Tennis Stadium in Queens, a larger venue, but it was only in 1969 that it played Madison Square Garden—one of the hallowed spaces of the arena rock era—for the first time. Following two shows at the Garden in that year, the Stones would play the venue three more times in 1972 and six more times in 1975.[3] While the changes no doubt mark shifts in the Stones' own popularity as a touring band, they also index the broader changes taking place in the staging of live rock during the 1970s. Under such circumstances, competition between the most successful bands heightened. As a mode of production, arena rock brought a decidedly competitive form of capitalism to a rock industry that was undergoing remarkable growth.

More than the economic scale of rock was changing during these years, however. The curious reference to Bechuanaland tells us something further about the rise of arena rock, something that has as much to do with the cultural framework within which the phenomenon took shape as with sheer economics. Rock tours were, among other things, a form of tourism, all the more so when they involved travel overseas. Musicians were not tourists in a straightforward sense. Touring musicians were working, after all, whereas tourism proper has typically been analyzed as a leisure activity removed from the world of work.[4] Yet touring also involves many hours of unproductive time, during which musicians engage in many of the activities that constitute tourism. More to the point, in journalistic and popular representations, musicians on tour performed a sort of tourism for readers and fans. Through tales of their encounters with distant lands and exotic people, rock stars codified their own privileged status and acted as mediators between the familiar and the foreign, as figures who traversed boundaries that others did not have occasion to cross.

Such representations, in a sense, mirrored the expanding global reach of the rock industry, and rock touring in particular. When the Beatles extended their touring base to Hong Kong, Australia, and New Zealand in 1964, and to Japan and the Philippines in 1966, they opened new lines of cultural commerce that would be further consolidated over the next decade. By 1971 both Led Zeppelin and its U.S. arena rock counterpart, Grand Funk Railroad, would include large-scale concerts in Japan as part of their touring itineraries. When Kiss rose to mega-stardom later in the decade, it was almost a given that it would tour Japan as a mark of its expanding appeal. On another level, though, we can interpret the imagery evoked above to stand for an effort to make meaning out of the changing spatial dimensions of rock. The enlarged space of the rock concert and the growing contours of the rock tour were two sides of the changes that took hold in rock during the 1970s. Within this context, rhetoric and imagery based on the exoticizing tendencies of what John Urry (1990) has termed the "tourist gaze" assumed discursive power as a means of explaining the new scope of rock music and the rock industry.

Two bands exemplify these elements of arena rock during the 1970s. Kiss built a massive base of success through a regime of tireless touring and savvy marketing. Bursting into success during the American bicentennial year of 1976, the band moved onto the global stage the following year with a tour of Japan that exposed some of the more uneasy ideological elements that accompanied the movement of American rock into foreign terrain. A subsequent set of concert dates in Brazil showed how different locations were invested with very different meanings in the experience of a single band. Perhaps no band stood for the global dimensions of arena rock as powerfully as Led Zeppelin. As a British band that had achieved major touring success in the United States, Zeppelin was already working in an international frame. The group's travels through Asia and North Africa portrayed its members not only as expansive capitalists but as explorers whose endeavors held out the possibility for meaningful cultural exchange. Taken together, Kiss and Led Zeppelin embody the peculiar mix of global meanings that circulated within the spaces and along the paths of arena rock during the 1970s.

The two bands also indicate the centrality of heavy metal to the changes occurring in live rock performance during the decade. The critic Robert Duncan explored this connection in *The Noise*, his book on rock of the 1970s. Characterizing heavy metal as a distillation of the impulse toward

230 "loudness" that took hold in rock of the 1960s, Duncan described the genre in terms that fuse sound with economics: "*loudest* is not only the best and most important part of the heavy metal style, *loudest* is also why this style was so suited to the cavernous, sound-devouring arena and so to the economy of scale that would be the linchpin of mass production rock 'n' roll" (Duncan 1984, 39). While there were certainly many successful arena performers who did not fit the heavy metal category—from the aforementioned Stones to Elton John and Peter Frampton—heavy metal and its kissing cousin, hard rock, provided an abundance of bands that took full advantage of the new scale of rock performance.[5] Moreover, the arena became the paradigmatic live setting for the heavy metal concert. No other genre of the period assumed so much of its definition from the mass qualities of the arena gathering and the ritualized displays of power enacted within that space.[6]

Regarding the touring efforts of Kiss and Led Zeppelin, two sorts of tourism were most at issue: sex tourism and cultural tourism. In a sense, sex tourism is a central aspect of most heavy metal concert tours, or is at least central to the mythology surrounding such tours. Male musicians routinely seek female companionship on the road, and certain female fans are especially happy to fulfill that role—although the pleasure taken by female groupies is overdetermined by the male dominant sexual hierarchy at work in the world of rock. Within heavy metal, Kiss and Led Zeppelin have achieved considerable repute and infamy for their sexual exploits, which have been recounted in many of the media accounts and other publications surrounding the bands' respective careers. In this capacity it is not surprising that sexual exploits would become part of the larger circuit of narratives stemming from the travel of these bands overseas. However, such exploits arguably assume a different dimension in the context of foreign tours, where the sexual exchange system common to heavy metal is complicated by the cross-cultural exchanges that occur between Western musicians and non-Western female fans. Sex with local women becomes a part of what the male traveler seeks to consume, and the national or ethnic boundaries at play often promote the perception that those women exist as "imagined territories" awaiting libidinal conquest (Rojek and Urry 1997, 17).

Cultural tourism typically involves a very different set of practices. As the term implies, through cultural tourism, travelers seek direct contact with aspects of their destination that convey something distinct and meaningful about local customs, histories, or patterns of civilization and communication. Some of the most storied tourist destinations in the world are sites of cultural tourism, such as the pyramids of Egypt or the Sistine Chapel in Rome. More generally, cultural tourism tends to be highly mediated through various institutions—museums, churches, government agencies—that have been granted authority to represent the location to the traveling public. Tourists themselves are often aware of this mediated quality, but only the most privileged or the most savvy travelers are able to circumvent some of this mediation and achieve more unfiltered contact with the culture of their destination. Rock stars on tour belong to this most privileged class of travelers, at least when their tours are sponsored by major record corporations and professional management agencies. Whether these stars choose to use their privilege to gain more direct access to local cultures, though, varies considerably from case to case. As I will show, the members of Kiss tended not to prioritize such access, and to remain largely within their own self-designed "bubble." By contrast, the members of Led Zeppelin—especially singer Robert Plant and guitarist Jimmy Page—were dedicated and adventuresome cultural tourists whose explorations went so far as to have an impact on the band's music.

The cover of the second Kiss studio release, *Hotter Than Hell* (1974), featured a mélange of "Oriental" signifiers. A series of red and silver stripes form a frame around the cover image, suggesting the rays of the sun, while the band occupies the center of the cover, pictured as usual in full stage makeup and costume. The Kiss logo is in the upper left portion of the cover, in black and yellow letters against a red background; beneath the band's name are a set of Japanese characters written in blue, presumably spelling the Japanese translation of "Kiss." Similarly, each band member has his name spelled beside him in a vertical yellow bar with green lettering, in both English and Japanese characters. The album's title, "Hotter Than Hell," appears at the top center of the frame, presented as an arc of black letters against a yellow background; to the right of the title is another small strip of Japanese lettering in green, perhaps a translation of the cover though seeming to float in its own space. Viewed through this lens, the band's trademark black-and-white face makeup comes to resemble something out of the Japanese Kabuki theater, an association strengthened by Gene Simmons's hair style, tied into a bun atop his head. When asked about the Kabuki references, though, Gene Simmons denied any conscious effort on the band's part to draw upon Japanese traditions: "I didn't know the first thing about that. . . . The reason I put my hair in a top knot was so it wouldn't fall in my face. . . . When I looked at myself, I thought I looked like some ancient barbarian and I liked it. But certainly there wasn't meant to be any historical or cultural reference" (Swenson 1978, 100). Having disowned the attempt to draw upon Japanese culture, Simmons justifies the Kabuki-like quality of the cover by recounting how the Japanese loved it: "We put Japanese writing on it and everyone thought it was an album recorded in Japan" (Swenson 1978, 100).

Simmons's expressed attitude here foreshadows the perspective that Kiss would bring to its tour of Japan three years later, in 1977: Japanese cultural imagery is there to be used; the band members have no particular interest in the meaning of that imagery but are pleased that it earns them the appreciation of Japanese fans. According to C. K. Lendt, the former business manager for Kiss, the trip to Japan was largely organized as a publicity stunt to showcase the international reach of the band. To ensure that the tour received due notice, Kiss's management arranged for twelve U.S. journalists to accompany the band on tour, all expenses paid (Lendt 1997, 63). Among the more extensive accounts that resulted from this concerted effort at publicity engineering was a two-part story written by Jack Hiemenz, which appeared in *Circus*. Whereas *Circus* had chastised Kiss during an earlier overseas trip to London, the magazine upheld the band as veritable conquering heroes during its jaunt through Japan.[7] Journalist Hiemenz is particularly impressed by the sheer scope of the undertaking, as Kiss took its substantial entourage and extravagant stage props overseas to ensure that Japanese audiences received the full Kiss spectacle. Putting the band's achievement in perspective, Hiemenz observed, "Nobody, not even Bowie, has ever toured Japan with a set. Bringing it over in a 707 freighter has cost $80,000. Add to that the expense of bringing along thirteen crew members, ten executive staff members, and eleven journalists and what you get is a trial run costing over a half million" (Hiemenz 1977a, 39–40).[8] Commenting on the Kiss tour plan, Paul Stanley notes that he had felt "disoriented" during the group's tour of Europe due to the lack of familiar surroundings. "But, hey, if you bring thirty people along, you're set! We've taken our whole environment with us [to Japan]!" (Hiemenz 1977a, 40).

With privileged access inside the Kiss "environment," Hiemenz spends the second half of his two-part story discussing the more private dimensions of the tour. His ostensible topic is the difficulty of finding "friendship" on the road, but that emphasis quickly dissolves into a consideration of the sexual availability of Japanese women for the band. He expresses not only surprise, but almost offense, that Paul Stanley refrains from any sexual contact with the many Japanese women who offered their services to the members of Kiss. In a strikingly blatant statement of support for the logic of sex tourism that undergirds much of the myth of rock 'n' roll, Hiemenz proclaims, "Sex isn't just the urge for pleasure; it's curiosity. What better way of getting to know a foreign country . . . than by spending a couple nights with various womenfolk? . . . It's the promiscuous man who feels the greatest interest and zest for human kind in all its physical and social variety" (Hiemenz 1977b, 34). Fortunately for the writer, if Paul Stanley was unwilling to live out his program for the accumulation of sexual "knowledge," Gene Simmons was a ready participant. Hiemenz characterizes Simmons as a "satyr in the grand tradition" and happily notes that by this theory of sex as a path to cultural understanding, the bassist has "probably accumulated enough knowledge to fill a twenty-volume encyclopedia" (Hiemenz 1997b, 34). Portrayed as a sexual explorer, Simmons ensures that the band's demonstration of economic power in orchestrating a foreign tour of such massive proportions is fortified by a demonstration of sexual power.

On tour in Japan, the common rock practice of sex with groupies assumed the dimension of "eating the other," of playing upon racial and sexual difference as a means of heightening the pleasure of the sexual experience. As explained by bell hooks: "One dares—acts—on the assumption that the exploration into the world of difference, into the body of the Other, will provide a greater, more intense pleasure than any that exists in the ordinary world of one's familiar racial group" (1992, 24). Asian women have been especially subject to such desires as held by white American and European men. Stereotypes of "Oriental" women tend to emphasize their sexual desirability in terms of an odd mix of knowledge, innocence, and submissiveness. Simmons affirms these qualities in his autobiography, where he recalls in connection with the Japanese tour: "The interesting thing about Japanese women, in my experience, is that they have a little girl quality, a certain innocence about their sexuality. *Coquette* is a French word, and that concept just doesn't exist in Japan, at least as far as I saw. For instance, when Japanese girls orgasm, a peculiar sound emanates from them that almost sounds like a baby crying" (Simmons 2001, 133–34). Such crude typologies should not be surprising from a man who admits to having extensively catalogued his sexual exploits by photographing every woman with whom he had sex on tour. Distressing though his tendencies are, Simmons's exploits and his perception of the women he encountered cannot be explained by recourse to individual deviance. By hooks's terms, he was very much playing to type in his own right, as a man for whom racial difference accentuated the pleasure of sexual conquest.

Kiss toured Japan at a moment when its media presence was at its height. The tour of Japan consolidated the band's achievements, and showed it still expanding the horizons of its success. In 1980, by contrast, when Kiss's management began looking into the possibility of arranging concerts in Latin America, the band's fortunes had started to decline. No longer extending its commercial reach, the band was now in need of new markets, as the receptivity of American audiences was no longer as reliable as it had been just a couple of years earlier. Mexico was the first proposed location. A team of Mexican promoters presented a deal to the band that, at first, sounded exceptionally promising. Kiss would earn one million dollars for just four shows and would play in stadiums seating one hundred thousand people. When Kiss's management traveled to Mexico City to scout locations for the concerts, though, they were met with disappointment. By C. K. Lendt's account, "What they call stadiums in most Latin American countries are simply enormous concrete shells with tiers of concrete slabs for people to sit on. . . . I doubt there was enough electrical power in any of those places to run a toaster let alone 400,000 watts of sound and lights" (Lendt 1997, 210). Such facilities made the prospect of a Kiss concert seem "farcical" to Lendt, and the plan was abandoned.

Three years later, another prospect arose, this time in Brazil. Kiss was still facing unsure concert turnouts in the United States. In Brazil it would have occasion to play to as many as two hundred thousand people in a single stadium. The conditions were not dramatically different from those in Mexico, but the Brazilian promoter did the legwork to ensure that the tour could happen. In June 1983, Kiss arrived to play concerts in three Brazilian cities, the first of which in Rio de Janeiro was the largest of the band's career. Over one hundred thousand came to Maracana Stadium in Rio to see the band, which played a slightly scaled-down version of its full show. Writing about the concert, Lendt was struck by the difference of

the Brazilian concert dynamic from that in the United States: "The audience streamed through the gates and into the stadium all night, even after
Kiss went on around 10:30 p.m. Some people obviously had tickets, many
didn't. . . . The sound was often sludgy, with blotchy patches of feedback
cutting into the guitar solos. . . . But the fans were rabid over Kiss" (Lendt
1997, 279). Despite the success of the event, however, Lendt also recalls the
ambivalent response of the band members. Kiss principals Gene Simmons
and Paul Stanley—at this point the only two original members still in the
band—noted the impressive scale of the concert, but somehow "it didn't
seem to count with them. It wasn't America. Or England. Or Europe. Or
Australia. It was the Third World, a stew pot of cultures. It wasn't that important" (Lendt 1997, 280).

Lendt's remarks might seem the uncharitable views of a former employee. Yet it is telling that in Simmons's autobiography, the Brazilian concerts only merit about three sentences of indirect commentary, as opposed
to the three pages devoted to the Japanese tour. Simmons contrasts the
large audiences of Brazil with the band's dwindling fortunes in the United
States, and sums up his impressions as follows: "Even though the experience was depressing in some respects, it opened our eyes to the idea that
no one city and no one marketplace is definitive" (Simmons 2001, 188).
For Simmons, then, the Brazilian concerts had a purely economic meaning, educating the band in the utility of visiting uncharted markets. Regarding Japan, Simmons offers a very different characterization. Having
disowned his band's effort to deliberately draw upon Japanese cultural
imagery, he nonetheless claims an affinity between Kiss and the Japanese
audience. "We later learned that the Japanese fans felt a great kinship with
us because of our makeup, which looked like kabuki theater makeup," he
states, and then elaborates, "In the same way that some of our early American fans were black, because they didn't see us as either white or black,
the Japanese took to us because they didn't see us as American or Asian"
(Simmons 2001, 133). For Simmons, then, the enthusiasm of Japanese
fans indicated not so much the particular attraction of those fans as the
universalism of Kiss's appeal, which was grounded in the band members'
masks and their fabricated personae. Because Japan was a civilized—albeit
exotic—location, the interest of the Japanese in Kiss had an impact on the
band that the more "third world" surroundings of Latin America could not.
Nevertheless, both concert tours demonstrated the capacity for arena rock

to be reproduced abroad along with the more routine commodities that have contributed to the global distribution of popular music.

Spring 1970: Led Zeppelin members Robert Plant, singer, and Jimmy Page, guitarist, retreat to an isolated cottage in Wales after spending the first two years of the band's existence maintaining a grueling tour schedule. Bron-Y-Aur, as the cottage was named, provided much desired rural tranquility for a band that had spent the preceding months immersed in the intensively public sphere of the rock concert tour. For Page and Plant, though, their stay at Bron-Y-Aur was no mere idyll. Having written and recorded the songs for their second album in between the concerts of an American tour, the pair hoped to allow themselves time to renew their creative chemistry. In keeping with the rustic setting, Page and Plant concentrated upon writing songs that featured acoustic guitar, the only instrument that they had between them; as Page later recalled, "The only electricity [at the cottage] was in the cassette recorders we had for reference" (Resnicoff 1990, 54). Playing to the recorders, often in the midst of wandering the countryside, the two musicians wrote the basis for a number of songs that would appear on Zeppelin albums throughout the 1970s (Sutcliffe 2000). They would also determine the tone for their next record, *Led Zeppelin III*, which was received as a serious departure for the "heavy" band upon its release in late 1970. Featuring a mostly electric first side and a second side of predominantly acoustic songs, *Led Zeppelin III* also included a dedication to Bron-Y-Aur on its inside cover that credited the cottage for "painting a somewhat forgotten picture of true completeness which acted as an incentive to some of these musical statements."

As much as the tenure at Bron-Y-Aur shaped the immediate direction of Zeppelin's music, it was perhaps more important for its long-term influence. Said Page, recollecting the experience, "The songs took us into areas that changed the band, and it established a standard of travelling for inspiration . . . which is the best thing a musician can do" (Yorke 1993, 110). Unlike Kiss, for whom touring foreign locations was principally of financial consequence, Led Zeppelin partook of a far more culturally driven form of travel, one that wasn't strictly tied to the touring regimen. Indeed, travel became something of an escape from touring for the members of Zeppelin; travel was leisure, despite its productive results, whereas touring was done as labor. At the same time, travel allowed the members of Led Zeppelin to live out certain fantasies of exploration, with the band seeking musical spoils that they could exploit to expand their creative reach. Susan Fast notes this tendency in her study of Led Zeppelin, particularly in connection with the band's fascination with "the East." Discussing the band's predilection for roaming through musical cultures, she describes the group's effort to present itself as "a filter through which various musics are passed and then offered up, in an 'original' way, to the listener" (Fast 2001, 86). In the era of arena rock, such wide-ranging affinities could be taken to embody the expansiveness of the form. Like Kiss, Led Zeppelin brought rock to faraway territories, but unlike Kiss, the members of Led Zeppelin absorbed some of the substance of those locations into their music.

Six years prior to Kiss's tour of Japan, in 1971 Led Zeppelin staged its own first tour of the country. It was conducted with far less fanfare than Kiss's enterprise, Zeppelin never having been quite so preoccupied with the orchestration of publicity as its costumed counterparts. Nonetheless, it represented a milestone in the scope of Zeppelin's touring efforts, and opened what would be a continuing circuit of travel between members of the group and "the East"—the Far East, South and Southeast Asia, and the Middle East of Arabic North Africa. The lead song from *Led Zeppelin III*, "The Immigrant Song," had reached the number one spot on the Japanese music charts at the time of the group's arrival, so Led Zeppelin was poised for success with the country's audiences; and indeed, the tour was successful enough that the band carried out another visit to Japan the following year, 1972 (Davis 1985, 147).

As notable as Zeppelin's tour of Japan was, two other non-concert destinations reveal more about the band's traveling ethos. Immediately following the tour, while bassist John Paul Jones, drummer John Bonham, and manager Peter Grant returned to England, Jimmy Page, Robert Plant, and tour manager Richard Cole continued traveling to other parts of Asia. The first stop was Bangkok where the band engaged in a bit of cultural tourism, visiting some Buddhist temples and a museum, and indulged in a full-scale bout of sex tourism in the city's well-known red-light district that, according to Cole's account, taxed all their stamina to the point that Page remarked, "They must have invented the term 'fucking your brains out' here" (Cole and Trubo 1992, 196–97). The trio then flew to Bombay for a four-day stay, where Page harbored a different sort of desire, the desire to record and collaborate with local musicians. That desire would remain unfulfilled on this visit, but would prompt Page and Plant to return just a few months later, on the heels of the group's first concert tour of Australia and New Zealand.

ARENAS OF THE IMAGINATION

When the two bandmates returned to Bombay in March 1972, Page came equipped with a sophisticated Stellavox field recorder with which he walked the streets, seeking to capture the sounds of street musicians — an effort that was routinely made difficult by the crowds that would be drawn whenever Page set up his machine (Davis 1985, 157). The heart of the visit was a recording session arranged by Page and Plant with the help of a local contact, during which they performed arrangements of two of the group's most non-Western-inflected songs, "Friends" from *Led Zeppelin III* and "Four Sticks" from its newly issued fourth, untitled album. Several takes of each song were recorded, though none were officially released.[9] Plant recalled the difficulty of working with Indian musicians: "It's very hard for them to cope with the Western approach to music with their counting and everything. . . . Where we count four beats to the bar, their bars just carry on and on" (Sauer 2003). The British musicians spent much of the session trying to communicate the sound they wanted to their Indian counterparts, a dynamic that suggests that something less than full collaboration was pursued by Page and Plant; they seemed to want to train the Indian musicians to their already established perceptions of Indian music. Still, the session had considerable significance for the members of Led Zeppelin as a first effort to bring what Davis called their "East/West fusion dream" to fruition (Davis 1985, 158).

This "dream" of cultural fusion became a key part of the Zeppelin mystique over the course of the 1970s, weaving its way into stories about the band as well as into further elements of the group's discography. Profiling Led Zeppelin for *Circus*, upon the release of its album *Houses of the Holy* in 1973, Barbara Graustark commented upon the influence of the band's travels upon its members' songwriting, citing a verse from the album's opening track as evidence of the group's global imagination: "California sunlight, sweet Calcutta rain/Honolulu starbright — the song remains the same" (Graustark 1973). Interviewed by the same magazine in 1975, Robert Plant made much of his taste for adventure and for encountering unfamiliar locations. He discussed a recent expedition made by himself and Page to the West Indies, casting the local population as a group of primitives who balance Catholic observance with "their beliefs from way, way back," and expressing excitement over arriving at a location with "seventy-thousand black people . . . and about a hundred whites" (Demorest 1975, 29). His greatest enthusiasm, though, was reserved for his memory of a visit to Morocco, which served as inspiration for Led Zeppelin's most epic

piece of exotica, "Kashmir," a song included on the newest album by the
band, *Physical Graffiti*.[10] Plant's account of the experience is worth citing
in full:

> I went to Morocco. It was the first time I started gettin' away to other
> lands without an entourage of people or as a member of a band. . . .
> The nearer I got to the Sahara, this atmosphere beckoned me to open
> my eyes in another way. . . . The people in the mountains, the Berbers
> and the people beyond there, have all these dances to Pan and I knew
> they were there. Occasionally you could ride into the hills and see these
> people watching as you went by and you got this fantastic feeling, as if
> you were going through a no-man's land between Kashmir and India.
> There's an area there, a no-man's land between the borders, where all
> the Bhutan warriors sit with their horses and muskets, waiting for the
> tourists . . . I really dig adventure. So lyrically something like "Kashmir"
> extends that. And at the end of the song I'm almost satisfied as if I've
> just done the whole trip (Demorest 1975, 29).

The desert, in Plant's story, assumes significance as a location the vast-
ness of which changes the way he looks at the land in front of him. No
longer a particular place in Morocco, it becomes an almost mythical "no-
man's land" where Plant feels his difference from his surroundings most
acutely. Intriguingly, this supposedly unpopulated landscape gains some
of its power from the sense that native eyes are watching, perhaps with a
threatening gaze. This sense of being watched becomes part of the uncan-
niness of the experience for Plant, but as such generates not fear but the
"fantastic feeling" of being in a truly unfamiliar type of place, the nature
of which he sought to express in his lyric for "Kashmir."

By the time Plant visited Morocco, it was already a much-hallowed place
among a certain subset of American and European bohemia. The literary
scholar Greg Mullins has drawn attention to the unique character of the
Moroccan city of Tangier in particular, which was established in 1923 as
an "international zone" to keep the strategic port city open to trade and
to avoid its domination by any single foreign power (Mullins 2002, 4).
Over the next several decades, a coterie of influential artists and intellectuals made Tangier into a destination, and often a place of self-imposed
exile, where they could enjoy the pleasures of a genuinely cosmopolitan
city while also having ready access to the "old" ways of the Arabic world.
Among these figures was the American Paul Bowles, who made Tangier his

permanent home, though perhaps more prominent were the writers of the Beat Generation, especially William Burroughs, who took up residence in Tangier for a number of years beginning in the mid-1950s. Burroughs and his companion and creative partner Brion Gysin were among the first Westerners to bring attention to the distinctive musical life of the area, and through their influence a number of musicians made veritable pilgrimages to Morocco, the most famous of whom was Brian Jones, the guitarist for the Rolling Stones, who released a recording that he made of the Master Musicians of Jajouka in the late 1960s.[11]

Plant gives little indication of having followed in the footsteps of these figures in his travels—he is most impressed not by the trappings of Tangier or the sound of local musicians, but by the sheer space he encounters in the desert. Jimmy Page is a different matter, though. In 1975 he was interviewed by none other than Burroughs for *Crawdaddy* magazine. The article, titled "Rock Magic," begins with Burroughs offering his own impressions of a Led Zeppelin concert. The sheer volume, combined with the "evocation and transmutation of energy" that he perceives, leads the writer to associate Zeppelin's musical effects with those achieved by Moroccan musicians. "The Led Zeppelin show depends heavily on volume, repetition, and drums," observed Burroughs, who continues, "It bears some resemblance to the trance music found in Morocco, which is magical in origin and purpose—that is, concerned with the evocation and control of spiritual forces" (Burroughs 1975, 35). When the interview commences, Burroughs immediately states this association to Page, who assents cautiously. The guitarist is forced to admit that he has not been to Morocco, but refers to "Kashmir" as evidence of the band's interest in such music, and asserts, "I'm very involved in ethnic music from all over the world" (Burroughs 1975, 39). For Burroughs, the association with Morocco is not merely one of style but of the dynamic between artist and audience, a subject that occupies much of the subsequent conversation. As the interview winds to a close, Page refers to the "rhythms within the audience" and suggests that "music which involves riffs . . . will have a trance-like effect, and it's really like a mantra . . . And we've been attacked for that" (Burroughs 1975, 40). Through his conversation with Burroughs, Page comes to explain the effect of Zeppelin's music as a channeling of energy based upon non-Western practices of disorienting the relationship between mind and body through the manipulation of sound.

Shortly after his interview with Burroughs, Page accompanied Plant on a trip to Morocco; he would later credit the novelist with having inspired him to do so (Tolinski and DiBenedetto 1997). The plan was similar to that governing their earlier travels in India, something of a field expedition to record and absorb the sounds of local musicians. Yet political conflicts between Spain and Morocco impeded their access; the privileges of stardom could only take them so far in the face of colonial tensions. Despite the limitations of the trip, Page still seemed to have been quite affected by it. Interviewed in March 1976 by *Melody Maker*, as the new Zeppelin album *Presence* was about to be released, Page attributed to Morocco a marked if undefined influence upon the band's current music: "I couldn't say that there was a number built around Moroccan rhythm on the new LP, but I definitely learned a lot from Morocco which I can relate to on songs" (Doherty 1976, 8). His subsequent explanation of the power of Moroccan music seemed to mimic his encounter with Burroughs; characterizing it as "trance music," he proclaimed that "when you see the sort of things that are done by the power of music as such, one couldn't help but sort of re-assess what one thought one knew already" (Doherty 1976, 8).

In the introduction to the collection, *Western Music and Its Others*, Georgina Born asks whether the musical appropriation of otherness can ever be understood apart from issues of domination, as a matter of "simple aesthetic difference" (Born and Hesmondhalgh 2000, 41). The spirit of her question underlies much of Susan Fast's analysis of Led Zeppelin with regard to its fascination with non-Western music. Seeking to avoid stark conclusions about the appropriative tendencies of Zeppelin, Fast asks, "What references to Eastern musics can be heard in Led Zeppelin and how are these heard?" (Fast 2001, 92). For Fast, the main implication of "Kashmir," a song she analyzes with impressive detail, is the way it stages a "blurring" of identities between East and West; and this blurring is largely indeterminate with regard to the broader politics of appropriation. She does not entirely let the band off the hook for its idealized interactions with the music and musicians of India and Morocco, but she does emphasize that Page and Plant have often seemed more self-effacing in these circumstances than have other musicians of similar influence.

Fast's emphasis upon the complexity of Led Zeppelin's Eastern front is well-taken, though in these matters I would tend to favor the views of Steven Feld, who argues that under the current globalization of musical commodities, the "escalation—of difference, power, rights, control, ownership, authority—politicizes the schizophonic practices artists could once claim more innocently as matters of inspiration, or as purely artistic dialogue of imitation and inspiration" (Feld 2000a, 264).[12] However, I am less concerned with staking a position in the debate over cultural appropriation than I am with situating Zeppelin's musical encounters in its time. The ventures of Page and Plant are part of a larger history of travel and tourism in which travelers seek to acquire something of the culture of their destination. One of the paradoxes of this form of cultural tourism has been pointed out by the tourism scholar Jennifer Craik: "the cultural experiences offered by tourism are consumed in terms of prior knowledge, expectations, fantasies and mythologies generated in the tourists' origin culture rather than by the cultural offerings of the destination" (Craik 1997, 118). Evidence of this dynamic can be seen in the largely unsuccessful effort at collaboration between Page and Plant and local musicians in Bombay, whom the rock musicians criticized for their inability to adapt to the regularities of Western musical practice. As much as Page and Plant were driven by a dream of cross-cultural collaboration, they could not leave their existing cultural assumptions behind them.

Connected as they are to larger patterns of tourism, the travels of Led Zeppelin are also, importantly, part of the history of rock music during the 1970s, a decade during which the group was consistently one of the top-drawing concert acts. That Page and Plant first visited India together on their way back from a tour of Japan evinces a connection between their musical adventurousness and the expanding circuit of concert performance during the decade; that they sought collaboration with Indian musicians but not with those in Japan suggests that there was still a gap between locations considered suitable for musical tourism and those that were targeted more strictly as markets. There is another key layer of significance here, which is alluded to by the critic Ann Powers's assessment of Zeppelin's appeal. "Jimmy Page and Robert Plant didn't become the world's foremost monster rockers on dumb luck—these two have a knack for making music big enough for any number of fans to live inside at once," states Powers. "This is why people hated them: they took up so much space. And it's why people loved them: that space could swallow you up, take you in" (Powers 1994, 69). Part of the way that Led Zeppelin "took up space" was through the band members' travels across geographic boundaries, and the traces their travels left upon their music. Meanwhile, their concerts, pushing at the capacity of the arenas and stadiums in which they played, dramatized the band's ability to fill space both literally and symbolically.

With the rise of arena rock, the rock concert became a new sort of commodity, not only due to its size but also due to its capacity to be reproduced and exported. The simultaneity of rock's move into the arena and its expansion into foreign markets was more than coincidence, but as the examples of Kiss and Led Zeppelin demonstrate, the processes involved and the meanings generated by these developments were far from unified. One can exaggerate the differences between Kiss and Led Zeppelin where their attitudes to foreign tours and non-Western locations were concerned. After all, the members of Led Zeppelin were as likely as those of Kiss to cast their travels through the Far East in terms of sexual adventure; as Robert Plant once said, "We can't be considered anthropologists or anything like that, but we knew of a few good brothels in the Far East" (Considine 1990, 60). Nonetheless, clear distinctions still exist.

Kiss and its surrounding organization perceived the band and its concerts to constitute a total environment to be exported and performed with little input from the surrounding destinations. In a sense, Kiss refined the process whereby the rock concert became a reproduced cultural form that generated revenue from a variety of sources, including ticket sales as well as a range of other merchandise—shirts, tour books, posters—for which the band had a pioneering marketing structure. Intriguingly, given the group's preoccupation with the bottom line, its foreign tours seemed to have been conducted as much to satisfy the demands of cultural capital as of strictly economic capital. How else to explain the remarkable outlay for publicity that the band undertook for its Japanese tour, ensuring that its exploits would receive ample coverage in the American rock press? A Japanese tour was itself a symbol of status in the expansionist world of 1970s rock, and the band's reception bolstered at least one member's conviction that the appeal of Kiss was universal. Latin America did not occupy the same space in the band's cultural imaginary, but again, status was as much at issue as finance. Facing diminishing concert attendance after years of performing to capacity crowds across the United States, Kiss played in Brazil as much to prove that it could still draw a crowd as to reap financial reward. In this regard, arena rock seems to have generated a self-perpetuating mechanism wherein the crowd itself was a measure of success, to be pursued at greater and greater lengths.

Led Zeppelin's ability to draw a crowd was rarely challenged. Even during the decline in the fortunes of heavy metal in the late 1970s, the band managed a triumphant festival performance at Knebworth in England in front of over one hundred thousand fans. Not that Zeppelin was immune from the dictates of capital where live performance was concerned. Led by its manager, Peter Grant, the group was infamous for taking the largest percentage of gate receipts (90 percent) of any touring band of the era. Where foreign tours and travels were concerned, though, the members of Zeppelin seemed to regard their pursuits as some odd combination of financial endeavor, luxury expense, and fieldwork. Regarding their fascination with "the East," variously conceived, the members of Zeppelin were arguably no less subject to exoticizing assumptions than Gene Simmons. Yet the species of cross-cultural imagination that Plant and Page evinced was one in which knowledge of the other culture was not so much taken for granted. Mingling their concert tours with other types of travel more akin to cultural tourism, the members of Led Zeppelin made the exploration of cultural and geographic difference an integral part of their creative process. In so doing, they put forth the possibility that the exportation of the rock concert to locations far afield could produce something other than strictly economic forms of exchange.[13]

Indeed, as other essays in this volume suggest, the visitation of Anglo-American rock stars to non-Western countries could have a galvanizing effect on local musicians and the formation of local music scenes, whatever the attitudes of the stars in question. Fortunately, where the politics of popular music are concerned, the ideologies that govern the work of cultural producers do not have a determining influence. Those ideologies remain a key part of the story of rock, though, for what they reveal about the values that internationally successful bands brought with them on tour, and the values that were transmitted in turn to the audience that read about their touring adventures in the rock press of the day. In that light, sex tourism and cultural tourism provided two prominent frameworks that gave shape to the global travels of star performers such as Kiss and Led Zeppelin. These two types of pursuit corresponded to two distinct fantasies, one in which masculinity was reinforced through the consumption of sexual and racial difference, the other in which creative artistry was strengthened through encounters with, and to some degree absorption of, foreign elements. Both of these fantasies were part of the rich mix of material and symbolic factors that combined to define the internationalization of heavy metal in the formative decade of the 1970s.

1   *Editors' Note*: Incidentally, "Bechuanaland" is the obsolete British colonial name for the country of Botswana, which in the present day happens to be home to one of sub-Saharan Africa's largest metal scenes (see Nilsson 2009).

2   The most thorough account of these changes can be found in Chapple and Garofalo 1977 (137–54). Chapple and Garofalo argue that the modern rock concert circuit began to crystallize in the late 1960s with the rise of ballrooms such as Bill Graham's Fillmore West and Fillmore East, in San Francisco and New York, respectively. These ballrooms, which typically held about two thousand people, were quickly rendered obsolete as the scale of rock concerts grew precipitously, and almost all had folded by 1971. At that point, arenas and stadiums were clearly established as the favored sites for rock concerts in the United States, and over the rest of the decade they would give rise to a concert industry that was notable for the sheer amount of revenue it generated, and for its concentration in the hands of a small number of promoters who exerted considerable power over the shape of tours.

3   The information here is drawn from a meticulously compiled Rolling Stones fan Web site created by Ian McPherson (2004), which provides a complete touring history of the band, broken down by country, region, and city. This site can be accessed at http://www.timeisonourside.com.

4   The classic account of tourism along these lines is by Dean MacCannell (1976). John Urry (1990) updates MacCannell's framework in many ways but largely retains the emphasis on tourism as a mode of modern leisure activity. For a more recent theoretical overview of the cultural and political dimensions of tourism, see Meethan 2001.

5   Deena Weinstein (2000) discusses the slippery boundary between heavy metal and hard rock. She characterizes Kiss as a band that was more properly termed hard rock than metal because of the melodicism of its music (20). Based on my research of the period, this seems an anachronistic judgment, as Kiss was routinely discussed in terms of heavy metal during much of its career in the 1970s.

6   Weinstein, again, argues for the central role of the concert in the construction of the heavy metal genre. See Weinstein 2000, 199–235.

7   Reporting on Kiss's appearance in London, Gary Herman likened the group to Nazi invaders, and said of the band in concert: "[Kiss] bully their audience, assault them and cajole them until, by the end of the set, everybody falls in line and gets up to stomp and shout" (Herman 1976, 27).

8   Lendt puts the figure at something closer to $250,000, still a substantial sum for 1977 (1997, 64).

9   These recordings have appeared on many bootleg releases of Led Zeppelin studio work. I have not had occasion to listen to them, unfortunately.

10 Fast (2001) analyzes "Kashmir" in extensive detail; see 92–111. I have also discussed the song at some length in Waksman (1999, 271–72), concentrating upon the remade version done by Page and Plant for their 1994 *No Quarter* project.

11 Details of Jones's travels in Morocco and his connection with Burroughs and Gysin can be found in Booth (1985, 332–42).

12 "Schizophonia" is a term coined by R. Murray Schafer to refer to the splitting of sounds from their geographic point of origin. Feld has developed a sophisticated rubric around the term in a series of essays. See Schafer (1977); Feld (1994).

13 *Editors' Note*: A further phase in metal concerts' global expansion is depicted in the film *Iron Maiden: Flight 666* (Dunn and McFadyen 2009), which follows the legendary British group on a worldwide tour in a modified jumbo jet piloted by Bruce Dickinson, the band's lead singer. This unique traveling arrangement allows the band to play concerts in places it had never visited before, including two dates in India (Mumbai and Bangalore) and the largest concert event ever in the history of Costa Rica. In February 2011, during their third tour to make use of the customized jumbo jet, Iron Maiden (a band mentioned more than twenty separate times in this book) traveled to Southeast Asia for the first time in its long career, playing concerts in Singapore, Jakarta, and Bali.

THUNDER IN THE FAR EAST

The Heavy Metal Industry in 1990s Japan

Kei Kawano and Shuhei Hosokawa

"To speak with irony, the Japanese heavy metal market resembles the Galapagos Islands." Thus Hiroshi Arishima, a music critic, underlined Japan's isolation from the worldwide evolution of a genre called heavy metal (interview, 1998). The Galapagos metaphor implied for him a local particularity disconnected from the wider world; proof of this isolation is in the fact that Japan embraces bands that are passé or have never been popular in the United States and the United Kingdom. According to an American music business guide, "There have also been many cases of rock performers who have gone out of fashion in *one part of the world* and *yet* are able to mount hugely successful tours in *other regions*" (Lathrop and Pettigrew 1999, 248, our emphasis). This passage can be said to prove true the sarcastic saying "big in Japan." The word "yet," relating here ("one part of the world") with there ("other regions"), is heavily loaded with a value judgment: fashionable versus obsolete. The judgment is often based on nothing more than the temporal and aesthetic closeness to or distance from American (and British) trends.

Some people believe that "catching up" with international trends is imperative and pleasurable in itself: being "international" is regarded as superior to being "national" or "regional." In order to look into the local cultural conditions that have introduced a temporal and aesthetic gap in a seemingly universal music market, in this essay we investigate how journalists and record companies treat and promote foreign acts, how genre rules function, and the kinds of local and global conditions that underlie the Galapagos metaphor. We will also focus on the editorial practices of *Burrn!*, the only major Japanese heavy metal magazine, which profoundly influences the contours of the genre's market, and argue that the importance of the Japanese heavy metal industry lies not only in the size of the market but also in its musical divergence from American and British trends and concepts. In our discussion we will use the term "transterritorial" to describe a particular type of geographical distribution of cultural (musical) products that extends beyond domestic borders to reach a distant territory without having to pass through a regional mass market first. We will also discuss the flexible position of heavy metal in both the mainstream and the fringe of the Japanese music industry.

The Japanese heavy metal community is characterized by (1) the marginality of homegrown bands; (2) the relatively large audience for bands from non-Anglophone countries; (3) a sustained following of "classical/traditional" heavy metal style (as defined by Weinstein, 1991, 8); (4) a scarcity of radio and television exposure; (5) the centrality of recorded sound in the audiences' experience; and (6) the power of *Burrn!* to define the movement and the genre. These intertwined characteristics result from the interplay between bands, agents, journalists, record labels, and fans.

Since we conducted this research around 1998–99, parts of the following picture may be less applicable to today. Ten years ago, for example, neither file sharing nor blogs were known and the impact of the Internet was still limited. However, glancing at the latest issues of *Burrn!*, we have noticed little change in the editorial policy and the magazine manages to maintain a high profile in the metal community.

From 1969 on, "hard rock" bands became so fashionable in the nascent rock scene that several Japanese (and Okinawan) bands adopted their style in the early 1970s. Most of these bands performed at American military bases and small venues because their music was not mass-oriented. In fact, the Japanese fan base for hard rock was so limited in the early 1970s that Led Zeppelin's Budokan concerts (October 1972) failed to sell out. Organizing Japanese tours for foreign artists in those days was, according to Kazuhiko Endô, the managing director of Udô Creative Artists—one of Japan's oldest and largest booking agents—a "very risky business" (interview, 1998). Only well-established groups could tour in the Far East, including Deep Purple (1972 and 1975), Cheap Trick, and Judas Priest (both in 1978). We should also note that the Budokan venue became internationally known not as a result of the Beatles concerts that took place there in 1966 (without an official "live" album documenting them), but through a series of "live" albums by hard rock groups. Hard rock, a genre privileging "live" recording, was not only symbolic of colossal spectacle: the release of "live" albums recorded in Japan also initiated Japan's entry into the global popular music market (see Waksman, this volume).

Since Japanese radio was reluctant to play hard rock, which did not always fit Japanese restrictive broadcast formats (AM was talk-oriented, while FM was dominated by pop and Western classical music), so-called rock cafés (*rokku kissa*) were principal sites for the hard rock audience in the 1970s. These small establishments, like jazz cafés, owned superb playback equipment and extensive record collections and played music that was usually undervalued by the mass media at a volume that would be prohibitive in the average Japanese residence. The patrons at these establishments were required to keep silent for the sake of concentrated listening. Some rock cafés invited knowledgeable DJs/collectors to present special events such as "Hard Rock Night." Throughout the 1970s, many future rock and heavy metal critics disseminated a sound little recognized by the Japanese mass media through rock cafés, where the recorded sound was crucial.

According to the owner of Shinjuku Record, a famous rock record shop, heavy metal came to be recognized as such in 1980 when Masanori Itô introduced the British band Iron Maiden to Japan (interview, 1998). Many acknowledge the key role played by "Heavy Metal Soundhouse," a show Itô presented at the Tsubaki House in Shinjuku, Tokyo, beginning in March 1981. His inspiration was DJ Neale Kay's heavy metal disco in London, one of the igniting sparks of the New Wave of British Heavy Metal (NWOBHM) (Itô 1993, 90). The difference between Tsubaki House and a typical rock café was its audience capacity (approximately one thousand people) and the lack of seats. Therefore the Soundhouse could simulate a real concert better than a rock café. The Japanese tours by Iron Maiden and Saxon in 1981 also clearly contributed to the formation of a metal community.

Jun Fukatami, the vice director of the Foreign Music Department at Mercury Records, Universal's label, remembers the sudden increase of titles in the rack marked "Hard Rock/Heavy Metal" around 1981 in a record shop where he worked part-time: "Expensive British imports—3,500 to 4,000 yen (approximately US\$30–35)—sold like crazy" (interview, 1998). Fukatami's career path from a part-time clerk to the editor-in-chief of *Metal Gear* magazine (*Burrn!*'s short-lived rival) to record company vice director is not atypical. He is among the many enthusiasts-cum-businesspersons in the heavy metal industry, because working in a niche market requires highly specialized knowledge and contacts.

BURRN!: THE WORLD'S HEAVIEST HEAVY METAL MAGAZINE

In October 1984 the first heavy metal magazine in Japan, *Burrn!*, was launched with Ozzy Osbourne on the cover. In contrast to many heavy metal periodicals in the United States and Europe that are weekly or bi-weekly, tabloid, and news-oriented, the monthly *Burrn!* tends to feature longer articles and sophisticated artwork. Its self-characterization as "the world's heaviest heavy metal magazine" could be interpreted literally: a typical issue is 200 pages and weighs 450 grams.

The editors of *Burrn!* boasted that it was the "largest Western popular music magazine in Japan" with a self-reported circulation of 150,000 copies (Sakai 1991, 205). The magazine sold more than general rock and pop magazines. In Kô Sakai's view, this was because heavy metal fans are more eager to know about music and artists than the general audience for rock and pop (Sakai 1991, 221). Singers who sell millions of records do not necessarily sell millions of magazines. Information on mainstream rock and pop is omnipresent in Japan, and their fans are more or less content with predigested, readily available material. The success of *Burrn!* may be due to the otherwise limited media exposure of heavy metal and the relatively high ratio of dedicated listeners to casual ones.

The inauguration of *Burrn!* fortuitously coincided with both the ascension of metal bands based in Los Angeles (known as L.A. metal) and the expansive growth of Japan's economy. Bands such as Mötley Crüe, Quiet Riot, and Dokken launched highly successful Japanese tours in the mid-1980s. With its growing entertainment industry, Japan was no longer a risky venture for foreign artists but a promising one. *Metal Gear* magazine estimated (August 1989, 115) that the share of heavy metal records in total foreign music sales rose from less than 5 percent in 1985 to more than 15 percent in 1988 (note that the market share of foreign music was approximately 35 percent of total record sales in Japan at the time). The late 1980s arguably marked the peak of popularity of heavy metal in Japan. The subsequent diversification of the genre into commercial metal, death metal, and many others from the 1990s onward made it difficult for Japanese metal fans to maintain unity under one flag.

Burrn!'s interviews with the artists featured on its covers are a main attraction for the magazine's readers. These are a way for journalists to gain credibility with the bands and their agents, who, in turn, allow the *Burrn!* writers to attend recording sessions and concerts abroad in order to provide advanced publicity for Japanese readers. Interviews in Japan are arranged through agreements between the artist's agent, the booking agent, the record company, and the magazine. Good interviewers can gain the trust of artists. In 1987 Masanori Itô, heavy metal's "guru"—a title used with both respect and irony—was named the exclusive band interviewer for Bon Jovi by Jon Bon Jovi himself (Itô 1993, 82). The interviews thus reinforce relationships not only between the artists and the readers/listeners but also among various intermediaries in the industry. Many of the interviews in *Burrn!* are accompanied by the word "EXCLUSIVE" in large letters. However, a member of KISS once mockingly told the magazine's editor-in-chief that the "exclusivity" makes sense only when applied to the world's top artists: "Who else wants to interview [obscure German bands] Gamma Ray or Heaven's Gate?" (Hirose 1994, 34).

In addition to interviews, *Burrn!* publishes columns dealing with the off-stage antics of foreign musicians. Usually the band members travel throughout Japan assisted by the staff of their Japanese booking agent, the A & R person, and at least one *Burrn!* writer. While interviews with musicians usually emphasize their transcendental artistry, the off-stage report purports to reveal the true-to-life personalities and everyday lives of the same individuals.

Such sympathetic portraits maximize the illusion of intimacy with fans. Creating a sense of intimacy, or "humanizing the celebrity," is one of the most fundamental tactics for mass appeal in the Japanese mass media (see Stevens and Hosokawa 2001). These columns seem to be addressed more to female readers than to male readers due to their rhetorical similarity to celebrity coverage in Japanese women's magazines (judging from the reader's letters, not a few women regularly read the magazine). The columns never refer to sex, drugs, violence, or alcoholism, evils often associated with heavy metal. Such a moral code stems from a concern with protecting individuals and the community from social condemnation, rather than from simple self-censorship. Violence, overdoses, and promiscuity, the magazine tacitly insists, are old myths that today's heavy metal has left behind (Itô 1993, 101). The humanized depiction of visiting artists thus "sanitizes" the scene.

Burrn!'s "international" importance is indexed by copy such as "subscriptions from overseas" and "We are looking for your demo!" printed in English. No other music periodicals in Japan exhibit such a friendly stance toward non-Japanese new bands and readership. The demo tapes/CDs and self-produced albums received by *Burrn!* come not only from Japan, the United States, and the United Kingdom but also from Argentina, Brazil, Finland, Italy, and many other countries. These receive brief comments in the "Demolition" column.

Any genre-specific magazine sooner or later faces the conundrum of defining the genre. A genre is defined through commercial needs and fans' expectations (Frith 1996). For Keith Negus, genre expectations are circulated through the media and can provide incentives and impose constraints upon musicians (1999, 29). Robert Walser notes that heavy metal magazines usually hold contradictory policies: on the one hand, they strive to appear as inclusive as possible in order to attract as many readers as possible. On the other, they must cautiously exclude bands that fans do not accept as metal because including them will "weaken the magazine's credibility"; the magazine thus becomes "a site for contestation of the term." (1993a, 4). An extended definition may dilute the "essence" of a genre, but a restrictive one may make the magazine detached from the latest fashion and cause a drop in circulation. *Burrn!* repeatedly raises the question of what heavy metal is and is not, especially when new sounds challenge the genre rules. It seems to us that the magazine tries to be more authoritative than its Western counterparts. Kazuo Hirose, *Burrn!*'s editor-in-chief at the time, recognized the impossibility of strict definition and believed that it was the editorial staff that set genre rules (interview, 1998). Therefore the "heavy metal" of *Burrn!* can be different from that defined by other magazines. The former editor-in-chief proudly claimed that the other metal magazines established around the late 1980s (folding shortly thereafter) were merely a "pseudo-metal press" (Sakai 1991, 208). The more the magazine defined the genre by its own rules, the more the Japanese notion of heavy metal diverged from American and British ones, to the extent that the head of the foreign music department at Victor claimed bluntly, "There is no heavy metal in America as *Burrn!* defines it" (Katsunori "KATZ" Ueda, interview, 1998). This was, of course, less a reality and more the impression of one particular heavy metal expert. Significantly, he regards the imagined difference between the definitions as positive: the United States, in his view, has loosened the genre definition while Japan continues to respect it.

CLASSICIZING METAL

The predilection for "classical/traditional" (or "old wave") heavy metal among Japanese fans is often explained by a domestic sensibility of *yôshikibi*, which means "stylistic beauty" or "style aesthetic." The term is often applied to Japanese classical/traditional arts that are related to the discipline and practice of *kata*, an aesthetic of pattern-style-form (see Hosokawa 1999, 524 ff.). In the case of heavy metal, the style aesthetic includes the power chord introduction, an intense riff, stable 4/4 meter, "lyrical" melodic line (preferably in a minor key, which is supposed to touch Japanese heartstrings), chord progressions based on predictable functional harmony, "weeping" guitar, a superb solo, a dramatic storyline (in the case of a concept album), adaptation of orchestral music, and other elements. According to one music writer, the "style aesthetic" is especially dominant in Japan and Germany (Tôgô 1998).

One element of this "style aesthetic" is singing in English. Heavy metal, along with jazz vocals, is explicitly English-language dominant, which distinguishes it from global genres in which the use of local languages is more frequent. Members of the Japanese audience can judge whether the vocal delivery is consistent with their style aesthetic, though English lyrics are not always semantically intelligible. The "gibberish" can articulate the "vibration." Singing in English, one of the requirements for becoming "international" (Negus 1999, 156 ff.), is part of the universalism inherent to heavy metal and often relates to an aspiration to become "international" among band members (bands can also be bilingual, singing in their first language and English as many Latin American bands do). Singing in Japanese will potentially appeal to the wider public yet at the same time alienate the core audience of metal enthusiasts.

Masanori Itô once called heavy metal music "a great art the twentieth century has produced" (Itô 1993, 35). Heavy metal, he insists, should return to its origin, or its basic *kata* [formula-pattern] and *seishin* [spirit] (1993, 153). The "origin" is the British hard rock he experienced in his oft-narrated British odyssey in the 1970s. He and his sympathizers depict the ideal of heavy metal as "solitary and lofty" (*kokô*), an image of a religious hermit who believes in his ideals in spite of society's conventions. This notion implies independence, intransigence, pride, and self-confidence. It was not until the 1990s that Japanese metal devotees discovered these tropes for "authenticating" the genre. The "art" discourse replaced a "revolt" one, a discourse that had made heavy metal legitimate in the master narrative of rock history. Metal's decreasing share in the domestic music market meant not a decline but a distance from the mainstream that affirmed a high state of spirituality. Fans might identify themselves less as "proud pariahs" (Weinstein 1991) as American fans did and more as ascetics and at the same time hedonistic aesthetes. The authentication discourse became necessary when the genre was no longer trendy, when the commercial viability and general approval of metal music was questioned. It was surely connected to the lost momentum of NWOBHM and L.A. metal in Japan, and the deviation from the hard rock canon caused by the diversification of substyles. This inclination toward the classical/traditional was likely reinforced by the centrality of recording in the process of reception and by the archival passion for discography and record collecting among influential critics. The technological possibility of repeatedly listening to the fixed sound is thus partly responsible for the canonization of the past masters.

"Style aesthetic," a music critic notes, "is used as praise for those who love it, but as a scornful word for those who do not" (Onoshima 1991, 111). When the aesthetic pattern of heavy metal was perceived as hackneyed by outsiders, the parody began. The *Animetal* TV series and CD compilations of theme songs from TV animation programs arranged in classical heavy metal style became faddish in the 1990s. The cartoon series was intended as well as received as a novelty. An abbreviation of "heavy metal," hebi-meta, a word that signifies the domestication of the genre in two senses (Japanization and taming), has become current despite the feelings of aficionados, for whom the term belittles, rather than simply abbreviates, the genre's name (Itô 1993, 120). A letter from a Japanese fan of Ozzy Osbourne questioned why heavy metal was regarded as rubbish. "Have more faith in Ozzy" was a summary of the editor's reply (*Burrn!*, August 2003, 87). Their dialogue may sound overtly religious: a priest guides a stray sheep. The hierarchy between the editor and the readership is eloquently demonstrated in this instance.

Toward the end of the 1970s, heavy metal, as is often described, emerged as a genre in opposition to the punk and new wave movement. A decade later, it was heavy metal that was challenged by grunge, hardcore, and alternative rock. Heavy metal critics loudly sang a chorus of disapproval against the newcomers from Seattle and other American cities: "Nirvana, Pearl Jam, Red Hot Chili Peppers, none of them are HM [heavy metal]. Even if one categorizes them HM, it is not the HM I love. They have a very different pattern than basic HM and none of the spirit of HM. The tunes are cheap and very far from 'solitary and lofty HM'" (Sakai 1991, 105). Grunge/alternative, the then-editor-in-chief thought, was an inferior derivative of authentic heavy metal rather than a developed form of metal or the result of an entirely different lineage. Hiroshi Arishima, the critic we cited in the beginning of the chapter, was regarded as a "traitor" in existing heavy metal circles when he began appreciating grunge/alternative. Itô wondered aloud if the fans of the new bands were as responsive to the NWOBHM music of the 1980s as fans of NWOBHM had been to their great predecessors from the 1970s (1993, 254). In other words, the lack of historical consciousness (reverence for the classical) was symptomatic of the faddishness of grunge/alternative, a novelty without roots. This is why, unlike *Kerrang!* and *Metal Hammer*, for example, *Burrn!* was not receptive to the new sound that would become a major trend from the 1990s on. The younger bands were mentioned in the magazine yet they were hardly featured and reviewed there as they were in other popular music periodicals.

According to a Disc Union staff member, many customers purchased both heavy metal and Nirvana at her shops where no specific racks for heavy metal and grunge were ever made (Ikuko Takayama, interview, 1998). Probably those customers located themselves away from the symbolic struggle in the popular music press. Meanwhile, *Burrn!*, by narrowing its focus, had come to target a more exclusive readership in a niche market.

THE RECORD INDUSTRY: MULTINATIONAL AND DOMESTIC

We regard the record industry not (merely) as a mindless manipulator dedicated to selling standardized products, nor as an exploitative mediator oppressing homegrown music for the benefit of multinational pop music, but as a collective agency that not only mediates between the musicians and the listeners to market and sell their products but also intervenes financially as well as socially in the process of music production/creation. Besides the statistical and macro-sociological investigation, we need to understand the "day-to-day working world or way of life within the organization" and the "daily micro-political maneuvering that characterizes the industry" (Negus 1999, 63, 79). To put it differently, it is necessary to conduct ethnographic research on the "business world" (along the same lines as Howard Becker's "art world") in which personnel in different roles, performances, and locations, with conflicting values and aesthetics and earning decidedly uneven salaries, strive to maximize economic profits and psychological satisfaction in a sometimes cooperative, sometimes hostile working environment.

The previous English-language literature on the Japanese record industry has been concerned either with the success stories or the failures to sell Western pop music in Japan and/or promote native artists worldwide. In both cases, the authors emphasize the differences in access to information, images, and sounds; in audience expectations; and in the behavior and value of corporate staff between Japan and the West.

One of the keys to analyzing the Japanese record industry is the conflict between multinational (or foreign-capital-based) labels and domestic ones (Victor Entertainment, Avex, Toy's Factory, Pony Canyon, King, and so on). This is not a variation of big business versus small business or major versus minor because the domestic labels are as competitive as the multinationals in the Japanese market. It is in part the behavior of domestic labels that made the Japanese heavy metal market unique in the worldwide scene. They attempted to discover and sign bands that had been abandoned or undiscovered by the multinational labels.

According to an A & R man at Pony Canyon, "Our mission is to pick up in Japan the overseas artists who are no longer profitable. This is our basic concept" (Hiroyuki Ônishi, interview, 1998). Pony Canyon artists in-clude Praying Mantis, Kamelot, and Yngwie Malmsteen. But Japan is not a strange junkyard of past acts that merits the derision of American and British observers. Rather, it is a reservation of sorts for powerful acts for-gotten by their not-so-loyal American and British audiences. Japanese crit-ics thus valued the "magic of pure passion shared by Japanese heavy metal fans" that "has revived many bands and artists in the past" (Itô 1993, 184).

With the increasing diversification and geographical segmentation of neighboring rights, issues of legal control have become more and more complicated. Generally speaking, Japanese labels have preferred the acqui-sition of regional (East Asian) or domestic licensing to the ownership of master recordings ("master rights") because the latter was riskier, espe-cially in the case of lesser-known bands. Label contracts (or package con-tracts that include the entire past catalogue) were rarer than individual ones with each band or album. Japanese labels were much more prudent than is usually expected by foreign bands and labels. Only when an artist's sales are guaranteed in Japan (for example, Yngwie Malmsteen) do labels purchase the (regional) master rights.

The relationship between the two types of record companies was akin to that between multinational record retailers and domestic ones. The latter usually run smaller but more numerous than the former. To compete with gigantic multinationals, domestic shops tended to stock the bands of the domestic labels that are marginalized, if not excluded, from stores like HMV. For example, a Disc Union employee in charge of heavy metal told us, "We have a close connection with the domestic labels. We want to keep a good relationship with the maniac [specialized] labels. We have had a deal with Zero Corporation since their start. Small labels come to shops like Disc Union because the major stores neglect their software [CDs]" (Ikuko Takayama, interview, 1998). By the same token, Kazuo Hirose, the editor-in-chief of *Burrn!*, also showed loyalty to the domestic labels: "The record company is like a pal to work with. Pony Canyon, Teichiku, Victor . . . We may collaborate with them to make their artists big. It could happen and it has happened. They [domestic labels] rely on this collaboration and our closeness results in good things" (interview, 1998).

Typical of this kind of collaboration is the case of the German band Helloween. The band, after winning a Swedish contest, was discovered by Itô, who introduced it to Victor. A Victor A & R man liked the band and gave its members a contract. An editor of *Burrn!*, excited by the album, wrote two lengthy articles (June and July 1987) about the group, and the band's Japanese tour was a great success. Helloween's popularity reinforced the connection of German metal bands with Victor. The band's success in Japan was therefore produced by a synergy of the critic, the domestic label, and *Burrn!*.

The advantage of domestic labels is that they can take the initiative in production and publicity while the multinationals usually have to accept the basic schedule and plan decided upon by company headquarters. The Japanese employees of multinational labels sometimes complain that they are relentlessly urged by headquarters to market bands that are popular in the United States yet incompatible with the expectations of the Japanese audience *and* Japanese gatekeepers. The American executives, they say, take for granted (erroneously) that American bestsellers are automatically Japanese ones.

The Japanese branch of a multinational record company usually decided whether or not it would release a Japanese CD of an album sent to it by headquarters. Compared to an imported CD, the Japanese release has the advantage of sleevenotes in Japanese (usually containing redundant praise of the album and the band), Japanese translations of lyrics, plus, in many cases, extras such as bonus tracks and posters. Another advantage of domestic releases is their solid nationwide distribution network: one can purchase or order them at any record shop in Japan. Japanese releases helped heavy metal penetrate provincial and rural areas before Internet shopping and MP3 file sharing drastically changed how recordings are accessed in the country.

Sometimes, especially when the catalogue of the multinational was weak (that is, did not sell well in the Japanese market), the branch attempted to sign bands that headquarters had disregarded ("third party" contracts, or "fishing" [*ipponzuri*] in their jargon). The third party contract, according to Fukatami (Mercury), is not desirable for the headquarters (which wishes to control the activities of the branch) but is necessary to achieve the required sales performance of the branch. Therefore the A & R department of the multinational had to pay attention to the demo, the imported album, and other information just as their counterparts at domestic labels do.

It is the duty of the A & R person of domestic labels to listen to huge numbers of demo tapes mailed either by bands or their management offices. We found that many bands had studied well the expectations of

They were keenly conscious of their marginality in the world market, as well as their commercial potential in Japan. Reading *Burrn!* must surely be helpful for their market research.

The first thing Masahiko Kishimoto did when he founded the Metal Mania label, a part of Teichiku Record, was to purchase plenty of imported records from the specialized shops in Shinjuku, Tokyo, probably the most concentrated zone of rock record shops in the world (interview, 1998). If a promising band had not yet signed with a Japanese label, he wrote a letter or called its management's office. Indie records usually contain contact information precisely for this purpose. Such serendipitous but direct contact is still common for Japanese A & R departments (though a search through the Internet is more practical today).[1]

Information on new bands and albums also came from writers, record shop owners, collectors, music publishers, promoters, and so on. Knowing how to position oneself effectively in social information networks and how to use one's specialized knowledge were the keys to being an efficient A & R person. Often A & R personnel signed contracts with their discoveries without ever meeting the band members in person or seeing a live performance. At this stage, what was important was that the recorded sound was suitable for home and headphone listening. This was a sharp contrast to the situation in the United States, where A & R men and women go to see gigs and band members when they are interested in the band's demo. There are obviously exceptions. Tetsuyuki Miyamoto, an A & R man of Toy's Factory, immediately signed the Hellacopters (Sweden) upon his first view of its live performance video at the Interdomestic Music and Publishing Market (MIDDEM) conference held in Cannes (interview, 1998). He was fortunate not only to see the video by chance but also to have the capacity to offer a contract without persuading his boss first.

A & R persons are mostly music enthusiasts. In Miyamoto's words, "The first absolute is my excitement. Without it, I couldn't get anyone else excited. I am a metal fan and want to be so forever" (interview, 1998). Such affective dedication and loyalty is shared by the editors of *Burrn!*, who want the magazine to be a "fanzine" rather than a purely commercial publication (Sakai 1991, 216). But the passion of A & R personnel must be cooled in the second act of the drama: the negotiation with the executive. Domestic labels usually had only one or two A & R staff members in charge of heavy metal. Their tastes and ideas were easily translated into the orientation of the catalogue, and they had considerable liberty to sign bands if the executives trusted them. The executives, who were usually more or less ignorant of the musical quality of the band (Miyamoto: "They don't judge if In Flames is good"), were concerned about the band's future, the target audience, the feasibility of promotion, and so on (Negus 1992, 48). The A & R people had to explain the marketability of the objects of their passion. Miyamoto's strategy for maintaining a reputation of reliability within the organization was to propose both narrowly targeted styles and widely accepted ones. Thus he could play with the experimental and the commercial. He advised that the A & R department should have flexibility in negotiating with the marketing department, and should also keep in mind the business profile and orientation of the label as well as the commercial potential of bands. The A & R people must be reliable at both ends—the band and the label. As Itô notes, they are central components that stimulate the scene and determine the orientation of labels (Itô 1993, 170).

The transfer of a band from a domestic label to a multinational (and vice versa) is quite common. The band Ten (of the United Kingdom), voted the "Brightest Hope" in the 1996 reader's poll of *Burrn!*, was first contracted with Zero Corporation but two years later moved to Mercury. Miyamoto's Hellacopters moved to Universal in 2001. Many A & R people from domestic labels resented these transfers, as though bands whose careers they had cultivated had been "snatched" by powerful hands. Bands from Anglophone countries (especially the United States) usually have many more chances to sign with multinational labels than those from non-Anglophone countries. To avoid difficult competition from the multinationals, Japanese labels tended to sign bands from Central European, Mediterranean, Latin American, and other non-English-speaking countries. These include Royal Hunt (Denmark), Blind Guardian (Germany), Rhapsody (Italy), and Angra (Brazil). (Asian bands are almost invisible, except those from Korea that seem to be tied more with today's "Korean pop culture boom" than with the existent heavy metal community.) The third party contract of the multinationals noted above was often employed with mid-level bands from "small countries." But such contracts did not automatically guarantee an American release. In multinational record companies, even "priority artists" on a smaller label are overshadowed by arena rock artists. They were sometimes handled badly and many experienced drops in popularity. Some bands value their personal bonds with A & R people and the previous track record of Japanese labels more than an ambitious yet uncertain contract with a multinational.

The harsh competition was not only between the multinational and the domestic but also among the Japanese labels. This results in an increase in royalties and advances. Some bands relied heavily on the force of the Japanese market because they—especially the classical/traditional heavy metal bands—knew that they could be successful almost exclusively in Japan and a small region. The financial investment of Japanese labels was proportionate to the level of their artistic intervention. Japanese A & R personnel, together with authorities/critics, often gave advice to "their" bands as more than ordinary gatekeepers. Their advice ranged from the title selection and order of tracks to issues of musical expression (more melodic, more ballads, more guitar solos, get a better drummer, and so forth). Given the commercial relevance of Japanese releases, the bands tended to accept these suggestions in order to accommodate the Japanese market.

PROMOTION AND EMOTION

The promotional division of a multinational label can play the power game on its turf. "Promotion is like *shôgi* [a Japanese chess-like game]," claims Jun Fukatami. For example, he explains, when he thought that Zakk Wylde alone was weak in media appeal, he packaged him along with promotional material for Kiss that promised to offer ("coming soon") materials for Paul Gilbert and the band Ten. The timing, combinations, channels, and contact persons for such campaigns are very carefully selected. By reflecting on the commercial value (in the present and near future) and sales capacity of his "chessmen" (and employing techniques of decoy, lure, and sacrifice), Fukatami can play favorably with the media.

A Warner A & R man took a "waiting tactic" when he promoted *Van Halen III*. Instead of generously exposing the album to publicity sources as one usually does, he just waited for contact from the media. He did not distribute free advanced tapes but asked writers and DJs to come to his office if they wanted to listen to the new album. However, he did not give them free samples but allowed them only to listen to the album in the office. Thus the intermediaries treated the release of *Van Halen III* with special attention. "What we need is experience, wisdom, and ideas. Our industry is a power game" (Kuni Takenouchi, interview, 1998).

Such a tactic was only possible for megastars; the promotional staff of lesser-known bands must struggle for the limited space and time allowable for heavy metal in the Japanese commercial media. To make basic sales predictable and to achieve effective promotion, the formation of a core audience was fundamental. Miyamoto, in his plan for promoting the Hellacopters, first organized its Japan tour before the release of the CD in order to form a core fan group. This promotional plan was the reverse of the standard one (CD releases usually precede tours) but live performance was, for him, central to the band's appeal.

Miyamoto's distinction between marketing and promotion was succinct: "To adapt band to media is not promotion but marketing. It's just for increasing the sales of a commodity. Promotion is different. It's to sell a band, not to adapt it to the media" (interview, 1998). Promotion to Miyamoto was more than an attempt to increase financial profits: it was to maximize the number of fans of his favorite music. What mattered was sharing his passion with the maximum number of listeners. Thus, media exposure is not the ultimate goal but is itself instrumental. Miyamoto succeeded in balancing his emotion with promotion by way of his tactics to form an epicenter for developing future fandom.

Even in the case of a superstar, the core heavy metal audience should not be dismissed. Fukatami, in his promotion of Bon Jovi's album, treated the core audience as a "fundament" without which the whole market would collapse. He paid tribute to the fan community that had supported the band ever since its disastrous live concert debut in Japan, though these fans are a miniscule minority in Bon Jovi's immense following. Without embracing the core, he believed, Bon Jovi would become merely a pop group, and that should not be. His respect for the core audience of course derives from his own long-standing commitment to heavy metal and not every pop metal band is treated this way (on the difference between a mass audience and a core audience, see Weinstein 1991, 179 ff.).

The labeling of a band as "heavy metal" ensures its appeal to a specific audience group but simultaneously weakens it for a mass audience that has a fixed idea of the genre. When promoting acts to a general audience, neutral or allusive terms such as "pure rock," "power rock," "loud rock," and "pop" were preferred to "heavy metal," a genre label with significant cultural baggage. Even Van Halen, according to a Warner A & R man, received less media coverage in Japan than, say, Madonna, even though the band's Japanese record sales were comparable. An Avex chief director tried to avoid the label "heavy metal" in his promotional materials as much as possible, spotlighting ballad songs that are more radio-friendly (closer to pop format) than typical metal tunes (interview, 1998). He also mentioned that Avex, a domestic label known for its dance music and pop catalogue, generally treated heavy metal coldly. Though Avex had a "pedigree" in the domestic heavy metal community, it probably started handling metal acts only because of the genre's stable core market. For similar reasons, various other domestic labels set up metal divisions in the 1990s.

The visual stereotypes of heavy metal may limit the range of its media exposure and popularity. Yôko Ichikawa, an A & R woman at Roadrunner Japan, a branch of the international indie distribution label, attributes the relative unpopularity of Type O Negative to the incompatibility between the band's image and its sound: "Type O Negative sells better than Sepultura on a worldwide level. They are a top priority band, but not so in Japan because their visuals don't fit their sound. They put on all black and have long hair, and play gothic. You'd think that band must be good for *Burrn!* because it's gothic. But it's wrong because their sound fits better for *rockin'on* or *Crossbeat* [rock magazines]" (interview, 1998). In other words, this band, she believes, did not fit well for the existing genre-by-genre route of promotion. As a result, it was, so to speak, "small in Japan."

Even now, for all the broadening of Internet shopping and MP3 file exchange, the record shop is still in Japan an important site where fans encounter CDs. Shop displays, volume and species of background music, flyers displayed, and classification of racks are all indicative of the orientation and quality of a shop. Whether one puts a CD in "Euro-metal," "melodic metal," or "melodic hardcore-thrash/Nordic" is important for targeting and "educating" customers. A & R people sometimes called influential retailers to give them tips for increasing sales because shop clerks and record label sales departments were often badly informed about niche genres. As an incentive for customers, some record shops publish free papers (for example, Disc Union's *Kôtetsu Damashii* [Steel Spirit]), to which both stocking clerks and music journalists contribute. What shops fear more than bad sales is overstocking. For the purposes of rational management, shops have to calculate the appropriate stocking amount under the pressure of record companies. Most of the albums disappear from the racks after a month or so and this quick turnover is in part due to increases in the species and quantity of new releases and the almost fixed size of the fan community. For fans and record shops in rural areas, where there is little new information available, *Burrn!* is by far the most reliable source for selecting CDs. Rural metal fans may have little chance to attend live performances, but they often own incredibly extensive CD collections.

The coverage and reviews in *Burrn!* are crucial factors that influence initial retail orders: "We stock the artists we don't think are heavy metal if *Burrn!* writes about them" (Ikuko Takayama, Disc Union, interview, 1998). This was especially the case for shops without a resident heavy metal expert. According to a Teichiku A & R man, the score of a record review in the magazine (which usually ranges between 60 and 95 out of 100) was relied upon more by record shops than by fans. What he meant was that retailers use *Burrn!* for forecasting consumer behavior—which is to say, it functioned both as a fan magazine and a trade magazine. Though an album's score was not always proportional to its sales, *Burrn!*'s commercial influence was undeniable. Through establishing a set of shared musical values, *Burrn!* strengthened the aesthetic and commercial bonds between the industry and the audience.

Because of its strong influence, *Burrn!* is always under pressure from record labels. As with other genres and other countries, heavy metal popular music journalism in Japan must fight to be independent from record companies. Journalists and editors may be intimidated by the threat of the withdrawal of ads from a magazine or by the deprivation of privileges the label has granted the magazine's writers. *Metal Gear*, according to its former editor-in-chief Fukatami, closed in part due to the pressure from Sony Music on its publisher, CBS Sony Publication. In other words, the longevity of *Burrn!* is owed in part to the fact that its publisher, Shinko Music Publication, has no formal alliance with a particular record company, though interviews in recording studios are arranged and paid for by labels and/or Japanese booking agencies. The labels knew through the accumulated album reviews and other articles which writer was in tune with which kind of sound and band character, and who was relied upon by fans. They could offer information about upcoming recordings and propose a paid interview. The editorial board has of course its own policy for how to deal with the proposal in order to preserve the magazine's (apparent) neutrality and autonomy. The negotiations that take place among the label, the artist's agency, the local booking agency, and the editorial staff are evidently tough.

Japan has the second largest music market in the world. Consequently, even a small portion of the overall pie can be significant in the world's genre markets. Heavy metal is one such market. In Japan, a heavy metal magazine has a larger circulation than general rock magazines. No single magazine can determine the popularity (or marketability) of Radiohead, for example, as clearly as *Burrn!* does for particular metal acts. No other genres in Japan feature such a centralized evaluation system and are so guided by a single authoritative voice. At least this was what the professionals in the genre industry believed. Whether the magazine is contested by alternative voices, how the tastes of the Japanese heavy metal audience are formed (Are they as purist as the magazine's or as eclectic and capricious as many other listeners of popular music? What about the gender ratio and age differentiation among metal fans?), and how the Internet has relativized the status of *Burrn!* are issues for future research. Despite the unison chorus among industry people and fans acknowledging the central position of *Burrn!* in the genre market, as yet there is no scientific research to prove it.

The purism and classicism found in the pages of *Burrn!* are key components of genre boundaries. The persistent attachment to the "classic" stems in part from the "style aesthetic" mentioned above, but this traditionalist and nationalist concept alone does not suffice to explain it, since a similar tendency can be found not only in such genres as tango, hula, and bluegrass in Japan but also in heavy metal communities in many other countries. This reminds us of a famous episode in which Muddy Waters was asked to play the acoustic guitar, not his then-favorite electric, during a European tour in the early 1960s by fans who had discovered and admired his half-forgotten 78s. These blues enthusiasts did not belong to the underclass as the original listeners of those 78s had, but to the middle class with its spending power, discographical knowledge, and aesthetic passion. "Blues" became aesthetic objects to be collected, appreciated, and researched. The new audience in the old continent had a different sense of authenticity, a sense enabled by the existence of recorded sources and by historical consciousness. Did the Europeans, due to their reverence for cultural "heritage," fail to discover the "living" (electrified) blues? Were they behind the American times and how can we explain the lag?

Though much less dramatic, the purist aesthetic of Japanese heavy

metal fandom is also related to the effects of geographical distance and me-
chanical reproduction. Regardless of the original context, recording technology can offer any past sound in a purely sonic form (deprived of social,
racial, class, and other associations) to faraway places so that the centrality
of recorded sound in musical experience can encourage purism and classicism among aficionados. Instead of instantly consuming the present and
the brand new, committed fans value stylistic authenticity judged from a
certain angle of genre history. The tendency to value the past requires historical knowledge. Enthusiasts must have access to more-or-less exclusive
channels for information and sounds unavailable to the masses. This loyalty to a specific genre distinguishes fans from the dominant, amorphous
group of music consumers.

To counter the usual description of cultural industries as bureaucratic
and exploitative institutions, Keith Negus underscores their "dynamic
human quality" and the "activity of enthusiasts whose actions contribute
to the formation of music industries but whose cultural industry is far
from institutionalized" (1999, 171). "Much music," he continues, "is moving across the world through human cultural industry and not as a result
of institutional corporate strategy." What we have found in the Japanese
heavy metal industry is a slightly different portrait, a flexible mixture of
the passion and calculation of enthusiasts, fans, musicians, and corporate
executives. At least in the Japanese heavy metal community at the turn
of the century, many multinational label personnel were also enthusiasts
dedicated in one way or another to their favorite music. Heavy metal could
be both mainstream and niche, depending on the level of the organization
to which one refers.

The global music industry has customarily classified artists according
to three geographical terms: international, regional, and national (or domestic). This categorization draws on different promotional and marketing strategies and is applicable to heavy metal artists. "International" acts
do not need to be named, while Japanese heavy metal bands can be filed
under "domestic." But should a Spanish band whose obscure album is available only in Zaragoza and Shinjuku be considered an "international artist"? It is not "regional" in the same sense as Spanish-language pop. Such
bands are special cases whose activity is centered in Japan and their home
countries (and sometimes neighboring areas). We name these cases "transterritorial" in the sense that they go beyond domestic borders to para-
chute onto distant "enclaves" before reaching domestic or regional mass

markets. Their performance is addressed more to a vague transterritorial audience than to a local mass audience. Electronica, free improvisation, progressive rock, noise/industrial, and other minor genre communities possess similar structures. "Big in Japan" (or "big in Germany" or wherever) makes the power of American control over the global market relative. It decentralizes the global distribution of specific sounds and profits.

Below the thriving surface of "international repertoire" in the heavy metal world, there are stubborn transterritorial acts and related niche markets where scattered enthusiasts and musicians strive for social and aesthetic recognition. The Galapagos Islands are not, after all, uncomfortable for the indigenous.

NOTES

This chapter is based on Kawano's master's thesis, "Dokujisei no Seisan" (The production of originality: Considerations of the music industry seen from Western heavy metal), submitted in 1999 to the Graduate School of Value System and Decision Science, Tokyo Institute of Technology. Kawano and Hosokawa, his supervisor, have revised it for the current version. We acknowledge the support of those who granted interviews. The title comes from *Thunder in the East* (1985), the album by the Japanese heavy metal band Loudness. All translations from Japanese are ours.

1 Unlike that of their American counterparts, the work of Japanese A & R staffers ranges widely, from scouting talent and making the first contact to producing and supervising albums, launching promotions, arranging Japanese tours, scheduling, providing personal care for band members, to other miscellaneous tasks, depending upon circumstances. There are quite a few women A & R staffers in Japan.

PART 6
SMALL NATION/
SMALL SCENE
CASE STUDIES

METAL IN A MICRO ISLAND STATE

An Insider's Perspective

Albert Bell

BACKGROUND AND SCOPE

Heavy metal has carved a modest but significant niche in Malta's music scene. The genre's internationalized iconic bands and various purveyors of the music's more extreme forms worldwide have long had a cult following on the island. Moreover, a relatively large number of metal bands supported by a dynamic underground community underpin the multifaceted nature of Maltese metal. While symptomatic of broader social processes, the consumption and production of metal in Malta epitomize the genre's presence at the intersection between the global and the local; these considerations constitute the central concerns of this chapter. Shaped by my own long-term and ongoing involvement in Maltese metal, both as a fan and as the bass player in various bands for twenty-five years, this chapter shall examine the evolution of metal in Malta from its origins and rise in the mid-1980s, when the scene thrived with a vibrant community of pioneering bands, to the characteristic music and supporting subculture found today. I will also introduce readers to the metal subgenres present on the island and the principal protagonists and mediators active in their diffusion. In closing, I reflect on Maltese metal's longevity.

SOME AUTOBIOGRAPHICAL NOTES

My interest in metal became particularly pronounced during my mid-teens when, through some close friends at school, I first encountered influential 1980s underground metal bands such as Venom and Mercyful Fate. Before this introduction to underground metal, my LP and cassette tape collection centered on more mainstream heavy metal/hard rock bands such as AC/DC, Black Sabbath, Deep Purple, Rush, Rainbow, Scorpions, Judas Priest, and the Michael Schenker Group. Rather than waning over time, my interest in all things metal increased over the years. I started amassing LPs and all sorts of metal paraphernalia and became increasingly active in the Maltese metal circuit, attending gigs by leading early 80s Maltese heavy metal bands such as Stratkast and Overdose, and eventually forming my own speed metal band, Kremation (initially called Exorcist), in 1985.

Gradually, speed, thrash, and even death metal bands were started all over Malta. The subculture supporting the Maltese metal scene also flourished, with most bands attracting significant audiences (of 350 or more) at metal gigs, and Maltese metalheads connected through a country-wide tape-trading network. After a brief two-year stint with Vandals, a thrash band, my attention shifted to doom metal. The Maltese metal scene's marginal interest in this subgenre was spurred in the mid to late 1980s, particularly through the impact that Candlemass's *Nightfall* (1987) and *Ancient Dreams* (1988) albums had on the Maltese underground metal tape-trading network. Although the bassist Leif Edling's Black Sabbath–inspired "rifferama" and Messiah Marcolin's operatic baritone vocal style failed to attract the interest and adulation of many of the more extreme Maltese metal acolytes (who like myself were still heavily immersed in the music of bands from the San Francisco Bay Area and German thrash metal scenes), with time and particularly with the gradual dissipation of thrash metal's novelty, Candlemass built a small yet committed following on the island. My own doom metal epiphany, however, took a different route. In my case, apart from pervasive Black Sabbath and Celtic Frost influences, it was Trouble's eponymous 1990 release that proved to be the crucial milestone in my doom metal trajectory. This album embraces all of what I re-

gard as the essential qualities of doom metal: namely, behemoth, gargan-
tuan, *heavy* guitar riffs; driving, pulsating, ominous bass lines with a fat,
bottom-end-weighted timbre; wailing, melodic vocal harmonies ushering
tales of human suffering and woe; and solid, slow-to-mid-tempo drum patterns.

Trouble also spurred my search for like-minded doom metal fans/mu-
sicians in an attempt to bring this subgenre to the attention of the Maltese metal scene. This quest resulted in my teaming up with Forsaken, a
union that has lasted, despite diverse trials and tribulations, to this day.
In November 2006, I formed another doom metal band called Nomad Son,
also drawing inspiration from Trouble and similar bands. Nomad Son de-
buted on stage at the first edition of the Malta Doom Night in October
2007, with its debut album *First Light* released on Italy's Metal on Metal
Records in July 2008.

The observations in this chapter are undoubtedly shaped by this personal connection to the captivating realm of metal. A sociological study
(Bell 2009) privileging the narratives of other Maltese metalheads (*n*=25)
sheds additional light on metal's impact on the life-worlds of supporters of
the local metal scene; in order to further ground this chapter in the subjective reality experienced by local metal subculturalists, the present essay is
informed both by the interviews conducted for that study and by excerpts
from Maltese metal songtexts.

METAL'S GENEALOGY IN MALTA

Possessing a rich and evocative history of five thousand years, the Maltese Islands are a small central Mediterranean archipelago consisting of
seven islets totaling approximately 315 square kilometers. A population of
390,000 inhabits Malta and Gozo, the two largest islets of the archipelago.
Land resources are limited and Malta's population density is one of the
highest globally (Sultana and Baldacchino 1994, 10).[1] A European Union
member state since May 1, 2004, the Republic of Malta is a parliamentary
democracy headed by a president. It gained its independence from Great
Britain on September 21, 1964. The effective closure of all British military
installations on the island on March 31, 1979 was another important milestone in Malta's eventful history.

Malta's sociocultural terrain has been imprinted by an endless stream
of colonial rulers attracted to the island's strategic geopolitical position in

the heart of the Mediterranean between the frontiers of northern Africa and southern Europe. As Baldacchino (2002a, 56) maintains, Malta may be best defined "as a 'crossroads' Island with a 'cosmopolitan' and 'polyglot' population reflecting the ethnic and linguistic mixture of Phoenician, Arab, Sicilian and British colonial influences." This ubiquitous mixture of cultures is made manifest in both the island's institutional framework (including its legal, parliamentary, electoral, and education systems) and on the phenomenological level, in the day-to-day lives of the Maltese people (Sultana and Baldacchino 1994; Clark 1999). Rather than monolithic, specific, and unambiguous, Maltese culture is better characterized as an assimilative, integrative, or hybrid culture, spurred in part by the strong magnetism that Britain (Malta's colonial ruler for well over 150 years) and Western culture, particularly American-British popular culture, hold for the Maltese (Baldacchino 2002b). While Maltese popular culture remains a mélange of indigenous and foreign influences (Grixti 2004), one cannot deny that Am-Brit imports have made strong inroads into the routine life experiences of the Maltese. Understanding Malta in the twenty-first century without reference to cable and MTV, Budweiser, Red Bull, McDonalds, KFC, and Burger King, Hollywood blockbuster movies, cell phones, and U.S./U.K. chart music is unfathomable. Music subcultures in Malta are also closely aligned with essentially Am-Brit music forms—including metal.

Given Malta's affinity with Am-Brit popular cultural forms, it is not surprising to find a long-standing, albeit quintessentially marginal, fascination with the metal genre on the island. However, to dismiss metal in Malta as merely another case of "cultural cloning" (Baldacchino 2002b) would be to subscribe to a rather simplistic assessment, if not a superficial one, of this intriguing sociological phenomenon. A detailed inspection of the genre's development across the island reveals a more intricate process, in which expatriate and indigenous cultural forces collide and intertwine. For this reason Maltese metal and other local music subcultures should be considered distinctive, valid (sub)cultural outgrowths calling for more reflective scrutiny. As Grixti (2004, 23) clearly posits, "When cultures come in contact the influence is likely to go in both directions, so that (as indeed is happening throughout the world) traditional Maltese youth culture is not so much getting replaced by a global mass culture as coexisting with it and being inflected by it."

The modest yet significant incursions the Maltese metal scene has recently made into the global metal community, particularly through the exposure of a small number of contemporary Maltese metal bands signed to enterprising foreign underground labels (including Apotheosis,[2] Beheaded,[3] Forsaken,[4] Martyrium, Nomad Son, Slit, Weeping Silence, and Abysmal Torment), might lead one to believe that the presence of metal in Malta is recent. However, this is certainly not the case. Maltese metal has an intricate genealogy with its origins rooted in the efforts of various rock bands and mediators whose creative endeavors from the mid 1970s to the present provided the necessary foundation for metal's relatively profuse growth in Malta. It is difficult to pinpoint a precise date for metal's origins in the country, and it is also quite arduous to designate a particular band or solo artist as progenitor. These tasks are further complicated by the fact that documentation on the subject remains sparse. A partial attempt to redress the matter was made with my contribution (Bell 1994) to an edited volume of selected sociological papers addressing diverse processes and issues within the Maltese societal milieu. Admittedly, that initial attempt was anything but comprehensive and it is hoped that the following overview will address the lacunae that still exist.

A list identifying a series of catalysts in the development of metal in Malta would be quite lengthy, with diverse players leaving their imprint on the process. Undoubtedly, the mid-1960s to mid-1970s "beat band" generation played a tacit yet influential role in the development of Maltese metal. For example, the early 1970s bands were purveyors of a DIY (do-it-yourself) and garage-based ethos that still pervades the metal scene today. Like several of their earlier progenitors, contemporary underground metal bands in Malta still operate from remote garage complexes subject to eviction, which leads too often to a coerced hiatus. Moreover, until the mid-1990s metal shows were housed in venues that had hosted beat bands and Saturday night "dances" prior to the latter's slow demise following the surge of progressive and hard rock in the mid-1970s and the punk, new wave/electronic, and metal scenes of the 1980s. More recently, Maltese metal performances have relocated to the St. Julians/Paceville entertainment haven and other locales in the vicinity. One may thus argue that the early beat band movement was essential for creating the "space" required to nourish the metal and other underground music scenes. Also, some of the local metal scene's most influential figures had roots in the 60s sounds and the beat bands teeming on the island during the period. Marc Storace, the vocalist and frontman with the Swiss hard rockers Krokus, is an example.

276   Maltese metal may be viewed as a natural outgrowth of the worldwide
rediscovery of the genre with the rise of the New Wave of British Heavy
Metal (NWOBHM) movement in the late 1970s. Around this time foundational Maltese hard rock/metal bands, including Stratkast (or Stratokaster
Disaster), B3, Valderkraay, Atlam (based in Zabbar), Spider Trash Band (of
Gozo), biker band Acid, and later Dark Medallion, Purple Haze, the Rush-
inspired Sphinx, Overdose (one of the few early bands to have a female lead
singer), and Birkirkara rockers The Unexplained, forged the backdrop for
a more easily definable Maltese hard rock/metal scene in the 1980s. While
still strongly influenced by Sabbath, Purple, Zeppelin, and other icons of
the 1970s, Malta's incipient metal scene also drew heavily from NWOBHM
pioneers such as Iron Maiden and Saxon.

Inspired by the more extreme faction of the NWOBHM juggernaut
(especially Venom) and the subsequent San Francisco Bay Area and German speed/thrash metal scenes of the mid-1980s, a new wave of bands
including Vandals,[5] Kremation,[6] and Passion Blade[7] then worked their
way to the forefront of the local metal scene. This is not to say, however,
that other metal variants were not represented on the island. Bands like
Ivory Cross (progressive hard rockers), Coven (highly influenced by Iron
Maiden), Tamarisk, Epicure, Hellequin, and Kraken were equally important to the Maltese metal scene during the 1980s, as were Brainstorm's and
Entract's glam metal.

The scene was rejuvenated in the 1990s with the eruption of a large number of emphatically more extreme bands, who brought the Maltese scene
closer to the diverse subterranean metal genres gaining ground internationally. Maltese metal in the 1990s was in fact characterized by a tightly
knit community of bands proudly allying themselves with extreme metal.
Prior to death metal's rise to popularity in the mid-1990s, Maltese thrash/
speed metal bands such as Manslaughter, Extremity, Realida, In Memo-
riam/Norm Rejection, Dark Sanctuary, and later Sanity, Trial by Fate,
Terra, Dirt, Obscurity, and Subtraction[8] remained a crucial part of the local
metal scene. As Death, Morbid Angel, Pestilence, and Obituary propelled
death metal to international acclaim, the presence of this subgenre rose
noticeably on the island. Bands like Beheaded, Lithomancy, Segregation,
Disinterred, Dilapidated, Biblical Infamy, Gruesome Funeral, Amentia, En-
shroud, Sceptocrypt,[9] and Stench of Necropsy represented the first wave
of early 1990s Maltese death metal. This was later followed by bands like
Arachnid, Dysmenorrhea, Canniria, Abysmal Torment, Erythuria, Hem-

lock, Seismic, Ktinodia, Defaced, Dying Signals, Tendency Charge, and Putrid Birth. While each of these bands presents its own interpretation of the death metal idiom, it is possible to identify some commonalities among the death metal bands presently engaged in the local scene. Local death metal bands tend to favor the archetypical, guttural "death grunts" or growled vocals with precisely timed phrasing of nihilistic or splatter/ gore lyrics (popularized by global scene leaders such as Cannibal Corpse). These are complemented by downtuned twin guitar riffs, hyper-fast beat-per-minute "blast beats," double-pedal kicks, and aggressive drumming. Although different individual bands have carved their own niches with some interesting departures from these standards, veteran band Beheaded has remained the leader of this genre in Malta for close to two decades, serving as a strong source of inspiration for up-and-coming death metal bands.

Doom metal in Malta is perhaps presently best represented by the scene veterans Forsaken and the newly formed Nomad Son. Forsaken and Nomad Son band members are strict adherents to the classic doom metal idiom, employing clean, dramatic vocals and powerful, mid-to-slow tempo riffs and, particularly in Forsaken's case, nods to the power/thrash and epic metal of the 1980s. Victims of Creation and Deluge of Sorrow remain the principal doom-death metal flag-bearers on the island, although the recently re-formed Oblique Visions may be considered as a forerunner in this regard, particularly through its self-released CD *Seas of Serenity* (1995). Undergoing a kind of renaissance in the mid-1990s, the doom scene in Malta at that time also featured Orbus Vitae (comparable to the United Kingdom's Serenity) and Born Too Late (a doom metal tribute band featuring members from Forsaken and thrashers Realida) and other doom-death metal bands such as Masada and Unknown Serenity.

Marking the increasing involvement of women in the Maltese metal scene, the female-fronted band Weeping Silence juxtaposes alto vocals with double-guitar harmonies and elaborate keyboard patterns pursuing atmospheric and goth-metal soundscapes in the vein of bands like The Gathering (The Netherlands) and Theatre of Tragedy (Norway). Goth-metal references also strongly influence other female-fronted bands such as Sidereal (which draws significantly from progressive rock) and the folk/ goth metal newcomer Memento Nostri.

Combining goth and black metal influences, the band Martyrium blends keyboards and female vocals with high-pitched screeches,[10] furiously paced twin guitar riffs, and fast up-tempo drum beats. Martyrium's aura of gothic horror and dark imagery is reinforced by the band's members' use of "corpse paint" (a form of facial makeup widely used in black metal to heighten the grimness of the music) and ominous pseudonyms such as "Count Mortem" and "Vargblood." Lyrically, Martyrium explores the netherworlds of Dionysian erotica, particularly in its self-released CD of 2002, *Withering in Voluptuous Embrace*. In contrast, Thy Legion, featuring former members of Martyrium, persists in the more purist, "old-school" tradition of the black metal genre, following the path of bands like the now disbanded Achiral,[11] Obscuritas Aeturnus, and Apotheosis. Prior to its dissolution, the symphonically charged dark metal of Archaean Harmony[12] added further diversity to the local black metal scene. It ventured toward the technical, progressive features of avant-garde black metal bands such as Arcturus, replete with virtuoso guitar soloing, atmospheric keyboard arrangements, and intricate, syncopated drum patterns. Archaean Harmony's black metal roots were apparent in its vocal style and its mystical, occult-oriented lyrics, though by and large the band departed from this subgenre's conventions.

Metal-core groups, such as Slit,[13] Loathe,[14] Core Frequency, Item, Clubmurder, and Knockturn Alley, embody the local metal scene's inclusion of hardcore sensibilities. In contrast to the more traditionalist perspective of Maltese power metal bands like Blind Saviour and Angel Crypt or the progressive-laden domains of bands like Twenty Two Other Worlds and old-school thrashers like Thrashacre, these bands represent the growing plurality and hybridity of the Maltese metal scene.

Apart from the music's producers, various intricately networked "mediators" have played an important role in the rise of metal culture in Malta. In her account of the rise of underground metal culture worldwide, Weinstein (2000) singles out small yet committed independent record labels and distributors, used record stores, the rise and dissemination of extreme metal 'zines and more glossy magazines throughout the globe, rogue radio stations with well-informed metal DJs playing extreme metal music, annual extreme metal festivals, and the Internet as the key players in the globalization of underground metal. Similarly, Harris (2000b) argues that the strong DIY ethic and the idiosyncratic nature of marginal subterranean metal scenes have helped extreme metal to move beyond the exclusive boundaries of Anglo-America.

The development of the scene in Malta confirms these assertions. A vigorous tape-trading network incorporating most metalheads on the island was one major instigator of the genre's dissemination in the 1980s. In the initial absence of "metal-friendly" record stores,[15] most Maltese headbangers were introduced to landmark albums like Metallica's *Kill 'Em All* (1983) and Exodus's *Bonded by Blood* (1985) through the circulation of poorly recorded C90/C60 cassette tapes. With original LP owners only loaning their hallowed possessions to a select few, cassette copies of such albums were much-coveted trophies in metalhead circles. Friends or relatives going abroad were given lengthy "must buy" lists. The items brought back were added to extensive trade lists that often circulated beyond Malta, introducing local metal enthusiasts to underground metal material and tape traders from all over the world (see Kahn-Harris, this volume). Copies of band demos and albums were given to acquaintances in Malta and abroad. Some fans outside of Malta avidly sought Maltese releases, which prior to the mid-1990s were difficult to find. Undoubtedly, Maltese metal first departed the country through tape trading. Technologies like the Internet and MP3s have changed the nature of this trading network, making Maltese metal much more accessible to metalheads worldwide. Most Maltese bands today have a backlog of professionally recorded material, offer downloadable samples of their music on their MySpace pages and Web sites, and disseminate their releases through online metal-oriented mail order distributors.

Over the years various print and Web-based 'zines produced by fans emerged in support of the local scene. Early printed 'zines including *Rancid Soup*, *Metal Manifest*, *Call of Angels*, the Gozitan-based *Mistbreed Zine*, *Arch Music Mag*, and *Forbidden Rite* (none of which is still in publication) emphasized local bands while also tracing developments in the metal world abroad. As has happened elsewhere, Internet-based Web-zines such as Pestilent.net, for example, have become more common in recent years. Significantly, Internet-based social networks now provide the predominant means of communication between Maltese metalheads and bands and their foreign counterparts, marking the shift of local metal toward global virtual community.

Locally produced radio metal shows, such as the perennial *Grinta* on 93.7, provide another platform for the scene's dissemination. These shows frequently host local metal bands and enthusiastically promote metal-oriented events. The Maltese metal scene has also benefited from periodic annual metal marathons that combine experienced and upcoming talent.

Festivals such as the Grim Reaper (2001 and 2002), Broadband (2004 and 2005), the Extreme Maltese Metal (2007, 2008, and 2010), the Mediterranean Metal Gathering (2010), and the Malta Doom Metal (2009 and 2010) festivals epitomize such efforts and have proven central to the continuing expansion of Malta's metal scene.

MALTA'S METAL SUBCULTURE: INTERSECTING THE GLOBAL WITH THE LOCAL

Various social processes converged on postcolonial Malta to create an increasingly culturally heterogeneous landscape. In the first section I established the importance of the island's colonial past and the Maltese affinity for a wide array of expatriate cultures. Yet Malta's postcolonial social and economic development (giving rise, among other things, to increased spending power), increasing democratization,[16] and openness to global influence (illustrated by the island's wholesale embrace of information and communication technologies in recent years) are equally crucial influences on Malta's effervescent contemporary cultural terrain: "Whilst many of Malta's traditional values remain, the social landscape in which they operate has changed wholesale. The forcible division of Church and State coupled with growing affluence and consumerism has led to a far wider range of social practices and social issues similar to those in Northern European states" (P. Kelly 2004, 24).

Malta in the twenty-first century presents a secularized and "open" sociocultural milieu, where a plurality of traditional and novel behavioral patterns coexist, allowing for convention and innovation to collide and intertwine. As Giddens (1994, xxvii–xxix) asserts, traditional mores in any society are being confronted by the encroachment of globalization. Maltese society is not being spared from this process:

> Globalisation intrudes into, and alters structures of day-to-day life, at the same time as those structures of day-to-day life have an impact upon the larger social world. Together with technological changes affecting the workplace, transformations in the nature of industrial and business organizations, and changes affecting gender and the family in dramatic ways, the landscapes of social life are becoming altered everywhere. . . . Malta cannot be studied, it is demonstrated over and over again, as though it were an isolated unit. It is part of a wider global so-

One may assert that the impact of the "global" on Maltese society directly influences the current proliferation of alternative tastes, lifestyles, and interests across the islands. The Maltese metalhead or "rocker" (the moniker Maltese metalheads use to describe themselves and by which they are generally known in their surrounding social world) stand resolutely as a signifier of subcultural "otherness" in Malta's current sociocultural landscape, despite decreasing visibility, particularly when compared to the 1980s and mid-1990s when metal (due to its far-reaching popularity at the time) articulated a more substantial part of that generation's youthful rebellion in both Malta and Gozo. This perception of difference stems mostly from metalheads' preference for a musical genre that stills lacks acceptance by the "mature," adult world.

As I shall examine in more detail below, various factors impinge on the possibility of an individual's manifest and protracted involvement in the Maltese metal scene. For many local metalheads the passage into adulthood is therefore generally marked by decreasing scenic participation. This phenomenon accentuates Maltese metal's decidedly adolescent to young adult orientation, allowing the music's detractors to dismiss or deride it as a crude flirtation with the need to shock typical of "growing up." However, the music's connection to "mindless" youthful rebellion is not the only constraint affecting its acceptance in the wider society. Notwithstanding Malta's increasing embrace of liberal attitudes and the presence of more vocal alternative lifestyle groups, the influence of traditional, deep-rooted worldviews remains pervasive. Metal in Malta, with its conventionally dissonant semiotic repertoire, remains tangential to steadfast definitions of "good taste" and moral rectitude. Transformations of the island's value systems over recent years have not helped to push metal upward in the echelons of respectability.

Moreover, the Maltese metalhead's brusque subcultural style has also contributed toward this persevering "otherness." Typically male and in his late teens to mid-twenties (notwithstanding the increasing gender and age differentiation in contemporary Maltese metal subculture), the Maltese metalhead is typically of an upper-working-class or middle-class background, possibly pursuing postsecondary education, and sporting long hair, jeans, and the quintessential black, short- or long-sleeved T-shirt fronted with the unintelligible logo of a death-grind or black metal band. The attire of those in the "nü-metal/metal core" mold runs to Adidas/Nike leisure wear, hip hop-styled baggy trousers, the essential goatee, assorted jewelry, nose and other facial piercings, tattoos and a baseball cap. Keen on role-playing games, on-line war-gaming, "shoot-'em-up" PlayStation games, slasher movies, online chatting, and downloading MP3s, the Maltese metalhead and his subcultural style express disenchantment (albeit at times obliquely) with a confusing, hypocritical adult world marred by stifling partisan politics, unappealing and archaic institutional structures, political patronage and nepotism, an oppressive and politically charged media, and a disapproving, intrusive, and judgmental wider social milieu. Norm Rejection, a radical metal/crossover Maltese band, vehemently articulates such acrimonious sentiments in "Straightjacket," a song from its self-released album titled 0002 (2002):

> I'm gonna devastate
> The makers of my hate . . .
> Oppress, no more
> Revolt, galore . . .
> My fist into your face . . .
> Freedom—I wanna taste.

The otherness that the Maltese metalhead experiences is evident in the way conventional authorities treat the subculture's principal rallying and uniting factor—metal music. Metal in Malta is still relegated to the margins. It remains out of favor with radio station managers who dictate playlists on the airwaves, and it is generally shunned by state- or corporate-sponsored mass entertainment events. Gig promoters and concert organizers have yet to accept metal, and visits from foreign metal bands, unless mediated by Maltese metal bands, are few and far between. While big business may have shied away from metal because, unlike dance or party music, it is simply not lucrative enough to justify investment, the state remains generally oblivious to its existence, politely ignoring it in state-sponsored music events while the subculture and its music lurk ominously in underground Maltese culture.

Clearly there are other social groups that represent "the other" in contemporary Maltese culture. In recent years, for example, there has been increasing interest in "new age" or "holistic" practices (Meli 2000). The island's increasing contact with alternative belief systems and lifestyles seems to have exacerbated this process. As a result, Maltese "new agers" are burrowing deep into the authority of traditional religion, marking a nexus between globalization, secularization, and the de-territorialization of traditional Maltese culture. While traditional Catholic values and dogma have not lost their significance in the Maltese Islands, research in this area reveals a growing Maltese tendency to seek out more personalized religious experiences:

> In more scientific terms, the religious decline, in a situation like that of Malta, may only be a stage in the secularisation process, incorporating desacralisation. In this sense, this decline may be reflecting a change from a type of religiosity which is 'sacral' to one which is more secular. It is the passage from a religion which emerges in the individual from the outside, deductively, as a result of a predominant and highly institutionalised Church, to a religion emerging from the individual's internal feelings and convictions. In the latter the individual does not resort to stereotyped symbols to manifest his/her religion, but strives to create one's own, reflecting more sincerely one's innermost feelings and personal convictions (Tabone 1994, 296).

The surge of revisionary Christian and non-Christian movements in Malta illustrates an increasing trend for personal interpretation of beliefs and cultural mores that were left unchallenged for decades, if not centuries. This is clearly related to the modernization processes discussed previously and has profound ramifications for the island's sociocultural fabric. There are indeed copious challenges to tradition in present-day Malta. The Maltese are now eager to interpret absolutes subjectively, to "desacralize" conventional truths and thereby leave their own imprint on society. This decline in the appeal of convention clearly resounds in the songtexts of Maltese metal bands. The following quote exemplifies the dissenting, defiant posture that binds affiliates to metal culture together:

> So many rules were spoken in my childhood days
> They've kept me blind but sane
> As I start to see, shall I lose my brain?
> The paths I now shall tread shall be decided by me
> Shall I rule my own destiny?
> In this world alone I travel to seek . . .
> what is what I seek?

284   This extract from "Wandering Knight" by the "old school" black/thrash metal band Achiral (from its *Wander Ignite* MCD, self-released in 2001) underscores the theme of "chaos," which Weinstein (2000, 38) describes as one of metal's major thematic complexes. As Weinstein observes (2000, 39), the tendency of metal lyrics to represent the "metaphysical rebellion against the pieties and platitudes of normal society" is universal across the metal world. However, the pervasive presence of religion and the Catholic Church in the Maltese social context is key to Maltese metal's particularly pronounced preoccupation with religion and penchant for "chaotic" song-text themes. The following lines from Beheaded's "Perpetual Mockery," the title track of its MCD released on Sweden's X-treme Records in 1998, illustrate this:

> Perpetual mockery
> All faith is being severed
> By the fallacies that are revered
> Obscured minds, impaired veracity
> Fertile ground for Christianity.

Yet Maltese metal songtexts do not merely express skeptical attitudes toward Christian belief or "desacralizations" of other forms of traditional wisdom. Unambiguous references and critical reflection upon the domination and superimposition of confessional values on Maltese society (which may also be applied to overseas social contexts) also abound. Subtraction's "Humanity Undone," the band's only recorded track, which appeared on an all-Maltese metal compilation titled *Core of Creation* (1996), indicates Maltese metal culture's critical engagement with and sensitivity to political issues.

> We own mental claws
> That prohibit us to think . . .
> Reduction of human rights
> Embalming the colour
> As if it was a contaminating disease.

One can also find examples of metal songtexts that overtly attack the machinations of local politics, which alongside religion remains a major preoccupation for the Maltese, with the island's two major political parties (the Malta Labour Party and the Center-Right Nationalist Party) infiltrating all levels of Maltese society (P. Kelly 2004, 24). Norm Rejection's song

"Malta Not for Sale," with its infectious chorus line—"*Inqumu mir-raqda* [Let's wake from our slumber], Malta not for sale"—is undoubtedly a case in point. One of the few local metal songtexts to be partially sung in Maltese,[17] this track critiques the island's environmental degradation, a spiraling deficit in public finances, rampant tax evasion, widespread political corruption and greed, and the increasing subservience to global corporate interests. The song's title is clearly a statement against the privatization of national interests, as epitomized at the time by HSBC's takeover of Mid-Med Bank, one of Malta's publicly controlled banking institutions. Perhaps Norm Rejection's leftist, Marxian politics stands out even more pronouncedly in its track "Caged"—a highlight on its *Deconform* album from 1998:

> We're suppressed
> We've regressed: that's life
> Unfed, asleep, estranged, entrapped: what's life?
> We're slaves, possessed, perpetuate . . .
> Masters force the alienation
> Plug what's numb inside your brain . . .
> Caged. *Mahkumin*! [Dominated!]

A critically engaged nature is not necessarily de rigueur in Maltese metal subculture. However, as these songtexts clearly demonstrate, this music subculture can offer a potent critique of Maltese society. Moreover, although it possesses a unique narrative, which in some ways may be distinct from how the genre and its concomitant culture evolved in Western countries, Maltese metal is an important representation of the global metal community and demonstrates the intensification and internationalization of heavy metal culture. These developments even merited specific mention in Weinstein's (2000, 283) observations on metal's global reach: "Even Malta, a tiny Mediterranean Island north of Libya and south of Italy has professional metal bands, as do Israel, Iceland and Egypt."

While exemplifying the genre's ability to penetrate comparatively insular social contexts, Maltese metal also demonstrates how taste and stylistic preferences may be mediated at the global level and reproduced by indigenous, homespun, "glocalized" interpretations. Some of Maltese metal culture's focal ideological concerns have already been noted in previous references to local bands' songtexts. However, a closer look at the subculture's organization can also shed light on metal culture's "glocal" dimensions. Although the music, its plethora of subgenres, leading performers, and iconography may be common reference points for metalheads worldwide, Maltese metal culture entails subcultural practices that highlight its idiosyncratic and autonomous nature.

The "metal gig" unquestionably plays a central role in Maltese metal subculture. While both state and private secondary schools act as "breeding grounds" for prospective metal acolytes (Bell 2009), subcultural ties and self-categorizations as "metalhead" are specifically fostered and reinforced at metal gigs. Maltese metalheads generally gather at the few venues where gigs by local bands are presently possible. Advertisements for gigs, metal nights, and other events are generally circulated via e-mail flyers on Facebook, Myspace and other virtual social networks or through online discussion groups and forums, such as Yahoo Groups' "Malta Music Scene."

Despite Maltese metal fans' increasing reliance on Internet use (resonating with the island's increasing openness to information technology), the metal gig still remains the rallying point for Malta's metal subculture. Despite the scene's increasing fragmentation, with local headbangers professing allegiance to disparate and often rival subgenres, the gig remains the highlight for many a Maltese metalhead's weekend. It is here where the latest gossip on local and foreign band line-up changes is exchanged, where prospective band members may be recruited into an established band's fold, where new bands longing for a record deal are formed, and where fans are expected to support the bands onstage with spontaneous and quite raucous "pit" formations, obligatory horns-up salutations, and by purchasing local bands' merchandise. This last is critical, and for many the defining facet, of "belonging" to the Maltese scene. While many people are content to download MP3s, "burn" foreign bands' albums on CDRs, and disseminate such material freely among peers, the local release seems to hold a special status in the Maltese metal scene. Maltese metalheads acknowledge and repond to the reality that local demo and album sales are necessary for the Maltese variant of the music to survive and thrive, and possibly allow the next watershed opus, which could potentially end once and for all the island's isolation from the global metal world. Thus, the purchase of releases by local bands, even if the individual's personal taste does not include the band's metal subgenre, demonstrates loyalty to Maltese metal and the scene (passionately referred to as "*ix-xena*" in Maltese) in general.

Apart from their symbolic dimensions, local metal gigs also serve an important economic function. Maltese metal bands rely on their own mettle and entrepreneurial prowess—a DIY ethos that makes the autonomy of the local metal scene possible. Earnings from gig attendance and merchandise returns are the principal source of revenue for financing professional recordings, tours abroad, and band promotion, particularly if the band in question cannot rely on some sort of backing from a foreign label or distributor. However, while the quality of studio recordings by local metal bands has improved significantly over the years, most of the island's music retail outlets still do not stock Maltese metal merchandise. Album releases, T-shirts, and so forth are informally procured at underground gigs and through bands' social networks. This ensures supporters' immediate and continuous face-to-face interaction with one another and with bands. All of this renders the gig a pivotal focal point for scene economics and, moreover, a site for valued scenic practices and important forms of "subcultural capital" (Thornton 1995; Kahn-Harris 2007) to come to the fore.

Two aspects are central to the creation of an individual's subcultural capital in Maltese heavy metal—longevity in the subculture and subcultural production/mediation. Those few people who withstand the test of time and a host of outside pressures to abandon the music (or, as some outsider detractors may argue, adults who remain fixated on chasing their adolescent dreams) are accorded a cherished, veteran status in the local metal culture. This may not be exclusive to the Maltese metal scene. Weinstein (2000, 110) observes for example that the U.S. metal scene is also markedly youthful and that older metalheads, rather than being treated as "generational oddities," are seen "as an affirmation of the metal culture itself."

However, the duration of a typical Maltese "rocker's" subcultural career tends to be shorter than his or her U.S. or European counterpart's. From my personal experience in the scene, it is comparatively very difficult to encounter metalheads more than thirty-five years old at local gigs or actively playing in Maltese metal bands. This is unlike what one usually encounters in metal communities abroad—particularly those that have formed around the more distinctively underground and nostalgic metal genres such as doom metal and "true" or "classic" heavy metal. Many aging Maltese metalheads apparently forego their interest in the genre and its concomitant scene altogether, while a minority retain their "outsider" status, perhaps occasionally surfacing for a gig or listening to metal CD/LP collections in private (Bell 2009). Thus fewer fans persevere in the Maltese metal subculture, giving "old hands" an influential position in the scene's informal hierarchy.

Those who have persisted in the scene well past their mid-twenties generally claim some personal history with bands, recording, or in other scene activities such as 'zine production, gig promotion, band management, sleeve design, metal DJing, and so forth. Veteran Maltese metalheads, attending gigs and engaged in some form of subcultural production, are crucial reference points for the younger individuals in the scene, attesting to the fact that one may take up adult roles without shedding one's passion for the music and all its trappings.

The dynamic subcultural production evident in local metal today, from Web-zine design to recorded output, exhibits the vital creativity of the Maltese metal subculture in contrast to the rather sterile picture indicated by general cultural trends on the national level. Data from the National Statistics Office (2002) reveal that cultural participation in Malta centers mostly on consumption. Creative cultural production remains a rare activity. The production of metal music by a host of up-and-coming and established bands and a wide plethora of scene-supporting activities help to redress this imbalance.

This brings us to another crucial source of subcultural capital in the Maltese metal scene: music production. Quality musical performance is the zenith of achievement within the scene, particularly if it is supported by professional recordings that have gained international recognition through record deals with foreign labels and tours abroad. Breaking into the international metal arena, even in small ways, gives performers prestige within the scene. It is useful to recall the introductory discussion on "cultural cloning" at this juncture. Sultana and Baldacchino (1994, 11), writing about local academia, trace aspects of this phenomenon in the way individuals who pursued postgraduate studies abroad tend to be treated upon their return to Malta. They are hailed as conquering heroes by "discerning peers and clientele" and considered superior to those academics who did not have the opportunity to continue specializing abroad. Such reverence is also reserved for local metal bands with exposure abroad. Yet the marked difference in the metal scene is that it does not discount bands that are still striving for foreign exposure. The scene's pervasive sense of community ensures that it remains supportive of bands still looking out for that lucky break. Rather, perseverance and an ability to network and locate oneself effectively within a particular subgeneric niche rather than mere talent are the main factors that affect a band's ability to reach outside Maltese shores. As the scene primarily privileges accomplished musical performance, the accumulation of subcultural capital centers on this pivotal aspect. Record deals with foreign labels are thus secondary to foreign performances, yet they are much-sought-after add-ons.

In this sense metal in Malta strongly inspires artistic development. A large percentage of Maltese metalheads eventually become metal band members themselves and most undergo the passage from fan to musician/band member within the span of one to two years. Only a few remain strictly on the fandom periphery. This explains the large number of bands that have been started in recent years. Maltese metalheads are not content with solely consuming the music; rather, they attempt to produce metal, using as reference points the standards for musical production developed by the genre's leaders within the Maltese and wider, global contexts.

MALTESE METAL AND ITS RESISTANCE TO "DECAY"

It is appropriate to close with some reflections on why Maltese metal has resisted what Weinstein (2000, passim), drawing on Ronald Byrnside's (1975) earlier work on musical styles, describes as "decay" or "exhaustion." Weinstein holds that after periods of formation and crystallization (that is, the periods during which the musical style becomes recognized as a distinct entity), most rock music styles become formulaic and thus fail to sustain the interest of followers and music producers alike. This period of decay renders musical styles ineffectual and eventually obsolete. Weinstein contends that, unlike other rock music genres, metal has managed to retain its mystique, and she identifies the growth and internationalization of metal subculture and the music's division into different subgenres as the principal factors in the genre's longevity. Perhaps these factors can also explain the perseverance of Maltese metal and the relatively isolated Maltese metal scene.

In the previous pages, I examined some of the characteristics and primary concerns of the Maltese metal subculture as well as the various metal subgenres present on the island. Considering the many restraints on the propagation of metal music in Malta (such as the island's conservatism, insularity, and geographical isolation from the European heartland), the continued presence of metal in Malta and, moreover, the existence of a vibrant metal scene are quite extraordinary. Clearly, Maltese metalheads' commitment to the music and the community's ability to continually rejuvenate itself has played an important role in ensuring metal's longevity in Malta.

Despite the pressures on Maltese metal, its supporting scene benefits from the notable capacity to attract streams of new "converts" into its fold. This guarantees support for established bands and the perpetuation of Maltese metal culture's core codes, including commitment to the scene, its DIY ethos, and independence from mainstream commercial music interests. Conversely, however, the scene's apprentices also provide up-and-coming musicians, fans, and mediators who produce novel experiences of and new meanings for being "metal." Undoubtedly, Maltese metal's ability to resist decay may be located along the dialectic between constant revitalization and the custody of the culture and the music's crystallized conventions. Thus while Maltese metal is indeed fragmented, encompassing diverse and often rival subgenres from metalcore to death, black, doom, and power metal, these variants or elements coexist within an all-embracing, identifiable whole—Malta's metal underground community.

In my view, the endurance of Maltese metal's "underground" character has been equally pivotal in ensuring the music's survival in Malta. As the fate of diverse rock music styles (even on the island) clearly indicates, it is when such styles are endorsed and propelled by mainstream forces that decay sets in. Malta's metal home brew, despite its tendency to mimic and reproduce an essentially imported cultural form, remains entrenched on the fringe, ostracized by the local music industry. Bonding among a music scene's supporters is more likely to retain its allure and significance if the music remains attached to the margins. In turn, the more exclusive a music subculture remains, the more it is possible to ensure that its core codes are not prejudiced or compromised, increasing the subculture's potential for nurturing a passionate and supportive community. As Kathryn Fox (1987) observed in her study of the punk rock scene in a city in the southwestern United States, music subcultural groups are more able to retain commitment from their affiliates if they foster and sustain a clear differentiation from the larger society. The group's demarcation from dominant society is revered by subculturalists and imbues "their self-identity with a sense of seriousness and purpose" (K. Fox 1987, 353). The reverence of the music's concomitant subculture.

While not necessarily a "self-sufficient universe," which is "uniquely the expression of [its] creators" (Canclini [1990] 1995, 5), Maltese metal remains essentially owned and produced by local metalheads. Moreover, the subcultural ties in Malta's metal scene are alive and well. As with other fringe Maltese music cultures, it is here that one may identify a mosaic of attitudes, practices, and styles that retains an emphatic distance from co-optational forces on the island. This dynamic syncretism has bestowed upon Maltese metal a mutable yet constant nature that has ensured its longevity. It is unlikely that this longevity is exhausted. By constantly re-articulating itself, and retaining its independence, Maltese metal should persevere well into the future.

NOTES

1 Amounting to around 1,250 persons per square kilometer (Baldacchino 2002a).

2 A Gozitan-based, one-man-project black metal band, Apotheosis released its debut album *Furthest from the Sun* (2002) on Norway's Nocturnal Art Productions, which is owned by Samoath, a member of the band Emperor.

3 Formed in 1991, Beheaded is presently signed to Unique Leader Records, a death-grind label based in the United States. The band unleashed its debut demo *Soul Dead* in 1995, signing to X-treme Records (Sweden) for its first official release— *Perpetual Mockery* in 1998. Beheaded issued an MCD titled *Resurgence of Oblivion* in 2000, followed by its second full-length CD, *Recounts of Disembodiment* in 2002 on Denmark's Mighty Music, after ending its ties with X-treme Records. Beheaded has toured extensively abroad, including the United States, Germany, and Eastern Europe.

4 Featuring myself on bass since the band's first four-track demo, 1991's *Requiem*, Forsaken started out as Blind Alley in 1990. The band's demo release was followed by the release of *Virtues of Sanctity*, a two-track 7" EP with Arkham Productions (France) in 1993, and a full-length album, *Evermore*, in 1996 with Storm Records (Malta). Following a forced hiatus due to the tragic demise of Daniel Magri, a central member of the band's twin guitar set-up, Forsaken returned with an MCD titled *Iconoclast* in 2002 and two full-length albums, *Anima Mundi* and *Dominaeon*, in 2004 and 2005 respectively, all with Golden Lake Productions (United Kingdom), while also securing prestigious appearances at various European metal festivals. The band is now signed to Sweden's I Hate Records.

5 Resurfacing recently as X-Vandals, this band has played a long-standing and influential role in the Maltese metal scene. Starting off as a trio, Vandals was a highly charged live act with the double-bass drum attack of tracks like "Speed

Crusher" and "Warrior" and the anthemic "Who Dares Wins" proving strong fan favorites during gigs. Toward the early 1990s (at one time also featuring myself on bass), the band moved away from its earlier speed metal/punk sensibilities and ventured toward thrash-oriented pastures. A videocassette single titled "Crusading Sinners" (1990) and an official live rehearsal demo (1991) are representative of the band's thrash-metal-oriented output.

6 Kremation (initially called Exorcist) was formed in 1985 during the heyday of the international speed/thrash metal explosion. Featuring Karl Fiorini (vocals), Mike Rizzo (guitars), Ritchie Rizzo (drums), and myself (bass), Kremation was a very active live band in the mid-1980s. In 1987 the band released its only official recording, *Guardian of the Realm*.

7 One of Malta's most popular metal bands during the 1980s, Passion Blade was a powerhouse metal act with a penchant for both invigorating original material and convincingly done covers. The band gradually shed its speed metal references and steered toward a more polished hard rock/metal direction in the mid-1990s. In 1998, under the shortened epithet Blade, the band released its only full-length album, *Rockomotive*, on the Maltese record label Storm Records.

8 Most of these groups disbanded some time ago, however not without a legacy of demo material for scene enthusiasts to plunder. Significant milestones here include Extremity's and Manslaughter's untitled demos (both 1991), Masada's *Untrodden* (1995), Realida's *Facing Reality* (1994), and Sanity's three-track untitled demo (1995).

9 Sceptocrypt's unconventional brand of death metal is evidenced in its *Wild Code of Reverie* demo (1996) and perhaps more pronouncedly in its *26 hrs 72 mins . . . The Need to Differ* promo CD (1999). Like most early 1990s Maltese death metal bands, Sceptocrypt disbanded at the tail end of the 1990s. Beheaded and Lithomancy are notable exceptions in this regard.

10 In contrast to death metal's low-end guttural growls, treble high-end vocal timbres are typical in black metal (see Hagen, this volume).

11 Debuting in 1998 with its *Dark Waters* demo, Achiral, consisting of old-school Venom/Bathory "worshippers," was one of the most prolific bands in the live Maltese underground metal circuit until its recent disbanding. Its 2001 *Wander Ignite* CD continues to mark the band's penchant for uncompromising thrash/black metal combined with eclectic influences.

12 Archaean Harmony's output includes *Nihility Mundane Soul* (2000) and its debut rehearsal demo *Resentment of an Evanesce Aeon* (1997).

13 Debuting with its *Vision of Life* demo in 2000, Slit released its *Mandra* promo CD in 2002 to widespread acclaim in the local and foreign metal press. The band released *Ode to Silence* on Anticulture Records (United Kingdom) in 2006 after releasing another full-length album titled *Chronaca Nera* on Retribute Records (United Kingdom) in 2005.

14 In a review of one of Loathe's early gigs supporting local death metal icons Beheaded (April 5, 2003—Allstars Pub, Paceville), Schembri (2003, 11) summarized Loathe's performance that day as an "excellent brew of old/brutal metal and Nu-

metal"—a description that may also be easily applied to the band's self-released debut promo MCD entitled *Abort/Retry/Fail* (2004).

15 A rock/metal CD outlet in Valetta called The Rock Shop was a notable exception in this regard. The owners of the shop also ran a record label called Storm Records, which was another fundamental player in the promulgation of home-brewed metal. Coming to the fore during the mid-1990s, Storm's releases included a number of Maltese metal releases, such as Blade's *Rockomotive* (1998) and Forsaken's *Evermore* (1996) full-length CDs. Storm Records also released two milestone all-Maltese metal samplers dubbed *The Storm Has Begun* (1995) and *The Core of Creation* (1996).

16 The Malta Labour Party's ascent to power in 1971 ensured that in its infancy as an independent country, Malta underwent a modest yet sustained economic development that also acted as the foreground for the creation of a strong welfare state crystallized in the establishment of a national health service, industrial law reform, and the introduction of home-ownership schemes and wide-ranging social security benefits, including children's allowances and cost of living increases (Briguglio 2001). Malta's socialist government was a key stakeholder in the island's incipient economic and social development with significant amounts of state-owned capital directed toward social and infrastructural projects (Delia 1987, 36). After the more neoliberally inclined Partit Nazzjonalista's election to the government in 1987, the island gravitated toward market-oriented, non-state interventionist policies, leading to devolution of power and wider participation in the decision-making process. The demise of state monopolies in the broadcasting and communications sectors, the institution of municipal authorities, and the increasing devolution of statutory powers to local councils have been important milestones toward this nascent democratization.

17 The Maltese language is a hybrid tongue possessing etymological roots that may be traced to both Semitic and Romance origins. In the more affluent and middle-class oriented parts of the island English and Maltese are combined, creating a variant of the language that demarcates social prestige and exclusiveness (Sciriha 1994; Clark 1999). Most Maltese bands have shied away from the Maltese idiom in their songtexts. In addition to Norm Rejection, the avant-garde death metal band Sceptocrypt also proved an exception to this rule, with its tracks "Isegoria 2000" and "Oratorio Mortem" containing Maltese song texts. The former, focusing on the challenges and opportunities raised by the island's integration in the European Union, also includes the band's rendition of the Maltese national anthem toward the end of the song.

NOISY CROSSROADS

Metal Scenes in Slovenia

Rajko Muršič

Perhaps it may seem unnecessary to write about the metal scene in Slovenia, a little-known country located on the periphery of Europe with a population of two million. However, small is beautiful, isn't it? But parts can speak for the whole. Metal is, roughly speaking, a global phenomenon—although not developed to the same extent around the globe—and its noisy messages can be heard today in many remote places. And Slovenia is not a sequestered nook. After all, the tiny twenty-one-year-old Republic of Slovenia lies at the crossroads of Europe.

It is difficult to speak of the development of popular music in Slovenia before World War I, because Slovenia was then a rather provincial and agricultural part of Austria-Hungary. However, in the first decades of the twentieth century, popular music began to crisscross the country from all directions. The first jazz band in Slovenia, Original Jazz Negode, was formed in 1922 (see Amalietti 1986). Slovenians learned about popular music genres and styles through direct contact with musicians from neighboring coun-

as well as through records, radio, the music press, and sheet music. At the
end of the century, the situation remained essentially unchanged, other
than the addition of the Internet and satellite television. These gave an
additional strong push to the development (or, in some cases, stagnation)
of the local popular music scene. Slovenia's metal scene, like those of other
European countries, developed within the general historical and social
frameworks of the late twentieth century.

IN THE TURMOIL OF HISTORY

The former Yugoslavia, reestablished after World War II as a socialist fed-
eration, was a country of huge internal differences and radical political
shifts. During the first three years following the war, Yugoslav Communists introduced Stalinist totalitarianism. That meant that Western music,
especially jazz, did not receive official approval, although a professional
jazz orchestra was reestablished in Ljubljana immediately after liberation.
Jazz therefore was not actually forbidden, but many jazz musicians suffered hard times (see, for example, Tomc 1989). Circumstances did not
change even after Tito's break with Stalin in 1948. Only in the second half
of the 1950s did things gradually change, and popular music, in its various
forms, became not only acceptable but an integral part of the development of so-called "self-management" socialism. At first, the previously-
suppressed jazz scene was developed, and rock music didn't gain much appeal in the late 1950s. Only after the first appearances of rock music on
film, which took place only in the early 1960s (Cliff Richards and The Shadows), did rock bands begin to play in dance halls. Electrified "pop" bands
then started to appear in Ljubljana and in the industrial towns of Maribor
and Koper (cf. Barber-Keršovan 1989).

Kameleoni (The Chameleons) was the most important Slovenian rock
band from the 1960s. It was very popular in all of the former Yugoslavia
(see Hmeljak 1995). In its later phase, in 1968, its sound turned more
toward distorted electric guitar. Kameleoni's soundtrack for the film *Sončni
krik* (Sun-Scream), directed by the famous Slovene director Boštjan Hlad-
nik, may be the first appearance of heavy-metal-sounding guitars in Slovenia as well as in all of what was then Yugoslavia.[1] The band's guitarist,
Marjan Malikovič, became one of the first Yugoslav guitar heroes.

In the late 1960s and early 1970s, Yugoslav popular music bloomed, especially electrified rock, which was by then called "pop." Popular music became an important part of the profitable national cultural industry, which defined the era of socialist consumerism in the former Yugoslavia. As travel abroad became possible, and the economic situation gradually improved, people went shopping in the nearest commercial centers in Italy and Austria. Among other things, they purchased records, and thus received fresh information on the most recent trends in music. Radio was also an important source of information, especially the famous Radio Luxembourg. Slovene rock groups from the late 1960s and early 1970s began to play more "updated" rock music, including hard rock, glitter rock, psychedelic, progressive, funk, jazz rock, and, for the first time, more distorted rock. The early 1970s was the time of the first Yugoslav guitar heroes (Radomir Mihajlović Točak from the group Smak was perhaps the most famous). Almost all of the most popular Yugoslav rock groups from the first half of the 1970s were influenced by hard rock (Time and Parni Valjak [Steamroller] from Croatia, Yu grupa [Yu Group], Pop mašina [Pop Machine], and Smak [Armageddon] from Serbia, Bijelo dugme [White Button] from Bosnia and Herzegovina, and even the Slovene underground group Buldožer [Bulldozer]). However, there were some groups with a sound closer to the heavy metal of the time, especially from Bosnia. Teška industrija (Heavy Industry) and Divlje jagode (Wild Strawberries) could have been considered the first hard rock/heavy metal bands in the former Yugoslavia, followed by the first Serbian heavy metal group, established in 1977, Gordi (Narcissus).

In Slovenia, in the first half of the 1970s, mainstream rock bands Oko (The Eye) and Jutro (The Morning) played hard rock. At the same time, local bands with a hard rock orientation were appearing, such as TNT and Grive (Thatches). The guitarist Mijo Popovič got his start with Grive and later became the lead guitarist of Pomaranča (Orange), the first Slovene heavy metal group.

In the 1970s the Yugoslav music industry blossomed. Recordings of the most famous groups of the time were regularly released, under license and with little delay, so the current records of AC/DC, Motörhead, Iron Maiden, Judas Priest, and others were readily available. Concerts by Uriah Heep, Iron Maiden, Saxon, Girlschool, Motörhead, and others were organized as well. These groups obtained many followers, especially in peripheral small towns in the regions of Primorska (Adriatic area) and Gorenjska (Alpine zone) (Prezelj 1999, 88). At that time, social stratification in the socialist country was rather minimal. Although young people from well-situated families had easier access to hi-fi equipment and records, even working-class youth could afford to buy records and attend concerts. In general, it was more difficult to purchase music equipment because it had to be imported. Therefore, the active musicians were predominantly young people from better-situated families.[2]

In 1980, Pomaranča (Orange) appeared: the first—and still today the most famous—heavy metal group in Slovenia. There were other bands as well, but they played heavy metal or hard rock only occasionally (for example, Ultimat [Ultimatum] and Flam). In larger urban centers, punk rock became the leading rock style, but heavy metal still had its audience, especially in smaller towns and in the countryside. Rock crowds were clearly divided between punk rockers, "hippies,"[3] and metalheads. Some mainstream rock bands, like Šank rock, Bombe (The Bombs), and Mery Rose (see Prezelj 1999, 84) occasionally played some heavy metal as well.

ON ROOTS AND ROUTES: "ETERNAL HEAVY METAL"

In the late 1970s and early 1980s, a majority of heavy metal and hard rock fans were recruited from technical schools with predominately male students in smaller industrial towns. During the second half of the 1970s, youth generally differentiated themselves along the lines of rock versus disco. However, in the 1970s the rock scene itself began to differentiate. Fans of early British heavy metal and hard rock bands like Black Sabbath, Deep Purple, Uriah Heep, Led Zeppelin, and others differentiated themselves from "hippies," who were still listening to the so-called old rock of the 1960s and 1970s or, in the early 1970s, had switched to "progressive" rock. Differentiation became more pronounced in the late 1970s, when punk rockers formed a strong and important scene in larger centers of the former Yugoslavia (particularly in Ljubljana, Rijeka, Zagreb, and Belgrade). But generally, rock fans would still collect a broad range of records. At that time, in the former Yugoslavia, records were inexpensive—the price was usually less than one third of the price in Western European countries. Fans were thus in a position to collect not only several dozen LP records, but also to make collections of several hundred or even several thousand LPs.

At the same time, local groups encountered many difficulties in releasing LP records on local labels. The labels were market-oriented, and they expected their records to return their investments. Therefore, with the exception of a few subsidized musicians (in jazz, classical, or traditional music), only groups with apparent commercial potential were given the opportunity to make recordings: Pomaranča, Oko, Šank rock, and a few others. Therefore, before the establishment of small independent labels in the late 1970s and early 1980s, the initial rock scenes in Slovenia (and the former Yugoslavia) were based on live performances in small youth clubs, in medium-sized venues and halls, and—for the most popular bands—in stadiums. In the 1960s, "guitar competitions" (*kitarijade*) were organized in large halls, while in the 1970s large festivals were more in favor (for example, the Boom Festival).

Numerous local bands played in every town of the former Yugoslavia, though they often only reproduced the musical models of the best-known international rock celebrities. The standard repertoire was Led Zeppelin, Deep Purple, and glitter rock. But an underground was developing as well, concentrated in Ljubljana under the influence of Radio Študent, the first independent local radio station in this part of the world. It was established in 1969 (http://www.radiostudent.si/) and since then has played all kinds of contemporary music with a special focus on progressive and alternative rock, as well as on improvised music and free jazz. It was the only channel for current underground information. Then, punk happened.

In the late 1970s and early 1980s, punk rock became synonymous with dominant Slovene rock and its alternatives. The punk movement in Slovenia was so strong and important that, for several years, all other rock genres were almost completely marginalized in public discourse (on the Slovene punk scene, see Malečkar and Mastnak 1985; Mastnak 1994; Tomc 1994; Muršič 1995, 1998, 2000a, 2002). My personal engagement at that time was with the punk-as-a-synonym-for-alternative movement in the town of Maribor. Although some interesting intersections between alternative styles appeared (for example, crossover bands like Anarchromixz from Maribor, and early speed metal bands), punk rockers and other rock fans considered heavy metal to be a dead end. But it survived.

At the end of the 1970s and at the beginning of the 1980s, there were very few heavy metal bands in Slovenia and quite a number of punk rock bands. But at the same time, heavy metal fans were much more numerous than punk rock fans. Foreign heavy metal bands usually played in the largest halls and stadiums while punk rockers performed in small venues.

It is beyond the scope of this chapter to examine the various reasons that   **299**
heavy metal was so undesirable in the eyes of the rock elite.

NEITHER GOOD NOR BAD: PURE POWER

Contrary to the utopian or revolutionary visions of rational(ized) societies elaborated in the writings of nineteenth-century social philosophers
Fourier, Comte, and Marx, the second half of the twentieth century actually brought a plurality of communal forms, which can be described as subcultures, scenes, or even tribes, and are characterized by a "collective feeling of shared puissance, this mystical sensibility that assures continuity"
(Maffesoli [1988] 1996, 24). Following Maffesoli, modernity is not the
epoch of rationalism or individualism, but exactly the opposite. According to his understanding, "tribes"—modern emotional communities—are
not only incomprehensible in terms of the older social constructions: they
are expressions of an incomprehensible "barbarity." And which communities are among the most apparent and fearful examples of "degenera-
tive" tribalism if not metalheads? Even in the dominant popular music
discourse, heavy metal was rarely discussed. Although one might get the
impression from such discourse that heavy metal culture was simply too
trivial to analyze, the truth was quite the opposite. A closer look actually reveals that heavy metal may be too complex to deal with without
extensive ethnographic and phenomenological methodologies (valuable
examples are Berger 1999a; Weinstein 1991, 2000; K. Jones 2003). It is almost impossible to say anything reasonable about metal without detailed
ethnography. Otherwise, silence and ignorance (in both meanings of the
latter word) are unavoidable.

I admit that in my Ljubljana and Slovenia entries in the *Encyclopedia of
Popular Music of the World* (Muršič 2005b and 2005c), I didn't even mention metal. And not many other writers in Slovenia have written scholarly articles on metal (exceptions are Prezelj 1999 and Kranjc 2002). Even
internationally, the scholarship of heavy metal is not very large. And even
among scholarly works, speculative or unsubstantiated discussions of the
effects of metal on suicidal behavior and other deviant and violent behaviors predominate (see, for example, Took and Weiss 1994; Thompson and
Larson 1995; Bryson 1996; Ballard, Dodson, and Bazzini 1999; Scheel and
Westefeld 1999; Lynxwiller and Gay 2000; Rubin, West, and Mitchell 2001;

Burge, Goldblat, and Lester 2002; Smith and Boyson 2002). To be sure, there are well-grounded empirical works as well, but even many of them were provoked more by public attacks on heavy metal (and rap) and accompanying moral panics than by the subject matter itself (on the public and political attacks on popular music, including heavy metal, see Martin and Segrave [1988] 1993; Cloonan 1996; Owen, Korpe, and Reitov 1998; Cloonan and Garofalo 2003). Studies largely deal with the social context of heavy metal culture(s) (see, for example, Gross 1990; Straw [1983] 1990; Hinds 1992; Weiner [1973] 1996; Harris 2000b; Beckwith 2002), and only a few discuss music (cf. Berger 1997, 1999b; Walser 1993a, 1997; Mulvany 2000).

Because such a wide variety of music is omnipresent today, it is now difficult for people to cultivate truly unified musical cultures. At a time when we are faced with conceptual splits between musical and cultural denominations—as say, with hip hop and electronic dance musics—enduring heavy metal scenes are perhaps the last bastion of music-and/as-culture unity. Therefore we have to take into consideration both music and culture, in an anthropology of music or musical anthropology (as developed by, for example, Merriam or Blacking). As an anthropologist (and philosopher) without a musicological background, I primarily discuss culture. But I have to say something about music first.

In my approach, the starting point in understanding any kind of music is that sounds themselves carry no particular message. Any sound, as well as any articulated piece of what we perceive as music in various cultural contexts, can achieve a variety of meanings. External meanings are typically attached to music and, uncritically, we miscomprehend these "meanings" (which actually come from lyrics, stories, titles, performance contexts, and so on) as the meanings of music. But the power of music communication is rooted at a much deeper level. Music is primarily an illocutionary/performative means of communication. Though it is undoubtedly a symbolic practice, its symbolism is inherently unclear. Music makes differentiation of meanings possible exactly because it does not speak the same way as a language does. If we understand music, in all its possible facets, as nonverbal sound games (see Muršič 1993, 2005a), it appears to us as an intentional construction of sounds and their organization in time. Basic elements of music are neutral, neither "good" nor "bad"; their message is (in) our perception. I do not wish to make a simplistic analogy between phonemes and the basic sounds of music, but there is a parallel, in

that the very essence of musical expression lies in expressing something
ultimately unspeakable (on that point see Jankélévitch 1987). How would
it otherwise be possible to find the same music in one case completely apo-
litical while in another context strongly politicized? For what other reason
can we find that satanic ideology is ascribed to heavy metal, while at the
same time we can also find purely Christian heavy metal? It is not only due
to the polysemic essence of music, it is because music makes symbolic differentiation possible. Every sound is essentially a *crossroads*: it can lead to
any interpretation. And, as we know of crossroads, these are dangerous
places, places of evil, places of destiny.

I have never been a heavy metal fan. I grew up with alternative music,
rooted in punk, and heavy metal scenes were foreign territories for me.
Only after closer examination of the Slovene metal scenes in 2003 did I become aware of how important this scene was for Slovenian popular music
in general.

STAY HEAVY!

Metal survived among the continually changing rock styles of the past
two decades. In the early 1980s the New Wave of British Heavy Metal
(NWOBHM; in Slovenia called "new metal"), with groups like Iron Maiden,
Motörhead, Def Leppard, Saxon, and Tygers of Pan Tang, and other British
groups like Judas Priest were influential enough to give a push to the rather
dispersed and marginalized heavy metal scene of Slovenia. But the first important Slovene metal bands were rooted in hard rock and heavy metal
from the 1970s. Pomaranča (Orange), under the leadership of the guitarist
Mijo Popovič, became a concert attraction in the early 1980s, followed by
the bands Sneguljčica (Snow White), Cvetje zla (Flowers of Evil), and Lene
kosti (Lazy Bones) (see Prezelj 1999, 86). In some ways, the situation may
have been similar to the scene in the United States. As metal fragmented
into a variety of styles, influenced by bands like Metallica and Slayer, some
commercially successful groups appeared in the mid-1980s playing hard
rock and pop metal (the term "lite" was not used in Slovenia). The most
successful was the still active Šank rock (Pub Rock), which is based in the
small mining town of Velenje and has generated a series of locally successful recordings.

Pomaranča is a legendary Slovenian heavy metal band. Even the young-
est metalheads today listen to its famous recordings from the 1980s. The

group occasionally still performs, and it remains a superb concert attraction. Its appeal was based on virtuosic lead guitar and strong rhythm, backed up by keyboards. Singers sang in Slovene, English, and Croatian. The band's first album, *Peklenska Pomaranča* (with a double meaning: a Slovene translation of *A Clockwork Orange*, and, literally, The Orange from Hell; 1981), was entirely Slovene, while the second (*Madbringer*, 1983) was made in English for an international audience. The album gained appeal in France and other European countries, and was even noticed in Japan. The socially engaged stance of the group, expressed in lyrics about alcoholism, militarism, violence, atomic war, authenticity, and so forth, came to the forefront on this recording. The band's third, much "softer" album, *Pomaranča/Orange III* (1985), was in Croatian/Bosnian and English, influenced by its new lead singer from Sarajevo. After a compilation from 1993, the group recorded its fourth album, *Takoj se dava dol* (Let's Have Sex Right Now, 1995), again in Slovene.

Another push followed soon after the appearance of the first local heavy metal groups in the early 1980s, this time inspired by thrash metal from the United States and bands like Metallica, Slayer, Megadeth, and Anthrax. In the alternative rock scene, under the strong influence of post-punk, hardcore, and industrial/experimental music, many crossover metal and hardcore groups appeared. Among these groups from the mid 1980s were No Limits, Quod Massacre, and Razzle Dazzle. At the same time, hardcore bands incorporated a NWOBHM sound as well (for example, hardcore groups Odpadki civilizacije [Dropouts of Civilization], G. U. Z. [Ugly, Dirty, Evil], and III. Kategorija [Third Category]). The fast tempo of hardcore was occasionally interrupted by distorted riffs in much slower tempo, which provided a unique dramatic atmosphere. Many bands were known only locally (for example, TNT from Maribor). In the 1980s hardcore and metal fans united for a while in their common "struggles" against disco fans, both in small towns and in Ljubljana, where an open fight between the youth groups actually occurred (Prezelj 1999, 88).

If the first wave of Slovene heavy metal was located in the capital city of Ljubljana and other large urban areas, the second wave was based in smaller towns. In Slovenia, "small towns" may be defined as those with a population of less than twenty thousand. Among the most important bands playing various kinds of thrash metal in the second half of the 1980s were Pragwald (from the central Slovenian town of Polzela), Epidemic Zone (from the town of Žalec), Sarcasm (from Škofja Loka), Game Over (from Jese-

nice), and Salem (from Koper), followed by Interceptor (also from Žalec)
and the progressive heavy metal band Skytower (from Postojna). Their appearance was connected with the emergence of new metal subgenres, such as doom, speed, death, and black metal, and the further development of crossovers. Local scenes in Ljubljana and in the above-mentioned smaller towns were becoming stronger and stronger (cf. Prezelj 1999, 89).

These groups may have been less virtuosic than Pomaranča, but they sounded much more intense and extreme. In strong and sharp riffs and less accentuated melodies, they expressed a small-town anger or frustration: they found themselves situated in parochial surroundings, yet at the same time cultivated seemingly unreachable ideals with their peers. Singers didn't even try to seduce with high-pitched vocals. Electric guitars became more and more distorted. Some of their recordings were reviewed in international journals and fanzines (*Rock Hard*, *Metal Hammer*, and so forth) (Prezelj 1999, 90). In the late 1980s the instrumental crossover group Polska malca (from Krško) appeared with an original sound reminiscent of experiments at the time by bands on the California-based postpunk label SST. But they were never recognized as a part of the Slovene metal mainstream.

If fans were still attracted to legendary groups like Iron Maiden or Motörhead, younger fans were searching for new inspiration. The most important breakthrough in the development of the Slovene metal scene was the appearance of Metallica and its first very influential albums. Metallica was a catalyst, provoking unprecedented mixes and developments. In the turbulent times of the late 1980s, it was no longer possible to speak of a uniform Slovene metal scene; instead there were many highly localized and internally diversified styles.

Along with bands that played a crossover blend of thrash metal and hardcore (like Železobeton [Reinforced Concrete] from Murska Sobota), many alternative rock bands started to use metal idioms (for example, Strelnikoff from Celje, which combined hardcore with drum machines, electronics, noise, and metal riffs). In the mainstream, grunge became influential as well (Nirvana, Soundgarden), but true metalheads were searching for more metal. Extreme metal emerged as their first choice.

Extreme metal gained immediate appeal in Slovenia. This is partly a result of the radicalization of the Slovene rock scene, caused by ongoing developments in punk and hardcore in the early and mid 1980s. During the late 1980s, Slovene extreme metal bands were initially influenced by the grindcore label Discharge and bands like Extreme Noise Terror, Napalm Death, and Bolt Thrower. Their first followers in Slovenia were Extreme Smoke 57 and D.T.W. (Prezelj 1999, 86). If the first heavy metal bands in the 1980s sang in the Slovene language, things dramatically changed in the late 1980s and the early 1990s. From that period on, many Slovene rockers used the English language in order to have international appeal, with the exception of punk/hardcore, crossover, and mainstream/commercial rock groups. The Slovene audience understands English well, for the language has been taught in primary and secondary school since the 1950s. Slovene metal groups were among the first to start to sing in English. With the appearance of metal groups from other parts of the world—not only from Great Britain and the United States—English became an international standard. Communication among fans and promoters increased, through fanzines, mail order catalogues, and fan clubs, from an underground, regional scope toward a more and more global network.

In the early 1990s new influences on Slovene metal came from different parts of the world. These influences were much more decentralized, although most information (and distribution channels) still came from the United Kingdom and the United States. Influences came from the strong industrial rock scene in Slovenia (Laibach) and Western Europe (Einstürzende Naubauten) and from the dark margins of the metal scene. These darker elements were already present in classic works by Black Sabbath, Motörhead, and Venom and were augmented by those found in Slayer's 1983 *Show No Mercy* album and the music of groups such as Kreator, Possessed, Celtic Frost, Bathory, and Sepultura.

The first group to synthesize these influences in Slovenia was Xenophobia. Subsequently, other groups gained a much wider audience than expected: Obscurity, In-a-Spleen (initially named Auschwitz), Scaffold, and Noctiferia. Despite making recordings and orienting themselves toward a broader audience, the first two bands, which experimented with many styles ranging from death metal to hard rock, did not lose their popularity with their local audience in Tolmin. Since 1994 progressive death metal was represented by the group God Scard (from Kranj), while the first representatives of the initial wave of progressive metal in the early 1990s were Non Finire Mai (Žalec) and Skytower (Postojna) (Prezelj 1999, 87). God Scard is still among the best-known Slovene melodic or hybrid extreme metal bands.

In the 1990s the most important influences gradually came to be from other parts of Europe, especially Scandinavia and Germany. The new generation of Slovene metal has definitely turned to the North, and death/black metal became the most developed and important part of the whole Slovene metal scene. It culminated with the unexpected local success of Noctiferia. The band from Ljubljana was established sometime around 1994 when its members went to primary school. During these years the band developed a unique version of death/black metal with a strong emphasis on harmonic progressions. Guitar solos and feedback are interchanged with strong riffs, sometimes backed up by synthesizers. Its hit "Fond of Lies" introduces acoustic guitars, followed by blast beats, enormous churning guitar riffs, and exceedingly growled vocals (but with understandable English lyrics). In 2002, its video "Fond of Lies" climbed to the top of the video chart on Slovene national television—and stayed there for quite a while. It was a big surprise even for the most fanatical metalheads. Moreover, the success of Noctiferia was a result of a massive mobilization of the dispersed Slovene metal scenes in the preceding few years. By using mobile phones and the Internet, they "voted" for Noctiferia—and won. This model of success worked efficiently for some other groups, too.

The video "Fond of Lies" was made in a clear black metal fashion, and was designed to be very provocative. At the end of the video, a character representing liberated, personified "evil" saws a wooden crucifix. This symbolic act of de(con)struction was challenging for the national audience. Fortunately, Noctiferia avoided trouble: apparently not many ordinary people could bear the brutal music all the way until the end of the video. In any case, Noctiferia made the internal breakthrough of the new Slovene metal scene. Starting with progressive metal stalwarts Prospect, other metal groups followed in their footsteps. At the same time, Noctiferia received good reviews in the international metal press, and its record was released in the United States on the American label Arctic Music Group. The Slovene scene has developed since then with many new bands, newspapers, Web pages, and venues.

THE ETERNAL PRESENT: ON INFLUENCES AND CONNECTIONS

The story of the Slovene metal scene(s) would not be complete without an examination of fans' preferences, influences, and local experiences. Back in 2003, I conducted a short survey, based on an open questionnaire posted on the Web page of the most important Slovene heavy metal fanzine, *Para-*

noid (http://www.paranoid-zine.com).⁴ My sample size was sixty-three respondents.

Female respondents comprised less than 10 percent of my sample, which reinforces my overall finding that the active metal scene is still predominantly male. There may be some indications that gender roles are equalizing slightly, however, especially in certain subgenres of metal such as gothic and melodic (Ajda Jelenc, personal communication; on gender in popular music, see Bayton 1998; on gender roles in heavy metal, see Krenske and McKay 2000). Things are changing somewhat, and there are now a handful of female instrumentalists and singers in Slovene metal groups. Female metal fans communicate intensively on Internet forums. Some of them play in metal groups (Metalsteel has a female drummer), and they also participate in other activities in the scene. But there are not as many actively involved female fans in the scene as male fans. Expert knowledge of metal is very important for both men and women (Klinec 2003).

Heavy metal fans who responded to the Web questionnaire were young, generally between fifteen and twenty-five years old. They were also quite well educated: almost all of them were either involved in or had completed secondary education, or were university students. Thus, one could claim that the metal community is to some extent recruited from the most promising parts of the younger population. In a certain way, they comprise a kind of elite, and not only in their self-identity as being special, though marginal. In some cases, for present-day young people, metal scenes are among the few remaining social spaces in which one can express difference, group solidarity, and a critical stance toward the "real world." Empirical investigations show that present-day young people are generally not rebellious (Miheljak 2002), though there are some who express criticism of liberal democratic society and prefer punk. Through metal, fans come to constitute modern "neo-tribes" (Maffesoli [1988] 1996) and build their own worlds.

Slovene metal follows the general historical pattern of heavy metal cultures, in that it emerged as an atypical urban formation, and not one that first appeared in the prosperous centers. As happened elsewhere in the heavy metal world, in Slovenia heavy metal attracted younger people in the 1970s from either depressed industrial regions or dispersed individuals in suburbs (cf. Straw [1983] 1990). Later, it developed, albeit sporadically, in both urban centers and on the semi-rural periphery. After an economic crisis in the 1980s the small factories were the first to be closed. At that time, some areas of the country were facing unemployment rates of 15 percent or even 20 percent. However, it is not the case that stronger local metal scenes would necessarily emerge in these regions. Instead, issues of local infrastructure and general "atmosphere" (that is, conservatism, the power of the church, small-town pressure, and so forth) seem to be more important factors. Younger people who attend high school in a nearby small town would later, most probably, attend the university in Ljubljana, Maribor, or Koper. The majority of heavy metal fans in Slovenia are recruited from among these students. It is thus impossible to define their social class. But if one defines class in terms of the social status of their parents, then it would seem that the majority would fit into the "middle class."

Though metal is still very attractive to young people in industrial regions facing ongoing uncertainty, it is also attractive to youth in small towns and in the countryside. Slovenia has only two cities with populations of more than one hundred thousand. Therefore, it is no surprise that almost 40 percent of my respondents live in the countryside and another 30 percent in small towns. This definitely has an effect on the development of the Slovene metal scene: while concerts featuring international groups are usually organized in larger towns and cities (mostly in Ljubljana), domestic concerts are much better attended in the interior. So, with the stubborn voluntarism of individual enthusiasts, local centers may dynamically appear, but then disappear, and the overall situation may appear fairly sluggish, especially when observed from the capital. At one moment one could find a vibrant scene in Žalec or Pivka; a few years later some groups could appear in Brežice or Murska Sobota. For more than twenty years, the small town of Škofja Loka has remained an important center with numerous local metal fans.

Even in a small country within which it is generally possible to get to a concert anywhere by car, live performance is not necessarily the crucial criterion of a band's success. The band must release a record, and media coverage helps considerably as well. When bands only promote themselves through live performance, their popularity is typically limited to the local scene(s). Slovene metal scenes are indeed quite localized, and one can identify more than ten apparently localized scenes in the country.

During my investigation of the Slovene metal scene(s), I identified more than two hundred bands involved in metal (excluding hard rock and old-school rock bands) in the past two and a half decades. Considering the anonymity of many bands, it may be possible to claim that somewhere between one hundred and two hundred bands are active in Slovenia at the time of this writing, and that a total of up to six hundred bands have performed different kinds of metal in the recent decades of Slovenian history. Pomaranča/The Orange was the most admired Slovene metal band. However, when asked to mention "the best" metal bands in Slovenia, respondents put Noctiferia at the top. Its death/black metal obviously found particular appeal in Slovenia. The second most attractive band at the moment is the progressive metal (or classic metal) group Prospect, also from Ljubljana. Other bands mentioned more than five times were the thrash metal bands Sarcasm from Škofja Loka and Root A' Baloota from Koper (with two female members); the death metal bands Scaffold and Magus Noctum from Ljubljana, Supremacy from Šoštanj, and Torka from the coastal area; the hardcore and crossover metal band Kaoz from Velenje; and the melodic, hybrid, and classic metal bands God Scard from Kranj, Requiem from Ljubljana, Sabaium from Ceršak, and Obidil from Železniki. In the past few years some very promising nü-metal bands have appeared, for example, D-Fact from Koper, Corkscrew from Kamnik, Wicked Crew from Ljubljana, and C.R.A.S.H Crew from Radlje ob Dravi. These groups have broader appeal among listeners of alternative and mainstream rock, as well as among Slovene hip hop fans.

Not all bands have survived since 2003 when the survey was made. Noctiferia is still very active, but there are some new bands around, for example Negligence, Metalsteel, Burning Legion, Last Day Here, Xephagos, Rock Shock, and so forth. Some older bands like Interceptor and Kaoz are still very productive.

Generally, the common ground of all metal fans lies in the works of the most famous heavy metal groups of the past: Iron Maiden, Metallica, Morbid Angel, Slayer, Death, Sepultura, AC/DC, Black Sabbath, and Judas Priest. Also very influential are Darkthrone, Dream Theater, and Cannibal Corpse. Responses to more detailed questions about the influences from different regions revealed two ways in which fans get in touch with current worldwide metal. The primary means of getting information is live concerts and festivals. A second way is provided through media and records. Respondents commonly indicated that they were starving for larger concerts. Slovenia is simply a small country. Therefore, it is generally not possible to attract an audience of more than ten to fifteen thousand at the largest concerts, although Metallica and Iron Maiden, who have both performed in Slovenia in recent years, attracted such numbers. At the same time, there is a continual flow of European groups who perform a gig or two in Slovenia while on tour in central and southeastern Europe. Thus, the Slovenian audience can become acquainted with young and promising groups from central, northern, and western Europe. The proximity of Munich, Vienna, and Milan guarantees that the flow of interesting performers will not cease.

The considerable abundance of metal concerts impacts domestic metal production. Due to the limited market, it may not be strategic for more ambitious performers to use the Slovene language and thus be relegated only to domestic spaces. However, at the same time it is much more difficult to break out of national boundaries and into the highly competitive wider European arena. It is perhaps most difficult for non-extreme heavy metal groups that hold appeal in highly localized scenes to achieve substantial international success.

Important factors also include a band's general attitude, the messages in the lyrics, and, most importantly, the subtle specificities of musical taste that are shaped at local, national, or regional levels. Popular music itself is not only locally and regionally shaped, but nationally as well. This shaping of popular music taste occurs such that important distinctions are made and sustained. It is clear that, even after twenty-one years of Slovene independence from Yugoslavia, the popular music of the former Yugoslavia is still much more attractive in Slovenia than the popular music of neighboring Austria or Italy. And, vice versa, emotions and messages as embodied in specific regional (or "national") sounds may not be acceptable in other regions. At the same time, local exoticisms may sometimes become attractive to a wider audience. This is completely unpredictable and remains a mystery of commercial success of popular music in general.

On the other hand, narrow cultural spaces are often more open to the formation of extreme scenes. Therefore it is not unexpected that, according to an almost unanimous opinion of my respondents, death and black metal are the most developed subgenres of metal in Slovenia. Almost any band with fresh ideas can find a venue in which to play, and beginners can make their recordings quickly as well. At least some metal fans will attend the concert, and at least some fans will buy the record, especially if the band sells it at a reasonable price. They cannot depend on promoters or major distribution chains, so they find other channels for their promotion. As a matter of fact, it is quite difficult to find Slovene metal albums in regular record shops. Even in specialized rock and heavy metal shops, well supplied with international products, it is often impossible to find even one-third of the actual record production of Slovene metal bands. In many cases such records are only sold through direct mail order, or at concerts.

Individual musicians often quit playing, confronted with the realization of how laborious the pathways to stardom are. Perhaps the realization that one can personally meet the entire potential audience dampens enthusiasm. Musicians can make only their first steps toward stardom rapidly and with ease. Many groups become locally successful long before they gain adequate skill to make a greater breakthrough.[5]

Typically, beginners receive offers from local promoters to play as openers at concerts of other Slovene bands, or of bands from adjoining countries. In that regard, scenes are connected to those located in Slovenia's neighboring states. Thus, bands from the western part of Slovenia are better acquainted with the Italian metal scene, while groups from the northeastern part of Slovenia are more tied to the Austrian scene.

Remarkably, fans are quite well acquainted with metal scenes in central Europe and the Baltic states, probably due to the concert tours and international distribution of such well-known acts as Vader, Behemoth, and Krabathor. However, they do not know very much about Mediterranean metal scenes. In any case, the survey showed that the most important source of influences for present-day Slovene metal (after the United Kingdom and the United States) is Scandinavia. Respondents list more than one hundred groups from that region. They are also very well informed about other groups from Europe (other than the United Kingdom). That metal has already become a global phenomenon is substantiated by the fact that groups such as Sepultura, Angra, Kataklysm, Annihilator, and Krisiunare are frequently mentioned.

From the survey answers it is clear that the global distribution of heavy metal recordings functions well, and that there are channels through which to obtain albums. However, these channels are far from decentralized. Despite many mail order distribution centers in peripheral countries and despite access to information via the Internet, the majority of channels of both information and music remain centralized within the well-known "majors" and their distributors. Only a small portion of international exchange is independent of these sources.

Slovenia is too small to comprise a major music market in and of itself. In the former Yugoslavia, the rock market was much larger, but only the most successful groups were in a position to make recordings with major labels. Therefore, alternative ways of making recordings were exploited. For example, groups made demo recordings and distributed them on cassettes. Also, rock groups began to release LP records and CDs on their own labels or with small independent labels that appeared in the mid-1980s and at the beginning of the 1990s. Among them were metal labels like Impaled, Black Out Records, and Reek Records (Prezelj 1999, 90).

Some additional independent labels and distributors have appeared in the past few years. They are in many ways stimulating the new Slovene metal groups and scenes. Worth mentioning are the Master of Metal Shop from Ljubljana (it released a Slovene metal compilation and is a distributor for Nuclear Blast Records), On Parole Productions from Kamnik (see http://www.on-parole.com), and a new metal newspaper, *Metal Planet*, from Celje (see http://www.metalplanet.si). It is therefore understandable that there would be an inclination toward more radical music genres and subgenres. Even the international success of Laibach confirms that observation. We can expect that at least some of the groups mentioned above, if persistent enough, will gain international appeal. With rare exceptions they sing in English. However, only if they develop something like a specific Slovene "sound" or "atmosphere" in their music can they count on success. The subgenres that are quite well developed in Slovenia include death metal, black metal, everlasting heavy metal, thrash metal, and also progressive metal and various kinds of crossover metal. There is a notable lack of power, doom, speed, gothic, and epic metal.

According to my survey, metal fans in Slovenia are most clearly opposed to rap and electronic dance music. Also, there is a clearly established dualism that is obviously attractive to people who search for information at the *Paranoid* Web page. Metal fans who responded to my questionnaire in *Paranoid* are evidently deeply rooted in moral/aesthetic dualism (on dualism, see Hills 2002), and even black-and-white Manicheism. Perhaps as a result, they typically did not recognize nü-metal as metal at all (it is worth mentioning that there is a quite lively nü-metal scene in Slovenia, led by D-Fact). At the moment in Slovenia, there are many promising bands, in addition to Noctiferia. Crossover will likely remain a vital part of metal scenes in Slovenia. However, it is possible that the future is in melodic metal, reinforced by innovative harmonic explorations (for example, Obidil, Sabaium).

NOTES

1 To be sure, its music was more psychedelic than hard or heavy. Nevertheless, it was clearly the beginning of a new sound.

2 Unlike other socialist countries, the former Yugoslavia didn't provide instruments, equipment, or rehearsal facilities for the production of popular music. Instruments and equipment made in Yugoslavia (and other socialist countries) were far from the same quality as imported equipment. In the 1960s people often constructed their own equipment themselves.

3 "Hippies" here refers to long-haired admirers of rock from the 1960s and 1970s who in some ways resembled hippies of the 1960s counterculture in the United States and the United Kingdom. Another term used for them was *hašišarji* (hashish smokers).

4 I would like to thank the editors of *Paranoid*, Ajda Jelenc, Peter Gregorc, and others who put the open questionnaire on the Web. The questionnaire asks about the most important heavy metal groups (with regard to regions, for example, the United States, the United Kingdom, and western, eastern, southern, and northern Europe), genres, concerts, the Slovene metal scene, and other basic data. It was accessible for a period of one month. I find that respondents were generally *Paranoid*'s regular readers, not merely occasional "visitors" to the Web site. This leads me to posit that the answers may be instructive for the Slovene scene in general. Talking to fans at concerts I noticed that the vast majority of them knew and read *Paranoid*.

5 At the same time, an audience may demand much more than beginners—or not yet highly-skilled groups—can offer. As a matter of fact, the Slovene audience is very demanding, especially of domestic acts. Typically, discussions in *Paranoid* exhibit various ways of commenting upon concerts and bands—with only occasional voices of support. This is characteristic of other scenes here as well.

NAKO

The Metal in the Marrow of Easter Island Music

Dan Bendrups

The globalization of heavy metal has resulted in the genre's extension beyond original performance contexts into what Robert Walser describes as
"a variety of musical discourses, social practices and cultural meanings"
(1993a, 2). On the remote Polynesian island of Rapanui (Easter Island),
metal has played a small but significant role in the development of the
local popular music scene, though its specific influence is nested within the
impact of broader processes of colonization and globalization on Rapanui
performance culture. Metal arrived on Rapanui as a consequence of these
processes, but the ways in which indigenous musicians have adopted,
adapted, and appropriated aspects of metal music and imagery provide
a fertile ground for the reflective study of metal as a global phenomenon.

As observed by Jeremy Wallach (2003a) and Paul Greene (2001), the
translocation of heavy metal music can lead to entirely new cultural constructions around the lyrics, gestures, music techniques, and images of
the genre. In the case of Rapanui, heavy metal influences have been in-

corporated into local performances in ways completely divorced from the music's original sociocultural contexts, as a mainstream musical form among other rock-derived genres. This chapter therefore constructs metal as a mainstream, commercial popular music phenomenon rather than as a form of subcultural expression, first because the subcultural study of metal is well served in the extant literature, and second because the Rapanui engagement with metal is a result of the genre's presence within mainstream, Anglo-American, commercial modes of musical transmission and dissemination.

The Rapanui adoption of elements of heavy metal music is an intergenerational phenomenon represented by the two bands that are the basis for this chapter. In the 1970s metal provided inspiration for performances by a popular musician known publicly as Zopzy and his band Rangi Moana (Blue Sky). Between 2000 and 2004, metal informed the performances of the four young musicians—Ata, Funfu, Teuira, and Profe—who formed the progressive hard rock band Nako (Marrow).[1] These bands defy specific categorization as heavy metal or any of its subgenres because their use of metal is eclectic, interspersed with influences from other music genres and combined with aspects of traditional indigenous Rapanui music. Metal is, however, undeniably present in their music, and its presence deserves recognition and interrogation because it provides these musicians with the musical materials that differentiate them from other Rapanui musicians and which underpin their significant contributions to the history of Rapanui popular music.

Zopzy's incorporation of heavy metal musical elements in the 1970s situated metal as a signifier of musical otherness, without interrogating the position of metal within Western popular culture itself. Thirty years later, Nako's metal-inspired experimentations led to new modes of musical expression on Rapanui that arguably align with generalized interpretations of metal as a transgressive genre (Walser 1993a, 9; Binder 1993). Composed of three Rapanui islanders in their early twenties and one Chilean music teacher, Nako challenged the conceptualization of Rapanui identity in music by replacing traditional signifiers of indigeneity with heavy metal sound preferences and free improvisation. Their performance trajectory spanned only a few years, but their musical innovations had a generative influence on Rapanui performance culture, and their significance therefore resonates beyond the time-limited frame of the band's existence.

This chapter's analysis of Nako in the context of Rapanui popular music is informed by my ethnomusicological fieldwork on Rapanui in 2002, 2003, 2004, and 2008. During 2003 I conducted extensive participant-observation research with Zopzy, Nako, and members of their families who are involved in other aspects of music-making on Rapanui, and this chapter is an attempt to represent their perspectives and their interpretations of the culture-scape that they inhabit. The histories and descriptions that follow are based on oral testimony, imparted over the course of many months and in hundreds of separate conversations, and on the knowledge that I have gained from deep immersion in Rapanui performance culture. A particular focus of the chapter is Nako's participation in the Tapati Rapa Nui (Rapa Nui Week) festival of 2002. Tapati Rapa Nui (henceforth Tapati) is a very significant annual event in the Rapanui calendar, established in the 1960s and reconceptualized in the 1990s as a medium for protecting and reinvigorating traditional Rapanui performance culture (see Bendrups 2008). It is therefore significant that Nako's most prominent and contentious public performance occurred within Tapati, disrupting the usual performances of perceived traditional music with their metal-derived sound.

SITUATING RAPANUI POPULAR MUSIC

In order to understand the place of metal in Rapanui popular music, some details concerning the island's colonial history and music traditions are required. Introduced influences in Rapanui music are usually positioned in relation to the island's perceived traditional music canons, which contribute significantly to the Rapanui conceptualization of cultural identity in contemporary life. Each new wave of music to arrive on Rapanui is, therefore, either enthusiastically adopted or shunned depending on the extent to which it reinforces or contradicts perceived traditional musical practices. However, the specific cultural context within which new musical forms have arrived on Rapanui can also have a significant impact on the manner of their reception and adoption.

Contemporary Rapanui is socially and politically defined by the island's status as a Chilean colony since 1888. This relationship with Chile, at times antagonistic (McCall 1975), is a state of being that Rapanui islanders variously negotiate, embrace, and contest through the ways that they "perform" their cultural identity. Polynesian voyagers settled Rapanui some time before the year 800 AD. Together with Hawai'i and Aotearoa/New Zealand, Rapanui constitutes a corner of the so-called Polynesian Triangle,

which represents the geographic extent of Polynesian settlement throughout the Pacific. The current population of around four thousand people re-
sides mainly in the town of Hangaroa—the island's only settlement—and
is composed of both indigenous Rapanui islanders and Chilean residents.
Modern-day Rapanui is a place of constant cultural exchange where colonialism and tourism have resulted in waves of influence in introduced material culture, language, customs, and entertainment. International tourism has been a driving force behind cultural change on Rapanui since its
inception in the 1970s, and multiple weekly flights connect the island to
both Tahiti and mainland Chile throughout the year. Contemporary Rapanui music reflects local and introduced influences, incorporating pre-
contact musical practices on the one hand with Latin American and other
Western popular music influences on the other.

Within this variegated soundscape, perceptions of musical and cultural
authenticity are mediated by the expectations of tourist audiences and the
listening preferences of young islanders who are increasingly engaged with
international popular music trends. Performance opportunities abound
for groups that cater to tourists with modernized performances of perceived traditional repertoire, complete with traditional performance dress,
as is common throughout the Pacific. Since the 1970s, occasional performance opportunities have eventuated for local groups performing rock or
reggae covers, often to a mixed audience of tourists and locals. The community is, however, so small that more specialized performances (including
the metal-derived sound of Nako) receive far less local support, and virtually no interest from a culture-tourism market more interested in traditional performances. Meanwhile, the globalized listening tastes of many
Rapanui youth are satisfied through recordings encountered and accessed
online, rather than through local live performances.

Pre-contact Rapanui music tradition comprises song styles that reflect
ceremonial and social functions, including a large body of songs and chants
that relate to ancient legends and historical events, which have been well
documented (Bendrups 2006, 2007; Blixen 1979; Campbell 1971; Loyola
1988; Urrutia Blondel 1958). Traditionally, these performances were accompanied by a range of stone percussion instruments, and there was little
in the musical texture to interfere with the vocal line of the song, which
was considered the most important aspect of the music.

The preeminence of songtexts within traditional Rapanui music is an
enduring characteristic in Rapanui performance culture more broadly, as

it provided the framework for the incorporation of guitars and ukuleles into the Rapanui musical tradition. Omnipotent symbols of pan-Pacific pop, these "stringband" instruments reached Rapanui via Tahiti and Chile from the 1930s onward, and they were fully integrated into Rapanui performance culture in the 1960s. Since then, the stringband has become a required accompaniment in various types of perceived traditional Rapanui music to the extent that being a musician on Rapanui implies an ability not only to sing but also to play guitar. The function of the guitar in perceived traditional music is usually restricted to strummed chords that accompany the vocal line.

The dissemination of commercial popular music on Rapanui began through routes of trade and contact established in the nineteenth century. On the one hand, links to Tahiti that were established by missionaries and traders in the 1860s provided a line of communication with French Polynesia. On the other hand, increasing Chilean involvement in Rapanui from the 1920s onward (Porteous 1981) resulted in the dissemination of a variety of popular culture influences directly from Latin America. An example of this process is the dissemination of Argentine tango on Rapanui in the 1930s, brought about by the arrival of a new military governor and his family, who owned a gramophone and a collection of then-popular tango recordings from Chile. Tango was such a hit with Rapanui audiences that it generated a local music and dance genre called *tango Rapanui* that remains popular today and is so venerated that it is regarded as a traditional performance genre in its own right.

Throughout the first half of the twentieth century, intensification of contact with Chile led to the adoption of Spanish as the main language for communication with colonial authorities and a reliance on commercial goods and produce from Chile. This cultural colonization of Rapanui engendered some changes in local popular music, including the adaptation of guitars and various types of Latin percussion in local performances, as well as the adoption of Latin American genres that were popular in Chile in the 1950s, such as *ranchera* and *corrido*. In time, traditional Rapanui music became referred to as *folklore*—the term used by Chileans to describe their own music traditions.

Rock music was introduced to Rapanui in the 1960s by United States Air Force personnel who were stationed there between 1966 and 1969 (Esen-Baur and Walter 1990, 162). These North American troops were a significant influence on many aspects of Rapanui social life, and their presence constituted a direct link to entertainment industry goods, including sound recordings that were unavailable in Chile and otherwise beyond the reach of Rapanui audiences. Islanders who were in their teens and early twenties during this period fondly recall parties that the American troops held on or near their base, with impressive sound systems and occasional guitar and banjo performances from the soldiers themselves.

In the early 1970s, the establishment of regular commercial flights between Chile and Tahiti via Rapanui facilitated further local access to Western popular music as it provided the Rapanui with access to two distinct spheres of commercial sound recording distribution: Latin American Chile and French-controlled Tahiti. The distribution of LPs on Rapanui was initially restricted by the prohibitive cost of the discs and the equipment required to play them. However, the arrival of portable (battery powered) cassette tape players on Rapanui around 1978 made recordings of Western popular music much more accessible. The durability of cassettes, as well as their compact size, made them far easier to transport from overseas locations, and the boom box quickly became the nucleus for local gatherings and festivities. The avowed Rapanui metal fan Iovani Paoa, who grew up in the 1970s, recalled, "In those times, the people who had tape players were the center of attention. Everyone would follow them around. The party was wherever the owner of the music was located" (interview, author's translation, April 7, 2003).

Most of the commercial recordings to arrive on Rapanui were of groups that had already proven their popularity in international markets. To this end, headlining rock and metal groups including AC/DC, Deep Purple, Black Sabbath, and even Dire Straits came to be well known and widely followed on Rapanui, while more alternative performers remained unknown. Globalized Latin American metal groups like Sepultura received no particular attention from Rapanui audiences, though the direct contact with Chile meant that, in the 1990s, some Rapanui islanders became familiar with groups like Criminal from the nascent Chilean metal scene.

THE SYMBOLISM OF METAL

The assertive, overtly masculine imagery of heavy metal provided a cultural reference point that young Rapanui men were keenly able to identify with in the 1980s. At first, these images were known only from album covers and printed media, but the introduction of television to Rapanui in 1984 included occasional music videos featuring top-selling artists, which reinforced the sale and proliferation of recordings and the popularity of some metal bands on Rapanui. In the late 1970s and early 1980s, the Chilean military government provided unprecedented opportunities for Rapanui islanders to travel beyond their small island through military service. The association between heavy metal performance techniques—particularly amplified guitar distortion—and power, as noted by Théberge (2001, 6), resonates with the personal interest that metal held for those Rapanui who first experienced the music while undertaking military service in Chile at this time.

The idea of being a soldier complemented, to some extent, the traditional Rapanui conceptualization of the warrior figure, or *matato'a* in pre-contact society (see Bendrups 2006). By completing military service, many Rapanui men felt that they were fulfilling a traditional social role, and the opportunity to participate in military service was viewed favorably. However, by joining the Chilean military, the young Rapanui reservists were required to discard their independent Polynesian cultural identity and conform to the culture, values, and ideology of the Chilean armed forces. Their spoken communication was in Spanish, rather than the Rapanui language, and their commanders treated them as Chilean citizens first, ethnic Rapanui second.

A minority of men from this generation, now in their forties, still wear military fatigues as daily attire, symbolizing their service. These men comprise the most visible proponents of heavy metal on Rapanui as metal band T-shirts have become a standard component of their clothing and metal ranks high among their listening preferences. Their preference for hard rock and early metal bands is a reflection of the popular music that was available to them at the time of their travel and military service in Chile in the late 1970s; however, their preference for metal may also be seen as a desire to affiliate with a subculture that otherwise does not exist on Rapanui, except in rare and isolated instances. For those who struggled to find a place in Rapanui life after completing extended military service, the cultural imagery of metal provided a focus for their confusion, echoing Wallach's observations of "a major crisis of masculine identity, a crisis metal addresses with its ethos of heroic individualism and its compelling musical expressions of power and mastery" (2000, 1). Lacking any association with traditional Rapanui music, metal also functioned effectively as a vehicle for individual escapism. The role of metal in the construction of

Iconic AC/DC graffito along Atamu Te Kena Avenue, Rapanui, the only instance of graffiti on the entire main street. Photo by D. Bendrups, 2002.

a sense of alternative identity on Rapanui is epitomized by a man known publicly as "Black" (the English word is used), who could be seen on a daily basis throughout 2002 and 2003 dressed in army boots, camouflage pants, and a black Metallica T-shirt, sporting long black hair and listening constantly to compilations of hard rock and metal on his Walkman. To all intents and purposes, Black's attire, behavior, and demeanor reflect the symbolic power of metal, even in a place as geographically isolated as Rapanui.

THE INFLUENCE OF METAL IN LOCAL PERFORMANCES

Heavy metal influences were first incorporated into Rapanui performances in the late 1970s. Throughout the 1980s and 1990s, the influence of metal in Rapanui music was restricted to superficial references in the performances of only one or two musicians. The English lyrics of most songs placed them beyond any kind of thematic relevance to Rapanui, and the acoustic guitars that formed the basis of stringband music on Rapanui were not capable of reproducing the electrified sounds that characterized these recordings.

Other challenges limited the adoption of heavy metal influences in Rapanui music. Guitars on Rapanui were (and are) mainly used to provide accompaniments to vocal lines, rather than acting as melodic voices in their own right, which is far removed from the largely melodic role of the guitar in heavy metal (Walser 1993a, 50). Furthermore, self-taught Rapanui guitarists were not educated in the complexity of chords, chord progressions, and harmonic structures that underpin much heavy metal music (Walser 1993a, 41–48), making it difficult for them to reproduce the playing that they heard on commercial recordings. Perhaps because of this, the most popular heavy metal songs on Rapanui were often those that were technically less complicated, and later, the rock ballads featured in performances by mainstream heavy metal bands in the 1980s. This does not, however, necesssarily mark musical ineptitude: one Rapanui guitarist who has absolutely no association with heavy metal convincingly reproduced Guns N' Roses's cover of Bob Dylan's "Knocking on Heaven's Door," which he had learned by ear, during an impromptu performance in the Tapati festival of 2003.

Finally, and perhaps most importantly, before the 1970s, Rapanui lacked the electrical infrastructure and electronic sound technology that are the lifeblood of heavy metal. What was heard on the tape could not be reproduced without the aid of amplifiers, and this inability to reproduce what was easily available on cassette may have discouraged many Rapanui guitarists from seeking to add heavy metal to their respective repertories. Things changed, however, in 1973, when Zopzy took advantage of a trip to Chile to purchase a drum kit, electric guitar, keyboard, and amplifiers and brought them home to Rapanui.

ZOPZY AND RANGI MOANA

In 1973 Zopzy was already recognized by his peers as an accomplished musician, having inherited (by oral transmission) and maintained an extensive repertoire of traditional Rapanui songs from his elders. He had also been exposed to Western popular music during the period when U.S. troops were stationed on Rapanui, and he drew creative inspiration from their music. Realizing that sophisticated sound equipment was required in order to properly replicate these recordings, Zopzy sought an opportunity to travel to Chile to purchase it. He was widely supported by friends and family who helped to raise the money required for him to make these purchases.

Zopzy returned to Rapanui in 1973 with two electric guitars, a drum kit, and an assortment of amplifiers. These instruments became the basis for his interactions with other musicians, and by 1974 a small group called Rangi Moana had formed. Rangi Moana's first public performances took place in small bars that were established in the 1970s to cater to international tourists, as well as the recently established discotheque Torocco. The band's repertoire consisted mainly of Creedence Clearwater Revival covers and original compositions, many of which were based on traditional songs and songtexts. The new instruments provided a whole new background to these songs but also presented a range of problems in performance. While guitar techniques were easily transferable from acoustic to electric guitar, the guitar sound achieved by Rangi Moana was not informed by any technical training, resulting initially in a rough electric guitar sound and moments of uncontrolled feedback that approximated the Western techniques that they were trying to emulate, but without clarity or precision.

The sounds of power and distortion, rather than messages inherent in English song lyrics, were what attracted Zopzy and Rangi Moana to amplified instruments. The prominent urban and industrial themes of many metal songs were anathema to life on Rapanui, where there was (and is) no heavy industry. Unlike performances of heavy metal by bands in other remote locations (for example, Greene 2001, 173), Rangi Moana saw no need to translate the themes of heavy metal, focusing instead on their own song lyrics that reflected Rapanui island life from the very outset of their metal-inspired performances.

Zopzy, who already possessed a wide repertoire of songs, began by performing his own compositions, as well as some traditional songs, in the new electronic media. As in traditional Rapanui music, he regarded the song lyric as the most important aspect of the music, relegating the loud and powerful new instruments to a secondary role. The drums, bass, guitar, and keyboard were used to create a sonic background to the vocal line, and the electric guitar filled in the gaps between each verse, often with short melodic interjections, or simply strumming individual loud chords. As a result, Zopzy developed a performance style that privileged the vocal line, while retaining the impact of amplified sound.

In the 1980s, particularly following the introduction of music video to Rapanui, Zopzy's performances began to incorporate the imagery of the performers he admired. To this day he sports massive hair, held up with a "stars and stripes" bandanna, tight black jeans, and heavy boots. His posture while performing emulates famous hard rock performers such as Axl

Rose, and he also guitar-hops from one side of the stage to the other in the manner of AC/DC's Angus Young. Zopzy's most recent CD (he has three) features a metallic blue cover photograph of his full body with electric guitars grafted onto his arms in place of his hands, and a large gothic typeface for the album's title (Zopzy 2004).

Rangi Moana dissolved in 1976 when Zopzy returned to Chile for an extended period, but he continued to perform and compose in his favored electronic medium. Without the collaboration of fellow musicians, Zopzy began to exploit the potential of the synthesizer to provide drum, bass, and keyboard accompaniment all at the same time. He learned how to program these effects into his synthesizer, leaving his hands free to play guitar while singing over the top. His performances today continue to exploit the programming capacity of his Roland EM10, and he often performs alone, with synthesized accompaniment. While this has its disadvantages, it does allow him greater freedom over the performance, and he has recently begun to incorporate spontaneous and improvised lyrics into his music. This creativity, together with the perception that Zopzy is capable of handling more than one instrument at the same time, has helped to consolidate his status in the local community. Zopzy is also considered an important local musician by many islanders on the strength of his lyrics alone, and he is admired by a new generation of musicians such as the emerging artist Roberto Pakomio (Pakomio 2007), whom he has helped to nurture.

NAKO: THE VOICE OF A NEW GENERATION

The members of Nako, all born around 1980, grew up in a variegated sound environment, replete with local, Polynesian, Chilean, and North American musics. As far back as they can remember, recordings of prominent rock groups like AC/DC had been present in this environment, blending in with other introduced musics. Like many of their peers, the members of Nako were increasingly drawn toward introduced music in their listening habits. Unlike other young Rapanui musicians, however, the members of Nako had access to instruments and audio equipment that allowed them to replicate the sounds of amplified music. This access was provided by a key figure in the group's development, Ata's blues-enthusiast father, who keenly encouraged an appreciation of blues music in his son. He took particular pleasure in jamming with the young Ata and his friends, encour-

Zopzy rehearsing
at home. Photo by
D. Bendrups, 2003.

aging musical experimentation and improvisation, and provided a small collection of instruments (guitars, drums, and synthesizer) with which to do so.

These jam sessions frequently took the form of synthesizer duets, where the young friends would learn simple blues vamps on the keyboard, with the father soloing over the top. They became accustomed to the sounds that could be produced by electronic piano and guitar, and learned quickly about the relationships of chords and improvisation within the stylistic context of the twelve bar blues. In this respect, they came to possess a blues-based musical knowledge that was shared by few other Rapanui musicians, and which set the members of Nako apart from their peers. This difference was manifested most clearly in Nako's use of prominent instrumental melodies and improvisations—elements that are largely absent from traditional Rapanui performance styles that emphasize vocals and lyrics. While Zopzy's earlier musical innovations restricted the use of simple guitar riffs to the space between vocal phrases in his songs, Nako's musical formation focused on instrumental proficiency and harmonically complex accompaniments.

In their first attempts at forming a band, Ata, Funfu, and Teuira collaborated with Ito, a guitarist and vocalist, and performed under the name Taimana (Diamond) to fellow high school students on Rapanui. Taimana incorporated a variety of popular music influences into their compositions, particularly the characteristic backbeat of rock-and-roll drums and a reggae-influenced preference for "skank" guitar style. Taimana focused their creative energies on original compositions rather than covers of introduced music. As members' instrumental proficiency improved, they began to experiment with new musical elements—adding more percussion (bells, woodblock, tom-toms, and more cymbals) to the drum kit, and experimenting with different kinds of guitar distortion. Meanwhile, Ito contributed his own song lyrics, composed and performed in the crooning melodic style of Tahitian singers like Angelo Ariitai Neuffer.

Taimana eventually split up as a result of artistic differences, in which the influence of metal was a key factor. As the band's lead singer, Ito became increasingly concerned that the heavy use of guitar distortion in all of their songs was obscuring the vocal line, and his soft, emotive lyrics were spoiled by the raw energy of the accompaniment. Conversely, Ata and Funfu were themselves concerned that the even, formulaic structures of Ito's songs restricted their improvisations and that this was in turn stifling their creativity. Ito split from the group, eventually rising to local popularity as a soloist with his album *Moana* (2002)—which became a feature of the Tapati festival of 2003.

After Taimana, Ata, Funfu, and Teuira continued to play together, forming Nako with the help of a Chilean violinist and multi-instrumentalist known to the group as Profe (Professor), who had arrived on the island as a secondary school music teacher in early 2000. In his dealings with Ata, Teuira, and Funfu as music students, Profe became intimately aware of the way that these friends supported each other emotionally through music. In response, Profe began to offer them more of his own time, and his presence was slowly integrated into the social fabric of the group's rehearsals.

The young musicians, who had come to trust Profe, began to ask for advice in regard to musical matters, and the answers that he provided were put to effective use. In the beginning, this centered around simple, straightforward issues like tuning up, playing difficult chords, or executing famous guitar riffs, but the subject areas soon moved on to more difficult and conceptual issues such as the motivations for performance, the messages involved, the implications of performing without a vocalist, and writing songs without lyrics. Profe provided Nako with access to a wealth of musical experiences, enriching the bandmates' understanding of music with discussions of form and function in European art music, on the one hand, and his anecdotes as a performer in Chile on the other. He added more complex guitar and piano techniques to their improvisations and finally convinced them to include his violin in their jam sessions. This last addition was facilitated after listening to a variety of John McLaughlin and Mahavishnu Orchestra recordings, which reminded the bandmates of the wild improvisations that they were already executing. They began rehearsing with renewed vigor and chose the name Nako—which translates literally as "marrow"—as a symbol of the profundity that they were trying to achieve with their music.

Toward the end of 2001, Nako began to develop a reputation for performing challenging new music. The members of Nako spent their summer vacations in lengthy rehearsals, with the goal of developing a public profile. To begin with, this consisted of occasional gigs in pubs and restaurants around the island, mirroring the efforts of Rangi Moana three decades earlier. Nako ventured into these performances with a spirit of experimentation rather than commercialism, being grateful for the opportunity to perform rather than expecting any payment for it. This was fortunate, as their performances so confounded the tourist expectation of a Rapanui band that they rarely met with paying audiences. Their reputation grew among the local population, however, and a small following (mostly of friends and classmates) began to develop around the group.

Over the summer of 2001, the members of Nako were subjected to a string of complaints from their neighbors, who had begun to tire of the band's continuous rehearsals. The band members were threatened publicly, stones were thrown at them and at the house where they rehearsed, and neighbors cut their electricity on a number of occasions. This frustration was understandable, given that Nako played very loudly and that their rehearsal space had only thin fibro-cement walls, but the resultant attitude of the band members was one of self-righteousness: their reaction-

Ata (drums), Profe (violin), and Funfu (guitar) jamming in their coveted home rehearsal space. Photo by D. Bendrups, 2002.

Nako's rehearsal space was situated above a common access road for nearby homes and hidden behind a thick wall of bamboo. Photo by D. Bendrups, 2002.

ary neighbors represented a kind of cultural conservatism that they were trying to subvert. As the band's public profile grew, however, the neighborhood community began to develop more of an understanding of Nako's creative intent, and the complaints gave way to general acceptance, and later, outright support, often demonstrated in gifts of food left at their rehearsal studio by neighbors passing through.

By the end of 2001, Nako had developed enough original compositions to warrant the production of a demo recording. Recording facilities were not available on the island at this time, so the group arranged a weeklong trip to the populous Chilean capital, Santiago, where Profe had some music industry contacts. With the help of some of Profe's university friends, Nako recorded a demo CD containing nine works, mostly lengthy improvisations, which were usually recorded in one take.

Matters came to a head for Nako shortly afterward in February 2002 when they were offered an opportunity to perform during the annual Tapati festival. Tapati consisted mainly of traditional music and dance presentations and competitions, with special evenings set aside for new music. Nako requested, and was granted, performance time on one of these nights, though with some trepidation on the part of the festival organizers who did not have a clear idea about exactly what sort of music Nako intended to perform. This trepidation was reinforced on the night in question when some ominously black storm clouds began to accumulate above the open-air stage shortly before the band's scheduled performance.

Nako started with a series of long, slow improvisations over a background of low synthesized strings, employing layered effects of delay and reverb, and producing a gradually thickening and garbled harmonic texture. In anticipation of the direction that this performance was about to take, Profe interjected across the rising tension of the music with the words, "Ladies and gentlemen, you may not like what you are about to hear, but . . . good" (author's translation, February 14, 2002). The stage amplification for Tapati comprised twelve large speakers, which had been used solely for the relay of acoustic guitars and voices up until this point. When Nako finally burst into their full-volume instrumental style, the stadium-scale amplification sent their music across the entire town of Hangaroa, clearly stating the band's presence to all listeners within a two-kilometer radius. The rain held off until the end of the band's performance, at which point it began to pour down to such an extent that all following acts for that night were cancelled.

During Nako's performance, the audience response was overwhelmingly positive, with shouts of encouragement and applause throughout. In the following days, however, Nako was accused by some Rapanui authorities of corrupting the cultural festival, and it was suggested that the band should be banned from future public events. Many criticisms were leveled directly at Profe, who seemed to have transgressed his pedagogical and pastoral role as a teacher. A number of critics suggested that he was such a bad influence that he should be expelled permanently from the island.

The criticisms of Nako's performance were largely due to a perception that the heavy music they presented was somehow anti-cultural, bearing little resemblance to the stringband music that the community was more accustomed to. Nako regarded these commentaries as examples of the conservatism of the wider community, responding to their detractors by pointing out that the acoustic guitar was itself a foreign introduction to Rapanui music, and that heavily amplified music was nothing more than an extension of an existing process of acculturation.

THE METAL IN THE MARROW: CONTEXTUALIZING NAKO'S PERFORMANCE STYLE

When Nako took to the stage at Tapati in 2002, their performance tested the boundaries of the relationship between music and identity that is so significant to contemporary Rapanui culture. Significantly, the transgressive elements of their performance at this most prominent of public events drew from heavy metal performance practice. Nako's members were not deliberately seeking out heavy metal techniques to emulate, but employed them when they suited the structural and stylistic intentions of the music. The eclectic influence of heavy metal was, therefore, dispersed throughout Nako's music rather than being concentrated in any specific part of their repertoire, but Nako's sound would have been unrecognizable without it.

On the Tapati stage, the most prominent aspect of Nako's sound was the guitar distortion employed by Funfu, who changed rapidly between different effects and registers. Funfu demonstrated significant skill in the execution of improvised solos that were rhythmically dense and complex, shifting across many keys and utilizing a wide melodic range. Owing to his use of both distortion and reverb, the rapid harmonic changes clashed upon themselves, resulting in a harmonically dissonant effect that further distorted the sound. The blues influence in Funfu's guitar style was subtle but clearly perceptible, recalling Harris's exaltation of the "blues-oriented features" (2000c, 124) of heavy metal music.

Teuira's bass solos drew inspiration from the improvisations set up by Funfu, blending another layer of electric guitar distortion into the already heavy sound. In contrast to the rapidly moving guitar solos, however, the bass line provided short riffs returning to a central tone within a couple of bars. This dialogue between guitar and bass recalled Moore's description of the "alternation between power chord and repeatedly plucked bass string" (Moore 2001, 130) as a characteristic of metal. The overall effect of this combination was a high degree of guitar dissonance and distortion—described by Walser as being indispensable to metal (1993a, 41–42)—rendered powerful by virtue of being anchored to a fixed bass line. Ata's drumming rarely contributed any stabilizing influence; rather, he also drew rhythms from Funfu's solos, exchanging ideas and instigating rhythmic changes in an improvised manner. Soaring above this dense musical texture, Profe's piano and violin lines provided rich melodic layers to the highly charged music, with occasional violin solos in counterpoint to the guitar.

In this manner, Nako developed their performance according to individual ideas, themes, and moods. When the need for change within a song was identified, they switched dramatically and instantly between dense, high-paced distortion, and thinner, rhythmically simpler ideas, turning off all effects or dropping one or two instruments out altogether. The ultimate effect was a kind of organized improvisation: a cumulative structure based on a series of small ideas developed individually and strung together.

The Rapanui community's conservative reaction to Nako's festival performance in 2002 resembles the mass-media reception of metal as a dangerous or transgressive genre in the West (Binder 1993, 758). Nako were seen as immature and transgressive, their music loud and irritating, and their communal lifestyle of constant rehearsal an idle waste. More significantly, Nako's decision to perform without a vocalist contradicted notions of musical authenticity in a culture where the vocal line is regarded as the most important element of the music. Reactions to their music ranged from physical threats to public commentary from a local politician denouncing their sound as "devil's music." Nako were also accused of drunkenness and drug use, linking their music to general antisocial activity.

These moralistic arguments against Nako were never followed up with concerted action, nor did they reflect the breadth of public support for the young musicians' experimentation, but they do reflect an important issue in contemporary Rapanui culture. The island's traditional cultural heritage provides a buffer against the ever encroaching commercial and cultural influences that reach Rapanui from Chile and through international tourism, and music is a prominent and important part of this heritage. While gradual changes to performance practice have been incorporated into Rapanui tradition over time, the sudden changes wrought by Nako's performance in 2002 represented a threat emanating from within the very festival that was charged with protecting this cultural heritage, and Nako's subversive power was therefore greater than its members might otherwise have imagined.

CONCLUSION

Nako continued to rehearse and occasionally perform through 2002 and 2003, but a series of personal setbacks led to the band's decline in 2004. Nevertheless, new musicians and recording projects came to occupy the conceptual space that Nako's innovative performances had created. Groups such as the reggae-influenced Varua and Mito y Fusión Rapanui began experimenting with new instrumentation, and a number of Rapanui guitarists began to develop proficiency in electric guitar performance. In 2007, the traditional cultural performance troupe Kari Kari collaborated in an unprecedented recording project with the famous Chilean progressive folk group Los Jaivas.

The members of Nako found a range of new creative outlets after their break-up in 2004. Profe turned his focus back to teaching and in 2006 obtained assistance from the Chilean government to establish a children's string orchestra on Rapanui. Both Ata and Teuira were invited to join the popular Rapanui cultural performance troupe Matato'a on an international tour and CD project in 2004 (Matato'a 2004), and they continued to perform with Matato'a until 2008. They also supported Roberto Pakomio's recording project (Pakomio 2007), infusing his country guitar style with their heavier performance aesthetics.

In 2008 the heavy metal influence on Rapanui was no longer manifested in live performance, but the rapid expansion of modern communication technology—including high speed Internet and mobile telephones—now provides the Rapanui people with unrestricted access to globalized popular culture. The history of heavy metal influence in Rapanui music presented in this chapter reflects an earlier era of restricted cultural flow, but it also reveals that the power of heavy metal music has a long-standing trajectory transcending the standard industrial and commercial frameworks of popular music dissemination. The musical explorations of Nako, like Zopzy and Rangi Moana before them, stand as testimony to the influence of heavy metal in the most geographically isolated music culture on the planet.

NOTE

1 The name *Nako*, the Rapanui word for marrow, refers to the band members as a collective and will be referred to in the plural, as will the names of the other Rapanui musical groups discussed in this chapter.

AFTERWORD

Robert Walser

Studies of global cultural flows hang precariously between capitalism and culture, pulled toward homogenization by the relentless subjugating powers of the cash nexus, tugged back by the specificities of place and experience, the rich resources and limiting hurts of history. What is at stake, as always, is not just the actual nature of a reality that is to be represented, but the context of the representing, its purpose. One may warn of cultural greyout as giant corporations reach for greater economies of scale, or celebrate the creative syncretism of people who fashion new meanings from the collision of old and new, near and far. The search for common threads of humanity has come to seem old-fashioned as postcolonialists have worked to undermine Enlightenment universalism and ethnomusicologists have striven to illuminate irreducible differences that distinguish musical practices. However, the danger of assimilating the Other has perhaps been allowed too much to overshadow its opposite, the fetishizing of difference to the point that respect for others becomes more theoretical than empathetic, and such that scholars of differing musical cultures feel that they have no shared concerns, nothing relevant to say to one another.

For Edward Said, the essence of being an intellectual was to insist otherwise: "For the intellectual the task, I believe, is explicitly to universalize the crisis, to give greater human scope to what a particular race or nation suffered, to associate that experience with the sufferings of others" (1996, 44). This kind of universalizing, however, depends upon empathy with a shared or kindred human struggle and is the very opposite of the essentializing that produces archetypes. The "Eternal Feminine" designates a timeless essence and by so doing turns our attention away from the specifics of lived lives; what appears to flatter women by uniting them in a mystically powerful union with all other women has the effect of trivializing their particular identities and experiences. Similarly, overtones, mathematical resultants of a fundamental pitch, remind us how acoustic phenomena seem grounded in nature. Yet the guitar timbres of heavy metal, filled with the rich array of overtones we call distortion, are only heard as powerful in certain historical and social contexts, rather than as failure, the inability of audio equipment to reproduce a signal clearly. As I argued in *Running with the Devil* (1993a, 136), gender identities are just as unnatural; they circulate socially as unfulfillable promises, passed like bad checks.

Certainly, there are material and biological factors that shape gendered behavior, but they are far more complex and varied than is usually assumed, as the scientific literature has recently been making ever clearer. Homosexuality, for example, is routinely stigmatized as a peculiarly human, perhaps even urban, vice, yet over three hundred species of vertebrates are known to practice it. Nearly half the sexual relations of bonobos, a species of ape that is among our closest relatives, are homosexual (Balcombe 2006, 109, 114). Popular sociobiological assumptions have been decisively undercut by recent findings that in the animal world, bodies and genders do not conform to a binary model, sex roles are reversible, same-sex sexuality is common, secondary sex characteristics are not just relevant to heterosexual mating, and mating is not primarily a matter of sperm transfer but rather one of maintaining relationships (Roughgarden 2004, 169–71).

And so among the other admirable features of this collection, it is a particular pleasure to encounter a variety of unforeseen masculinities. Dan Bendrups's study of Easter Island, "the most geographically isolated music culture on the planet," shows how heavy metal mediates familiar anxieties of masculinity for its audience of forty-something men, but with a nationalistic twist. Metal was the music of these fans' youth and their military service in Chile, but since it is so strongly identified with North America, the music became a symbol of Easter Island's independence from Chilean dominance. It thus was quite naturally fused with the traditional culture of the island, as when the band Nako blended Anglo-American metal with Rapanui sounds and lyrical topics.

Jeremy Wallach's comparative study of metal in Indonesia, Malaysia, and Singapore also shows how regional scenes can be connected to global networks. Again, there are familiar tensions of masculinity, centering on not having the means to realize the lifestyle that is celebrated in advertising and popular culture. But in distinguishing the working-class ethno-nationalism of Malaysia and Singapore from the broad popularity of metal in Indonesia across class, region, and ethnicity, Wallach nonetheless shows how all three metal scenes are anchored in preexisting male sociality patterns. And in all three we see the exscription of women, but not any of the other gender strategies I had identified in mainstream American metal culture.

Most intriguingly, Cynthia P. Wong analyzes the surprising discursive fusions of Tang Dynasty, which sounds and looks like a Western metal band (with some use of traditional instruments), but features lyrics that have been modeled on the classical poetry of its namesake era, the seventh and eighth centuries. These musicians and their fans respond to familiar conflicts between media images and lived experiences of masculinity by connecting to the past, recovering traditions and history that had been lost to Communist erasure. The result is a tough and aggressive but also poetic and contemplative masculine ideal.

These authors and others in the collection exemplify productive dialogue in popular music scholarship. They draw upon previous work on heavy metal in ways that enable them to produce their own generative studies. Not content with seemingly natural stereotypes and archetypes, they delineate and account for similarities and differences in differing social contexts. Looking behind the norms of social status and cultural hierarchy, they uncover surprising instances of creativity, as people who are considered marginal cultural actors thrash their way toward better understandings of their lives and ways of making them more worth living. Like Susan Fast's *In the Houses of the Holy* (2001), Harris M. Berger's *Metal, Rock, and Jazz* (1999a), and Glenn Pillsbury's *Damage Incorporated* (2006), this new contribution to what might as well be called heavy metal studies could not be more different from the impoverished stereotypes that most often circulate as representations of heavy metal's essence. It aims to register fully the complexities of the cultures and lives in which metal is meaningful, and to encourage a kind of scholarly dialogue that repatriates the findings of specialized studies as contributions to shared humanistic concerns. In these ways, it thereby seriously aspires to fulfill the intellectual's task as Edward Said so boldly defined it.

ACKNOWLEDGMENTS

This project took over ten years to bring to fruition, and we have many people to thank. The editors would like to express our appreciation to our families and friends, as well as all the individual contributors to this volume for their insights, hard work, and patience. Jeremy especially thanks Esther A. Clinton for editorial assistance that really merits far more than a mere mention in the acknowledgements. He would also like to extend his gratitude to Maxine Barry, Isaac Brunner, Matthew A. Donahue, David Harnish, Brian Hickam, Michael Mooradian Lupro, David A. McDonald, Katherine Meizel, Sarah Morelli, Adam Murdough, Benjamin Hedge Olson, and Kristen Rudisill for their valued input and assistance with this project. Harris is grateful to Giovanna P. Del Negro, Judith Hamera, and Jesse L. Rester. Paul would like to thank Gert-Matthias Wegner, Shamsher B. Nhuchhen-Pradhan, and the musicians of UgraKarma and X-Mantra. All three of us are grateful to the College of Liberal Arts at Texas A&M University for its generous support of this project. We are thankful as

338   well to editorial director Ken Wissoker, Leigh Barnwell, Neal McTighe, and everyone else at Duke University Press who helped bring this project to fruition. An early version of a portion of chapter 6 appeared in the *Journal of Latin American Cultural Studies* 12 (3): 329–46. We gratefully acknowledge the kind permission of the journal to reprint it here. For additional images and links to songs and videos mentioned in the text, please see our Web site, www.metalrulestheglobe.com.

WORKS CITED

A., V. Orias. 2001. Answered by Valfar. *Majesta Webzine*, October 1. http://www
.windir.no/, accessed February 26, 2011.

Achiral. 1998. *Dark Waters*. Demo cassette. Self-released.

———. 2001. *Wander Ignite*. MCD. Self-released.

Ahmad, Jasman, Siti Zaiton, and Sulaiman Zakaria, eds. 1996. *Dikir barat*. Petaling
Jaya: Setiamas.

Alexandre, Ricardo. 2002. *Dias de luta: O rock e o Brasil dos anos 80*. São Paulo: Dórea
Books and Art.

Ali, Lorraine. 1998. Rebirth of Loud. *Spin*, August, 87 ff.

Amalietti, Peter. 1986. *Zgodbe o jazzu: Razvoj afroameriške glasbe med leti 1619–1964*
[The story of jazz: Development of Afro-American music between 1619 and
1964]. Ljubljana: Državna založba Slovenije.

Amorphis. 1994. *Tales from the Thousand Lakes*. CD. Nuclear Blast, NB 097-2.

———. 1996. *Elegy*. CD. Relapse Records.

Anderson, Benedict. 1983. *Imagined Communities: Reflections on the Origin and
Spread of Nationalism*. London: Verso.

Apotheosis. 2002. *Furthest from the Sun*. CD. Nocturnal Art Productions.

Appadurai, Arjun. 1990. Disjuncture and Difference in the Global Cultural Economy. *Public Culture* 2 (2): 1–24.

Arallu. 2002. *Satanic War in Jerusalem.* CD. Raven Music.

Archaean Harmony. 1997. *Resentment of an Evanesce Aeon.* Demo cassette. Self-released.

———. 2000. *Nihility Mundane Soul.* CD. Solemn Music.

Arnett, Jeffrey. 1993. Three Profiles of Heavy Metal Fans: A Taste for Sensation and a Subculture of Alienation. *Qualitative Sociology* 16 (4): 313–31.

Ascah, Matthew. 2003. "I've Felt the Hate Rise Up in Me": Intersections of Race, Violence, and Masculinity in the Music and Performance of Slipknot. M.A. thesis, Bowling Green State University.

Atkins, E. Taylor. 2001. *Blue Nippon: Authenticating Jazz in Japan.* Durham, N.C.: Duke University Press.

———, ed. 2003. *Jazz Planet.* Jackson: University Press of Mississippi.

Avelar, Idelber. 2001. Defeated Rallies, Mournful Anthems, and the Origins of Brazilian Heavy Metal. In *Brazilian Popular Music and Globalization*, ed. Christopher Dunn and Charles Perrone, 123–35. Gainesville: University of Florida Press.

———. 2003. Heavy Metal Music in Postdictatorial Brazil: Sepultura and the Coding of Nationality in Sound. *Journal of Latin American Cultural Studies* 12 (3): 329–46.

Ayik, Ilgin. 2008. Pentagram (a.k.a. Mezarkabul): Founders of Turkish Heavy Metal. Paper presented at "Heavy Fundametalisms: Music, Metal, and Politics," Salzburg, Austria, Nov. 3–5.

Back, Les. 2002. Wagner and Power Chords: Skinheadism, White Power Music, and the Internet. In *Out of Whiteness: Color, Politics, and Culture*, ed. Vron Ware and Les Back, 94–132. Chicago: University of Chicago Press.

Balcombe, Jonathan. 2006. *Pleasurable Kingdom: Animals and the Nature of Feeling Good.* New York: Macmillan.

Baldacchino, Godfrey. 2002a. A Nationless State: Malta, National Identity, and the European Union—2: The Onset of Partisan and Religious Hegemony. *Sunday Times*, Dec. 15: 56–57.

———. 2002b. A Nationless State: Malta, National Identity, and the European Union—3: Searching for "Nation-ness." *Sunday Times*, Dec. 22: 56–57.

Ballard, Mary E., Alan R. Dodson, and Doris G. Bazzini. 1999. Genre of Music and Lyrical Content: Expectation Effects. *Journal of Genetic Psychology* 160 (4): 476–87.

Balzamon. 1997. Letter to the editor. *Nordic Vision* 8: n.p.

Barber-Keršovan, Alenka. 1989. Tradition and Acculturation as Polarities of Slovenian Popular Music. In *World Music, Politics, and Social Change: Papers from the International Association for the Study of Popular Music*, ed. Simon Frith, 73–89. Manchester: Manchester University Press.

Barber-Keršovan, Alenka, Rajko Muršič, and Jože Vogrinc, eds. Forthcoming. *Popular Music and National Culture: Viewing the World from the Balkans.* Hamburg: Lit Verlag.

Barcinski, André, and Ivan Finotti. 1998. *Maldito: A vida e o cinema de José Mojica Martins, o Zé do Caixão*. São Paulo: Editora 34.

Barcinski, André, and Sílvio Gomes. 1999. *Sepultura: Toda a história*. São Paulo: Editora 34.

Barendregt, Bart, and Wim van Zanten. 2002. Popular Music in Indonesia since 1998, in Particular Fusion, Indie, and Islamic Music on Video Compact Discs and the Internet. *Yearbook for Traditional Music* 34: 67–113.

Barnard, Timothy P., ed. 2004. *Contesting Malayness: Malay Identity across Boundaries*. Singapore: Singapore University Press.

Barnouin, Barbara, and Changgen Yu. 1993. *Ten Years of Turbulence: The Chinese Cultural Revolution*. Publications De L'institut Universitaire De Hautes Études Internationales, Genève. London: K. Paul International.

Baulch, Emma. 1996. Punks, Rastas, and Headbangers: Bali's Generation X. *Inside Indonesia* 48. http://www.insideindonesia.org/edit48/emma.htm, accessed June 18, 2003.

———. 2003. Gesturing Elsewhere: The Identity Politics of the Balinese Death/Thrash Metal Scene. *Popular Music* 22 (2): 195–215.

———. 2007. *Making Scenes: Reggae, Punk, and Death Metal in 1990s Bali*. Durham, N.C.: Duke University Press.

Bauman, Zygmunt. 1998. On Glocalization: Or Globalization for Some, Localization for Some Others. *Thesis Eleven* 54 (1): 37–49.

Bayles, Martha. 1994. *Hole in Our Soul: The Loss of Beauty and Meaning in American Popular Music*. New York: The Free Press.

Bayton, Mavis. 1998. *Frock Rock: Women Performing Popular Music*. Oxford and New York: Oxford University Press.

Beckwith, Karl. 2002. Black Metal Is for White People: Constructs of Colour and Identity within the Extreme Metal Scene. *M/C Journal* 5 (3). http://journal.media-culture.org.au/0207/blackmetal.php, accessed June 2, 2008.

Beheaded. 1995. *Soul Dead*. Cassette demo. Self-released.

———. 1998. *Perpetual Mockery*. CD. X-treme Records.

———. 2000. *Resurgence of Oblivion*. MCD. Mighty Music.

———. 2002. *Recounts of Disembodiment*. CD. Mighty Music.

Bell, Albert. 1994. Rock Music and Counter-Culturalism in Malta. In *Maltese Society: A Sociological Inquiry*, ed. R. G. Sultana and G. Baldacchino, 421–39. Malta: Mireva Publications.

———. 2009. Extreme Subterranea?: Heavy Metal Subculture in Malta. Ph.D. diss., University of Malta.

Bendrups, Dan. 2006. War in Rapanui Music: A History of Cultural Representation. *Yearbook for Traditional Music* 38: 18–32.

———. 2007. Oceanic Encounters on Record: The Social History and Significance of the Rapanui Song *Sausau*. In *Oceanic Music Encounters: The Print Resource and the Human Resource—Essays in Honour of Mervyn McLean*, ed. Richard Moyle, 35–45. Auckland: RAL.

————. 2008. Pacific Festivals as Dynamic Contact Zones: The Case of Tapati Rapa Nui. *Shima* 2 (1): 14–28.

Berger, Harris M. 1997. The Practice of Perception: Multi-Functionality and Time in the Musical Experiences of a Heavy Metal Drummer. *Ethnomusicology* 41 (3): 464–88.

————. 1999a. *Metal, Rock, and Jazz: Perception and the Phenomenology of Musical Experience*. Middletown, Conn.: Wesleyan University Press.

————. 1999b. Death Metal Tonality and the Act of Listening. *Popular Music* 18 (2): 161–78.

————. 2004. Horizons of Melody and the Problem of the Self. In *Identity and Everyday Life: Essays in the Study of Folklore, Music, and Popular Culture*, by Harris M. Berger and Giovanna P. Del Negro, 43–88. Middletown, Conn.: Wesleyan University Press.

————. 2009. *Stance: Ideas about Emotion, Style, and Meaning for the Study of Expressive Culture*. Middletown, Conn.: Wesleyan University Press.

Berger, Harris M., and Michael T. Carroll, eds. 2003. *Global Pop, Local Language*. Jackson: University Press of Mississippi.

Berger, Harris M., and Cornelia Fales. 2005. "Heaviness" in the Perception of Heavy Metal Guitar Timbres: The Match of Perceptual and Acoustic Features over Time. In *Wired for Sound: Engineering and Technologies in Sonic Cultures*, ed. Paul D. Greene and Thomas Porcello, 181–97. Middletown, Conn.: Wesleyan University Press.

Better Red Than Dead. 2002. *The World Needs a Hero*. RAC Records, CD 634479152320.

Binder, Amy. 1993. Radical Rhetoric: Media Depictions of Harm in Heavy Metal and Rap Music. *American Sociological Review* 58 (6): 753–67.

Birch, Nicholas. 2008. 2008: A Metalhead Odyssey in Istanbul. *Eurasianet*, Feb. 25. http://www.eurasianet.org, accessed March 15, 2008.

Blabbermouth Web site. 2003. It's Official: Cannibal Corpse Are the Top-Selling Death Metal Band of the SoundScan Era. Nov. 17. http://www.roadrunnerrecords .com/blabbermouth.net/news.aspx?mode=Article&newsitemID=16769, accessed April 16, 2008.

————. 2008. 60,000 Tickets Sold for This Year's Wacken Open Air Festival. March 4. http://www.roadrunnerrecords.com/blabbermouth.net, accessed March 15, 2008.

Black Sabbath. 1995. *Forbidden*. CD. IRS.

Blade. 1998. *Rockomotive*. CD. Storm Records.

Blixen, Olaf. 1979. Figuras de hilo tradicionales de la Isla de Pascua y sus correspondientes salmodias. *Moana* 2 (1): 1–106.

Blood & Honour. 2003. Why We Fight. Blood & Honour Web site. http://www .skrewdriver.net, accessed Jan. 14, 2003.

Bloom, Howard. 1973a. Led Zep vs. Alice: The Battle of the Bucks. *Circus*, July, 50.

————. 1973b. Led Zep after the Tour: Bigger Than the Beatles? *Circus*, October, 66–70.

Booth, Stanley. 1985. *The True Adventures of the Rolling Stones*. New York: Vintage.   **343**

Borger, Julian. 2003. Metallica Is Latest Interrogation Tactic. *The Guardian*, May 20. http://www.guardian.co.uk, accessed Jan. 17, 2004.

Born, Georgina, and David Hesmondhalgh, eds. 2000. *Western Music and Its Others: Difference, Representation, and Appropriation in Music*. Berkeley: University of California Press.

Bourdieu, Pierre. [1979] 1984. *Distinction: A Social Critique of the Judgement of Taste*. London: Routledge.

——. 1991. *Language and Symbolic Power*. Cambridge: Polity Press.

——. 1993. *The Field of Cultural Production*. Oxford: Polity Press.

Breen, Marcus. 1991. Stairway to Heaven or Highway to Hell? Heavy Metal Rock Music in the 1990s. *Cultural Studies* 5 (2): 191–203.

Briguglio, Michael. 2001. Ideological and Strategic Shifts from Old Labour to New Labour in Malta. M.A. thesis, University of Malta.

Brooks, Van Wyck. 1947. *The Times of Melville and Whitman*. New York: E. P. Dutton.

Brown, Timothy S. 2004. Subcultures, Pop Music, and Politics: Skinheads and "Nazi Rock" in England and Germany. *Journal of Social History* 38 (1): 157–78.

Brunner, Isaac. 2006. Taken to the Extreme: Heavy Metal Cover Songs—The Impact of Genre. Ph.D. diss., School of Communication Studies, Bowling Green State University.

Bryson, Bethany. 1996. "Anything but Heavy Metal": Symbolic Exclusion and Musical Dislikes. *American Sociological Review* 45 (2): 884–99.

Burge, Micah, Corrie Goldblat, and David Lester. 2002. Music Preferences and Suicidality: A Comment on Stack. *Death Studies* 26: 501–4.

Burghart, Devin. 1999. *Soundtracks to the White Revolution: White Supremacist Assaults on Youth Music Subcultures*. Chicago: Center for New Community.

Burnett, Robert. 1996. *The Global Jukebox: The International Music Industry*. New York: Routledge.

Burroughs, William S. 1975. Rock Magic. *Crawdaddy*, June, 34–40.

Bushnell, John. 1990. *Moscow Graffiti: Language and Subculture*. Winchester, Mass.: Unwin Hyman.

Byrnside, Ronald. 1975. The Formation of a Musical Style: Early Rock. In *Contemporary Music and Music Culture*, ed. Charles Hamm, Bruno Nettl, and Ronald Byrnside, 159–92. Englewood Cliffs, N.J.: Prentice-Hall.

Caiafa, Janice. 1985. *Movimento punk na cidade: A invasão dos bandos sub*. Rio de Janeiro: Jorge Zahar.

Campbell, Ramón. 1971. *La herencia musical de Rapanui: Etnomusicología de la Isla de Pascua*. Santiago: Editorial Andres Bello.

Canclini, Néstor García. [1990] 1995. *Hybrid Cultures: Strategies for Entering and Leaving Modernity*. Trans. C. L. Chiappari and S. L. López. Minneapolis: University of Minnesota Press.

Candlemass. 1987. *Nightfall*. LP. Metal Blade Records.

——. 1988. *Ancient Dreams*. LP. Active Records.

344   Castells, Manuel. 2000. *The Rise of the Network Society: The Information Age: Economy, Society and Culture Vol. I*. 2nd ed. Malden, Mass.: Blackwell.

———. 2004. *The Power of Identity: The Information Age: Economy, Society and Culture Vol. II*. 2nd ed. Malden, Mass: Blackwell.

Celtic Frost. 1984. *Morbid Tales*. LP. Noise Records.

Chapple, Steve, and Reebee Garofalo. 1977. *Rock 'n' Roll Is Here to Pay: The History and Politics of the Music Industry*. Chicago: Nelson-Hall.

Chopyak, James D. 1987. The Role of Music in Mass Media, Public Education, and the Formation of a Malaysian National Culture. *Ethnomusicology* 31: 431–54.

Christe, Ian. 2003. *Sound of the Beast: The Complete Headbanging History of Heavy Metal*. New York: Harper Collins.

Clark, Marilyn. 1999. The Pursuit of a Criminal Career among Maltese Male Youth: A Biographical Approach. Ph.D. diss., University of Sheffield.

Clifford, Mike. 1983. *The Harmony Illustrated Encyclopedia of Rock*. New York: Salamander/Crown.

Clinton, Esther A. 2010. In the Ear of the Beholder: Aesthetics and Musical Taste. Paper presented at the Society for Ethnomusicology 55th Annual Meeting, Los Angeles, Nov. 11–14.

Cloonan, Martin. 1996. *Banned! Censorship of Popular Music in Britain: 1967–92*. Hants: Arena.

Cloonan, Martin, and Reebee Garofalo, eds. 2003. *Policing Pop*. Philadelphia: Temple University Press.

Coffin Joe. 1996. Banda é o segredo da origem do tudo. *Folha de São Paulo*, Caderno Ilustrada, Nov. 6, 4–5.

Cole, Richard, and Richard Trubo. 1992. *Stairway to Heaven: Led Zeppelin Uncensored*. New York: Harper Collins.

Comaroff, Jean, and John Comaroff. 2005. Millennial Capitalism and the Culture of Neoliberalism. In *The Anthropology of Globalization and Development: From Classical Political Economy to Neoliberalism*, ed. Marc Edelman and Angelique Haugerud, 177–87. Malden, Mass.: Blackwell.

Conover, Rachel Patrick. N.d. A Report on the Metal Scene in Alcalá de Henares, Spain. Unpublished paper, Bowling Green State University.

Considine, J. D. 1990. Led Zeppelin. *Rolling Stone*, Sept. 20, 57–60, 109.

Conte Oliveros, Jesus. 1994. *Isla de Pascua: Horizontes sombríos y luminosos*. Santiago: Centro de Investigación de la Imagen.

Coogan, Kevin. 1999. How Black Is Black Metal?: Michael Moynihan, *Lords of Chaos*, and the "Countercultural Fascist" Underground. *Hit List* 1 (1): 32–49.

The Core of Creation. 1996. Compilation CD. Storm Records.

Corona, Ignacio, and Alejandro Madrid. 2008. *Postnational Musical Identities: Cultural Production, Distribution, and Consumption in a Globalized Scenario*. Lanham, Md.: Lexington Books.

Corte, Ugo, and Bob Edwards. 2008. White Power Music and the Mobilization of Racist Social Movements. *Music and Arts in Action* 1 (1): 4–20.

Cowell, Henry, and Sidney Cowell. 1955. *Charles Ives and His Music*. New York: Oxford University Press.

Craik, Jennifer. 1997. The Culture of Tourism. In *Touring Cultures: Transformations of Travel and Theory*, ed. Chris Rojek and John Urry, 113–36. London: Routledge.

Cressy, Simon. 2008. A Darker Shade of Black. *Searchlight Magazine*, July. http://www.searchlightmagazine.com/, accessed Aug. 11, 2008.

Cullison, Alan. 2004. Smoke on the Volga: Among Russian Fans, Deep Purple Reigns. *Wall Street Journal*, Dec. 10, A1.

Cusick, Suzanne G. 2008. "You Are in a Place That Is out of the World . . .": Music in the Detention Camps of the "Global War on Terror." *Journal of the Society for American Music* 2 (1): 1–26.

Darkthrone. 1993. *Under a Funeral Moon*. CD. Peaceville.

Dasein, Deena. 1991. King's X: Algebra Harmonies, Six String Soul. *Illinois Entertainer*, March 17, 46–47.

Davis, Stephen. 1985. *Hammer of the Gods: The Led Zeppelin Saga*. New York: Ballantine.

de Kloet, Jeroen. 2001. Red Sonic Trajectories: Popular Music and Youth in Urban China. Ph.D. diss., Amsterdam School for Social Science Research.

De Launey, Guy. 1995. Not-So-Big in Japan: Western Pop Music in the Japanese Market. *Popular Music* 14 (2): 203–25.

Delia, Emanuel P. 1987. *The Task Ahead: Dimensions, Ideologies, and Policies — A Study on the State of the Economy*. Malta: Confederation of Private Enterprise.

Del Negro, Giovanna P. 2004. *The Passeggiata and Popular Culture in an Italian Town: Folklore and the Performance of Modernity*. Montreal: McGill-Queens University Press.

Del Negro, Giovanna P., and Harris M. Berger. 2004. Identity Reconsidered, the World Doubled. In *Identity and Everyday Life: Essays in the Study of Music, Folklore, and Popular Culture*, 124–58. Middletown, Conn.: Wesleyan University Press.

Demoniac. 1999. *The Fire and the Wind*. CD. Osmose Productions.

Demorest, Steven. 1975. The Circus Magazine Interview: Robert Plant. *Circus*, June, 26–31.

Denski, Stan, and David Sholle. 1992. Metal Men and Glamour Boys: Gender Performance in Heavy Metal. In *Men, Masculinity, and the Media*, ed. Steve Craig, 41–60. Newbury Park, Calif.: Sage.

Derschmidt, Eckhert. 1998. The Disappearance of the "Jazu-kissa": Some Considerations about Japanese "Jazz Cafés" and "Jazz Listeners." In *The Culture of Japan as Seen Through Its Leisure*, ed. Sepp Linhard and Sabine Frühstück, 303–315. Albany: State University of New York Press.

Die Böhse Onkelz. 1984. Deutchland. *Der nette Mann*. LP. Rock-O-Rama.

DiMatteo, Enzo. 2002. Hate Rock Revival. *Now Magazine*, June 20. http://www.thefreeradical.ca/Hate_rock_in_toronto1.htm, accessed Aug. 11, 2008.

Dimmu Borgir. 2003. *Death Cult Armageddon*. CD. Nuclear Blast.

Ding, Jian, and Elaine Yee-Man Chan. 1999. *The Chinese Democracy Movement and*

Tiananmen Incident: Annotated Catalog of the UCLA Archives, 1989–1993, *International Studies and Overseas Programs*. Los Angeles: University of California Press.

DJ. 2004. Re: A Question of Blast Perception. http://pub104.ezboard.com/, accessed Feb. 22, 2004.

Doherty, Harry. 1976. Past, Presence, and Future. *Melody Maker*, March 20, 8–9.

Dolabela, Marcelo. 1987. *ABZ do rock brasileiro*. São Paulo: Estrela do Sul.

Dorsal Atlântica. 1985. *Ultimatum*. EP. Self-released.

———. 1986. *Antes do Fim*. LP. Lunário Perpétuo Records.

———. 1988. *Dividir e Conquistar*. LP. Heavy Records.

———. 1990. *Searching for the Light*. LP. Heavy Records.

Duncan, Robert. 1984. *The Noise: Notes from a Rock 'n' Roll Era*. New York: Ticknor and Fields.

Duncombe, Stephen. 1997. *Notes from Underground: Zines and the Politics of Alternative Culture*. London: Verso.

Dunn, Sam, and Scot McFadyen, dirs. 2005. *Metal: A Headbanger's Journey*. Seville Pictures.

———. 2008. *Global Metal*. Seville Pictures.

———. 2009. *Iron Maiden: Flight 666*. Sony-BMG.

Eddino Abdul Hadi. 2008. Metal's Iron Rule. *The Straits Times* [Singapore], Sept. 12.

Eddy, Melissa. 2002. Rock Group Charged with Hate Crimes. *Washington Post*, Sept. 30, A22.

El Evil Emperor. 2007. Interview: Wasted Land. *Metal-Waves*, Aug. 25. http://www.metal-waves.com, accessed March 15, 2008.

Emperor. 1996. *Anthems to the Welkin at Dusk*. CD. Century Black, 7848-2.

Encyclopaedia Metallum. 2007. http://www.metal-archives.com/index.php, accessed July 4, 2007.

Enslaved. 2002. *Monumension*. CD. Osmose Productions, OPCD 119.

Esen-Baur, Heide-Margaret, and Christian Walter. 1990. L'île de Pâques aujourd'hui. In *L'île de Pâques: Une Énigme?*, ed. Francina Forment and Heide-Margaret Esen-Baur, 160–66. Brussels: Verlag Philipp von Zabern, Musées Royaux D'art et D'Histoire.

Exodus. 1985. *Bonded by Blood*. LP. Torrid Records.

Extremity. 1991. Untitled demo cassette. Self-released.

Fast, Susan. 2001. *In the Houses of the Holy: Led Zeppelin and the Power of Rock Music*. Oxford: Oxford University Press.

Feld, Steven. 1988. Notes on World Beat. *Public Culture* 1 (1): 31–37.

———. 1994. "From Schizophonia to Schismogenesis: On the Discourses and Practices of World Music and World Beat." In *Music Grooves*, ed. Charles Keil and Steven Feld, 257–89. Chicago: University of Chicago Press.

———. 2000a. "The Poetics and Politics of Pygmy Pop." In *Western Music and Its Others: Difference, Representation, and Appropriation in Music*, ed. Georgina Born and David Hesmondhalgh, 254–79. Berkeley: University of California Press.

———. 2000b. A Sweet Lullaby for World Music. *Public Culture* 12 (1): 145–71.

Feng, Jicai. 1996. *Ten Years of Madness: Oral Histories of China's Cultural Revolution.* San Francisco: China Books and Periodicals.

Ferzacca, Steve. 1996. In This Pocket of the Universe: Healing the Modern in a Central Javanese City. Ph.D. diss., Dept. of Anthropology, University of Wisconsin-Madison.

Firestarter. 1997. Compilation CD. Century Black, 7900–2.

Fischer, Hermann. 2001. *Sombras sobre Rapa Nui: Alegato por un pueblo olvidado.* 2nd ed. Santiago: LOM Ediciones.

Fisher, Ian. 2004. The Struggle for Iraq: Prisoner; Iraqi Tells of U.S. Abuse, from Ridicule to Rape Threat. *New York Times,* May 14.

Folha de São Paulo. 1994. Sepultura e Ramones percorrem o país em turnê inédita. Caderno Folhateen, Nov. 7, 6–7.

―――. 1996. Queremos ajudar a pôr o Brasil na história: Entrevista com Igor Cavalera. Caderno Mais!, April 14, 5.

―――. 1999. Sepultura conquista súditos na Inglaterra. Caderno Ilustrada, June 7, 5.

Formosa, Joseph J. 2000. Solemn Music. *Sunday Times* [Malta], Sept. 17: 18.

Forsaken. 1991. *Requiem.* Demo cassette. Self-released.

―――. 1993. *Virtues of Sanctity.* 7″ EP. Arkham Productions.

―――. 1996. *Evermore.* CD. Storm Records.

―――. 2002. *Iconoclast.* MCD. Golden Lake Productions.

―――. 2004. *Anima Mundi.* CD. Golden Lake Productions.

―――. 2005. *Dominaeon.* MCD. Golden Lake Productions.

Fox, Aaron. 2004. *Real Country: Music and Language in Working-Class Culture.* Durham, N.C.: Duke University Press.

Fox, Aaron, and Christine Yano, eds. Forthcoming. *Songs out of Place: Country Musics of the World.* Durham, N.C.: Duke University Press.

Fox, Kathryn Joan. 1987. Real Punks and Pretenders: The Social Organization of a Counterculture. *Journal of Contemporary Ethnography* 16 (3): 344–70.

Freund, Charles Paul. 2003. Baghdad Rock (Heavy Metal Dissent). *Reason,* June. http://reason.com/hitandrun/001015.html, accessed Jan. 17, 2004.

Frith, Simon. 1983. *Sound Effects: Youth, Leisure, and the Politics of Rock 'n' Roll.* London: Constable.

―――, ed. 1989. *World Music, Politics, and Social Change: Papers from the International Association for the Study of Popular Music.* Manchester, U.K.: Manchester University Press.

―――. 1996. *Performing Rites: On the Value of Popular Music.* Cambridge, Mass.: Harvard University Press.

―――. 2000. The Discourse of World Music. In *Western Music and Its Other: Difference, Representation, and Appropriation in Music,* ed. Georgina Born and David Hesmondhalgh, 305–322. Berkeley: University of California Press.

From Heaven to Hell: The Ultimate Metal Collection. 1998. Compilation cassette. Pony Canyon, PMCL 064-4.

FTG. 1998. *Aku Tak Peduli* [I don't care]. Pony Canyon, PMCL 065–4.

―――. 2000. *FTG.* Pony Canyon, PMCL 104-4.

Fuchs, Michael. 1992. Die Rockbands der Skinheads: Eine Botschaft des Hasses. *Die Welt*, Dec. 28, 8–9.

Fu Su Yin, Kelly, and Liew Kai Khiun. 2008. From Folk Devils to Folk Music: Tracing the Malay Heavy Metal Scene in Singapore. In *Sonic Synergies: Music, Technology, Community, Identity*, ed. Gerry Bloustien, Margaret Peters, and Susan Luckman, 115–23. Ashgate Popular and Folk Music Series. Aldershot, Hampshire, England: Ashgate.

Gaines, Donna. 1991. *Teenage Wasteland: Suburbia's Dead End Kids*. New York: Pantheon.

Gaonkar, Dilip Parameshwar. 2001. On Alternative Modernities. In *Alternative Modernities*, ed. Dilip Parameshwar Gaonkar, 1–23. Durham, N.C.: Duke University Press.

Geertz, Clifford. 1983. "From the Native's Point of View": On the Nature of Anthropological Understanding. In *Local Knowledge*, 55–70. New York: Basic Books.

Gellner, David. 1992. *Monk, Householder, and Tantric Priest*. Cambridge: Cambridge University Press.

Ghazal, Rym Tina. 2004. Band Hoping to Rock Iraq. *Toronto Star*, Jan. 25. http://www.thestar.com, accessed Jan. 26, 2004.

Gibbs, Jason. 2008. How Does Hanoi Rock?: The Way to Rock and Roll in Vietnam. *Asian Music* 39 (1): 5–25.

Giddens, Anthony. 1994. Foreword. In *Maltese Society: A Sociological Inquiry*, ed. R. G. Sultana and G. Baldacchino, xxvii–xxxiv. Malta: Mireva Publications.

Gilroy, Paul, and Errol Lawrence. 1988. Two Tone Britain: White and Black Youth and the Politics of Anti-Racism. In *Multi-Racist Britain*, ed. P. Cohen and H. Bains, 121–55. London: Macmillan Education.

Giulianotti, Richard, and Roland Robertson. 2004. The Globalization of Football: A Study in the Glocalization of the "Serious Life." *British Journal of Sociology* 55 (4): 545–68.

Glanzer, Perry L. 2003. Christ and the Heavy Metal Subculture: Applying Qualitative Analysis to the Contemporary Debate about H. Richard Niebuhr's *Christ and Culture*. *Journal of Religion and Society* 5: 1–16.

Gleason, Phillip. 1983. Identifying Identity: A Semantic History. *Journal of American History* 69: 910–31.

G.O.D. 1995. Interview. http://vandenis.sc-uni.ktu.lt/~vystan/god.html, accessed Aug. 21, 2002.

Goh, C. 1971. *The May Thirteenth Incident*. Kuala Lumpur: Oxford University Press.

Goodbye, Zhang Ju (Zaijian Zhangju). 1997. Audiocassette tape. Scorpion Culture [Beijing].

Goodrick-Clarke, Nicholas. 1985. *The Occult Roots of Nazism: The Ariosophists of Austria and Germany 1890–1935*. Wellingborough: Aquarian Press.

———. 2002. *Black Sun: Aryan Cults, Esoteric Nazism, and the Politics of Identity*. New York: NYU Press.

Gopal, Sangita, and Sujata Moorti, eds. 2008. *Global Bollywood: Travels of Hindi Song and Dance*. Minneapolis: University of Minnesota Press.

Gracyk, Theodore. 1996. *Rhythm and Noise: An Aesthetics of Rock*. Durham, N.C.: Duke University Press.

Grad, David. 1997. Interview with Jello Biafra. *Bad Subjects*, Feb. 30. http://eserver .org/bs/30/grad.html, accessed Feb. 11, 2002.

Graham, Laura. 1995. *Performing Dreams: Discourses of Immortality among the Xavante of Central Brazil*. Austin: University of Texas Press.

Grandin, Ingemar. 1989. *Music and Media in Local Life: Music Practice in a Newar Neighbourhood in Nepal*. Linköping: Department of Communication Studies.

Graustark, Barbara. 1973. *Houses of the Holy*—A Schizoid Led Zep Roars out of Hiding. *Circus*, May, n.p.

Greene, Paul D. 1995. Cassettes in Culture: Emotion, Politics, and Performance in Rural Tamil Nadu. Ph.D. diss., University of Pennsylvania.

———. 2001. Mixed Messages: Unsettled Cosmopolitanisms in Nepali Pop. *Popular Music* 20 (2): 169–87.

———. 2003. Nepal's *Lok Pop* Music: Representations of the Folk, Tropes of Memory, and Studio Technologies. *Asian Music* 34 (1): 43–65.

———. Forthcoming. Intense Emotions and Human Rights in Nepal's Heavy Metal Scene. In *Popular Music and Human Rights, Volume II, World Music*, ed. Ian Peddie. Burlington, Vt.: Ashgate Press.

Greene, Paul D., and David R. Henderson. 2000. At the Crossroads of Languages, Musics, and Emotions in Kathmandu. *Popular Music and Society* 24 (3): 95–116. Reprinted in Berger and Carroll 2003.

Greene, Paul D., and Thomas Porcello, eds. 2005. *Wired for Sound: Music and Technologies in Sonic Cultures*. Middletown, Conn.: Wesleyan University Press.

Greene, Paul D., and Yubakar Raj Rajkarnikar. 2001. Echoes in the Valleys: A Social History of Nepali Pop Music, 1985–2000. *Wave Magazine* [Nepal] 63: 16–18, 21.

Grixti, Joe. 2004. *Broadcasting and the Young Adult Consumer: Local and Global Media Influences on Maltese Youth Culture*. Malta: Broadcasting Authority.

Gross, Robert L. 1990. Heavy Metal Music: A New Subculture in American Society. *Journal of Popular Culture* 24 (1): 119–30.

Guilbault, Jocelyne. 1996. Beyond the "World Music" Label: An Ethnography of Transnational Musical Practices. *Beitrag zur Konferenz Grounding Music*, May. http://www2.hu-berlin.de/fpm/texte/guilbau.htm, accessed Feb. 2, 2002.

Hahn, Tomie. 2006. "It's the RUSH": Sites of the Sensually Extreme. *TDR: The Drama Review* 50 (2): 87–96.

Halford, Rob. 1985. Foreword. In *Heavy Metal Thunder: The Music, Its History, Its Heroes*, by Philip Bashe, viii–ix. New York: Doubleday.

Hall, Stuart. 1996. The Question of Cultural Identity. In *Modernity: An Introduction to Modern Societies*, ed. Stuart Hall, David Held, Don Hubert, and Kenneth Thompson, 595–634. London: Blackwell.

Han, Minzhu, and Hua Sheng, eds. 1990. *Cries for Democracy: Writing and Speeches from the 1989 Chinese Democracy Movement*. Princeton, N.J.: Princeton University Press.

350   Hannerz, Ulf. 1992. *Cultural Complexity: Studies in the Social Organization of Meaning*. New York: Columbia University Press.

Harbert, Benjamin. 2007. Fade to Black: The Catalysis of Politics and Aesthetics in Egyptian Heavy Metal. Paper presented at the joint conference of the U.S. and Canadian Branches of the International Association for the Study of Popular Music, Northeastern University, Boston, April 27–29.

Harrell, Jack. 1994. The Poetics of Destruction: Death Metal Rock. *Popular Music and Society* 18 (1): 91–104.

Harris, Keith D. [now Keith Kahn-Harris]. 1997. "Music Is My Life"?: Discourse Analysis and the Interview Talk of Members of a Music-Based Subculture. Working Paper 4, Department of Sociology. London: Goldsmiths College.

———. 2000a. An Orphaned Land?: Israel and the Extreme Metal Scene. Paper presented at the 3rd Crossroads in Cultural Studies International Conference, Birmingham, England, June 21–25.

———. 2000b. "Roots"?: The Relationship between the Global and the Local within the Extreme Metal Scene. *Popular Music* 19: 13–30.

———. 2000c. "Darkthrone Is Absolutely Not a Political Band": Difference and Reflexivity in the Global Extreme Metal Scene. In *Changing Sounds: New Directions and Configurations in Popular Music*, ed. Tony Mitchell, Peter Doyle, and Bruce Johnson, 124–29. Proceedings of the 1999 biannual conference of the International Association for the Study of Popular Music (IASPM). Sydney: University of Technology.

Hart, David S. 1988. Heavy Metal Thunder: "White Metal" Is the New Grassroots Movement. It's Loud. It's Radical. And It's Growing. *Contemporary Christian Music*, January, 18–20.

Hebdige, Dick. 1981. Skinheads and the Search for a White Working Class Identity. *New Socialist*, September/October, 38–41.

Hecker, Pierre. 2005. Taking a Trip to the Middle Eastern Metal Scene: Transnational Social Spaces and Identity Formations on a Non-National Level. *NORD-SÜD Aktuell* 19 (1): 57–66.

———. 2008. Heavy Metal in a Muslim Context: The Rise of the Turkish Metal Underground. Paper presented at "Heavy Fundametalisms: Music, Metal, and Politics," Salzburg, Austria, Nov. 3–5.

———. 2009. Public Perceptions of Masculinity and Femininity in Turkish Metal. Paper presented at the "Heavy Metal and Gender" Conference, Cologne, Germany, Oct. 8–10.

Hellhammer. 1990. *Apocalyptic Raids*. Noise Records, N00083.

Henderson, David. 2003. Who Needs "The Folk"?: A Nepali Remodeling Project. *Asian Music* 34 (1): 19–42.

Herman, Gary. 1976. Kiss Blitzes London. *Circus*, Aug. 10, 26–27.

Hernandez, Deborah Pacini, Héctor Fernández L'Hoeste, and Eric Zolov. 2004. *Rockin' Las Américas: The Global Politics of Rock in Latin/o America*. Pittsburgh: University of Pittsburgh Press.

Hicks, Michael. 1999. *Sixties Rock: Garage, Psychedelic, and Other Satisfactions.* Urbana: University of Illinois Press.

Hiemenz, Jack. 1977a. A New Stage, a New Act, and a Grand Entourage Bring Two Rock Worlds Dizzyingly Close Together. *Circus*, June 23, 38–41.

———. 1977b. Part Two: Kiss in Japan. *Circus*, July 7, 31–34.

Hills, Matt. 2002. *Fan Cultures.* London: Routledge.

Hinds, Elizabeth Jane Wall. 1992. The Devil Sings the Blues: Heavy Metal, Gothic Fiction, and "Postmodern" Discourse. *Journal of Popular Culture* 26 (3): 151–64.

Hirose, Kazuo. 1994. Interview with KISS. *Honoo* 2: 34.

Hmeljak, Franko. 1995. *Kameleoni 1965–1995.* Koper, Slovenia: Capris—društvo za oživljanje starega Kopra.

Hodkinson, Paul. 2002. *Goth: Identity, Style, and Subculture.* Oxford: Berg.

Hogg, Chris. 2004. It's Only Iraq'n'roll but I Like It. *BBC News*, Jan. 12. http://news .bbc.uk/go/pr/fr/-/2/hi/ middle_east/3390149.stm. accessed Jan. 15, 2004.

Holt, Fabian. 2007. *Genre in Popular Music.* Chicago: University of Chicago Press.

Honig, Emily. 2002. Maoist Mappings of Gender: Reassessing the Red Guards. In *Chinese Femininities, Chinese Masculinities*, ed. Susan Brownell and Jeffrey N. Wasserstrom, 255–68. Berkeley: University of California Press.

hooks, bell. 1992. Eating the Other. In *Black Looks: Race and Representation*, 21–40. Boston: South End Press.

Hooper, John. 2000. Race-hate Rock CDs Seized in East Germany: Police Impound Neo-Nazi Music after Killing Shocks Country. *The Guardian*, Sept. 6. http://www .guardian.co.uk/world/2000/sep/06/johnhooper, accessed March 3, 2011.

Hosokawa, Shuhei. 1999. "Salsa No Tiene Fronteras": Orquesta de la Luz and the Globalization of Popular Music. *Cultural Studies* 13 (3): 509–34.

Huang, Liaoyuan. 1994. Zhongguode Bon Jovi [China's Bon Jovi]. In *Beijing-yaogunbuluo* [The Beijing rock tribe], ed. You Zhou, 36–50. Tianjin: Tianjin Social Sciences Association Publisher.

Huizinga, Johan. 1955. *Homo Ludens: A Study of the Play Element in Culture.* Boston: Beacon Press.

Human Rights Watch. 1998. *Academic Freedom in Indonesia: Dismantling Soeharto-era Boundaries.* New York: Human Rights Watch.

Hunt, Chris. 1987. Independents' Day. *Solid Rock*, n.n., 36–37.

Huq, Rupa. 2005. *Beyond Subculture: Pop, Youth, and Identity in a Postcolonial World.* New York: Taylor and Francis.

Ihsahn, and Samoth. 2007. Exclusive EMPEROR Guitar Lesson and Tabs. *Revolver Magazine.* http://www.revolvermag.com/, accessed March 7, 2011.

Islam Online. 2003. U.S. Tortures Iraqi POWs with Heavy Metal. May 21. http:// www.islamonline.net/, accessed Jan. 15, 2004.

Itô, Masanori. 1993. *Dangen.* Tokyo: Burrn! Corporation.

Jacobs, Karrie. 1993. Germany Stomps Skinhead Music. *Rolling Stone*, Nov. 11, 18–19.

Jankélévitch, Vladimir. 1987. *Muzika i neizrecivo* [Music and the unspeakable]. Novi Sad, Serbia: Književna zajednica Novog Sada.

Jasper, Tony, Derek Oliver, Steve Hammond, and Dave Reynolds. 1983. *The International Encyclopedia of Hard Rock and Heavy Metal*. New York: Facts on File.

Johannessen, Christine. 1967. Norwegisches Burschenbrauchtum: Kult und Saga. Ph.D. diss., University of Vienna.

Jones, Danko. N.d. Singer's clinic with Derrick Green. http://www.badtasterecords .se/files/public/singers_clinic_part_1.m3u, accessed Oct. 20, 2004.

Jones, Karl. 2003. *"A Blaze in the Northern Sky": Black Metal Music and Subculture; An Interactionist Account*. Sociology Working Papers 36. Manchester: University of Manchester.

Jones, Mike. 1998. Marketing British Pop: The Promotion of British Pop Acts and British Pop Records in Japan. In *Popular Music: Intercultural Interpretation*, ed. Toru Mitsui, 99–105. Kanazawa: Kanazawa University.

Judas Priest. 1976. *Sad Wings of Destiny*. Koch Records, B00003TFN7.

Kadmon. 1995. *Aorta No. 20: Oskorei*. Vienna: Aorta Publications.

Kahn, Joel S. 2006. *Other Malays: Nationalism and Cosmopolitanism in the Modern Malay World*. Honolulu: Asian Studies Association of Australia in association with University of Hawai'i Press.

Kahn-Harris, Keith. 2002. "I Hate This Fucking Country": Dealing with the Global and the Local in the Israeli Extreme Metal Scene. In *Music, Popular Culture, Identities*, ed. R. Young, 133–51. Amsterdam: Editions Rodopi.

———. 2004a. The Failure of Youth Culture: Reflexivity, Music, and Politics in the Black Metal Scene. *European Journal of Cultural Studies* 7 (1): 95–111.

———. 2004b. Unspectacular Subculture? Transgression and Mundanity in the Global Extreme Metal Scene. In *After Subculture*, ed. Andy Bennett and Keith Kahn-Harris, 107–18. New York: Palgrave Macmillan.

———. 2007. *Extreme Metal: Music and Culture on the Edge*. New York: Berg.

———. 2008. "Metal Studies"—A Bibliography. http://www.kahn-harris.org, accessed Nov. 16, 2008.

Kampfar. 1997. *Mellom Skogkledde Aaser*. CD. Century Black, 7931–2.

Kapchan, Deborah. A. 1994. Moroccan Female Performers Defining the Social Body. *Journal of American Folklore* 107 (423): 82–105.

Kaplan, Jeffrey. 1998. Religiosity and the Radical Right: Toward the Creation of a New Ethnic Identity. In *Nation and Race: The Developing Euro-American Racist Subculture*, ed. Jeffrey Kaplan and Tore Bjørgo, 102–25. Boston, Mass.: Northeastern University Press.

Kawabata, Shigeru. 1991. The Japanese Record Industry. *Popular Music* 10 (3): 327–45.

Keil, Charles, Angeliki V. Keil, and Dick Blau. 1992. *Polka Happiness*. Philadelphia: Temple University Press.

Kelly, Paul. 2004. Cultural Policy in Malta: A Critical Analysis of the State of Culture in Malta, Its New Cultural Policy, and the Appraisal of This Policy by the Council of Europe. M.A. thesis, De Montfort University.

Kelly, Sean. 2006. Communities of Resistance: Heavy Metal as a Reinvention of Social Technology. In *The Resisting Muse: Popular Music and Social Protest*, ed. Ian Peddie, 149–62. Burlington, Vt.: Ashgate Press.

Kemper, Peter. 1992. Immer Aggressiverer Flirt mit dem Grauen: Das international Phänomen Gewalt; Rock ist zum Integrationsfeld jugendlicher deutscher Rechtsradikaler geworden. *Frankfurter Allgemeine Zeitung*, Nov. 14, 29–31.

Kiss. 1974. *Hotter Than Hell*. LP. Casablanca.

Klinec, Mirjana. 2003. Biti ženska v moškem svetu: Položaj žensk v heavy metalu [Being female in a male world: The situation of women in heavy metal]. Diploma thesis, Department of Ethnology and Cultural Anthropology, University of Ljubljana.

Kong, Lily. 1996. Popular Music and a "Sense of Place" in Singapore. *Crossroads* 9 (2): 51–77.

Kozorog, Miha. 2001. Glasba—prostor—identiteta: Primeri iz Tolmina po letu 1945 [Music—space—identity: Examples from Tolmin after 1945]. Diploma thesis, Department of Ethnology and Cultural Anthropology, University of Ljubljana.

Kranjc, Darja. 2002. O vlogi mitologije dobrega in zla v besedilih power epic metala—Rhapsody [Mythology of good and evil in the texts of power epic metal group Rhapsody]. *Glasnik Slovenskega etnološkega društva* [Bulletin of the Slovene Ethnological Society] 42 (3): 23–27.

Krell, David Farrell. 1996. *Infectious Nietzsche*. Bloomington: Indiana University Press.

Kremation. 1987. *Guardian of the Realm*. Album cassette. Self-released.

Krenske, Leigh, and Jim McKay. 2000. "Hard and Heavy": Gender and Power in a Heavy Metal Subculture. *Gender, Place, and Culture* 7 (3): 287–304.

Kuo, Kaiser. 2000. Remembering the Good Old Days. *China Now*. http://www .chinanow.com/english/features/rocktalk/remembering.html, accessed July 2, 2002.

Kusno, Abidin. 2003. Remembering/Forgetting the May Riots: Architecture, Violence, and the Making of "Chinese Cultures" in Post-1998 Jakarta. *Public Culture* 15 (1): 149–77.

Lathrop, Tad, and Jim Pettigrew Jr. 1999. *The Business of Music Marketing and Promotion*. New York: Billboard Books.

Led Zeppelin. 1970. *Led Zeppelin III*. LP. Atlantic.

———. 1975. *Physical Graffiti*. LP. Swan Song.

Lendt, C. K. 1997. *Kiss and Sell: The Making of a Supergroup*. New York: Billboard Books.

Levi, Erik. 1990. The Aryanization of Music in Nazi Germany. *Musical Times* 131 (1763): 19–23.

LeVine, Mark. 2008. *Heavy Metal Islam: Rock, Resistance, and the Struggle for the Soul of Islam*. New York: Three Rivers Press.

———. 2009. *Headbanging against Repressive Regimes: Censorship of Heavy Metal in the Middle East, North Africa, Southeast Asia, and China*. Copenhagen: Freemuse.

Lian Kwen Fee. 2001. The Construction of Malay Identity across Nations: Malaysia, Singapore, and Indonesia. *Bijdragen tot de Taal-, Land-, en Volkenkunde* 157 (4): 861–80.

354   Lipsitz, George. 1994. *Dangerous Crossroads: Popular Music, Postmodernism, and the Poetics of Place*. London: Verso.

Liu, Menghan. N.d. When *Hybrid Theory*'s Knockin' on Mainland China's Door: Cultural Fusion Steers the Staging of E-age Generation. Unpublished paper, Bowling Green State University.

Llewellyn, Meic. 1998. Beyond the Transatlantic Model: A Look at Popular Music as If Small Societies Mattered. *Critical Musicology Journal: A Virtual Journal on the Internet* 2. http://www.leeds.ac.uk/music/Info/critmus/, accessed Nov. 2, 2001.

Loathe. 2004. *Abort/Retry/Fail*. Promo MCD. Self-released.

Lockard, Craig. 1991. Reflections of Change: Sociopolitical Commentary and Criticism in Malaysian Popular Music since 1950. *Crossroads: An Interdisciplinary Journal of Southeast Asian Studies* 6 (1): 1–111.

———. 1998. *Dance of Life: Popular Music and Politics in Southeast Asia*. Honolulu: University of Hawai'i Press.

Lööw, Helene. 1998. White Power Rock 'n' Roll: A Growing Industry. In *Nation and Race: The Developing Euro-American Racist Subculture*, ed. Jeffrey Kaplan and Tore Bjørgo, 126–47. Boston: Northeastern University Press.

Louie, Kam. 2002. *Theorising Chinese Masculinity: Society and Gender in China*. Cambridge: Cambridge University Press.

Loyola, Margot. 1988. Mis vivencias en Isla de Pascua. *Revista Musical Chilena* 170: 48–86.

Lynxwiller, John, and David Gay. 2000. Moral Boundaries and Deviant Music: Public Attitudes toward Heavy Metal and Rap. *Deviant Behavior* 21: 63–85.

Lystrup, Pål. 2003. Interview with Gaahl of Gorgoroth. http://www.gorgoroth.org/band/interviews/heavymeta12003eng.html, accessed Feb. 15, 2004.

MacCannell, Dean. 1976. *The Tourist: A New Theory of the Leisure Class*. New York: Schocken Books.

MacDougall, J. Paige. 2003. Transnational Commodities as Local Cultural Icons: Barbie Dolls in Mexico. *Journal of Popular Culture* 37 (2): 257–75.

Maffesoli, Michel. [1988] 1996. *The Time of the Tribes: The Decline of Individualism in Mass Society*. London: Sage Publications.

Malečkar, Nela, and Tomaž Mastnak, eds. 1985. *Punk pod Slovenci* [Punk under the Slovenes]. Ljubljana: Krt 17.

Males, Mike A. 1996. *The Scapegoat Generation: America's War on Adolescents*. Monroe, Maine: Common Courage Press.

Manslaughter. 1991. Untitled demo cassette. Self-released.

Manuel, Peter. 1988. South Asia. In *Popular Musics of the Non-Western World: An Introductory Survey*, 171–97. Oxford: Oxford University Press.

Mariappan, Kntayya. 2002. Ethnicity, Malay Nationalism, and the Question of Bangsa Malaysia. In *Ethnonational Identities*, ed. Steve Fenton and Stephen May, 198–226. Hampshire, U.K.: Palgrave MacMillan.

Marriott, McKim. 1976. Hindu Transactions: Diversity without Dualism. In *Transaction and Meaning*, ed. Bruce Kapferer, 109–42. Philadelphia: Institute for the Study of Human Issues.

Marshall, George. 1991. *Spirit of '69: A Skinhead Bible*. London: S.T. Publishing.   **355**

Martin, Linda, and Kerry Segrave. [1988] 1993. *Anti-Rock: The Opposition to Rock 'n' Roll*. New York: Da Capo Press.

Martyrium. 2002. *Withering in Voluptuous Embrace*. CD. Self-released.

Masada. 1995. *Untrodden*. Demo cassette. Self-released.

Masland, Tom, Karen Breslau, and Jennifer Foote. 1992. Muffling the Music of Hate: Germany Cracks Down on Skinhead Rock. *Newsweek*, Dec. 14, 53.

Mastnak, Tomaž. 1994. From Social Movements to National Sovereignty. In *Independent Slovenia: Origins, Movements, Prospects*, ed. Jill Benderly and Evan Kraft, 93–111. London: Macmillan.

Matato'a. 2003. *Fusion Natura*. CD. EMI [Chile/Bolivia].

———. 2004. *Tatoo*. CD. Tupuna Productions.

Mathews, Ben. 1995. *The Solid Singapore-Malaysia Joke Book*. Singapore: Angsana Books.

Mattila, Mikko, and Janne Sarna. 1999. For the Glory of Metal. *Isten 100*, n.p.

McCall, Grant. 1975. Sympathy and Antipathy in Easter Islander and Chilean Relations. *Journal of the Polynesian Society* 84: 467–76.

———. 1994. *Rapanui: Tradition and Survival on Easter Island*. 2nd ed. Sydney: Allen and Unwin.

McClary, Susan. 1994. Same as It Ever Was. In *Microphone Fiends: Youth Music and Culture*, ed. Andrew Ross and Tricia Rose, 29–40. New York: Routledge.

McDonald, Andrew [William Pierce]. 1978. *The Turner Diaries*. Fort Lee, N.J.: Barricade Books.

McDonald, Chris. 2009. *Rush, Rock Music, and the Middle Class: Dreaming in Middletown*. Bloomington: Indiana University Press.

McGowen, Chris, and Ricardo Pessanha. 1998. *The Brazilian Sound: Samba, Bossa Nova, and the Popular Music of Brazil*. Philadelphia: Temple University Press.

McIver, Joel. 2000. *Extreme Metal*. London: Omnibus Press.

McPherson, Ian. 2004. Gather No Moss: The Complete Rolling Stones Concertlog, 1962–2011: North America: The North Atlantic Seaboard. Time Is on My Side Web site. http://www.timeisonourside.com/atlantic.html, accessed Feb. 20, 2011.

Medway, Gareth. 2001. *Lure of the Sinister: The Unnatural History of Satanism*. New York: NYU Press.

Meethan, Kevin. 2001. *Tourism in Global Society: Place, Culture, Consumption*. New York: Palgrave.

Meintjes, Louise. 1990. Paul Simon's *Graceland*, South Africa, and the Mediation of Musical Meaning. *Ethnomusicology* 34 (1): 37–73.

Melankol X. 1996. Review of *Ancient Hymns of Legend and Lore* by Bishop of Hexen. *Nordic Vision* 7: n.p.

Meli, Janet. 2000. New Age: A Sociological Perspective. B.A. thesis, University of Malta.

Melzer, Alexander. 2002. J. R. R. Tolkien: A Metal Pioneer. *The Metal Observer*. http://www.metalobserver.com/gb/articles/tolkien.html, accessed Feb. 5, 2002.

356　Mendoza-Denton, Norma. 1996. "*Muy Macha*": Gender and Ideology in Gang-girls' Discourse about Makeup. *Ethnos* 6: 47–64.

Metalik Klinik 3. 2000. Compilation cassette. Rotorcorp/Musica, MSC.8346.

Metallica. 1983. *Kill 'Em All*. LP. Megaforce Records.

Metalstorm Website. 2008. Ragnaröck Festival-Lichtenfels, Germany, 30th–31st March 2007. http://www.metalstorm.ee/pub/article.php?article_id=337, accessed Aug. 1, 2008.

Miheljak, Vlado, ed. 2002. *Mladina 2000: Slovenska mladina na prehodu v tretje tisočletje* [The youth 2000: Slovenian youth at the turn to the third millennium]. Maribor: Aristej and MŠZŠ.

Miller, Daniel. 1995. Introduction: Anthropology, Modernity, and Consumption. In *Worlds Apart: Modernity through the Prism of the Local*, 1–22. New York: Routledge.

Mitchell, Tony, ed. 2001. *Global Noise: Rap and Hip-hop outside the USA*. Middletown, Conn.: Wesleyan University Press.

Mitsui, Toru. 1983. Japan in Japan: Notes on an Aspect of the Popular Music Record Industry in Japan. *Popular Music* 3: 107–20.

Mitsui, Toru, and Shuhei Hosokawa. 1998. *Karaoke around the World: Global Technology, Local Singing*. London: Routledge.

Moore, Alan. 2001. *Rock: The Primary Text*. 2nd ed. Aldershot, England: Ashgate.

Moretti, Eddy, and Suroosh Alvi, dirs. 2007. *Heavy Metal in Baghdad*. VBS.TV.

Moyle, Richard. 1991. *Polynesian Music and Dance*. Auckland: Centre for Pacific Studies, University of Auckland.

Moynihan, Michael, and Didrik Søderlind. 1998. *Lords of Chaos: The Bloody Rise of the Satanic Metal Underground*. Venice, Calif.: Feral House.

Mudrian, Albert. 2004. *Choosing Death: The Improbable History of Death Metal and Grindcore*. Los Angeles: Feral House.

Mullins, Greg. 2002. *Colonial Affairs: Bowles, Burroughs, and Chester Write Tangier*. Madison: University of Wisconsin Press.

Mulvany, Aaron. 2000. "Reawakening Pride Once Lost": Indigeneity and European Folk Metal. Ph.D. diss., Wesleyan University.

Muršič, Rajko. 1993. *Neubesedljive zvočne igre: Od filozofije k antropologiji glasbe* [Non-verbal sound games: From philosophy toward anthropology of music]. Maribor, Slovenia: Katedra.

———. 1995. *Center za dehumanizacijo: Etnološki oris rock skupine* [Center za dehumanizacijo: An ethnological description of the rock group]. Pesnica, Slovenia: Frontier, ZKO Pesnica.

———. 1998. Autochthonisation of Rock Music in Rural Slovenia. In *Popular Music: Intercultural Interpretations*, ed. Toru Mitsui, 281–88. Kanazawa, Japan: Graduate Program in Music, Kanazawa University.

———. 2000a. *Trate vaše in naše mladosti: Zgodba o mladinskem in rock klubu* [The story of the rock and youth club in Trate]. 2 vols. Ceršak, Slovenia: Subkulturni azil.

———. 2000b. Provocation and Repression after Socialism: The Strelnikoff Case. In *Changing Sounds: New Directions and Configurations in Popular Music; IASPM*

1999 *International Conference Proceedings*, ed. Tony Mitchell, Peter Doyle, and Bruce Johnson, 309–18. Sydney: University of Technology.

———. 2002. Local Feedback: Slovene Popular Music between the Global Market and Local Consumption. *Beiträge zur Popularmusikforschung* 29/30: 125–48.

———. 2005a. Ethnographic Experience, Understanding, and Narratives in the Discourse of Popular Music. In *Text and Reality*, ed. Jeff Bernard, Jurij Fikfak, and Peter Grzybek, 147–58. Ljubljana: Institute of Slovenian Ethnology at ZRC SAZU.

———. 2005b. Ljubljana. *Encyclopedia of Popular Music of the World, vol. 7*, 139. New York: Continuum.

———. 2005c. Slovenia. *Encyclopedia of Popular Music of the World, vol. 7*, 137–39. New York: Continuum.

Mutilated Mag. 1991. Review of demo tape by Incantation. *Mutilated Mag* 2 (11): n.p.

Nagata, Judith A. 1974. What Is a Malay? Situational Selection of Ethnic Identity in a Plural Society. *American Ethnologist* 2: 331–50.

National Socialist Black Metal Web site. 2003. White Power Music. http://www.nsbm.org/white_power_music, accessed March 10, 2003.

———. 2008a. CDs and T shirts. http://www.nsbm.org/store, accessed Aug. 11, 2008.

———. 2008b. Frequently Asked Questions about National Socialist Black Metal. http://www.nsbm.org/faq/, accessed Aug. 4, 2008.

———. 2008c. Media Page. http://www.nsbm.org/media/, accessed Aug. 11, 2008.

———. 2008d. NSBM Groups and Political Parties. http://www.nsbm.org/groups/, accessed Aug. 11, 2008.

National Statistics Office of Malta. 2002. *Kultura 2000: A Survey on Cultural Participation*. Malta: NSO.

Negus, Keith. 1992. *Producing Pop: Culture and Conflict in the Popular Music Industry*. London: Arnold.

———. 1999. *Music Genres and Corporate Culture*. New York: Routledge.

Ng, Benjamin Wai-ming. 2002/2003. Japanese Popular Music in Singapore and the Hybridization of Asian Music. *Asian Music* 24 (1): 1–18.

Nietzsche, Friedrich. [1872] 1967. *The Birth of Tragedy in the Spirit of Music*. Trans. Walter Kaufmann. New York: Random House.

———. [1888] 1974. *The Gay Science*. Trans. Walter Kaufmann. New York: Random House.

———. [1901] 1967. *The Will to Power*. Ed. Walter Kaufmann. Trans. Walter Kaufmann and R. J. Hollingdale. New York: Random House.

Nilsson, Magnus. 2009. Gender in Global and Local Metal: What Can We Learn from the Scene in Gaborone? Paper presented at the "Heavy Metal and Gender" Conference, Cologne, Germany, Oct. 8–10.

Nomad Son. 2008. *First Light*. CD. Metal on Metal Records.

No Remorse. N.d. Bloodsucker. *This Time the World*. CD. Panzerfaust Records.

Norm Rejection. 1998. *Deconform*. CD. Molotov Records.

———. 2000. 0002. CD. Self-released.

Oblique Visions. 1995. *Seas of Serenity*. CD. Self-released.

Ochoa, Ana María. 1999. El desplazamiento de los discursos de la autenticidad: Una mirada desde la música. *Antropología* 15/16: 171–82.

O'Conner, Alan. 2002. Local Scenes and Dangerous Crossroads: Punk and Theories of Cultural Hybridity. *Popular Music* 21 (2): 225–36.

Ogasawara, Yasushi. 1998. Mr. Big in Japan: Perception of Rock Music by Japanese Rock Fans. In *Popular Music: Intercultural Interpretation*, ed. Toru Mitsui, 182–84. Kanazawa: Kanazawa University.

Olsen, Dale. 2008. *Popular Music of Vietnam: The Politics of Remembering, the Economics of Forgetting*. New York: Routledge.

Olsen, Dale, and Daniel E. Sheehy. 2000. *The Garland Encyclopedia of Latin American Music*. New York: Garland.

Olson, Benjamin. 2008. I Am the Black Wizards: Multiplicity, Mysticism, and Identity in Black Metal Music and Culture. M.A. thesis, Bowling Green State University.

Onoshima, Dai. 1991. Toshi bunmei no yugami wo utsushidas jûkinzoku ongaku [Heavy metal music: A reflection of distorted urban civilization]. *Music Magazine*, December, 117–23.

Overdose. 1985. *Século XX*. Split LP with Sepultura, *Bestial Devastation*. Cogumelo.
———. 1987. *Conscience*. LP. Cogumelo.

Owen, Ursula, Marie Korpe, and Ole Reitov. 1998. Smashed Hits: The Book of Banned Music. Special issue, *Index on Censorship* 72 (6).

Pakarati, Ito. 2002. *Moana*. CD. Nuku te Mango [Chile].

Pakomio, Roberto. 2007. *O Tatou*. CD. Tokerau Producciones.

Panggilan Pulau Puaka II (Call of the haunted island II). 1999. Compilation cassette. Psychic Scream, PSCL9010-4.

Parvo, David. 2003. Strelnikoff: Censorship in Contemporary Slovenia. In *Policing Pop*, ed. Martin Cloonan and Reebee Garofalo, 140–50. Philadelphia: Temple University Press.

Pedersen, Jostein. 2000. Look to Hell! Look to Norway. *Listen to Norway* 8 (2): 6–11.

Perlman, Marc. 1999. The Traditional Javanese Performing Arts in the Twilight of the New Order: Two Letters from Solo. *Indonesia* 68: 1–37.

Perrone, Charles. 1989. *Masters of Contemporary Brazilian Song: 1965–1985*. Austin: University of Texas Press.

Perry, Elizabeth J., and Nara Dillon. 2002. "Little Brothers" in the Cultural Revolution: The Worker Rebels of Shanghai. In *Chinese Femininities, Chinese Masculinities: A Reader*, ed. Susan Brownell and Jeffrey N. Wasserstrom, 269–86. Berkeley: University of California Press.

Pickles, Jo. 2000. Punks for Peace: Underground Music Gives Young People Back Their Voice. *Inside Indonesia* 64. http://www.insideindonesia.org/edit64/punk1 .htm, accessed June 18, 2003.

Pillsbury, Glenn T. 2006. *Damage Incorporated: Metallica and the Production of Musical Identity*. New York: Routledge.

Pizek, Jeff. 2003. Dark Tranquility. *CRC Pulse*, December, 5 ff.

Poberžnik, Polona. 2002. *Popularna godba skoz lokalne godbene prakse na primeru Koroške* [Popular music through local music practices in the case of the Koroška region]. Paper presented at the IASPM-Slovenia meeting in the Gromka Club, Feb. 14.

Pomaranča. 1981. *Peklenska Pomaranča*. LP. PGP RTB.

———. 1983. *Madbringer*. LP. PGP RTB.

———. 1985. *Pomaranča/Orange III*. LP. PGP RTB.

———. 1995. *Takoj se dava dol*. CD. Panika Records.

Porteous, J. Douglas. 1981. *The Modernization of Easter Island*. Western Geographical Series 19. Victoria, B.C.: Department of Geography, University of Victoria.

Powers, Ann. 1994. To the Misty Mountain. *Village Voice*, Nov. 15, 69.

Prezelj, Mitja. 1999. Heavy Metal: Bojevniki peklenskega hrupa [Heavy metal: The Warriors of Pandemonium]. In *Urbana plemena: Subkulture v Sloveniji v devetdesetih* [Urban tribes: Subcultures in Slovenia in the nineties], ed. Peter Stankovič, Gregor Tomc, and Mitja Velikonja, 83–96. Ljubljana: ŠOU — Študentska založba.

Protzman, Ferdinand. 1992. Music of Hate Raises the Volume in Germany. *New York Times*, Dec. 2, A9–10.

Purcell, Natalie. 2003. *Death Metal Music: The Passion and Politics of a Subculture*. Jefferson, N.C.: McFarland and Company.

Quah, John S. T. 2000. Globalization and Singapore's Search for Nationhood. In *Nationalism and Globalization: East and West*, ed. Leo Suryadinata, 71–101. Singapore: Institute of Southeast Asian Studies.

Rafalovich, Adam. 2006. Broken and Becoming God-Sized: Contemporary Metal Music and Masculine Individualism. *Symbolic Interaction* 29 (1): 19–32.

Ranawana, Arjuna. 2000. Shake, Rattle, and Roll: Why Kids Won't Sing the Traditional Tune. *Asiaweek* 29 (23). http://www.cnn.com/ASIANOW/asiaweek/magazine/2000/0616/sr.kids.html, accessed Feb. 20, 2011.

Realida. 1994. *Facing Reality*. Demo cassette. Self-released.

Resistance Records Website. 2003a. Resistance History. http://www.resistance.com/history, accessed Jan. 16, 2003.

———. 2003b. Resistance Product Info. http://www.resistance.com/catalog/productinfo, accessed Jan. 10, 2003.

Resnicoff, Matt. 1990. In through the Out Door: Jimmy Page Goes Back to Led Zeppelin. *Musician*, November, 48–64, 72.

Ribeiro, Hugo L. 2004. Notas Preliminares sobre o Cenário Rock Underground em Aracaju-SE [Preliminary notes on the underground rock scene in Aracaju-SE]. Paper presented at the V Congresso da Seção Latino-Americana da Associação Internacional para o Estudo da Música Popular, Rio de Janeiro, June 21–25.

———. 2009. Heavy, Doom, and Death Metal in Brazil. Paper presented at the "Heavy Metal and Gender" conference, Cologne, Germany, Oct. 8–10.

Risério, Antônio. 1993. *Caymmi: Uma utopia de lugar*. São Paulo: Perspectiva.

Robertson, Roland. 1992. *Globalization: Social Theory and Global Culture*. Thousand Oaks, Calif.: Sage.

Robinson, Deanna Campbell, Elizabeth B. Buck, and Marlene Cuthbert. 1991. *Music at the Margins: Popular Music and Global Cultural Diversity*. Newbury Park, Calif.: Sage Publications.

Roccor, Bettina. 2000. Heavy Metal: Forces of Unification and Fragmentation within a Musical Subculture. *World of Music* 42 (1): 83–94.

Rockin' in the Islamic World: Underground Heavy Metal Scene Thrives Cautiously in Egypt. 2006. CBS News. http://www.cbsnews.com/stories/2006/08/13/ world/ main1890218.shtml, accessed June 27, 2007.

Rodel, Angela. 2004. Extreme Noise Terror: Punk Rock and the Aesthetic of Badness. In *Bad Music: The Music We Love to Hate*, ed. Christopher Washburne and Maiken Derno, 235–56. New York: Routledge.

Rojek, Chris, and John Urry. 1997. Transformations of Travel and Theory. In *Touring Cultures: Transformations of Travel and Theory*, ed. Chris Rojek and John Urry, 1–19. London: Routledge.

Roughgarden, Joan. 2004. *Evolution's Rainbow: Diversity, Gender, and Sexuality in Nature and People*. Berkeley: University of California Press.

Rubin, M. Alan, Daniel V. West, and Wendy S. Mitchell. 2001. Differences in Aggression, Attitudes toward Women, and Distrust as Reflected in Popular Music Preferences. *Media Psychology* 3: 25–42.

Said, Edward. 1996. *Representations of the Intellectual*. New York: Vintage Books.

Sakai, Kô. 1991. *Baimei Kôi* [Publicity stunt]. Tokyo: Shinko Music Pub.

Salem. 1986. *Destruction Till Death*. Demo cassette. Self-released.

———. 1989. *Millions Slaughtered*. Demo cassette. Self-released.

———. 1994. *Kaddish*. CD. Morbid Records, MR015.

———. 2007. *Necessary Evil*. CD. Season of Mist, B000PAAI30.

———. 2010. *Playing God and Other Short Stories*. CD. Pulverised Records.

Salleh, Halim. 2000. Globalization and the Challenges to Malay Nationalism as the Essence of Malaysian Nationalism. In *Nationalism and Globalization: East and West*, ed. Leo Suryadinata, 132–74. Singapore: Institute of Southeast Asian Studies.

Samuels, David. 2004. *Putting a Song on Top of It: Expression and Identity on the San Carlos Apache Reservation*. Tucson: University of Arizona Press.

Sanity. 1995. Untitled demo cassette. Self-released.

Sarkitov, Nikolay-Dautovich. 1987. Ot "khard-roka" k "khevi-metallu": Effekt oglupleniya ["Hard-rock" to "heavy-metal": The Stupefaction Effect]. *Sotsiologicheskie Issledovaniya* 14 (4): 93–94.

Sauer, Scott. 2003. String Arrangements: On This Day in Led Zeppelin History. March 29. http://groups.yahoo.com/group/LZHistory/message/325, accessed May 18, 2005.

Saunders, Mike. 1971. Kingdom Come: Sir Lord Baltimore (Review). *Creem*, May, 74.

Sceptocrypt. 1996. *Wild Code of Reverie*. Demo cassette. Self-released.

———. 1999. *26 hrs 72 mins. . . The Need to Differ*. Promo CD. Self-released.

Schafer, R. Murray. 1977. *The Tuning of the World*. New York: Knopf.

———. 1994. *The Soundscape*. Rochester, Vt.: Destiny Books.

Scheel, Karen R., and John S. Westefeld. 1999. Heavy Metal Music and Adolescent Suicidality: An Empirical Investigation. *Adolescence* 34 (134): 253–73.

Schembri, Mel. 2003. Beheaded and Loathe. *Dansezee* 10: 11.

Schwarzer Orden. 2002. *Kamaraden*. CD. Resistance Records, 1222.

Sciriha, Lydia. 1994. Language and Class in Malta. In *Maltese Society: A Sociological Inquiry*, ed. R. G. Sultana and G. Baldacchino, 117–31. Malta: Mireva Publications.

Segal, Charles. 1982. *Dionysiac Poetics and Euripides' Bacchae*. Princeton, N.J.: Princeton University Press.

Sen, Krishna, and David Hill. 2000. *Media, Culture, and Politics in Indonesia*. Melbourne: Oxford University Press.

Sepultura. 1985. *Bestial Devastation*. Split LP with Overdose, *Século XX*. Cogumelo.

———. 1986. *Morbid Visions*. LP. Cogumelo.

———. 1987. *Schizophrenia*. LP. Cogumelo.

———. 1989. *Beneath the Remains*. LP. Roadrunner.

———. 1991. *Arise*. LP. Roadrunner.

———. 1993. *Chaos AD*. LP. Roadrunner.

———. 1996. *Roots*. CD. Roadrunner.

———. 1998. *Against*. CD. Roadrunner.

———. 2001. *Nation*. CD. Roadrunner.

———. 2003. *Roorback*. CD. SPV.

Shagrath. 2003. Interview by Ross Hagen. Metalcoven Website. http://www.metalcoven.com/interview_dimmu_ross.html, accessed Dec. 15, 2003.

Shamsul Amri Baharuddin. 2001. A History of an Identity, an Identity of History: The Idea and Practice of "Malayness" in Malaysia Reconsidered. *Journal of Southeast Asian Studies* 32 (3): 355–66.

Shank, Barry. 1994. *Dissonant Identities: The Rock 'n' Roll Scene in Austin, Texas*. Hanover, N.H.: University Press of New England.

Shulman, David D. 1986. Battle as Metaphor in Tamil Folk and Classical Traditions. In *Another Harmony: New Essays on the Folklore of India*, ed. Stuart Blackburn and A. K. Ramanujan, 105–30. Delhi: Oxford University Press.

Shuman, Amy. 1993. Dismantling Local Culture. *Western Folklore* 52 (2/4): 345–64.

Silverman, Carol. 1989. Reconstructing Folklore: Media and Cultural Policy in Eastern Europe. *Communication* 11: 141–60.

Simmons, Gene. 2001. *Kiss and Make-up*. New York: Three Rivers Press.

Simon Wiesenthal Center. N.d. *The New Lexicon of Hate: The Changing Tactics, Language, and Symbols of America's Extremists*. Los Angeles: Simon Wiesenthal Center.

Singer, Milton. 1972. *When a Great Tradition Modernizes*. New York: Praeger.

Singh, Amardeep. 2000. "They Would Rather Listen to Samba or Death Metal": Channeling Global Subcultures. *Polygraph* 11 (1): 89–113.

Sivec, Jože. 1994. Opera. *Enciklopedija Slovenije* 8: 141–43.

Slit. 2000. *Vision of Life*. Demo CD. Self-released.

———. 2002. *Mandra*. Promo CD. Self-released.

———. 2005. *Chronaca Nera*. CD. Retribute Records.

———. 2006. *Ode to Silence*. CD. Anticulture Records.

362   Slobin, Mark. 1993. *Subcultural Sounds: Micromusics of the West*. Hanover, N.H.: Wesleyan University Press/University Press of New England.

Smith, Russ. 1997. Interview with Bishop of Hexen. *Mimes Brum: Storm Frå Vest*, n.p.

Smith, Stacy L., and Aaron R. Boyson. 2002. Violence in Music Videos: Examining the Prevalence and Context of Physical Aggression. *Journal of Communication* 52 (1): 61–83.

Soulfly. 1998. *Soulfly*. CD. Roadrunner.

———. 2000. *Primitive*. CD. Roadrunner.

Stallybrass, Peter, and Allon White. 1986. *The Politics and Poetics of Transgression*. London: Methuen.

State of Hate: White Nationalism in the Midwest 2001–2002. 2001. *Breaking New Ground*, Winter, 1–12. Chicago: Center for New Community.

Steinke, Darcy. 1996. Satan's Cheerleaders. *Spin*, February, 62–70.

Stevens, S. Carolyn. 2008. *Japanese Popular Music: Culture, Authenticity, and Power*. London: Routledge.

Stevens, S. Carolyn, and Shuhei Hosokawa. 2001. So Close Yet So Far: Humanizing Celebrity in Japanese Music Variety Shows, 1960s–1990s. In *Asian Media Productions*, ed. Brian Moeran, 223–46. Richmond: Curzon.

Stokes, Martin. 2004. Music and the Global Order. *Annual Review of Anthropology* 33: 47–72.

Störkraft. 1991a. Kampfhund. *Mann Für Mann*. LP. Rock-O-Rama.

———. 1991b. Kraft Für Deutschland. *Mann Für Mann*. LP. Rock-O-Rama.

———. 2003. *Das Waren Noch Zeiten*. CD. Resistance Records, 1167.

The Storm Has Begun. 1995. Compilation CD. Storm Records.

Stothard, Sheryll. 1998. Rage and Desire. In *Generation: A Collection of Contemporary Malaysian Ideas*, ed. Amir Muhammad, Kam Raslan, and Sheryll Stothard, 155–57. Kuala Lumpur: Hikayat Press.

Straw, Will. [1983] 1990. Characterizing Rock Music Culture: The Case of Heavy Metal. In *On Record*, ed. Simon Frith and Andrew Goodwin, 97–110. London: Routledge.

———. 1991. Systems of Articulation, Logics of Change: Communities and Scenes in Popular Music. *Cultural Studies* 5 (3): 368–88.

———. 2001. Scenes and Sensibilities. *Public* 22 (3): 245–57.

Striking Distance. 2001. *March to Your Grave*. CD. NGS Records, TR06.

Sultana, Ronald G., and Godfrey Baldacchino, eds. 1994. *Maltese Society: A Sociological Inquiry*. Malta: Mireva Publications.

Suryadinata, Leo, ed. 2000. *Nationalism and Globalization: East and West*. Singapore: Institute of Southeast Asian Studies.

Sutcliffe, Phil. 2000. Getting It Together at Bron-Y-Aur: The Story of *Led Zeppelin III*. Rock's Backpages Web site. http://www.rocksbackpages.com/, accessed Feb. 20, 2011.

Sutton, R. Anderson. 1996. Interpreting Electronic Sound Technology in the Contemporary Javanese Soundscape. *Ethnomusicology* 40 (2): 249–68.

Swenson, John. 1978. *Kiss*. New York: Tempo Books.

Sylvan, Robin. 2002. *Traces of the Spirit: The Religious Dimensions of Popular Music*. New York: NYU Press.

Tabone, Carmel. 1994. Secularisation. In *Maltese Society: A Sociological Inquiry*, ed. R. G. Sultana and G. Baldacchino, 285–300. Malta: Mireva Publications.

Talty, Stephan. 1996. The Methods of a Neo-Nazi Mogul. *New York Times Magazine*, Feb. 25, 40–43.

Tan Sooi Beng. 1989/1990. The Performing Arts in Malaysia: State and Society. *Asian Music* 21 (1): 137–71.

Tang Dynasty. 1992. *Tang Dynasty*. CD. Magic Stone.

———. 1999. *Epic*. Audiocassette tape. Jingwen Records (Beijing).

Taylor, Charles. 1995. Two Theories of Modernity. *Hastings Center Report* 25 (2): 24–33.

Taylor, Laura Wiebe. 2008. Nordic Nationalisms: Black Metal Takes Norway's Everyday Racisms to the "Extreme." Paper presented at "Heavy Fundametalisms: Music, Metal, and Politics," Salzburg, Austria, Nov. 3–5.

Taylor, Timothy. 1997. *Global Pop: World Music, World Markets*. New York: Routledge.

Tedjasukmana, Jason. 2003. Bandung's Headbangers. *Time Asia*, June 16. http://www.time.com/, accessed June 19, 2008.

Théberge, Paul. 1997. *Any Sound You Can Imagine: Making Music/Consuming Technology*. Hanover, N.H.: Univ. Press of New England.

———. 2001. "Plugged In": Technology and Popular Music. In *The Cambridge Companion to Pop and Rock*, ed. Simon Frith, Will Straw, and John Street, 3–25. Cambridge: Cambridge University Press.

Thompson, Eric. 2002. Rocking East and West: The USA in Malaysian Music. In *Global Goes Local: Popular Culture in Asia*, ed. Timothy Craig and Richard King, 58–79. Honolulu: University of Hawai'i Press.

Thompson, Robert, and Reed Larson. 1995. Social Context and the Subjective Experience of Different Types of Rock Music. *Journal of Youth and Adolescence* 24 (6): 731–44.

Thornton, Sarah. 1995. *Club Cultures: Music, Media, and Subcultural Capital*. Cambridge: Polity Press.

Titon, Jeff Todd. 1993. Reconstructing the Blues: Reflections on the 1960s Blues Revival. In *Transforming Tradition: Folk Music Revivals Examined*, ed. Neil V. Rosenberg, 220–40. Chicago: University of Illinois Press.

Tôgô, Kaoruko. 1998. *Asahi Shinbun*, Feb. 29.

Tolinski, B., and G. DiBenedetto. 1997. Jimmy Page: Days of Heaven. Guitar World Web site. http://www.guitarworld.com/, accessed May 20, 2005.

Tomc, Gregor. 1989. *Druga Slovenija: Zgodovina mladinskih gibanj na Slovenskem v 20. Stoletju* [The other Slovenia: History of youth movements in Slovenia in the twentieth century]. Ljubljana: UK ZSMS (Krt 54).

———. 1994. The Politics of Punk. In *Independent Slovenia: Origins, Movements, Prospects*, ed. Jill Benderly and Evan Kraft, 113–34. Houndmills, Basingstoke, Hampshire, London: Macmillan.

364   Tomlinson, John. 1991. *Cultural Imperialism: A Critical Introduction*. Baltimore: Johns Hopkins University Press.

Took, Kevin J., and David S. Weiss. 1994. The Relationship between Heavy Metal and Rap Music and Adolescent Turmoil: Real or Artifact? *Adolescence* 29 (115): 613–21.

Tourniquet. 1992. *Pathogenic Ocular Dissonance*. CD. Intense Records/Metal Blade, B000001C67.

Trouble. 1990. *Trouble*. LP. Metal Blade Records.

Tsing, Anna L. 2005. *Friction: An Ethnography of Global Connection*. Princeton, N.J.: Princeton University Press.

25 Ta Life. 1999. *Friendship, Loyalty, Commitment*. CD. NGS Records, 3011-2.

Ulriksborg, T.-E. Kari Rueslåtten. 2003. Interview with Kari Rueslåtten. http://home.online.no/~torleift/kari/disco2.html, accessed Feb. 29, 2004.

Ulver. 1997. *Nattens Madrigal*. CD. Century Black, 7858-2.

UN Data. 2010. Gross National Income Per Capita (PPP Int. $). http://data.un.org, accessed March 26, 2011.

Urrutia Blondel, Jorge. 1958. Reportaje de un músico a Rapa-Nui. *Revista Musical Chilena* 60: 5–47.

Urry, John. 1990. *The Tourist Gaze: Leisure and Travel in Contemporary Societies*. London: Sage Publications.

Vandals. 1990. *Crusading Sinners*. Video cassette single. Self-released.

———. 1991. Untitled live/rehearsal demo cassette. Self-released.

Vianna, Hermano. 1996. Sepultura e o samba do futuro. *Folha de São Paulo*, Caderno Mais!, April 14, 4–5.

Von Kuehnelt-Leddihn, Erik. 1993. *Liberty or Equality*. Front Royal, Va.: Christendom Press.

Waksman, Steve. 1999. *Instruments of Desire: The Electric Guitar and the Shaping of Musical Experience*. Cambridge, Mass.: Harvard University Press.

———. 2009. *This Ain't the Summer of Love: Conflict and Crossover in Heavy Metal and Punk*. Berkeley: University of California Press.

Walker, Seb. 2003. Pumped Up. *Baghdad Bulletin*, Aug. 17. http://www.baghdadbulletin.com, accessed Jan. 21, 2004.

Wallach, Jeremy. 2000. Opening Remarks: Rocking in the Free World; Global Perspectives on Heavy Metal (Panel Discussion). Society for Ethnomusicology 45th Annual Meeting, Toronto, Nov. 4, 2000.

———. 2002. Exploring Class, Nation, and Xenocentrism in Indonesian Cassette Retail Outlets. *Indonesia* 74 (October): 79–102.

———. 2003a. "Goodbye My Blind Majesty": Music, Language, and Politics in the Indonesian Underground. In *Global Pop, Local Language*, ed. Harris M. Berger and Michael T. Carroll, 53–86. Jackson: University Press of Mississippi.

———. 2003b. The Poetics of Electrosonic Presence: Recorded Music and the Materiality of Sound. *Journal of Popular Music Studies* 15 (1): 34–64.

———. 2005a. Engineering Techno-Hybrid Grooves in Two Indonesian Sound Studios. In *Wired for Sound: Engineering and Technologies in Sonic Cultures*, ed.

Paul D. Greene and Thomas Porcello, 138–55. Middletown, Conn.: Wesleyan University Press.

———. 2005b. Underground Rock Music and Democratization in Indonesia. *World Literature Today* 79 (3/4): 16–20.

———. 2008a. Living the Punk Lifestyle in Jakarta. *Ethnomusicology* 52 (1): 97–115.

———. 2008b. *Modern Noise, Fluid Genres: Popular Music in Indonesia, 1997–2001.* Madison: University of Wisconsin Press.

Wallis, Roger, and Krister Malm. 1984. *Big Sounds from Small Peoples.* London: Constable.

Walser, Robert. 1993a. *Running with the Devil: Power, Gender, and Madness in Heavy Metal Music.* Middletown, Conn.: Wesleyan University Press.

———. 1993b. Forging Masculinity: Heavy Metal Sounds and Images of Gender. In *Sound and Vision: The Music Video Reader*, ed. Simon Frith, Andrew Goodwin, and Lawrence Grossberg, 153–81. New York: Routledge.

———. 1997. Eruptions: Heavy Metal Appropriations of Classical Virtuosity. In *The Subcultures Reader*, ed. Ken Gelder and Sarah Thornton, 459–70. London: Routledge.

Waters, Malcolm. 1995. *Globalization.* New York: Routledge.

Wave [Nepal]. 1999. Know Your Band: Drishty. *Wave* 41 (August): 21.

Waxer, Lise. 2002a. *The City of Musical Memory: Salsa, Record Grooves, and Popular Culture in Cali, Colombia.* Middletown, Conn.: Wesleyan University Press.

———, ed. 2002b. *Situating Salsa: Global Markets and Local Meanings in Latin Popular Music.* New York: Routledge.

Weeping Silence. 2000. *Deprived from Romance.* MCD. Self-released.

Weiner, Andrew. [1973] 1996. Doom Patrol: Black Sabbath at the Rainbow. In *The Beat Goes On: The Rock File Reader*, ed. Charlie Gillett and Simon Frith, 19–28. London: Pluto Press.

Weinstein, Deena. 1991. *Heavy Metal: A Cultural Sociology.* New York: Lexington.

———. 2000. *Heavy Metal: The Music and Its Culture.* New York: Da Capo. [2nd ed. of Weinstein 1991].

Welch, Chris. 1970. Page on Zeppelin III. *Melody Maker*, Oct. 24, 11.

White Pride World Wide. 2001. Southern Poverty Law Center. *Intelligence Report* 103. http://www.splcenter.org/intel/intelreport/article.jsp?pid=328, accessed May 16, 2008.

Wikipedia. 2007. Heavy Metal. http://en.wikipedia.org/wiki/Heavy_metal, as accessed July 2, 2007.

Williams, Raymond. 1998. *Navadna kultura: Izbrani spisi* [Common culture: Selected writings]. Ljubljana: Studia humanitatis.

Wilson, Scott. 2008a. *Great Satan's Rage: American Negativity and Rap/Metal in the Age of Supercapitalism.* Manchester: Manchester University Press.

———. 2008b. From Forests Unknown: Eurometal and the Audio Political Unconscious. Paper presented at "Heavy Fundametalisms: Music, Metal, and Politics," Salzburg, Austria, Nov. 3–5.

Witchhammer. 1990. LP. *Mirror, My Mirror.* Cogumelo.

366   Wong, Cynthia P. 1996. We Define Ourselves! The Negotiation of Power and Identity for Asian Americans in Hip Hop. Paper presented at the Thirteenth National Conference of the Association for Asian American Studies, Washington, D.C., May 29–June 2.

———. 2005. Lost Lambs: Rock, Gender, Authenticity, and a Generational Response to Modernity in the People's Republic of China. Ph.D. diss., Columbia University.

Wong, Deborah, and René T. A. Lysloff. 1998. Popular Music and Cultural Politics. In *The Garland Encyclopedia of World Music, Vol. 4: Southeast Asia*, ed. Terry Miller and Sean Williams, 95–112. New York: Garland Publishing.

Wong, Kean. 1993. Metallic Gleam. *The Wire* 110 (April): 18–21.

Xue, Li. 1993. *Yaogunmeng* [Searching for rock dreams]. Beijing: Zhongguodianyin-chubanshe.

Yang, Mayfair Mei-hui. 1999. From Gender Erasure to Gender Difference: State Feminism, Consumer Sexuality, and Women's Public Sphere in China. In *Spaces of Their Own: Women's Public Sphere in Transnational China*, ed. Mayfair Mei-hui Yang, 35–67. Minneapolis: University of Minnesota.

Yorke, Ritchie. 1993. *Led Zeppelin: The Definitive Biography*. Novato, Calif.: Underwood-Miller.

Young, Nigel. [1997] 2000. The Deep Purple Diary. http://members.aol.com/nigelyoung, accessed April 4, 2008.

Yu, Mok Chiu, and J. Frank Harrison, eds. 1990. *Voices from Tiananmen Square: Beijing Spring and the Democracy Movement*. Montreal: Black Rose Books.

Zach, Paul. 2002. Urbankarma Digs Its Roots. *Straits Times*, Feb. 2, 2002. http://straitstimes.asia1.com.sg/columnist/0,1886,19–43939,00.html, accessed Feb. 5, 2002.

Zhou, You, ed. 1994. *Beijingyaogunbuluo* [The Beijing rock tribe]. Tianjin: Tianjin Social Sciences Association Publisher.

Zopzy. 2004. *Hakaora Koe*. CD. RAF Sound System.

IDELBER AVELAR is a professor of Latin American literature in the Department of Spanish and Portuguese, Tulane University. He is the author of *The Letter of Violence: Essays on Narrative, Ethics, and Politics* (2004) and *The Untimely Present: Postdictatorial Latin American Fiction and the Task of Mourning* (1999), the latter a recipient of the MLA Kovacs Award and translated into Spanish and Portuguese. He is the co-editor of a forthcoming volume on Brazilian popular music and citizenship, as well as the author of numerous articles published in the Americas and in Europe. He is currently at work on two manuscripts, one on masculinity in Latin American fiction and the other on race, rhythm, and nationhood in Brazilian popular music.

ALBERT BELL is the head of the Department of Youth and Community Studies at the University of Malta. His research interests include music subcultures and his doctoral dissertation focused on heavy metal culture in Malta. Albert also composes and plays bass for the Maltese doom metal bands Forsaken and Nomad Son.

DAN BENDRUPS is a senior lecturer in music at the University of Otago, Dunedin, New Zealand. His teaching and research combines ethnomusicology and popular music studies, and he has written on diverse topics pertaining to music and popular culture in Australia, New Zealand, and the wider Pacific. Dr. Bendrups is best known for his work on Rapanui (Easter Island) music, and he also works with Latin American and Latvian migrant musicians in Australasia. He is currently the recording reviews editor for *The World of Music*, New Zealand representative for the Australia/New Zealand branch of the International Association for the Study of Popular Music, and chair of the Australia/New Zealand Regional Committee of the International Council for Traditional Music.

HARRIS M. BERGER is a professor of music and the associate head in the Department of Performance Studies at Texas A&M University. He works at the intersection of ethnomusicology, folklore studies, popular music studies, and performance studies. His books include *Metal, Rock, and Jazz: Perception and the Phenomenology of Musical Experience* (1999), *Global Pop, Local Language* (co-edited by Michael T. Carroll, 2003), *Identity and Everyday Life: Essays in the Study of Folklore, Music, and Popular Culture* (co-authored by Giovanna P. Del Negro, 2004), and *Stance: Ideas about Emotion, Style, and Meaning for the Study of Expressive Culture* (2009). In 1996, he founded the Popular Music Section of the Society for Ethnomusicology and was the section's chair until the end of 2004. He served as the president of the U.S. branch of the International Association for the Study of Popular Music from 2004 to 2007 and is currently the president of the Society for Ethnomusicology. Dr. Berger is the co-editor of the Music/Culture series at Wesleyan University Press and has recently completed a five-year term as the co-editor of the *Journal of American Folklore*.

PAUL D. GREENE is an associate professor of ethnomusicology and integrative arts at Pennsylvania State University, Brandywine. His research focuses on music, technology, and religion in India and Nepal. He is the recipient, with Thomas Porcello, of the Society for Ethnomusicology's 2006 Klaus P. Wachsmann Prize, for the edited volume *Wired for Sound: Engineering and Technologies in Sonic Cultures*. His articles have appeared in *Ethnomusicology*, *Asian Music*, *The World of Music*, *Popular Music*, *Popular Music and Society*, and elsewhere. He has served as the recording review editor of *Ethnomusicology* and is outgoing chair of the Popular Music Section of the Society for Ethnomusicology.

ROSS HAGEN is an adjunct lecturer at Utah Valley University and has taught courses in Western music history, American music, and rock music. He studied music at Davidson College and received his M.M. and Ph.D. in musicology at the University of Colorado-Boulder. His dissertation compares modes of participatory fan activity in the Denver noise scene and in rock fan fiction to deconstruct codes of authenticity and ideology within music fandom. He is also active as a bassist and composer in the bands encomiast and Schrei aus Stein.

SHARON HOCHHAUSER is an independent scholar who specializes in the study of popular music and the entertainment industry. Her past work includes studies of the

Moody Blues and their relationship to their fans and filksong, a science-fiction-based musical practice. She holds a Ph.D. in musicology/ethnomusicology from Kent State University and currently works as an entertainment special-event producer.

SHUHEI HOSOKAWA is a professor at the International Research Center for Japanese Studies (Kyoto). He is the co-editor of *Karaoke around the World* (1998) and a contributor to the collections *Fanning the Flames* (edited by William W. Kelly), *Popular Music Studies* (edited by David Hesmondhalgh and Keith Negus), *Situating Salsa* (edited by Lise Waxer), and *Sonic Synergies* (edited by Gerry Bloustien, Margaret Peters, and Susan Luckman).

KEITH KAHN-HARRIS is an honorary research fellow in the Department for Psycho-Social Studies, Birkbeck College, London. He is the author of *Extreme Metal: Music and Culture on the Edge* (2007), the co-author of *Turbulent Times: The British Jewish Community Today* (2010), the co-editor of *After Subculture: Critical Studies in Contemporary Youth Culture* (2004), and for several years wrote for the metal magazine *Terrorizer*. He blogs at www.metaljew.org and his personal website is www.kahn-harris .org.

KEI KAWANO received his master's degree at the Graduate School of Social Engineering, Tokyo Institute of Technology. He is currently working at the New Delhi office of the Japan External Trade Organization.

RAJKO MURŠIČ is a professor of cultural anthropology at the University of Ljubljana, Slovenia, where he lectures in anthropological methodology, popular music, and popular culture. He is the author of *Center za dehumanizacijo: Ethnological Description of the Rock Group* (1995) and *Trate: Stories of the Rock and Youth Club* (2000), the co-editor of *Europe and Its Other: Notes on the Balkans* (2007), and the author of many articles on popular music, cultural anthropology, and theoretical issues in anthropology. He used to work for Radio Student and occasionally writes for the magazine *Nova Muska*.

STEVE WAKSMAN is an associate professor of music and American studies at Smith College. He is the author of *Instruments of Desire: The Electric Guitar and the Shaping of Musical Experience* (1999) and *This Ain't the Summer of Love: Conflict and Crossover in Heavy Metal and Punk* (2009). Currently, he is co-editing the *Sage Handbook of Popular Music* with Andy Bennett and researching the history of live music in the United States during the nineteenth and twentieth centuries. A guitarist since the age of nine, he is a particular fan of old-school 1970s metal, and remembers fondly the moment he figured out how to play a power chord. He blogs at themetalpunk-continuum.blogspot.com.

JEREMY WALLACH, an anthropologist and ethnomusicologist specializing in the cross-cultural study of popular musics, is an associate professor in the Department of Popular Culture at Bowling Green State University in Ohio. He is the author of *Modern Noise, Fluid Genres: Popular Music in Indonesia, 1997–2001* (2008) and numerous articles and book chapters on Southeast Asia, sound recording technology, world beat, punk, and metal. He is a founding member and current Chair of the Popular Music Section of the Society for Ethnomusicology.

ROBERT WALSER is a professor of music and the director of the Rock and Popular Music Institute at Case Western Reserve University. He is the author of *Running with the Devil: Power, Gender, and Madness in Heavy Metal Music*, the editor of *Keeping Time: Readings in Jazz History*, and a Certified Pro Tools Operator.

DEENA WEINSTEIN is a professor of sociology at DePaul University in Chicago, specializing in popular culture and social theory. Her recent publications include *Heavy Metal: The Music and Its Culture* (2000) and various journal articles and book chapters on the structure of rock bands, protest songs, rock criticism, celebrity, and religion, among others. In addition, she is a rock journalist, concentrating in metal.

CYNTHIA P. WONG is an ethnomusicologist who studies expressions of cultural, gender, and generational identity in popular music. Her dissertation research examined these identity issues in the lives and music of the pioneer generation of rock musicians in the People's Republic of China. Her earlier projects have focused on issues of cultural and masculine identity among Asian American rappers in the United States. She has also conducted extensive research on the impact of the Great Proletarian Cultural Revolution (1966–76) on the lives and careers of Chinese musicians in the United States. She has taught at SUNY-Stony Brook and is affiliated with Columbia University in New York.

Page numbers in italics indicate figures.

26, 90–92, 146–53, 164, 171–72, 178, 193–95, 198, 217; films about, 28 n. 4, 57 n. 1, 246 n. 13; globalization of, 4–5, 15–16, 20–23, 43–57, 89, 110–12, 133, 200, 229, 241–44, 266–67, 278, 310, 313–14, 331–32; hard rock vs., 13, 32–33 n. 22, 137–38, 229–30; history of, 36–43, 205–9, 216–17; hybridity of, 10, 19, 56, 58 n. 7, 103 n. 3; instrumentation of, 10–11, 65, 76–77, 184; journalism of, 48–49, 51–52, 57 n. 2, 206–7, 232–33, 250–53, 255–56, 264–65; loudness of, 12, 30 n. 12, 229–30; masculinity in, 19, 24–25, 40, 64–66, 82–83, 84 n. 6, 95, 233, 318–19, 334–35; modernity and, 7–8, 16–19, 27, 31–32 n. 17, 93–94; mythic/heroic imagery in, 31–32 n. 17, 37–38, 46, 56, 76–79, 83, 104 n. 9, 149–50, 164, 173, 179 n. 8, 179 n. 10, 190–95; negative reactions to, 135–36, 142, 326–28, 330–31; origin of the term, 37, 57 n. 2; politics in, 94–95, 129–32, 284–85; premodern past idealized in, 31–32 n. 17–18, 65–66, 68–69, 76–79, 82–83, 193–95; as psychological warfare, 34–35; punk vs., 13–14, 31 n. 15, 41, 118, 298–99; race issues in, 19, 25–26, 32 n. 18, 90–92, 168–69, 193, 203, 209–10, 219–21; on radio, 50–51, 142, 279; in record stores, 50, 101–2, 255–57, 263–64, 293 n. 15, 310; religious issues in, 17–18, 21, 32 n. 18, 42–43, 56, 110, 118–19, 124–28, 131, 190–91, 193–94, 197, 283–84; rhythm in, 13, 145, 186–87, 192; scholarship of, 9–10, 15–16, 26–27, 29 nn. 9–10, 37, 299–300, 335–36; subgenre proliferation in, 30 n. 11, 36, 38–43; as transgression, 18, 24, 31 n. 16, 32 n. 19, 89, 109–12, 127–28, 133–34, 213–15, 222–23, 329; vocals of, 12, 116–17, 130, 146, 184, 322; women "exscripted" from, 66, 84 n. 6, 95, 335; as working-

class phenomenon, 15–17, 54, 56–57, 335. *See also* guitar; *individual bands and subgenres*

metal musicians: attire of, 3, 38, 189, 191–92, 231–32, 235, 278, 322–23; attitude toward fans of, 124; band formation process of, 52–53; criminality of, 42, 180–81, 183, 195–98, 199 n. 9, 216–17; as martyrs, 80–82; sexual exploits of, 72–73, 230, 233–34, 237, 243; sociality among, 95–97, 325; in the studio, 95–98, 328; tape-trading networks of, 201, 205, 279; on tour, 228–44. *See also* metal scenes

metal scenes: in Africa, 25–26, 33 n. 23, 44, 245 n. 1; altruism in, 212–13; in Bali, 9, 31 n. 15, 95, 97–98, 138, 156–57 n. 2; in Brazil, 9, 15, 18, 135–36, 138, 141–43; in Chile, 318; in China, 19–20, 25, 56, 57 n. 4, 59 n. 19, 66–69, 82, 84 n. 9; cultural capital in, 21, 99, 205–19, 223, 287–89; "Do It Yourself" ethos in, 31 n. 15, 48, 104 n. 10, 118, 275, 278, 287; in Egypt, 3, 9; in Finland, 214; in Germany, 47; global vs. local, 54–55, 110–12, 121, 132–34, 138, 156–57 n. 2, 200–202, 218–19, 223, 247–48, 266–67, 285–86; identity performance in, 23–24, 213–15; in Indonesia, 15, 17, 20, 25, 47, 55, 57 n. 4, 87–89, 91–92, 95, 97–101, 103 n. 4, 335; in Iraq, 34–36; in Israel, 21–22, 201–4, 209–10, 218–19, 221–23; in Japan, 19, 22, 247–51, 253–56, 265–66; in Korea, 260; in Malaysia, 17, 20, 25, 49, 55, 87–91, 95–96, 99, 101, 103 n. 4, 335; in Malta, 18, 22–23, 271–72, 274–91, 291–93 nn. 2–15; in Nepal, 17–18, 20, 84 n. 7, 110–12, 115–24, 134 n. 1; in North America, 162, 168, 171–72; in Norway, 21, 31–32 nn. 17–18, 181–83, 190–99, 202, 214–17, 220–21; in Ohio, 4, 13–15, 104 n. 6, 118; in the Philippines, 105 n. 13; "play" within,

JEREMY WALLACH is an associate professor of popular culture at Bowling Green State University. He is the author of *Modern Noise, Fluid Genres: Popular Music in Indonesia, 1997–2001* (2008).

HARRIS M. BERGER is a professor of music and the associate head of the Department of Performance Studies at Texas A&M University. Most recently, he is the author of *Stance: Ideas about Emotion, Style, and Meaning for the Study of Expressive Culture* (2009).

PAUL D. GREENE is an associate professor of ethnomusicology and integrative arts at Pennsylvania State University, Brandywine. He is the editor, with Thomas Porcello, of *Wired for Sound: Engineering and Technologies in Sonic Cultures* (2005).

Library of Congress Cataloging-in-Publication Data

Metal rules the globe : heavy metal music around the world /
edited by Jeremy Wallach, Harris M. Berger, and Paul D. Greene.
p. cm.
Includes bibliographical references and index.
ISBN 978-0-8223-4716-3 (cloth : alk. paper)
ISBN 978-0-8223-4733-0 (pbk. : alk. paper)
1. Heavy metal (Music)—History and criticism.
2. Music and globalization.
3. Racism in popular culture.
I. Wallach, Jeremy. II. Berger, Harris M., 1966– III. Greene, Paul D.
ML3534.M534 2012
781.6609—dc23   2011027661